THE CONDOR TRIALS

THE CONDOR TRIALS

TRANSNATIONAL REPRESSION AND
HUMAN RIGHTS IN SOUTH AMERICA

•

Francesca Lessa

Yale UNIVERSITY PRESS   NEW HAVEN AND LONDON

Published with assistance from the
Mary Cady Tew Memorial Fund and with support from the
Fund established in memory of Oliver Baty Cunningham,
a distinguished graduate of the Class of 1917, Yale College,
Captain, 15th United States Field Artillery, born in
Chicago September 17, 1894, and killed while on active
duty near Thiaucourt, France, September 17, 1918,
the twenty-fourth anniversary of his birth.

Yale University Press books may be purchased in quantity
for educational, business, or promotional use. For
information, please email sales.press@yale.edu (U.S. office)
or sales@yaleup.co.uk (U.K. office).

Set in Scala type by Integrated Publishing Solutions, Grand
Rapids, Michigan. Printed in the United States of America.

Library of Congress Control Number: 2021952571
ISBN 978-0-300-25409-9 (hardcover : alk. paper)

A catalogue record for this book is available from the
British Library.

This paper meets the requirements of ANSI/NISO
Z39.48-1992 (Permanence of Paper).

10 9 8 7 6 5 4 3 2 1

A Fernando

CONTENTS

ACKNOWLEDGMENTS

Per aspera ad astra
—*Latin expression meaning that through hardships,*
one can reach the stars

For days, I tried to think of a way to write these acknowledgments so that they would speak of the immense gratitude I feel to everyone who supported me during this research project. But the friends, family members, and colleagues to be acknowledged are just too many, and I decided to write a collective tribute instead.

In early 2013, when I embarked on this new project, I longed to return to the Río de la Plata, which had become my second home since 2007. Often, in my Oxford office, I would close my eyes and be transported to beloved cafés on the streets of Buenos Aires or Montevideo. Eventually, beyond Argentina and Uruguay, I also ended up traveling to Brazil, Chile, Paraguay, the US, and Italy, where I was extremely fortunate to make new friends and colleagues who believed in the importance of my research, supported me in every possible way, and trusted me enough to share their personal stories, which were often tales of much pain, loss, and suffering, but also of resilience and hope in the face of immense adversity.

Then, in February 2017, a previously unknown group in Uruguay, the self-proclaimed "Commando General Pedro Barneix," sent death threats via email to a group of thirteen individuals including human rights lawyers, activists, jurists, public prosecutors, government authorities, and myself. I decided to speak openly about this life-changing experience, hoping that this public acknowledgment might help lift the veil on the long-silenced issue of threats and attacks that academics increasingly confront in Latin America (and elsewhere). I soon discovered that in fact I was not alone, and too many colleagues faced and continue to confront similar situations in their work. Such threats damage not only our physical and mental integrity but also our freedom of opinion and expression: silencing the voices of academic research sets dangerous precedents in all societies, as the tragic fate of Giulio Regeni reminds us.

Having to abandon Uruguay, where I had recently relocated in order to begin a second phase of my research, was the lowest moment of this project. Uruguay was my place in the world (*mi lugar en el mundo*), as my beloved friend Fernando used to tell me. Eventually, to keep the project going, I returned to Argentina, where I had lived between 2014 and 2016. Buenos Aires's streets, hustle and bustle, and beloved friends provided some longed-for normality in the midst of a complex situation. Against all odds, the time came to fly back to Oxford in 2018 and begin writing this book.

What you will find in the following pages is not only the product of years of my work, but also a collective project, one in which many people provided "a grain of sand" (*un granito de arena*). I cannot think of a better way to thank everyone who I encountered on this journey than by citing a fragment of the poem "Hagamos un trato" by Uruguayan poet Mario Benedetti:

> es tan lindo
> saber que usted existe
>
> it is so nice
> to know that you exist

Last but not least, I am extremely grateful to the funders who believed in and supported this project:

- the European Union's Horizon 2020 research and innovation program under the Marie Skłodowska-Curie grant agreement number 702004;
- the University of Oxford's John Fell Fund Grant numbers 0006189 (2019) and 122/686 (2013);
- the British Academy/Leverhulme Small Research Grant number SG142423;
- the University of Oxford's ESRC Impact Acceleration Account Grant number IAA-MT14-008;

- the Open Society Foundation's Human Rights Initiative;
- the AHRC-LABEX Grant number AH/N504580/1; and
- the University of Oxford's ODID Research Fund and the LAC/St Antony's College Malcolm Deas Fund.

Abbreviations

AAA	Alianza Anticomunista Argentina (Argentine Anticommunist Alliance), Argentina
ADT	Archivo del Terror (Archives of Terror), Paraguay
APDH	Asamblea Permanente por los Derechos Humanos (Argentine Permanent Assembly for Human Rights), Argentina
ARFRM	Ministerio de Relaciones Exteriores, Comercio Internacional y Culto (Ministry of Foreign Affairs, International Trade and Worship), Argentina
CEJIL	Center for Justice and International Law, USA
CELS	Centro de Estudios Legales y Sociales (Center for Legal and Social Studies), Argentina
CENIMAR	Centro de Informações da Marinha (Navy Information Center), Brazil
CGIOR	Centro General de Instrucción para Oficiales de Reserva (General Training Center for Reserve Officers), Uruguay
CIA	Central Intelligence Agency, USA
CIE	Centro de Informações do Exército (Army Information Center), Brazil
CIEX	Centro de Informações do Exterior (Center of Foreign Information), Brazil
CISA	Centro de Informações de Segurança da Aeronáutica (Aeronautics Safety Information Center), Brazil
CODEPU	Corporación de Promoción y Defensa de los Derechos del Pueblo (Corporation for the Promotion and Defense of People's Rights), Chile

CONADEP	Comisión Nacional sobre la Desaparición de Personas (National Commission on the Disappearance of Persons), Argentina
CNV	Comissão Nacional da Verdade (National Truth Commission), Brazil
DIA	Defense Intelligence Agency, USA
DOD	Department of Defense, USA
DINA	Dirección de Inteligencia Nacional (Directorate of National Intelligence), Chile
DIPPBA	Dirección de Inteligencia de la Policía de la Provincia de Buenos Aires (Directorate of Intelligence of the Buenos Aires Provincial Police), Argentina
DNII	Dirección Nacional de Información e Inteligencia (National Directorate of Intelligence and Information), Uruguay
DOPS	Departamento de Ordem Política e Social (Department for Political and Social Order), Brazil
DOS	Department of State, USA
ESMA	Escuela de Mecánica de la Armada (Navy Mechanics School), Argentina
FAB	Força Aérea Brasileira (Brazilian Air Force)
FAU	Federación Anarquista del Uruguay (Anarchical Federation of Uruguay)
FBI	Federal Bureau of Investigation, USA
GAU	Grupos de Acción Unificadora (Unifying Action Groups), Uruguay
INR	Bureau of Intelligence and Research, US State Department
JCR	Junta de Coordinación Revolucionaria (Revolutionary Coordinating Junta)
MAC	Memoranda of Enrique Arancibia Clavel
MIR	Movimiento de Izquierda Revolucionaria (Revolutionary Left Movement), Chile
MJDH	Movimento de Justiça e Direitos Humanos (Justice and Human Rights Movement NGO), Brazil
MLN	Movimiento de Liberación Nacional-Tupamaros (National Liberation Movement), also known as MLN-T, Uruguay
NSA	National Security Archive NGO, USA
OCOA	Organismo Coordinador de Operaciones Antisubversivas

	(Coordinating Organism for Antisubversive Operations), Uruguay
OCT	Operation Condor Trial, Argentina
OPR-33	Organización Popular Revolucionaria (Popular Revolutionary Organization), Uruguay
PCA	Partido Comunista de la Argentina (Communist Party of Argentina)
PCC	Partido Comunista de Chile (Communist Party of Chile)
PCR	Partido Comunista Revolucionario (Communist Revolutionary Party), Uruguay
PCU	Partido Comunista de Uruguay (Communist Party of Uruguay)
PFA	Policía Federal Argentina (Argentine Federal Police), Argentina
PIT-CNT	Plenario Intersindical de Trabajadores and Convención Nacional de Trabajadores (Inter-Union Workers and National Workers Convention), Uruguay
PM	Pubblico ministero (public prosecutor), Italy
PRT-ERP	Partido Revolucionario de los Trabajadores–Ejercito Revolucionario del Pueblo (Workers' Revolutionary Party–People's Revolutionary Army), Argentina
PVP	Partido por la Victoria del Pueblo (Party for the Victory of the People), Uruguay
ROE	Resistencia Obrero Estudiantil (Workers' and Students' Resistance), Uruguay
SDHPR	Secretaría de Derechos Humanos para el Pasado Reciente (Human Rights Secretariat for the Recent Past), Uruguay
SERPAJ	Servicio Paz y Justicia (Peace and Justice Service NGO), Uruguay
SID	Servicio de Información de Defensa (Defense Information Service), Uruguay
SIDE	Secretaría de Informaciones de Estado (State Information Secretariat), Argentina (1956–1976); Secretaría de Inteligencia del Estado (State Intelligence Secretariat), Argentina (1976–2005)
SIE	Servicio de Inteligencia del Estado (State Intelligence Service), Bolivia
SIJAU	Secretariado Internacional de Juristas por la Amnistia en

	Uruguay (International Secretariat of Jurists for Amnesty in Uruguay NGO), France
SNI	Serviço Nacional de Informações (National Information Service), Brazil
SSF	Superintendencia de Seguridad Federal (Superintendence of Federal Security), Argentina
TCA	Tribunal de lo Contencioso Administrativo (Contentious Administrative Court), Uruguay
TOF1	Tribunal Oral en lo Criminal Federal N° 1 (Buenos Aires Federal Criminal Court No. 1), Argentina
TOF6	Tribunal Oral en lo Criminal Federal N° 6 (Buenos Aires Federal Criminal Court No. 6), Argentina
UAL	Unión Artiguista de Liberación (Artiguist Liberation Union), Uruguay
UNHCR	United Nations High Commissioner for Refugees
UYFRM	Ministerio de Relaciones Exteriores de Uruguay (Ministry of Foreign Relations of Uruguay)
VDS	Vicaría de la Solidaridad (Vicariate of Solidarity), Chile

Introduction

Valparaíso de terremotos y escaleras
donde cada escalón es una casa en ascuas
Valparaíso de marineros y mercados
y costas de agua helada y transparente
había acogido a Anatole y Eva Lucía
cuando en diciembre del setenta y seis
aparecieron en la plaza O'Higgins
a la deriva y tomados de la mano.
—*Mario Benedetti*, Ni colorín, ni colorado[1]

The morning of December 22, 1976, two toddlers stepped out of a black car with tinted windows into O'Higgins Square in the port city of Valparaíso, Chile.[2] The owner of the rides in the playground area (fig. 1) allowed the kids, alone and holding hands, to play on various games throughout the day. But time passed and no one came to collect them. Hours later, and rather alarmed at this point, the owner called the Carabineros, Chile's military police, to report the abandoned toddlers. Who were these mysterious children who, according to the local newspaper *El Mercurio*, were well-dressed and spoke with "an accent and used expressions typical of the River Plate"?[3]

Four-year-old Anatole and nineteen-month-old Victoria Julién had materialized in Valparaíso on that austral summer day in what would be the last stop of an ordeal begun three months earlier on the other side of the Andes, in the Argentine capital Buenos Aires. Anatole and Victoria in fact lived in the locality of San Martín, in the province of Buenos Aires, with their parents Mario Roger Julién and Victoria Lucía Grisonas—Uruguayan political activists who

Figure 1. O'Higgins Square in Valparaíso, Chile. Image courtesy of Karinna Fernández Neira.

had sought asylum in Argentina. Mario had traveled first and secured refugee status in 1973 from the United Nations High Commissioner for Refugees (UNHCR). In 1974 the whole family was reunited in Buenos Aires, where in May 1975 Victoria was born.[4] The children's parents were politically active in the local Uruguayan exile community and participated in the founding in July 1975 of the Partido por la Victoria del Pueblo (Party for the Victory of the People; PVP). The latter, rooted in anarcho-syndicalism and critical Marxism, catalyzed resistance in Buenos Aires against the Uruguayan dictatorship and particularly became a target of transnational repression.

Indeed, in the context of recurrent operations against PVP activists in 1976, Argentine and Uruguayan security agents targeted the Julién family house on September 26. A large military deployment of two armored vehicles and numerous armed men, in both military uniform and civilian clothing, interrupted the peaceful siesta that Sunday afternoon, local resident Joaquín Castro recalled, and the neighborhood was "under siege" for hours.[5] Mario Julién shielded his children in the bathtub for protection from flying bullets,[6] and then attempted to flee from the backyard and hid in a nearby house; but he was soon recognized, seized, and murdered.[7]

Another neighbor witnessed how civilian officers took the little toddlers, who were crying and desperately asking for their mother, to a nearby gas station. One officer shut them up, screaming "You will not see that bitch of your mother

ever again" (*cállate que a la yegua de tu madre no la vas a ver más*).[8] Neighbor
Francisco Cullari watched in horror as four agents dragged Victoria Grisonas
by the hair on the ground and then repeatedly threw her onto the pavement,
until an officer ordered them to stop, since he said they needed her alive.[9]
Cullari offered to look after the toddlers until relatives could collect them, but
the agents responded that they were qualified to do so themselves.[10]

Reconstructing how the siblings appeared in Valparaíso has been a jigsaw
puzzle. Over the years, survivors' testimonies helped to establish that Anatole
and Victoria spent about ten days in the clandestine torture center known as
Automotores Orletti, located in Buenos Aires's Floresta district, where their
mother was interrogated and tortured.[11] Inside Orletti, Anatole spoke to Uruguayan prisoner Alvaro Nores and told him that he was there with his mother,
sister, and several other people. At an unspecified time around October 7, Anatole and Victoria traveled to Uruguay, probably alongside María Claudia García,
a pregnant Argentine prisoner, who looked after the two children during their
imprisonment in a second secret prison, this time on the ground floor of the
majestic building that housed the Uruguayan military intelligence service in
central Montevideo.[12] One day Anatole exchanged a few words with Julio César
Barboza, a guard there, telling him his name and his sister's.[13] According to
Barboza, Major José Nino Gavazzo—the person in charge—was quite fond of
the siblings, especially of Anatole, whom Gavazzo jokingly named "coyote,"
and brought them candies.[14] In late December the toddlers were taken to Chile.
Anatole later shared with me some recollections of that trip: "I remember
being on a small plane and someone telling me 'go to the cockpit.' That was the
first time I saw the shape of the plane controls, and I also stared at the Andes,
with their snow-capped mountain tops, which I had never seen before."

After being abandoned in O'Higgins Square, the children spent several
months in the Playa Ancha orphanage and in various adoptive households in
Valparaíso. In June 1977 the juvenile court magistrate granted temporary custody of the children to dental surgeon Jesús Larrabeiti and his wife, teacher
Silvia Yáñez, who, unlike other prospective families, were willing to adopt both
of the inseparable siblings.[15] But, just when Larrabeiti and Yáñez were about
to sign the final adoption papers in 1979, a tip-off from the Uruguayan exile
community in Venezuela helped the biological family locate the siblings in
Chile.

What had happened was that in February 1979, a Chilean social worker traveling through Venezuela had identified from a publication collating photos of
disappeared children the two abandoned siblings, whom she had assisted in

the orphanage at Valparaíso.[16] Then, in July 1979, a letter from France alerted Belela Herrera, the head of the UNHCR's office in Santiago at the time, of their potential location.[17] Herrera still remembers her disbelief when she learned of the possibility that the Julién siblings were in Valparaíso: "Of all places," she wondered, "how could those children have left Argentina, where they lived, and be in Chile?"[18] She asked a lawyer to go to Valparaíso to verify the claim, which turned out to be true.

Subsequently, Paulo Evaristo Arns, the archbishop of São Paulo and president of the Brazilian human rights NGO Clamor, arranged for the Uruguayan paternal grandmother, María Angélica Cáceres, who had been tirelessly looking for her grandchildren and their parents since their disappearance, to travel to Chile.[19] Herrera, Cáceres, two Clamor envoys, and two representatives of the Vicariate of Solidarity (Vicaría de la Solidaridad), Chile's major human rights NGO at the time, went to Valparaíso,[20] where the grandmother first broke the news to Mr. Larrabeiti, who had been summoned for a meeting at Anatole's school.[21] After extensive consultations with lawyers and psychologists, Cáceres and the adoptive family agreed that Anatole and Victoria should remain in Chile, as long as they regularly visited Uruguay to become acquainted with their biological relatives. This difficult decision particularly aimed to protect Anatole, who had witnessed and still recalled losing his parents just three years earlier: being separated from his second household could have caused him devastating emotional trauma.[22]

On July 31, 1979, Clamor officially announced the identification of the Julién siblings, who became the first disappeared children in South America to be reunited with their biological relatives. The news strongly reverberated throughout the Southern Cone,[23] and raised hopes that other disappeared children could also be found. Indeed, the grandparents of other Uruguayan toddlers who had disappeared in Argentina, including Simón Riquelo and Mariana Zaffaroni,[24] traveled to Chile to conduct investigations.[25]

The mystery of Anatole and Victoria's story has only been partially solved, and many questions still remain unanswered. Why had the siblings been taken from Buenos Aires to Montevideo, only to later be abandoned in Valparaíso?[26] Were they some kind of war booty (botín de guerra)?

Progressively, the struggle for truth and justice by survivors—including Anatole and Victoria themselves—victims' relatives, human rights activists, and lawyers helped answer some of these lingering questions and also resulted in the conviction, in five distinct criminal trials in Montevideo and Buenos Aires between 2009 and 2021, of eight Uruguayan and seven Argentine officers for the kidnapping and murder of Mario Julién and Victoria Grisonas and the abduction of their children.[27] However, as Uruguayan Mario Benedetti's poem about the vicissitudes of the siblings that opens this book states, the story is far from over ("el cuento no se ha acabado"). The search for answers continues.

Anatole and Victoria's ordeal is one of the most illustrative cases of the so-called Operation Condor, the secret repressive network that Argentina, Bolivia, Chile, Paraguay, and Uruguay created in late 1975 to target political opponents beyond their respective borders. This transnational arrangement helps explain how, in the three months between late September and late December 1976, the children's tribulations spanned three countries, from their initial abduction in Argentina, detention in Uruguay, and finally their abandonment in Chile. Their ordeal was especially enigmatic, since all other Uruguayan stolen babies were located in Argentina. Were Anatole and Victoria taken to Montevideo because one Uruguayan officer had wanted to adopt them but eventually realized that was unfeasible given Uruguay's small size and population? Had they been promised to a Chilean family who subsequently changed their minds and backed out? None of these hypotheses has ever been confirmed, but what is beyond doubt is that the Condor transnational network enabled these cross-border human rights violations to take place with complete impunity across the region.

Anatole and Victoria's tale powerfully illustrates the two main themes at the heart of this book: first, the transnational repressive coordination that South America's criminal states implemented throughout the 1970s to silence political exiles, and second, the transnational efforts by justice seekers who obstinately pieced together evidence about borderless terror and ultimately achieved accountability for some of these atrocities. The siblings' ordeal, while unique, also speaks to hundreds of other similar stories that South American exiled families lived through at that time: the initial despair and terror at the disappearance of loved ones, the unrelenting search for any leads of where they might be, the denial and impunity across the continent, and the silence and inaction from local authorities; but also the support of other families and survivors who bravely spoke out against state terror and injustice, international solidarity for refugees escaping persecution, and the enduring network of transnational activists who, in South America and beyond, have ceaselessly demanded justice.

Transnational Terror and Transnational Justice

This book reflects the growing interest in transitional justice since the late 1980s and draws attention to a largely marginalized aspect of this extensive literature: accountability for transnational human rights violations, which I define as crimes that cut across state borders. Indeed, transitional justice, which comprises different judicial and nonjudicial processes that countries embark on in tackling human rights violations after periods of dictatorship and conflict, has largely been dominated by a state-centric approach: consequently, human rights violations that did not conform to the borders of states were often left unaddressed.[28] Expert Pierre Hazan, the senior advisor on transitional justice with the Centre for Humanitarian Dialogue, notably admitted how the nation-state had been "a primary means of reflecting on and organizing transitional justice approaches."[29]

Indeed, the majority of the literature centered for a long time on the analysis of single-country studies or comparative volumes of transitions,[30] while other publications focused primarily on key actors such as the judiciary and civil society,[31] the role of distinct mechanisms—mainly prosecutions, amnesties, and truth commissions—and memory struggles.[32] Beginning in the 2010s, some scholars began to construct large-N country data sets to assess the impact of transitional justice mechanisms on human rights and democracy scores.[33] Despite their differences, all these contributions take the state as their main unit of analysis.

The state has, likewise, been the cornerstone of the international human rights system. In the past decade, however, issues such as environmental protection, the responsibility of transnational corporations, and the illegal rendition of suspected terrorists have encouraged scholars to pay more attention to the extraterritorial applicability of human rights provisions. Contemporary challenges, including deepening globalization, the fragmentation of states, and the rise of nonstate actors, have gradually questioned this overwhelming focus on the state. Steadily, international law has also begun to shift, and states have progressively yet reluctantly started to accept that their human rights obligations do not end at their borders; however, the top-down vertical relationship, according to which human rights must be primarily guaranteed within a state's territory, still prevails.[34]

This dominant state-centric approach has restricted the potential for the analytical study of and policy responses to only human rights violations that match the national boundaries of the states in which they occurred. This book complements the existing scholarship by proposing a shift to a two-level analysis which simultaneously encompasses the state and the international sphere. This transnational approach enables us to appreciate, on one hand, how from the late 1960s South American criminal states effectively suspended national borders in order to facilitate political repression and, on the other, how networks of transnational justice seekers working to achieve accountability for extraterritorial atrocities also required state borders to be transcended. In fact, the probing of transnational crimes involved a complex cross-border web of judges, lawyers, prosecutors, survivors, relatives, human rights activists, and experts in gathering evidence and supporting judicial proceedings both nationally and internationally.

I am not the first scholar to analyze transnational issues, and numerous publications exist within political science, international relations, law and sociology, with significant research having been conducted on both transnational activism[35] and international justice mechanisms.[36] A seminal publication is *Activists beyond Borders,* which probed the role and impact of transnational activist networks in changing human rights policies.[37] Further, Augusto Pinochet's 1998 arrest in London triggered abundant interest in transnational justice efforts and various types of strategic litigation for past atrocities,[38] including trials in foreign courts and the resort to universal jurisdiction.[39]

Building on these precedents, this book goes a step further and moves away from the prevailing focus on the jurisdictional venue employed to achieve justice—that is, domestic and international tribunals, to dedicate attention instead to the very nature of the crimes probed, which transcended the geographical borders of states and relied on the close collaboration between agents of various countries. Beyond the focus on extraterritorial human rights violations, this book also charts new terrain with regard to accountability processes for transnational atrocities, revealing the specific challenges—on top of those traditionally associated with accountability for domestic repression—related to the intrinsically complex and cross-cutting nature of extraterritorial crimes. It explores how these difficulties had to be overcome in investigating, documenting, and prosecuting transnational crimes, and how consequently transnational justice efforts were required to fully reconstruct the horrors perpetrated.

This book contributes as well to three other subsets of the transitional justice scholarship: first, publications exploring accountability outcomes through diverse explanatory variables and models;[40] second, contributions on the role of justice makers and innovators;[41] and finally, studies that monitor criminal trials for past atrocities.[42] I develop an analytical framework anchored in the notion of justice seekers to explain how individuals navigate complex transitional justice processes and overcome innumerable obstacles. Justice seekers were especially instrumental in revealing the atrocities of transnational repression as early as the late 1970s, when such crimes were being committed, and later in creating the momentum needed for judicial proceedings to take place. Indeed, a network of committed actors in both the domestic and international spheres filed criminal lawsuits at a time of impunity, supported the evidence-gathering process, and sustained these proceedings over time.

The focus on justice seekers contributes to transitional justice in two respects. First, it overcomes two prevailing dichotomies within the literature: namely, the frequent pitting of the national vs. the international spheres on one hand, and of civil society against the state on the other. Such binary framings leave numerous hidden nuances unaccounted for, and often are unable to capture how these distinctions are much more blurred in practice. In fact, justice seekers operate both domestically and internationally, as well as within civil society and state institutions. Second, it draws attention to proactive and strategic attempts by justice seekers to generate networks to support transitional justice processes. These individuals actively promote accountability, and their efforts at the national and international levels create the conditions necessary for justice to be achieved.

Last but not least, the book is also of interest to scholars and researchers investigating Operation Condor. Condor never ceases to attract attention and has been the subject of scholarly and journalistic research for decades, particularly since the discovery of the Archives of Terror in Asunción, Paraguay, in December 1992. Condor also has featured in numerous novels,[43] theater productions, documentaries, and art exhibitions,[44] and was in 2020 the subject of an extensive article in the *Guardian*.[45] The extant literature has extensively documented the political and historical origins of Operation Condor, and meticulously described its inner workings and dynamics. Significant publications have been released by North American[46] as well as South American scholars.[47] Interest in Condor intensified in 2015,[48] coinciding with the fortieth anniversary of its creation, and again after the latest round of declassification of US government documents in April 2019, which helped shed new light on previously unknown facets of this transnational operation.

The scholarship has, however, paid only limited attention to the search for accountability for Condor's atrocities. One important exception is the influential 2004 book by John Dinges, *The Condor Years,* where he outlined numerous initiatives in the US, South America, and Europe to provide justice for Operation Condor crimes in the 1990s and early 2000s. The present volume builds upon this precedent and takes it further, since Dinges's book was published when just a few such prosecutions had taken place. Since the late 2000s, there have been a rising number of criminal trials for Condor atrocities in South America and beyond.

This book contributes to this scholarship in two regards. First, it documents the post-2000 wave of prosecutions that have probed the atrocities of the transnational terror network, including two major trials in Argentina and in Italy that I closely monitored. Second, the Database on South America's Transnational Human Rights Violations, which was compiled between 2017 and 2020, systematically maps out for the first time the cases of victims of transnational human rights violations between 1969 and 1981 and contains information on 805 instances. This mapping exercise has allowed me to develop an original and new periodization of transnational repression in South America, which distinguishes five phases and outlines specific dynamics and core actors in each stage; this framing places Operation Condor within a broader historical and political context and thereby locates its origins within South America's local dynamics and prior traditions of police collaboration. These contributions complement the existing Condor literature, which largely focuses on the role of the US, by devoting closer attention to the local network of actors and dynamics in South America.

Methodology

This book relies on an interdisciplinary methodology that was especially developed by blending archival records, interviews, and judicial documents. This innovative research design transcends the traditional state-focused lens; regional and cross-regional studies have often been sidelined, but using such a framing can significantly contribute to our understanding of human rights violations, which rarely conform to state borders.

Blending data gathered from multiple and unexploited data sources, such as newly opened archives and recently completed criminal prosecutions, has enabled a richer account and a robust analysis of not only the geographical extent of transnational repression in South America, but also the role of criminal courts in redressing transnational crimes and how accountability may contribute to a sense of justice for victims, their families, and society. This approach can be seen as constituting a multisited ethnography for taking unexpected trajectories and operating in multiple sites of activity and connections.[49]

Between 2014 and 2018 I conducted extensive field research in South America and consulted ten state and NGO archives in Argentina, Brazil, Chile, Paraguay, Uruguay, and the United States, where I collated a compendium of 3,154 documents.[50] The archives are:

- *Argentina:* Ministry of Foreign Affairs, International Trade and Worship; Center for Legal and Social Studies; and memoranda by Chilean intelligence agent Enrique Arancibia Clavel;
- *Brazil:* Justice and Human Rights Movement; and the archives of the National Truth Commission;
- *Chile:* Vicariate of Solidarity;
- *Paraguay:* Archives of Terror;
- *Uruguay:* Historical and Diplomatic Archive of the Ministry of Foreign Affairs; and records of the Human Rights Secretariat for the Recent Past; and
- *US:* National Security Archive, which comprises documents from governmental agencies including the Central Intelligence Agency, the Federal Bureau of Investigation, the Department of Defense, and the State Department.

Further, I accumulated a corpus of twenty-seven legal documents relating to criminal proceedings for transnational crimes unfolding in Argentina, Chile, Uruguay, and Italy and also assembled a data set of forty-five criminal investigations, at different phases of the judicial process, taking place in Argentina, Chile, Uruguay, Italy, the US, Paraguay, Peru, Brazil, and France. Finally, I conducted 105 interviews in Argentina, Brazil, Chile, Italy, Paraguay, Peru, Uruguay, and the US, targeting survivors and relatives of victims of transnational repression and Operation Condor; historians, political scientists, journalists, and document analysts; and legal professionals and judicial actors, including lawyers, public prosecutors, and judges.

I was the only international scholar to monitor judicial proceedings on a regular basis in the Argentine Condor trial, of which I attended seventy-four hearings between October 31, 2014, and May 27, 2016, and in the Italian Condor trial, of which I observed eleven hearings between November 7, 2018, and July 9, 2021. This lengthy trial ethnography provided me with exceptional insights into the intricacies of justice dynamics and the innovative knowledge production that these prosecutions engendered.

Book Framework

This book is divided into two complementary parts, the first on transnational repression and the second on transnational justice. Accordingly, part 1 tackles the emergence of transnational political movements in South America from the 1960s and the ensuing transnational repression unleashed to suppress political opposition. During the 1960s and 1970s, both peaceful and armed political movements in South America became increasingly transnational in nature, largely owing to the movement of political exiles across the region. The Revolutionary Coordinating Junta (Junta de Coordinación Revolucionaria; JCR) was emblematic of this trend, bringing together four guerrilla groups from Argentina, Bolivia, Chile, and Uruguay in the early 1970s. Such transnational collaborations also occurred between political parties such as the Argentine and Chilean communist parties. These transnational movements induced South American states to begin coordinating their policies of repression on a continental scale: beginning in 1969, they progressively built a sophisticated network of collaborative practices that facilitated the elimination of political opponents no matter where they were physically located. Transnational repression effectively silenced opposition to South America's regimes by both revolutionary and peaceful groups, and even targeted individuals in exile in Europe and the US. Part 1 also employs illustrative cases of victims from Uruguay, Chile, Brazil, Paraguay, Bolivia, and Argentina to enhance understanding of the inner workings of these repressive ventures. Chapter 1 defines the concept of transnational repression and outlines five distinct phases. It then unpacks the first phase between August 1969 to January 1974, describing the political and historical context, beginning with the 1964 military coup in Brazil and outlining the downward spiral of dictatorial takeovers between 1971 and 1973 in Bolivia, Uruguay, and Chile. Chapters 2 to 5 analyze the remaining four phases of transnational repression and reveal the complex web of police, military, and intelligence actors who pursued exiled persons throughout South America. Condor constituted the apex of transnational repression, ushering in the most systematic, institutionalized, and centralized phase in which cross-border atrocities peaked between March 1976 and December 1978; cross-border atrocities then began to subside after early 1979.

While the terror was still unfolding, justice seekers bravely began to draw attention to this cross-border repression both domestically and internationally. As a result, a network of transnational activists emerged to gather the evidence required to reveal the crimes. The search for justice was transnational in two respects: first, traces and evidence relating to transnational crimes were collected and compiled throughout South America since the 1970s; and second, different tribunals and jurisdictions were strategically employed in numerous countries to overcome the prevailing impunity in the region. Part 2 examines the implications of transnational macrocriminality for subsequent justice-seeking efforts and the role of victims' relatives, human rights activists, and legal professionals in ensuring perpetrators were held to account. Chapter 6 sets out a novel analytical framework on justice seekers, while chapter 7 reviews their initial attempts, starting as early as 1976, to expose transnational repressive schemes. Chapter 8 then considers emblematic judicial proceedings that probed extraterritorial atrocities in Chile and Uruguay, further contributing to undermining broad policies of impunity in the region. Finally, chapters 9 and 10 tackle the *mega-causas* (large criminal proceedings comprising numerous victims and perpetrators) on Operation Condor in the courts of Buenos Aires and Rome, respectively. Finally, the conclusion recapitulates core lessons learned from the process of trying to achieve accountability for the Condor crimes and considers their potential relevance to contemporary manifestations of cross-border atrocities.

PART I
TRANSNATIONAL REPRESSION IN SOUTH AMERICA

1 • Five Phases of Transnational Repression

The *frontera seca*, literally "dry border," is an imaginary line that separates the border cities of Rivera (Uruguay) and Santana do Livramento (Brazil).[1] It demarcates an invisible boundary between the two nations and cuts across the city center that the two cities share, as well as a plaza fittingly called Praça Internacional (International Plaza), where one large Uruguayan flag and a Brazilian one tower on either side of the square.

At dawn on November 4, 1969, Uruguayan police officers crossed the *frontera seca* to return Wilson do Nascimento Barbosa to Brazil.[2] Barbosa was a *carioca*, a Rio de Janeiro native, and a history professor linked to the revolutionary guerrilla group National Liberation Action (Ação de Libertação Nacional), which had been established by Brazilian Communist Party dissidents in 1968. Two months earlier, on September 6, the Uruguayan police had arrested Barbosa as he visited a friend in Montevideo. Barbosa was in Uruguay to arrange for his wife and daughter to travel to Europe, after he had discovered that his name was on a list of people wanted by the Brazilian dictatorship. After his arrest, the police immediately took him to the fourth floor of Montevideo's police headquarters, where he was repeatedly tortured and interrogated. After two Brazilian army sergeants identified Barbosa at the ninth police precinct, he was incarcerated at a detention center located on the premises of the army's General Training Center for Reserve Officers (Centro General de Instrucción para Oficiales de Reserva; CGIOR) in Montevideo.

Barbosa's fate was the subject of close communication between Brazilian and Uruguayan authorities. On October 1 the Brazilian Ministry of Foreign Affairs (known as Itamaraty) learned of the arrest from the Brazilian Embassy in Uruguay, and Itamaraty's Center of Foreign Information (Centro de Informações do Exterior; CIEX) quickly informed all intelligence agencies that Barbosa had been about to travel to an "Iron Curtain" country, probably Cuba.[3] An agent of the Department for Political and Social Order (Departamento de Ordem Política e Social; DOPS),[4] Brazil's political police, also headed to Montevideo to coordinate with Uruguayan authorities on the ground.[5] In late October, after Itamaraty discovered that the Uruguayan Constitution gave detainees arrested during a state of emergency the option to leave the country, specific instructions were transmitted to the Brazilian ambassador on coordinating with the Uruguayan Interior Ministry for Barbosa's handover at the border.[6]

Consequently, on November 3, four Uruguayan police officers picked Barbosa up from the CGIOR and took him, handcuffed, to another police station where he was beaten until debilitated. He was a large man and a martial arts expert,[7] so only after he was incapacitated did the police officers place him on the floor of a Mustang car and, followed by a yellow vehicle with four additional officers, drove for Brazil. At 6 a.m. the following day, he was delivered to the Brazilian army's secret service at the Seventh Mechanized Cavalry Regiment in Santana do Livramento, where he was immediately interrogated and tortured. Subsequently, he was held in numerous prisons across Brazil, including Porto Alegre's DOPS and the eighth-floor secret prison within the Navy Information Center (Centro de Informações da Marinha; CENIMAR) in Rio de Janeiro.[8] In mid-January 1971, after a sixteen-month ordeal, he was freed on the condition that he leave Brazil and not return.[9]

In the late 1960s, Barbosa's tribulations were far from exceptional. Just weeks after his clandestine deportation, on November 28, 1969, the influential Uruguayan weekly magazine *Marcha* publicly denounced—in an article fittingly titled "Uruguay—Brazil: The End of Police Borders"—the plight of Brazilian refugees who had been arrested in Uruguay and, in some cases, subsequently reappeared in Brazil, including Barbosa, Jorge Miranda Jordão, José Calvet, Cláudio Antônio Weyne Gutiérrez, Euclides Garcia Paes, and brothers Sebastian Mendes Filho and Tarcino Guimarães Mendes.[10] Foreshadowing darker days to come, the article also related that DOPS delegate Sergio Fleury, the head of Brazil's death squads, would be traveling to Uruguay to meet high-ranking police officers to discuss internal security.

Barbosa's story, only one among a much larger number of cases, shows how Condor-style arrangements and practices had been unfolding in South America since the late 1960s. Accordingly, I propose the notion of transnational repression to capture how South America's criminal states perpetrated politically motivated extraterritorial human rights violations at least between 1969 and 1981. Transnational repression, as a concept, transcends the narrow focus on Operation Condor that dominates the existing scholarship. Throughout this book, I employ interchangeably the terms "transnational repression" and "repressive coordination" (from the Spanish *coordinación represiva*), since they both denote the same diverse yet interconnected processes of collaboration among South America's security forces to target political opponents beyond borders.

In this chapter, I outline five distinct phases within transnational repression, of which Condor was the apex: a three-year period when violence was centralized, institutionalized, systematic, and methodical. I analyze the first phase (Embryonic Interaction), by considering some illustrative episodes from the late 1960s and early 1970s in which Brazilian exiles were targeted in Uruguay, Chile, and Argentina, and afterwards clandestinely returned to their country of origin. The modus operandi in these episodes was undoubtedly more rudimentary than Condor's sophisticated system. But there are clear parallels which demonstrate that Condor arose from gradually increasing degrees of collaboration, which eventually consolidated in late 1975, when the novel system was set up and transcended all prior arrangements.

Transnational Repression

The Database on South America's Transnational Human Rights Violations elucidates how Operation Condor needs to be placed within a larger historical framework. Based on the insights from this original data set, I developed a periodization which differentiates five phases of transnational repression that permits a fuller appreciation of the origins, dynamics, and processes leading up to Condor and its subsequent downfall (fig. 2). I derived these stages by blending the trends emerging from the database with significant junctures in South America's history. Furthermore, this differentiation also captures shifting levels of violence, the participation of different actors, and diverse modes of collaboration (bilateral and multilateral) in each phase, and thereby lets us appreciate the increasingly higher degrees of centralization and sophistication that the regional coordination acquired over time.

The first period, labeled *Embryonic Interaction,* encompassed fifty victims between August 1969 and January 1974; August 1969 inaugurated this periodization, since the earliest case of cross-border persecution that I could trace occurred then. Between late 1969 and late 1972, only a few cases of victims of transnational repression took place per year until the Pinochet coup in Chile,

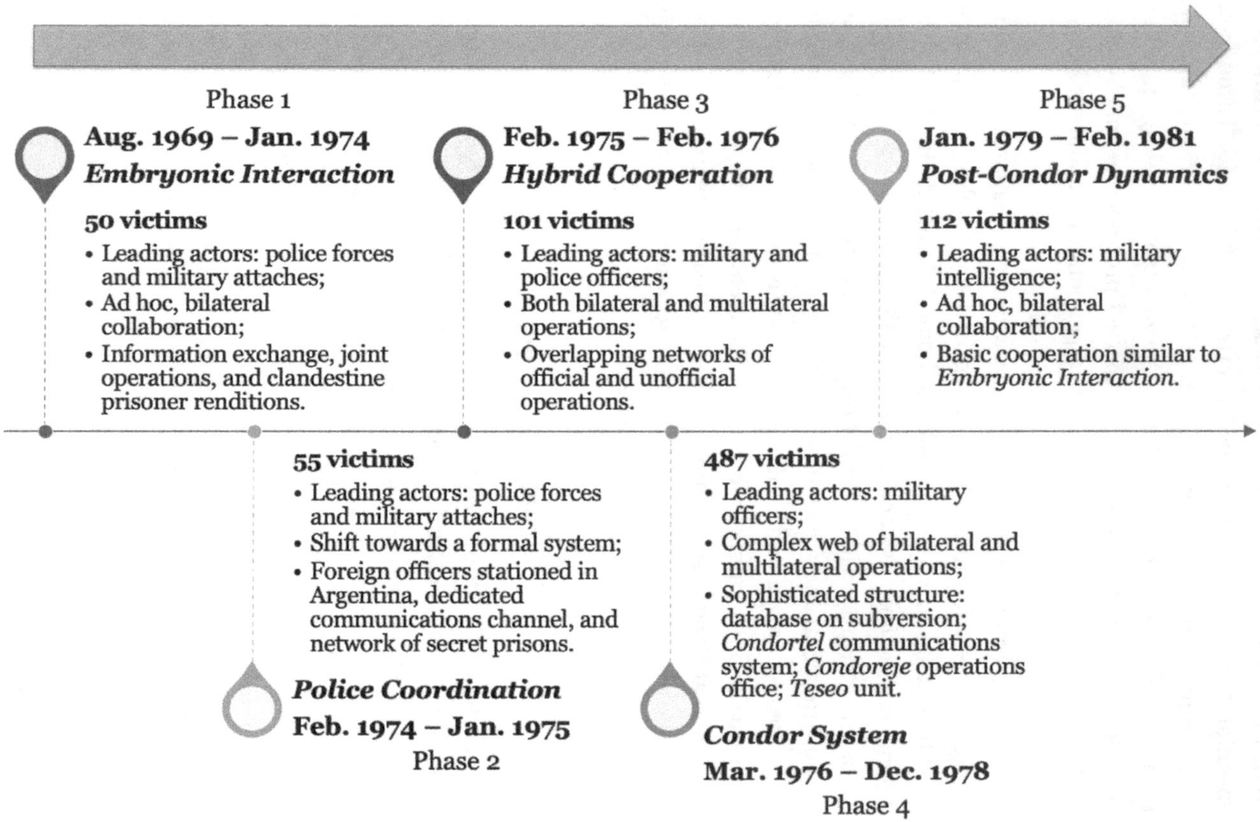

Phase 1

Aug. 1969 – Jan. 1974
Embryonic Interaction

50 victims
- Leading actors: police forces and military attaches;
- Ad hoc, bilateral collaboration;
- Information exchange, joint operations, and clandestine prisoner renditions.

Police Coordination
Feb. 1974 – Jan. 1975
Phase 2

55 victims
- Leading actors: police forces and military attaches;
- Shift towards a formal system;
- Foreign officers stationed in Argentina, dedicated communications channel, and network of secret prisons.

Phase 3

Feb. 1975 – Feb. 1976
Hybrid Cooperation

101 victims
- Leading actors: military and police officers;
- Both bilateral and multilateral operations;
- Overlapping networks of official and unofficial operations.

Condor System
Mar. 1976 – Dec. 1978
Phase 4

487 victims
- Leading actors: military officers;
- Complex web of bilateral and multilateral operations;
- Sophisticated structure: database on subversion; *Condortel* communications system; *Condoreje* operations office; *Teseo* unit.

Phase 5

Jan. 1979 – Feb. 1981
Post-Condor Dynamics

112 victims
- Leading actors: military intelligence;
- Ad hoc, bilateral collaboration;
- Basic cooperation similar to *Embryonic Interaction*.

Figure 2. Phases of transnational repression and key features.

in the aftermath of which a noteworthy spike of thirty cases unfolded between September and December 1973. My analysis of these cases provides the fundamental backdrop for the discussion in chapters 2 through 5: the defining features of transnational repression's modus operandi, including the close exchange of information and clandestine renditions, were already manifest in these early days. In this period, the region's police forces were the main actors that drove transnational repression and did so in close collaboration with military attachés: collaborative arrangements were relatively simple, and largely unfolded on an ad hoc and bilateral (i.e., between two countries) basis.

The second phase, defined as *Police Coordination,* unfolded between February 1974 and January 1975 and claimed fifty-five victims. The turning point that initiated this second period was the meeting of high-ranking regional police officers in Buenos Aires in late February 1974, during which a new system to target refugees in Argentina was formally agreed upon. It included, among other features, a secure communications channel and the permanent stationing of foreign officers. Although the number of victims in the first two phases may at first seem similar, the scope and extent of cross-border political persecution was more intense in this second phase, with fifty-five victims in just eleven months compared with fifty over the previous four years.

The third stage, named *Hybrid Cooperation,* involved 101 victims from February 1975 to February 1976; the number of cases almost doubled that of the previous phase and illustrates the deepening intensity of the repressive coordination. Since late 1974—but more openly after early 1975—there was also a shift in the actors involved, with military security and intelligence forces at this time acquiring more prominence in leading the regional collaboration. Additionally, bilateral forms of collaboration were gradually also complemented by rising instances of multinational cooperation involving three or more countries.

The fourth period, known as the *Condor System,* unfolded between March 1976 and December 1978, and had the highest number of victims, 487, corresponding to 60 percent of the total. Although the agreement that created Operation Condor was signed in late November 1975, that same document foresaw that signatory countries had until the end of January 1976 to ratify it and begin fully implementing the novel system. These provisions are reflected in the victim trends in the data set, which registers a marked rise in cases starting in March 1976. This month is thus taken as the starting point for this fourth phase, since the March 24 takeover in Argentina effectively removed any remaining barriers to unleashing the full terror upon thousands of political exiles who had been sheltering there for some time. During this phase, transnational repression was carried out through an impressive set of integrated, multilateral, and institutionalized arrangements, which comprised bilateral and multilateral operations, a shared information database, a secure and encrypted communications mechanism (Condortel), an operations headquarters (Condoreje), and planned assassinations in Europe (Teseo). Violence was at its most systematic and brutal in this phase, particularly between March and December 1976, when 31 percent of all victims were targeted within just nine months.

The final phase, called *Post-Condor Dynamics*, covers 112 cases between January 1979 and February 1981. During this period there was a return to the patterns of the initial phases, and large waves of arrests occurred in the context of the persecution against members of the guerrilla group Montoneros returning to Argentina. While operations still drew upon existing communications channels set up by Condor, transnational repression had become by then a watered-down version of the previous system: the multilateral and institutional aspirations of the Condor system phase had been abandoned because of resuming tensions between two core members, Argentina and Chile. The security forces remained key actors in this last phase, but operations returned to being bilateral and ad hoc, as in the early 1970s.

This periodization helps us better understand the gradual evolution and deepening of transnational repression, as well as its continuities and disruptions over time. Despite variation in each phase regarding the repressive actors involved, targeted victims, and modus operandi, four overall enduring trends can be discerned and taken to constitute the core features of transnational repression throughout. First, *persecution was squarely linked to political activism regarding the victims' country of origin*; indeed, victims were invariably targeted while in exile, but the reasons behind this were inextricably related to political activism linked to their native country. Second, there was a *fluid and rapid exchange of intelligence information* among South America's police and intelligence services, which included the meticulous monitoring of sought individuals both before and after detention. Third, *international task forces carried out joint repressive operations*; indeed, agents from interested countries, normally the victim's country of origin and where she or he currently lived, conducted operations together comprising unauthorized arrests, imprisonment, and interrogation under torture, before the final fate of detainees was decided. Most of these international operations unfolded in Argentina, which had initially been a safe haven for thousands of South American refugees, and over time turned into a "deadly trap."[11] Fourth, *clandestine rendition of prisoners* often took place after the initial arrest, with targeted activists then being forcefully returned to their country of origin via air, water, or land.

A Third World War?

Transnational repression in South America was facilitated by the diffusion of the National Security Doctrine (NSD) during the Cold War. The NSD, which has been defined as "an interrelated set of concepts about the state, development, counterinsurgency warfare, and, above all, security,"[12] began to spread in the 1950s and inspired the philosophies and operations of Latin America's armed forces and dictatorships. At that time, achieving national security was a fundamental objective that surpassed all other concerns. The doctrine also combined anticommunist sentiment and the threat of an internal enemy with a defense of Western Christian values. In 1950 anticommunism became explicitly central to US government policy when National Security Council Paper no. 68 gloomily depicted a battle for global hegemony taking place between the US and the Soviet Union.[13] This view gradually turned into an obsession and an ideological war, couched in the language of the Latin American militaries as a Third World War.[14] The experiences of French and US specialists in guerrilla wars in Algeria, Vietnam, and Cuba in the 1950s and 1960s further affected the NSD's counterinsurgency ideology.[15] According to this perspective, traditional rules governing conventional inter-state wars had been altered, and the new guerrilla wars were defined instead by an elusive and unconventional enemy, which was composed of irregular forces, avoided direct clashes, and was closely connected with the local population.[16]

Both the US and the French approaches directly influenced the doctrine of the Latin American militaries. In the late 1940s, the US began to train military forces from friendly nations, and hundreds of Latin American officers studied in Panama at the now infamous US Army School of the Americas (Escuela de las Américas), including learning counterinsurgency techniques.[17] In addition, US advisors were dispatched on the ground to instruct local police and intelligence officers. The case of Uruguay is representative here. Beginning in the mid-1960s, officers of the US Agency for International Development, especially of its Office of Public Safety, helped create, supply, and coordinate the intelligence apparatus of the Uruguayan police. Between 1969 and 1972, Uruguay was in fact one of the top four recipients in Latin America of US aid, alongside Brazil, Guatemala, and the Dominican Republic.[18] Dan Mitrione, among the many officers regularly stationed in Uruguay after 1964, especially promoted the use of torture and counterinsurgency techniques when coaching Uruguayan officers involved in fighting the Tupamaros guerrillas in the 1960s.[19]

In addition to US influence, the French experience with revolutionary wars in Algeria and Indochina particularly inspired the Argentine and Brazilian militaries. French military leaders advocated several concepts, including the division of territory to better control the population, the torture and disappearance of captured insurgents, and the importance of intelligence and interrogation methods.[20] In 1957, contact between the French and Argentine armed forces intensified, and several French advisors traveled to Buenos Aires to provide intelligence training and help the Argentines prepare for this new modality of war.[21] In 1960 the French and Argentine governments further signed a secret agreement to create a permanent mission of French assessors within the army's general staff in Buenos Aires, an arrangement that lasted until 1981.[22] It is noteworthy that the Argentine Army never used the US terminology of counterinsurgency, but instead followed French categories of "counterrevolutionary war" and "struggle against subversion."[23]

Against this geopolitical backdrop, authoritarian takeovers swept across South America, beginning in Paraguay in 1954 and followed by Brazil ten years later. There was a resulting snowball effect, and most of South America was under dictatorial rule by the mid-1970s. Coups occurred in Argentina in 1966, Peru in 1968 and 1975, Bolivia in 1971 and 1980, Uruguay and Chile in June and September 1973 respectively, and Argentina once again in 1976. These dictatorships mercilessly and methodically repressed all forms of opposition, pursuing members of left-wing armed groups and also politicians, intellectuals, teachers, students, workers, trade union leaders, and political activists. These regimes committed egregious human rights violations, including extrajudicial executions, unlawful imprisonment, enforced disappearances, torture and inhumane treatment, baby theft, and sexual violence. By the early 1970s, these policies of domestic political repression had acquired an additional and sinister dimension, owing to the expansion and intensification of regional collaboration, which allowed repression to transcend geographical borders.

The early origins of this regional network of cooperation, however, can be traced back to practices of police collaboration in South America that began in the late nineteenth century, when a close relationship already existed between the Brazilian and Argentine police forces. Information interchange, for example, can be dated back to 1902, when the identification services of the police forces of Rio de Janeiro and La Plata formally agreed to exchange their records.[24] In parallel, the concept of national security began being articulated: Argentina's 1902 National Residency Law specified that disruptive behavior that affected national security or public order could warrant the deportation of foreigners, and it was routinely used to summarily deport criminals, anarchists, and communists.[25]

In 1905 Croatian-born Juan Vucetich, who had pioneered fingerprinting methodologies in Argentina, coined the notion of "subversive criminals" in the context of emerging police collaboration in South America.[26] Furthermore, Vucetich and his assistant publicly proposed during the 1905 Third Latin American Scientific Congress in Rio de Janeiro the formation of a "South American Police Conference," to promote the creation of an international police force.[27] In October 1905 the first regional police conference was organized by the Buenos Aires Provincial Police and helped set the normative bases for this lasting police cooperation.

The minutes of this 1905 interpolice gathering (*conferencia interpolicial*) show that Vucetich's suggestion was approved, and that delegates began outlining the framework for collaborative policing, including arrangements to facilitate the exchange of criminal records of "dangerous individuals to society."[28] Argentine historian Diego Galeano notes how this broad category of "dangerous person" permitted the circulation of information among police forces regarding "a wide spectrum of suspects," ranging from urban thieves to international delinquents and labor activists.[29] Subsequently, the second South American International Police Conference (Conferencia Internacional Sudamericana de Policía) in February 1920 expanded this classification of potential enemies. Indeed, after the 1917 Russian Revolution, communist and anarchist movements were particularly in the spotlight, and Argentine, Chilean, and Brazilian police advocated the vigorous repression of any subversive act. Communications systems also became important at that juncture, so that police forces could quickly transmit information to verify the identity of suspected individuals. Moreover, conference countries also decided to promote the cooperation among police officers that was needed to monitor offenders and conduct criminal investigations outside of national territories.[30] These early practices of South American police cooperation would acquire renewed significance during the Cold War.

Ideological Borders

With the onset of military coups, particularly in Brazil on March 31, 1964, evidence began to surface regarding the surveillance and persecution of polit-

ical activists across borders in South America. National security and anticommunism defined the Brazilian regime, and consequently distinctions between
internal and external politics became increasingly blurred.[31] Ideological borders prevailed over territorial ones, since potential enemies could be found
anywhere, both inside and outside the country.[32] Politics rather than geography
increasingly defined borders, and, consistent with this Manichean vision, a
sharp line demarcated the Western Christian world from the communist one.[33]
Further, as organized political opposition increasingly disregarded borders, authoritarian regimes believed they should equally overlook national jurisdictions
when persecuting enemies. This new ideological reshaping of borders enabled
Brazil to harass its citizens abroad starting in the late 1960s, and to further
interfere in the internal politics of neighboring countries such as Bolivia and
Chile, where left-wing leaders had taken power, or in Uruguay, where the
Frente Amplio coalition seemed close to winning the 1971 elections.[34]

The large concentration in Montevideo of hundreds of leading exiled politicians, who included deposed Brazilian president João Goulart, and the governor of Rio Grande do Sul (hereafter RS) state Leonel Brizola, particularly
preoccupied the Brazilian dictatorship. Furthermore, *pombos-correios* (literally,
"carrier pigeons")—Brazilians who delivered information to exiles in Uruguay
and returned to Brazil with political guidelines—constantly crossed the porous
border.[35] Uruguayan authorities also became concerned about the political
activities that Goulart, Brizola, and other exiles were conducting in its territory, and considered imposing restrictions on their freedom of movement.[36]
In mid-1964, a DOPS/RS agent was already operating inside the Brazilian
Embassy to collate information and monitor Brazilians living in Montevideo.[37]
In 1965, yielding to pressure from Brazil, Uruguay's government confined
Brizola to the small resort town of Atlántida, near Montevideo, where he could
more easily be controlled.[38] Afterward, in 1967, the Uruguayan police was
placed on high alert, and instructed to closely watch exiles at the border in
Rivera:[39] the extensive *frontera seca* facilitated a continual flow of both fleeing
militants and security officers following after them.

Brazil's cross-border harassment of political opponents relied on a complex
web of civilian and military organs dedicated to intelligence gathering and
espionage.[40] At its heart stood the National Information Service (Serviço Nacional de Informações; SNI), established in 1964, which coordinated national
security information. Other organs, created between 1967 and 1970, included
the Army Information Center (Centro de Informações do Exército; CIE), the
CENIMAR, the Aeronautics Safety Information Center (Centro de Informações

de Segurança da Aeronáutica; CISA), the DOPS, and the Security and Information Divisions (Divisões de Segurança e Informações).[41] The Center of Foreign Information (CIEX) played a fundamental role in facilitating transnational repression. Inspired by the British MI6, Brazilian diplomat Manoel Pio Corrêa created it in 1966 to oversee his fellow citizens abroad: CIEX agents infiltrated refugee groups, exchanged intelligence information with local and foreign intelligence bodies, and constantly spied on individuals of interest.[42] Its activities were most intense in Montevideo and Buenos Aires, which were considered resistance hotspots, but it also operated in Paris, Prague, Moscow, and Lisbon.[43] Monitoring was permanent; eight years after the coup, for example, the Brazilian dictatorship still spied on Brizola in Uruguay.[44]

In 1968 political repression deepened further in Brazil. In June the dictatorship militarized several zones in the country, particularly near the southern border with Uruguay and Argentina, and declared them national security areas.[45] In December the sanctioning of Institutional Act No. 5 worsened persecution further, authorizing, among other provisions, torture, illegal detentions, the suspension of political rights, and censorship.[46] Although cases of disappearances dated back to 1964, this mechanism became especially emblematic of the terror regime from 1969 onward.[47] The late 1960s marked the start of Brazil's Years of Lead, and a second wave of exiles left for Uruguay. DOPS delegate Sergio Fleury also traveled at this time to Uruguay to train local military and police officers in antisubversive practices, and to improve collaboration with Brazilian intelligence. He also coordinated the monitoring of Goulart abroad; former Uruguayan intelligence agent Mario Neira Barreiro revealed to Brazilian newspaper *Folha de São Paulo* in 2008 how he had spied on the former president from mid-1973 until his mysterious death in December 1976 in Argentina.[48]

Brazil's repressive escalation coincided with Vice President Jorge Pacheco Areco (1967–72) taking over as Uruguay's president, after Óscar Gestido passed away a few months after taking office. During Pacheco's regime, authoritarianism crept into Uruguayan politics too, through the permanent use of constitutional emergency powers to suspend civil liberties and increasing use of police clampdowns to tackle mounting levels of economic and social crisis. In parallel, both right- and left-wing armed groups progressively became more violent. As Uruguay embarked on its downward spiral toward dictatorship, local authorities became increasingly interested in collaborating with their Brazilian counterparts. In this period, Uruguayan police arrested and illegally deported dozens of Brazilians, and cooperation between Brazilian and Uruguayan security forces also deepened in tracking Uruguayans.[49] For instance, DOPS/RS's search order 219/1972 transmitted information regarding Tupamaro member Enrique Ostrovski, who had escaped from the Uruguayan city of Salto and was allegedly heading to the Brazilian city of Rio Grande. Uruguayan authorities requested that their Brazilian counterparts discover the suspect's location and arrest him.[50]

Chilean Spring

In the late 1960s, as authoritarianism and repression intensified in Brazil and Uruguay, militants looked beyond the Cordillera (Andes Mountain range) to Chile for a safe refuge in which to regroup and sustain resistance. On November 4, 1970, the world anxiously watched the inauguration of Chile's new president, doctor and socialist politician Salvador Allende, whose political project seemed to combine "the best of the two worlds of the Cold War by achieving socialism through democracy."[51] Under his government (1970–73), Chile became a sanctuary for thousands of refugees fleeing political persecution in Bolivia, Brazil, and Uruguay. Up to 1,200 Brazilians, mainly left-wing guerrilla members, had arrived in Chile since 1968, and from there they repeatedly denounced Brazil's repressive downturn and the systematic use of torture. Concurrently, militants of the Bolivian National Liberation Army (Ejército de Liberación Nacional; ELN) recurrently sought refuge in Chile, escaping several waves of repression.[52]

Simultaneously, between 1,500 and 3,000 Uruguayans also landed in Chile, escaping persecution under Presidents Pacheco Areco (1967–72) and Juan María Bordaberry (1972–73).[53] Chile offered these militants not only a refuge but also a crucial space for their political activities, where they could fraternize and share experiences in a nonclandestine context.[54] Jorge Selves, a Tupamaro leader in Chile, recalled how "it was during the Chilean exile that the Latin American left had for the first time had the opportunity to get together and connect."[55] During the early 1970s crackdown against Uruguay's most famous urban guerrilla group, the Movimiento de Liberación Nacional-Tupamaros,[56] many political prisoners took advantage of constitutional provisions that allowed them to leave the country and settle abroad. Later on, dozens of these militants would be targeted by transnational operations in South America.[57] In Chile, Uruguayan militants in exile mostly stayed on the margins of local politics. Some Tupamaros, however, developed good relationships with the Chilean Socialist Party (Partido Socialista de Chile) and the Group of Personal Friends

(Grupo de Amigos Personales)—Allende's security team, with whom Tupamaros members, such as Natalio Dergan and William Whitelaw, closely collaborated.[58] These Tupamaro exiles also shared some ideological and political affinities with the Revolutionary Left Movement (Movimiento de Izquierda Revolucionaria; MIR), Chile's revolutionary guerrilla movement.[59]

A Continental Threat

This movement of militants across the Southern Cone from the late 1960s sparked a gradual emboldening and intensification of the repressive coordination among security forces. The Argentine Federal Police (Policía Federal Argentina; PFA) quickly took a leading role in conducting joint operations. Since 1966, Argentina had also been living under dictatorship, known as the "Argentine Revolution"—the prototype of O'Donnell's "bureaucratic-authoritarian state"[60]—that was headed successively by military rulers Juan Carlos Onganía (1966–70), Roberto Levingston (1970–71), and Alejandro Lanusse (1971–73). In this period, PFA officers conducted operations in close coordination with military attachés by closely exchanging intelligence information, carrying out unlawful arrests of sought individuals, participating in interrogation sessions, and arranging their repatriation—practices that would later become systematic on a regional scale.

Increasingly, collaborative arrangements among South American countries reflected their rising concern with the activities of revolutionary groups derived from the aftermath of the 1959 Cuban Revolution. The need for potential collaboration was articulated as early as August 1967, when Brazilian Foreign Minister José de Magalhães Pinto contemplated the prospect of bilateral cooperation with nearby countries if they sought assistance when facing the threat of subversion.[61] Steadily, regional collaboration in intelligence exchange and joint operations rose, ostensibly as a response to a parallel cooperation among the Southern Cone's revolutionary groups.

Documents from Paraguay's Archives of Terror further confirm these early concerted efforts by the region's authorities and security forces in monitoring the actions of subversive groups. In June 1969, for instance, Brazil informed Paraguay about the establishment of the so-called United Broad Front, which planned assassination operations in Brazil, Argentina, and Paraguay.[62] Further, another cluster of Paraguayans was apparently robbing banks in Foz do Iguaçu City to fund a counterrevolution in Paraguay, and trafficking arms into Brazil. Diplomatic missions regularly reported on how subversion, alongside its alleged implications for national security, was quickly expanding throughout South America.[63]

In mid-December 1970, the first major Argentine–Brazilian operation occurred in Buenos Aires,[64] during which Brazilian colonel Jefferson Cardim de Alencar Osório, his son Jefferson Lopetegui Osório, and his Uruguayan nephew Eduardo Lopetegui were unlawfully arrested and then deported.[65] Cardim, a close collaborator of Goulart and leader of the 1965 Guerrilha de Três Passos, had escaped from prison in 1968, aided by his son and former major Joaquim Pires Cerveira.[66] During his exile in Uruguay, in November 1970, Cardim had accepted Allende's invitation to become an advisor for his government to the Latin American Free Trade Association. Consequently, on December 11, Cardim, his son, and nephew set off from Montevideo to catch the ferry from Colonia to Buenos Aires, and then travel onward to Chile via Mendoza. A day earlier, the military attaché in Buenos Aires's Brazilian Embassy, Nilo Caneppa da Silva, who had received reliable information about Cardim's trip likely from Montevideo's CIEX agent Alberto Conrado Avegno,[67] set the arrest plan in motion, and contacted the PFA's Department for Foreign Affairs (Departamento de Asuntos Extranjeros).[68]

When Cardim and his travel companions arrived at Buenos Aires's harbor, they saw fifteen PFA vehicles waiting. Police officers informed them they were conducting routine inspections after receiving tip-offs that drugs were being transported.[69] Cardim whispered to his son, "Dançamos mesmo, tudo isso é mentira" (We are in real trouble, that's all a lie).[70] Next PFA officers took them to the Superintendencia de Coordinación Federal (Superintendence of Federal Coordination), a grim building located in central Buenos Aires, which housed a branch of the PFA that stood at the heart of political repression.[71] There they were imprisoned in separate cells and tortured for hours.

That same day, da Silva and Leuzinger Marques Lima, the deputy air attaché at Montevideo's Brazilian Embassy (who happened to be in Argentina for unrelated reasons), both went to the Coordinación Federal, where they checked confiscated documentation and the prisoners' property.[72] When an Argentine colonel approached them to inquire what should be done with the detainees, da Silva suggested that they be turned over to Brazilian authorities, since Argentine law allowed the expulsion of foreigners for subversive activities.[73] The colonel responded that arranging this would take a couple of days, given that the president himself had to authorize such a decision. The PFA's head, General Jorge Cáceres Monié, began the procedure straightaway. In parallel, soon after officers ascertained that Cardim's nephew worked for the Uruguayan military and was the son of a colonel, they put him on a commercial flight to Montevideo, after notifying the Uruguayan Ministry of Foreign Affairs.[74]

On December 12, da Silva briefed Ambassador Antonio Francisco Azeredo da Silveira about the arrests and requested permission, which was granted, for the prisoners' return to Brazil, escorted by Marques Lima and another Air Force officer.[75] The following day, Cardim and his son traveled on a Brazilian Air Force (Força Aérea Brasileira; FAB) plane alongside another prisoner, Para guayan Leonardo Pérez Leal.[76] Their ordeal continued in Brazil, where they were tortured at Galeão Air Base in Rio: there CISA agents Abílio Correa de Souza and Ferdinando Muniz de Farias questioned Cardim about his exile and trips to Cuba, Mexico, and Paris.[77] Meanwhile, in Buenos Aires, da Silva and PFA General Cáceres concurred on the convenience of close collaboration in addressing similar situations in the future.[78]

Archival records released by the Brazilian Truth Commission in 2014 indi cate that, just one month later, the Argentine government formally suggested to the Brazilian Foreign Ministry a confidential arrangement to promote the coordination between competent authorities regarding the activities and loca tion of "extremists."[79] The Argentines were keen to draw on diplomatic chan nels and proposed that the system "should aim for maximum speed in the exchange of information, in order to be effective."[80] The Brazilians welcomed the proposal; within a few months, this improved coordination arrangement was in place.

Unlike Cardim's earlier deportation, which had been signed off on by Ar gentina's president, any pretense of legality was abandoned during the kid napping of refugee Edmur Péricles Camargo in 1971. Camargo, also known as "Gauchão," had been the leader of a Brazilian guerrilla group that had op erated in Porto Alegre between 1969 and 1970. Since early 1971 he had been living as a political refugee in Santiago.[81] In a similar manner to the Cardim operation, on June 16 PFA officers forcefully dragged Camargo from a LAN-Chile plane, which had just landed at Buenos Aires's Ezeiza International Airport.[82] Camargo had been bound for Montevideo, where he was scheduled to undergo eye treatment, given that his sight had been compromised by tor ture.[83] His abduction was arranged among PFA officers, a CIEX agent nor mally based in Montevideo, and Brazilian military attachés in embassies in Santiago, Buenos Aires, and Montevideo.[84] At dawn on June 17, Camargo, who was escorted by Air Force attaché Miguel Cunha Lana and Paulo Sérgio Nery, the director of CIEX, was taken back to Rio de Janeiro on a FAB plane, which had been flown to Buenos Aires to collect him.[85] Camargo was never seen again.

The operations against Cardim and Camargo plainly demonstrate how in the early 1970s South America's dictatorships willingly and increasingly used extralegal methods to hunt down political opponents, and how more efficient mechanisms of coordination were beginning to emerge to facilitate the detention and rendition of exiled militants.[86] In these cases, the key role of the Argentine PFA as one of the core actors in charge of handling transnational repression was already forming, in addition to the rapid exchange of information and the mounting of operations through diplomatic channels that military attachés had access to. Similar coordination practices were likely in place between Argentina and Uruguay. Diplomatic correspondence of the Uruguayan Embassy in Buenos Aires shows that, in mid-December 1971, a Uruguayan police commissioner had traveled to Buenos Aires to interrogate three Uruguayan nationals, who had been arrested in a guerrilla camp in Córdoba and were being held incommunicado in the Coordinación Federal.[87]

Major newspapers in Argentina and Uruguay at the time repeatedly reported on the expansion of "communist subversion" in the continent. In June 1971, both Buenos Aires's *La Nación* and Montevideo's *El Día* recounted in detail an alleged terrorist plan to spread subversion by the "Revolutionary Movement of National Liberation" (Movimiento Revolucionario de Liberación Latinoamericana), which had been arranged at a meeting of "extremists" from numerous Latin American countries in Punta del Este weeks earlier.[88] In Argentina, concern with the Tupamaros' international activities and the likely establishment of an operational base in Argentina was significantly growing.[89] Indeed, Uruguayan militants had been fleeing in large numbers into Argentina since April 1972 (after the Uruguayan Parliament had declared a state of internal war against armed guerrillas), and numerous activists regularly traveled between the two countries.[90] Uruguayan groups (particularly the Tupamaros) were in fact collaborating with like-minded militants in Argentina, especially the Montoneros and the Workers' Revolutionary Party–People's Revolutionary Army (Partido Revolucionario de los Trabajadores–Ejercito Revolucionario del Pueblo; PRT-ERP).[91] Cooperation with the PRT-ERP,[92] one of Argentina's main guerrilla organizations, grew especially close in late 1972, as the specter of a military coup in Chile loomed nearer and hundreds of Tupamaros began retreating to Argentina from Chile.

Increasingly, the intensifying collaboration among revolutionary groups became a major concern in the eyes of the Southern Cone regimes, and one that warranted action. In January 1972 the Uruguayan ambassador in Chile, Manuel Sánchez Morales, pressed Foreign Minister José Mora Otero to nominate a military attaché who would help the embassy monitor Uruguayans coming into Chile. The ambassador lamented that the embassy could not keep track of exiles' activities and movements, despite knowing that individuals linked to subversive activities in Uruguay "constantly traveled in and out of Chile."[93] A military attaché, he believed, would provide invaluable assistance in efficiently scrutinizing refugees and would have better access to information and sources from the army and the Carabineros, which were off-limits to the diplomatic corps.

In a noteworthy step further, in September 1972 the Paraguayan Armed Forces and the Argentine Army signed a secret bilateral intelligence agreement, thus formalizing coordinated actions against subversive groups. The two countries would combine efforts to gather and exchange information and mutually collaborate through appropriate measures to discourage cooperation between revolutionary groups; when subversive activities persisted, the military would proceed to incarcerate activists in areas distant from the border.[94] These formal and informal measures multiplied throughout the 1970s as the region's dictatorships continued to join forces in response to the collaboration among the continent's revolutionary groups, especially the JCR.

Revolutionary Solidarity

The emergence of South America's dictatorships in the mid-1960s had triggered a widespread movement of political refugees in search of safety, first in Uruguay and then Chile. This exile had, in turn, "fostered the circulation of militants and ideas across the region" and encouraged coordinated action in fulfilling the objective of a continental revolution.[95] The notion of a global war against imperialism had been espoused in April 1967 by Ernesto Che Guevara in the *Tricontinental* magazine.[96] Che's failed experience and his later murder in Bolivia reinforced the willingness of South America's revolutionary groups to deepen their efforts and embrace armed struggle (*lucha armada*). Fidel Castro also endorsed the spread of the revolution throughout the American continent and promoted cooperation and solidarity among armed groups in July 1967 at the first conference of the Organization for Latin American Solidarity (Organización Latinoamericana de Solidaridad).[97]

Between 1966 and 1969, the Southern Cone's revolutionary groups developed "the firm conviction that revolution could be achieved in their own countries,"[98] and some organizations, largely the MIR, ELN, MLN, and PRT-ERP, started forging closer ties—initially mainly on a bilateral basis between 1968 and 1972—owing to their shared commitment to armed struggle.[99] Multilateral collaboration began in November 1972, when eight members of the MIR Political Commission, three PRT leaders, and three Tupamaro chiefs met in Santiago at a secret gathering, dubbed the *pequeño Zimmerwald*.[100] They unanimously approved a proposal by MIR's leader and the meeting's host, Miguel Enríquez, to "unify the revolutionary vanguard"[101] against imperialist domination and create a new international organization,[102] reflecting Guevara's idea of creating "coordinating juntas" (juntas de coordinación).[103] Indeed, through the JCR, these four groups could coordinate their actions without merging.[104] Several resolutions were also adopted, including the creation of a political magazine, the holding of a joint cadre school, and collaborative activities including the exchange of militants.[105] The first concrete action after this initial gathering was the MIR's hosting of the Cadre School (Escuela Internacional de Cuadros) in early 1973 in the Andean village of Farallones near Santiago.[106] This weeklong school provided political training to thirty middle-rank militants from Chile, Argentina and Uruguay,[107] enabled them to exchange experiences, and promoted the homogenization of their ideas.

During a second summit in June 1973 at Rosario, Argentina, larger delegations from each organization participated, and the ELN also formally joined this loose alliance; topics discussed included the PRT-ERP's proposal to launch a guerrilla war in Argentina's Tucumán province and the establishment of delegations to garner support overseas. Other collaborative activities involved public relations trips to Europe and Cuba, ransom kidnappings to gain funds, and the development of the JCR-1 submachine gun. In late 1973 Tupamaro leader Efraín Martínez Platero embarked on a trip to Cuba, Europe, and Algeria as the JRC's "official ambassador,"[108] in particular to seek Fidel Castro's blessing, which was, however, denied given El Comandante's dislike of the PRT-ERP. Simultaneously, the PRT-ERP, with MLN and ELN members, conducted three major kidnappings of businessmen in Argentina, including Exxon executive Victor Samuelson, and so secured $20 million, which the PRT-ERP partially shared with the other groups. Condor expert John Dinges aptly remarked how the JCR operated as a sort of "crypto Rockefeller Foundation of the radical Marxist left."[109] Finally, the manufacture of the JCR-1 submachine gun, designed by Argentine ELN leader Luis Stamponi and Chilean engineers who had copied the Swedish Carl Gustav,[110] began in a Tupamaros safe house on the outskirts of Santiago, but its production was moved in late 1973 to San Justo, near Buenos Aires.[111]

Between 1972 and 1973, Chile and the MIR had been at the heart of the JCR, but Pinochet's coup meant that the JCR and all its activities had to relocate to Argentina; starting in 1974, the PRT-ERP would increasingly take the lead in this coordination. Allegedly, the founding meeting of the JCR occurred in January 1974 in the small locality of Los Molles in Mendoza, in which a large number of guerrilla members from Argentina, Bolivia, Brazil, Chile, and Uruguay participated.[112] The PRT-ERP publicly announced the JCR's creation in mid-February 1974, when six journalists were picked up in Buenos Aires and taken to Villa Bosch, a town outside the capital, to attend a press conference. Eleven representatives of the JCR, MLN-Tupamaros, ELN, and PRT-ERP participated in the conference,[113] during which PRT-ERP leader Enrique Gorriarán Merlo distributed a pamphlet containing the JCR's constitutive declaration, known as *A los pueblos de América Latina* (To the People of Latin America). An announcement occurred concurrently in Lisbon.

The declaration was reproduced in November 1974 in the first issue of the political theory magazine *Che Guevara,* the JCR's official press organ, and explained these groups' decision to join efforts and conduct their political and ideological struggles more efficiently together against bourgeois nationalism, imperialism, and reformism, following in Che Guevara's footsteps. The JCR believed that a continental revolutionary strategy should match the international imperialist tactic, and it was open to other revolutionary organizations to join. The declaration was effectively a call to arms for a revolutionary war in Latin America directed to the working class, the *campesinos* (rural workers), students, intellectuals, and all the exploited classes.[114]

Foreigners in Pinochet's Chile

After the military coup on September 11, 1973, Chile became engulfed in an unprecedented spiral of bloodshed and brutality, characterized by illegal arrests, torture, and extrajudicial executions. On September 16 the security forces assassinated famous folk singer Víctor Jara in Santiago's Chile Stadium, which had become one of several improvised detention centers for political prisoners. By December the population of prison camps had climbed to eighteen thousand.[115] Furthermore, in just one month between September and October 1973, the infamous *caravana de la muerte* (death caravan) commanded by General Sergio Arellano Stark left behind a trail of ninety-six extrajudicial executions of political prisoners from Valdivia in the south to La Serena and Calama in the north.[116] The dictatorship quickly silenced all dissenting voices and detained former members of Allende's cabinet, including Defense Minister Orlando

Letelier, later sending them to a concentration camp in Isla Dawson in the remote Tierra del Fuego archipelago.

The military junta especially targeted the large community of South American exiles, estimated to be between ten thousand and thirteen thousand, accusing them of involvement in internal politics and of constituting a security threat for Chile.[117] On September 12 the dictatorship issued an ultimatum, and foreigners had to report to the closest police station or military division to explain why they were in Chile and all the activities they had undertaken since arrival.[118] On September 16 another communiqué warned "against foreign extremists who had come to kill Chileans," exhorting Chilean citizens to report them to the closest military authority.[119]

Simultaneously, the Uruguayan dictatorship, which was particularly preoccupied with a potential vast return of Tupamaros, closely collaborated with its Chilean counterpart and shared information on Uruguayans arrested in Chile "to determine if they were linked to the Tupamaros."[120] Interest in the activities of Uruguayan exiles in Chile predated the coup. In April 1973 the Uruguayan military intelligence service, the Defense Information Service (Servicio de Informacion de Defensa; SID),[121] had reported that a Tupamaro column had been active in Chile since 1971,[122] and this so-called *Guacha chica* group allegedly welcomed incoming Uruguayans in Chile, offering accommodation and other kinds of support.[123]

Right after the coup, preoccupation with Uruguayans in Chile intensified. On September 14 the SID transmitted a list of 159 Tupamaros thought to be in Chile to the Uruguayan Police's National Directorate of Intelligence and Information (Dirección Nacional de Información e Inteligencia; DNII).[124] Equally, Brazilian diplomatic missions in Chile, which had been monitoring Brazilian refugees since the late 1960s, also increased efforts to track their whereabouts, and the embassy worked in close collaboration with local authorities in Santiago.[125]

Cooperation extended beyond information exchange, since Uruguayan, Argentine, and Brazilian officers were physically in Chile, conducting operations with their local equivalents. A declassified report of the US Department of Defense revealed that four Uruguayan Army officers were in Santiago in mid-September 1973, noting how Uruguay had "a small staff working at the Chilean Army Headquarters in Santiago in order to review the status of all Uruguayans in Chile" and to "interrogate those in custody and investigate those seeking to return to Uruguay."[126] Furthermore, a memo by Enrique Arancibia Clavel, a Chilean secret agent stationed in Argentina (see chapter 2), revealed how nine Argentine police and intelligence officers, who reported to Argentine colonel Jorge Oscar Montiel, had conducted antisubversive operations in late 1973 with Chilean intelligence in the city of Puerto Montt.[127]

Estadio Nacional

Nowhere else was the collaboration between South America's security forces more evident than at the National Stadium (Estadio Nacional), another makeshift political prisoners' camp in Santiago, where plainclothes Uruguayan and Brazilian officers operated with the permission of the Chileans.[128] Over six hundred foreigners were imprisoned there, mainly Bolivians (147), Uruguayans (89), Brazilians (88), and Argentines (63), in a separate section (sección extranjería) headed by Major Sergio Fernández between mid-October and late November.[129] According to Fernández and other Chilean officers, including Brigadier Raúl Jofré (the assistant to the National Stadium's commander), Argentines, Brazilians, and Uruguayans were among the stadium's interrogators and had been deliberately sent from their respective countries to deal with detainees of those nationalities.[130] These foreign officers had access to specifically allocated offices on the second floor that were equipped with torture paraphernalia.[131]

Testimonies from National Stadium survivors, investigations by Amnesty International, and declassified US documents provide additional evidence of the presence of foreign agents. Several former prisoners, including Otto Brockes and Nielsen Pires, testified in a 2014 public hearing about the presence of Brazilian police officers at the stadium. Tomás Togni narrated how a Chilean police officer had interrogated him about an association of Brazilian exiles in Chile, the Brazilian left, and activities back home based on questions that five Brazilian police officers, who were standing behind him, wrote on pieces of paper as they attempted to dissimulate their identities.[132] Similarly, Osni Gomes recalled how three Brazilian agents openly interrogated him in Portuguese about his trip to China and the Communist Party of Brazil, using torture methods including the typical Brazilian pau de arara (literally, parrot's perch). Chilean officers witnessed Osni's session behind a glass wall and the victim overheard them say that "the Brazilians were professional torturers."[133] Luiz Carlos Guimarães, another prisoner, recognized in the stadium one of his interrogators, nicknamed "the doctor," as CENIMAR officer João Alfredo Poeck, who had tortured him months earlier; Poeck also told Guimarães that "they would resume the conversation interrupted in Rio de Janeiro."[134] CIE colonels

José Brant Texeira and Paulo Malhães (see chapter 5) also operated in Chile.[135] Correspondence from Santiago's Brazilian Consulate to the SNI from October 1973 further substantiates prisoners' accounts, since it noted how the vice consul, who had gone to the stadium to deliver a confidential letter containing the name of Brazilian prisoners whose return to Brazil was undesirable, encountered five Brazilian police officers accompanied by the Brazilian military attaché, who "were taking care of the situation of Brazilian detainees."[136]

Amnesty International, whose delegation visited the stadium in early November 1973, publicly denounced in 1974 the fact that Brazilian police officers not only assisted in interrogations but also provided training in interrogation techniques to the Chileans. The Brazilian team, led by torture specialist Poeck, had arrived in mid-October and interrogated approximately twenty Brazilian prisoners: the Chilean police admired and praised their "Brazilian methods."[137] The US Embassy in Santiago was also aware of this situation, since Brazilian prisoners had recounted to refugee workers that they had been interrogated by "individuals speaking fluent Portuguese and whom they assumed to be Brazilian police or military intelligence officers."[138]

Uruguayan prisoners, including nineteen-year-old Luis Giusti and history professor Heber Corbo, similarly spotted in early October officers from their country in civilian clothes who interrogated some of their comrades.[139] Another Uruguayan prisoner, Carlos Capelán, directly witnessed the consequences of the brutal torture that Alberto Corvalán, son of Luis Corvalán, secretary general of the Chilean Communist Party (Partido Comunista de Chile; PCC), had suffered at the hands of Uruguayan officers.[140] The latter were specialists in torture methods that did not leave lasting marks, and they shared their sophisticated methods with the Chileans, who were too brutal in handling prisoners and left enduring scars. Ostensibly, Uruguayan military officers spoke with complete impunity about their nationality, their mission in Chile, and their intention to interrogate Uruguayan prisoners at the stadium.

In late 1973 the repression against foreigners heightened throughout the Southern Cone. In Chile ten Uruguayans—mainly Tupamaro militants—were disappeared or murdered,[141] while the Argentine gendarmerie arrested and returned three Chilean militants, who had sought exile in southern Argentina a month earlier, to military officers and Carabineros at the Chilean border, where they disappeared. In December, an Argentine–Brazilian operation, probably commanded by delegate Fleury, resulted in the abduction from Buenos Aires of Joaquim Pires Cerveira and João Batista Rita, leading members of Brazilian guerrilla groups who had recently fled from Chile.[142] Afterward they were unlawfully returned to Brazil and were seen in January 1974 at the secret army prison on Rio de Janeiro's Barão de Mesquita Street, bearing evident signs of torture.[143] Their disappearance and that of Argentines Juan Raya and Luciano Pregoni in Rio in November 1973 were most likely connected, since Raya was at that time allegedly collaborating with Pires Cerveira's group.[144]

In late 1973 thousands of asylum seekers began to arrive in Argentina, escaping Pinochet's terror. Diplomatic missions closely monitored these refugees and, as early as mid-1973, Buenos Aires's Uruguayan Embassy had requested instructions from Montevideo on how to proceed when Uruguayan asylum seekers requested consular assistance.[145] The embassy also closely monitored prominent exiled Uruguayan politicians, especially Enrique Erro, Zelmar Michelini, and Héctor Gutiérrez-Ruiz,[146] and regularly informed Montevideo of developments regarding their legal status in Argentina and when they sought consular assistance, especially passport renewal.[147] Equally, the Chilean Ministry of Foreign Affairs oversaw the activities of Chileans abroad from December 1973, when all diplomatic missions received instructions to forward lists of Chilean citizens within their jurisdictions who had conducted or were leading campaigns against the military junta, alongside their connections to local politicians, the media, and international organizations.[148]

Final Reflections

This analysis of the Embryonic Interaction phase of transnational repression has shown how, from the late 1960s, the Southern Cone countries and Brazil progressively increased their collaborative arrangements to harass political opponents beyond the geographical borders of their territories. The pursuit of Brazilian refugees in Uruguay, Argentina, and Chile—alongside rising cases of Uruguayan, Chilean, and Argentine militants equally being targeted from late 1973—demonstrates how South American countries gradually began to coordinate their actions in response to the perceived threats from the revolutionary and political movements active on the continent. Victims of cross-border repression steadily rose in number. Operations by foreign military officers in Santiago's National Stadium in late 1973 constituted, in the words of former Brazilian prisoner Togni, the first tragic example of "international cooperation in torture and repression."[149] Not only did Brazilian and Uruguayan officers interrogate detainees of those nationalities, but they also disseminated their knowledge of torture and interrogation techniques to the Chileans.

It was not solely dictatorial regimes such as Brazil, Uruguay, and Chile that participated in regional terror. Argentina, which had held presidential elections in March and September 1973, electing Héctor Cámpora and Juan Perón respectively, also participated. Argentine security officers in fact clandestinely repatriated Chilean militants detained in Patagonia, collaborated in joint operations with Chilean and Brazilian officers, and began targeting Argentine citizens abroad in mid-1973.[150]

Transnational repression in this phase mainly unfolded through bilateral, ad hoc operations that persecuted specific militants, mostly Brazilian refugees. Brazil played a fundamental role from the late 1960s, when it pioneered the practice of pursuing its citizens abroad through the so-called *Plano de Busca no Exterior*[151] (Abroad Search Plan), and inaugurated practices such as the monitoring of exiles through its military attachés, joint detention and interrogation operations, and illegal deportations. Former Brazilian president General Ernesto Geisel admitted that agreements regarding information exchange were in place with Argentina and Uruguay since the government of General Emílio Garrastazu Médici (1969–74).[152] Beginning in 1969, Brazilian military and police intelligence officers—especially from DOPS/SP—further taught counterinsurgency methods for fighting urban guerrillas to Argentine, Chilean, Paraguayan, and Uruguayan officers who traveled to Brazil for training.[153]

By late 1973 the repressive coordination had significantly deepened. With military coups in Uruguay in June and Chile in September, South America's geopolitical context had changed significantly. Curbing all subversive threats, whether arising from revolutionary groups or political parties, became a shared priority for South American regimes. The next chapter illustrates how by early 1974 the existing ad hoc and bilateral arrangements no longer sufficed, and the aggregation of thousands of South American refugees in Argentina deeply troubled the dictatorships, which then put in place a more formalized mechanism for regional collaboration.

2 • Police Coordination in the Southern Cone

Rocha is a province in Uruguay of astounding natural beauty, facing the southern Atlantic Ocean: a land of sand dunes, fishing villages, crystalline waters, and sea lions on the coastline, and of lagoons, ranches, green pastures, and horses inland. The army's Twelfth Infantry Battalion is located in Rocha's homonymous capital, and this was where Antonio Viana Acosta was imprisoned in a cell near the communications room. In November 1972, when Captain Pedro Buzó Correa was forced to free Antonio, since no evidence had been found of his suspected participation in the MLN-Tupamaros, Buzó Correa uttered sinister words of farewell: "I am sure you are a Tupamaro and not a small fish. I will tie up loose ends and don't forget this, wherever you will go, anywhere in the world, I will find you."[1]

In the early 1970s Viana Acosta had been repeatedly arrested in Uruguay on suspicion of being a member of the Tupamaros, which he was. After this latest episode, he decided to move to Argentina in 1973 with his wife Estela. They lived a few blocks away from one of Buenos Aires's central train stations, Once de Septiembre, until February 1974, when Argentine PFA officers unlawfully arrested him. Taken to the secret prison on the premises of the Superintendence of Federal Security (Superintendencia de Seguridad Federal; SSF) near Congress—formerly Coordinación Federal—Uruguayan and Argentine officers tortured him about his Tupamaros activities in Argentina. Weeks later, he was forcefully repatriated to Uruguay. As predicted in Captain Buzó Correa's threatening words, the tentacles of transnational repression had indeed reached Antonio.

As discussed in chapter 1, coordinated repression had consolidated further after the coup in Chile, and the subsequent presence of thousands of refugees in Argentina meant that the prior cooperative practices were no longer adequate. A stronger system of regional collaboration was believed to be needed, and this began to form in late February 1974 at a high-level meeting in Buenos Aires, when the region's police chiefs agreed to launch a novel operational arrangement. Inspired by Interpol, this scheme envisioned the creation of a secure communications channel, an information headquarters, and the free movement of agents, among other elements.

During this *Police Coordination* phase of transnational repression, both high-profile victims and rank-and-file militants were equally targeted. Pinochet's intelligence agency, the Directorate of National Intelligence (Dirección de Inteligencia Nacional; DINA), dramatically assassinated exiled Chilean general Carlos Prats in Argentina, while Uruguayan and Argentine police officers increasingly harassed symbolic figures, particularly exiled Uruguayan politician Zelmar Michelini, and further pursued lower-profile militants, especially those belonging to the Tupamaros.

Two enduring features emerged at this time: first, Uruguayans began to be systematically targeted, and, second, Argentina was the main theater of extraterritorial operations. A large number of Paraguayan, Uruguayan, Bolivian, Chilean, and Brazilian exiles had indeed congregated by the mid-1970s in Argentina, the last Southern Cone country to retain a semblance of democracy where exiles could seek shelter. Amnesty International estimated there were about a hundred thousand refugees, but the true number is likely to have been higher.[2]

This chapter unpacks this second phase that, between February 1974 and January 1975, claimed at least fifty-five victims. Initially, it analyses events leading up to the secret February gathering and then the development of the new police coordination scheme. Subsequently, case studies of victims illustrate the practical implementation of this new format.

Fleeing Chile

Immediately after Pinochet's coup, many foreigners had found safe harbor in the embassies of Italy, France, Mexico, and Argentina, thereby being spared certain torture and potential death. Conversely, the diplomatic missions of Chile and Uruguay were used as crucial extensions of domestic repression, closely and actively monitoring refugees in order to transmit information back home and aid intelligence gathering. During the austral summer of 1973 and 1974, the watchful eyes of ambassadors, consuls, and military attachés tracked the movements of political refugees across South America. The Chilean Embassy in Argentina was particularly active. For instance, in January 1974 Ambassador René Rojas informed the consul in Buenos Aires that Argentina had become an important center for resistance activities against the Chilean junta and that information had to be gathered on the existence of guerrilla training camps, the movement of arms and people to and from Chile, and the formation of resistance groups.[3] The embassy regularly conveyed all relevant developments to Santiago, such as the entry of two MIR militants in January 1974 into the southern Patagonian Neuquén province, and their subsequent requests for political asylum.[4] The military attaché also transmitted this type of intelligence to the Chilean Army Intelligence Directorate and the Argentine State Information Secretariat (SIDE).[5] Further, the ambassador keenly sought information on Chilean refugees from local authorities, in particular the Argentine Ministry of Foreign Affairs.[6]

Uruguayan diplomatic missions similarly engaged in surveillance activities.[7] In January 1974 the consulate in Santiago compiled a list of all Uruguayans seeking asylum in embassies, especially those of Sweden, Argentina, and Venezuela;[8] one refugee included on the 251-strong list, Luis Latronica, would be murdered in one of the earliest joint Argentine–Uruguayan operations in Buenos Aires. Since mid-1973 the Uruguayan regime had kept an especially close watch on Tupamaro members resettling in Argentina from Chile. Uruguayan historians Clara Aldrighi and Guillermo Waksman have documented how, in March 1973, Tupamaro leaders determined to abandon Chile, for fear of an imminent coup, and moved to Buenos Aires.[9] In late 1973 numerous other militants clandestinely crossed into Argentina or arrived after securing asylum through diplomatic channels. In Buenos Aires, Tupamaro leaders aimed to be physically closer to Uruguay and participate in the JCR. But this relocation ultimately had deadly consequences. The Uruguayan security forces, extremely concerned with the Tupamaros' connections with the JCR, resolved between late 1973 and early 1974 to tackle these potential threats head-on. They soon unleashed an unprecedented wave of operations against exiled Tupamaros in Argentina to impede their consolidation and resurgence.

Rear Guard in Argentina

By 1974 Southern Cone militants faced a different scenario than in the early 1970s: the 1971 coup in Bolivia, followed by those in Uruguay and Chile in 1973, had shattered revolutionary hopes, but reaffirmed in these activists' view "the inevitability of armed struggle."[10] Uruguayan historian Aldo Marchesi has observed how, in the mid-1970s, Argentina became a strategic rear guard (*retaguardia*) for Uruguayan, Chilean, Bolivian, and Brazilian militants, where they could maintain political activities. However, Argentina too had begun a spiraling descent toward political violence and authoritarianism.

Over sixty thousand Uruguayans, whether they were political or economic migrants, now lived in Argentina, and Buenos Aires was a crucial site in the consolidation of resistance against the Uruguayan dictatorship, serving as "the operative base of organized political exile."[11] Since President Bordaberry's violent repression against the Tupamaros in 1972, this group had established its rear guard in Buenos Aires from where, influenced by the PRT-ERP, it was planning a *contraofensiva* (counteroffensive), a massive influx of militants back into Uruguay, which never materialized.[12]

Other Uruguayan political organizations similarly retreated to Argentina, including the Anarchical Federation of Uruguay (Federación Anarquista del Uruguay; FAU), with its mass branch, the Workers and Students' Resistance (Resistencia Obrera Estudiantil; ROE), and its military sector, the Popular Revolutionary Organization–33 Orientals (Organización Popular Revolucionaria–33 Orientales; OPR-33); and the Uruguayan Communist Party (Partido Comunista Uruguayo; PCU).[13] These also set up their *retaguardias* in Buenos Aires, which was strategically located near Uruguay but also enabled militants to easily travel to Cuba or Europe when needed.[14]

Meanwhile, the MIR's decision against exile ("¡No asilo!") after Pinochet's coup meant that few of its militants participated in the JCR in Argentina initially and did so largely only after the DINA murdered its leader Miguel Enríquez in October 1974.[15] Conversely, most ELN members had fled from Chile to Argentina, where they reencountered other exiled leaders of the Bolivian left—most important, former president Juan José Torres, who was working to consolidate the resistance against the dictatorship of Hugo Banzer (1971–78), which had overthrown him in 1971.[16] Torres assembled a coalition of opposition groups, called the Alliance of the National Left (Alianza de la Izquierda Nacional) to prepare its return to power; Major Rubén Sánchez, also the ELN's representative at the JCR, was the former president's closest collaborator in Chile and Argentina.[17]

The security forces perceived this high concentration of exiles in Argentina as a breeding ground (*caldo de cultivo*) for subversion.[18] As early as October 1973, the head of the SSF, Lieutenant Colonel Jorge Oscar Montiel, recommended that the Immigration Office expel a group of Uruguayan exiles who had recently arrived from Chile, arguing that their presence compromised national security in Argentina.[19] Further, the JCR's public appearance in February 1974 offered the perfect reason to justify consolidating a mutual system of repression by the region's security forces to respond to the increased coordination by revolutionary groups.[20] South America's criminal states believed that their response to the international communist threat should also be international.[21] In practice, transnational repression enabled the security forces to progressively dismantle the JCR and also to target numerous exiled nonarmed political opponents, which were equally considered a menace.

A Tupamaro in Buenos Aires

Antonio Viana Acosta had crossed the River Plate in March 1973 and was one of thousands of Uruguayans living in Buenos Aires. "There is no space for me in Uruguay, and I am a danger [queme] for the other comrades [compañeros]," he had told the leader of his Tupamaro column, who endorsed Antonio's decision.[22] In Argentina, Antonio was politically active within the Tupamaros and the JCR, and met regularly with senators Zelmar Michelini and Enrique Erro, whom he knew from Uruguay. He was also a volunteer social worker at the Ministry of Social Welfare, which was then the cradle of the infamous Alianza Anticomunista Argentina (Argentine Anti-Communist Alliance; AAA), a far-right group that, between 1973 and 1975 while Argentina was still technically a democracy, murdered hundreds of left-wing activists and political figures.[23] Created by President Perón's private secretary and minister of social welfare, José López Rega, the AAA drew members from the police, military, trade unions, and Peronism, whilst its leaders included PFA police inspector Alberto Villar and superintendent Juan Ramón Morales.

Antonio witnessed the AAA's gestation throughout 1973: weapons, illicitly bought in Paraguay, were stockpiled within the ministry's premises, and ambulances were used to move armaments around. One day Antonio noticed something unusual close to home. Ford Falcon cars and two or three people he had previously seen in the ministry were stationed on the same block as his house. After reporting this incident to his comrades, they advised him not to return to the ministry and said that they would transfer him to a different house. But before Antonio could move, an AAA task force, composed of PFA inspectors Villar and Luis Margaride and other individuals, violently broke into his home in the early hours of February 21, 1974, screaming "We know you are a Tupamaro, and we came to get you."

Days later, the Uruguayan Embassy notified the Ministry of Foreign Affairs of the incident, reporting that "the Federal Police, through information received from neighbors, became aware that Tupamaro elements had sought refuge in the house located in Anchorena 82. After inspecting the site, Antonio Viana Acosta, Estela Angela Barboza, and Eduardo Dutra Soria were detained. All Uruguayan citizens. Viana Acosta admitted he had handwritten a list of Uruguayan security forces' agents, from Rocha province, against whom attacks were being planned."[24]

Antonio was taken to the SSF headquarters, where Argentine and Uruguayan police and military officers, including Uruguayan police commissioner Hugo Campos Hermida and Major Manuel Cordero of the SID, tortured him. The presence of Uruguayan officers did not surprise Antonio, who had seen them previously roaming the streets of Buenos Aires. Using psychological and physical torments, his interrogators questioned him about the PRT-ERP, the Tupamaros, and the addresses of numerous sites belonging to these groups.

A Meeting during Carnival

Less than a week after Antonio's kidnapping, the heads of the police forces of Argentina, Bolivia, Chile, Paraguay, and Uruguay held a secret meeting in Buenos Aires. Unlike Condor's founding summit, this February 1974 gathering has received little attention except from US political scientist Patrice McSherry, who first highlighted its significance.[25] Information about this meeting is limited, but fortunately more details have recently come to light.

The Argentine PFA hosted this summit between February 27 and March 4, which was Carnival week. Representatives from Bolivia, Chile, Paraguay, and Uruguay participated. Brazil did not attend, citing the meeting's occurrence during Carnival as the reason for their absence.[26] Delegates included the PFA's head, General Miguel Ángel Iñiguez, inspectors Villar and Margaride, and Uruguayan police inspector General Víctor Castiglioni, director of the DNII. A three-person mission traveled from Chile, composed of General Ernesto Baeza Michaelsen, the director general of Chile's Investigations Police, René Navarro Verdugo, his legal advisor, and Air Force Colonel Mario Jahn Barrera, the deputy director of DINA, to participate in this international meeting organized to study and exchange experiences about subversive groups operating on the continent.[27] Details on delegations from Paraguay and Bolivia could not be confirmed.

Uruguayan investigative journalist Roger Rodríguez unearthed details on this gathering that were originally published in an article in December 1975 in

El Auténtico, a newspaper of the Argentine Peronist Party.[28] The authenticity of the verbatim record of the talks contained therein could not be independently verified; however, the content of what was discussed matches subsequent events, and the format of police repression that followed lends credence to the transcription's accuracy. The article notes how, during this summit, the heads of the region's police forces established ideological and operational foundations for the persecution of thousands of Chileans, Uruguayans, Paraguayans, and Bolivians in Argentina.

PFA head Iñiguez inaugurated the event on February 27 and welcomed all the delegations.[29] Afterward, the Chileans suggested a proposal for a six-point system:

> first, setting up within each embassy a Security Attaché, whether from the armed or police forces, whose basic functions would be to coordinate with local security forces. . . . second, similarly to Interpol, establishing an Information Headquarters. . . . third, planned and unforeseen movement of officers, having access to the security organisms of each country. . . . fourth, the necessity of developing a communications channel. . . . fifth, creating a system of scholarships, for formal training or work experience, . . . sixth, a photo album [fragment ends].[30]

All the delegates wholeheartedly endorsed the proposed scheme and suggested additional elements. Uruguayan Castiglioni highlighted the importance of collaborating in critical areas, such as border regions. Villar offered full cooperation and noted that Chile and Bolivia could send officers to the border cities and areas of Mendoza, San Juan, Salta, and Jujuy as appropriate. He fully supported the idea of foreign agents operating on Argentine soil. He also proposed that refugees should be monitored on a weekly basis and their movements restricted, so they could not reach border areas. Additionally, Villar observed how albums containing photos of sought individuals were being prepared and that the safest communications mechanism would be through military attachés, "since civilian personnel may have different ideas from ours."[31] Villar further recommended using "narcotics commission" as a code word when contacting the PFA about these matters, "so we already know what this is about."[32] In late March this police coordination system received the blessing of Argentine President Perón.[33]

Significantly, this summit took place just days after the abduction of Viana Acosta and less than two weeks after the PRT-ERP's public announcement of the JCR. Coordination among South America's security forces was already an open secret. In May 1974 the US ambassador in Santiago, David Popper, cabled to the State Department regarding the Chilean junta's desire "for closer communication with sympathetic neighbors" and the existence of "close intelligence and security police ties between Chile and Argentina, Brazil, Paraguay, etc. to combat leftist terrorism."[34] Several declassified CIA documents from the late 1970s further denote a long history of cooperation in combating subversion in South America, and mention February 1974 as its starting point.[35] A June 1976 CIA publication on "Latin American Trends" explicitly affirmed that

> In early 1974, security officials from Argentina, Chile, Uruguay, Paraguay, and Bolivia met in Buenos Aires to prepare coordinated actions against subversive targets. They agreed to establish diplomatic security liaison channels, to exchange intelligence information on a regular basis, and to facilitate the international movement of security officers on official business.
>
> Since then, [text redacted], the Argentines have conducted joint countersubversive operations with the Chileans and with the Uruguayans. Until recently, however, there was no evidence that this cooperation was extensive or very effective.[36]

This information significantly matches the details contained in the *El Auténtico* article, but the CIA assessment on the repressive coordination prior to 1976 is misrepresentative. At least 156 individuals were in fact targeted between 1974 and 1975, and many were assassinated or disappeared. The emblematic cases summarized on the following pages clearly expose the extent and reach of police cooperation in the Southern Cone. US intelligence bodies underestimated, or purposefully hid, the threat posed by South America's growing collaboration in repressive practices, and they later would approach Condor in a similar fashion.

Flight 158

After his initial detention and torture inside the SSF, Antonio was moved to Devoto and Caseros prisons, and finally to a small police cell in Buenos Aires's twenty-first police precinct. During his peregrinations, he managed to send a message to Senator Erro, who arranged for two renowned lawyers, Rodolfo Ortega Peña and Silvio Frondizi, to help Antonio. They immediately filed a habeas corpus writ before the tribunals and also attempted to secure asylum for him in a third country, since Antonio was terrified of being returned to Uruguay.

The filing of the habeas corpus most likely forced the PFA to change or accelerate its plans. On April 4 officers suddenly returned Antonio to the SSF, where he was told he would be handed over to the Uruguayan authorities. Driven in a Ford Falcon car to Aeroparque Jorge Newbery, Buenos Aires's central airport, and tied to a heater on the premises, Antonio waited to board Pluna airline flight 158 to Montevideo. Antonio tried to resist repatriation, but officers threatened him: "Well, we can always drop you in the middle of the River Plate to feed the fish."[37] On the plane's staircase, Antonio was left in the pilot's custody, while on board he was reunited with his wife, who had been detained at the Immigration Office the same day as Antonio.

Flight 158 landed in the early hours of April 5 at Carrasco International Airport. DNII officers immediately took Antonio to the Montevideo police headquarters for questioning. Four days later, Captain Buzó Correa and Officer Néstor Silvera Fonseca traveled to Montevideo to pick him up. Buzó Correa, lifting the hood covering Antonio's face, reminded him: "I kept my word: had I not told you I would come find you? Well, here I am."

The officers returned Antonio to Rocha's Twelfth Infantry Battalion, where he was repeatedly interrogated. Fellow detainees, including Tupamaro leaders such as José Mujica and Eleuterio Fernández Huidobro, remember the vicious tortures "El Pantera" (Antonio's nickname) suffered. Given his refusal to talk, he was sent to the Eleventh Infantry Battalion in the city of Minas. There Major José Nino Gavazzo, officers from the Coordinating Organism for Antisubversive Operations (Organismo Coordinador de Operaciones Antisubversivas; OCOA),[38] and even General Gregorio Álvarez, Uruguay's future head of the armed forces between 1978 and 1979, persistently tortured Antonio. Questions centered on the political activities in exile of Senators Erro and Michelini, and of Tupamaro militant Washington Barrios, whom Antonio did not know. Eventually, in October 1974, Uruguayan authorities formally recognized Antonio's detention and transferred him to the country's male political prison, Libertad. There prison guards and doctors subjected him to medical experiments and inhumane treatment until 1981, when he was given advanced release and successfully fled to Sweden.

Denouncing Refoulement

Meanwhile, life continued seemingly as normal for the large community of Uruguayan exiles in Buenos Aires. On April 19 a gathering of four thousand commemorated the events leading to Uruguay's independence in 1825, and two former senators took the stage. The crowd had widely applauded and cheered Senator Erro, who severely reproached the Uruguayan regime for having filled prisons with students, workers, and politicians, and accused the military of being "torturers" who held onto power with no regard for the people's suffering.[39] The Uruguayan Embassy permanently spied on such exiles' events and the activities of key political figures, who constantly denounced the atrocities of the Uruguayan dictatorship in Argentina and beyond, and then reported back to the Ministry of Foreign Affairs.

After Antonio's detention, police persecution against refugees intensified in Argentina. Indeed, throughout 1974, right-wing paramilitary groups constantly harassed exiles, some of whom were tortured at the hands of security agents from their countries of origin in Argentine police stations.[40] Chilean intelligence was especially preoccupied with Argentina's apparent inability to control refugees, and the DINA informed the Chilean Embassy in Buenos Aires that Argentine authorities were unable to effectively monitor Chilean exiles who moved freely around the country.[41] Further, Chilean intelligence services had detected that extremist groups composed of South American citizens had fled to Argentina in late 1973 and requested that the ambassador raise these matters with the Argentine government and demand that they be relocated away from border areas.

Between late April and early May 1974, the PFA detained at least fifteen Bolivian, Chilean, and Uruguay exiles; some of them were later expelled to their country of origin, where their safety was at risk.[42] Indeed, on May 6, four Uruguayans were deported from Buenos Aires; they had been originally detained in late April by the PFA's Department for Foreign Affairs for illegal permanence in Argentina, and later investigations accused them of involvement with subversion, which ultimately warranted their expulsion.[43] Carlos Antonio Rodríguez Coronel was put on a midday Air France flight for Montevideo, while Juan Carlos Iparraguirre Almeida, Julio Cesar Saavedra Duarte, and Justo Pilo Yañez traveled on the evening ferry.[44]

After learning of these events, the UNHCR local representative, Frank Krenz, visited the Uruguayan Embassy inquiring about Rodríguez Coronel.[45] According to Rodríguez Coronel's lawyer, Leandro Despouy, this case exemplified the early collaboration between the Argentine and Uruguayan forces and the crucial role of the PFA in deciding on his transfer to Montevideo. Despouy himself suffered threats; on the same day of his client's deportation, he received an intimidating phone call with heartbreaking groans and screams of pain from someone being tortured, possibly Rodríguez Coronel himself.[46]

UNHCR's intervention and mounting international pressure resulted in the men being freed in late June in Uruguay. In this case, the Uruguayan dictatorship delivered mixed messages, affirming in August that Rodríguez Coronel was wanted by the armed forces for his alleged connections to subversion,[47] but then backtracking in October by asserting that "there had never been an extradition request regarding these individuals to the Argentine authorities."[48]

By mid-1974 four features of this second phase were apparent. First, the PFA stood at the heart of regional coordination, detaining and torturing targeted individuals in the clandestine prison on the SSF's premises, and deciding whether they should return to their country of origin. Second, habeas corpus petitions rarely guaranteed victims' safety and potentially triggered their expulsion. Third, the repatriation of foreign citizens accused of subversion constituted another deadly mechanism that allowed home countries to capture sought individuals. Finally, anyone attempting to help victims, most often lawyers, was routinely intimidated or even murdered: in July and September 1974, the AAA assassinated the two lawyers who had tried to help Antonio, with Ortega Peña being the first official victim of the AAA's spate of killings.

A Southern Winter

We will go to Australia if necessary to get our enemies.[49]
—*Manuel Contreras, DINA's Director*

Similarly to the brutal crushing of all opposition that unfolded in Chile in late 1973, the Uruguayan regime began closing in on many exiled opposition leaders in 1974, including Senator Erro, from the traditional Blanco (Nationalist) Party. In June 1973 the Uruguayan military had accused Erro of links with the Tupamaros and demanded that Parliament strip him of immunity from arrest and prosecution. When legislators refused to grant this request, President Juan María Bordaberry and the armed forces exploited this denial as a pretext on June 27 to shut down Parliament.[50] Since escaping to Argentina, Erro had been a vocal opponent of the Uruguayan dictatorship and actively assisted arriving Uruguayan refugees,[51] quickly becoming a focal point for the local exile community.

In May 1974 the Argentine government, likely acquiescing to Uruguayan pressure, tightened its grip on Erro. The Immigration Office severely restricted his freedom of movement, prohibiting him from residing or traveling through the Argentine capital or the provinces bordering Uruguay, including Buenos

Aires and Corrientes.[52] Meanwhile, Ambassador Adolfo Folle Martínez regularly notified Montevideo of the senator's political activities, such as his participation in an homage to Oscar Mendieta, an activist of the Uruguayan Revolutionary Communist Party (Partido Comunista Revolucionario; PCR)[53]—murdered by Uruguayan security forces a year earlier—and during which Erro powerfully criticized both Uruguayan and Argentine authorities.[54] Therefore the PFA demanded Erro's expulsion, due to his defiance of his refugee obligations not to participate in political activities.

Senator Michelini, from the left-wing coalition Frente Amplio (Broad Front), was also in the crosshairs. In March 1974 he had given a powerful testimony to the Russell Tribunal II in Rome, which was probing the situation in Latin America, and had fully exposed for the first time the dramatic situation in Uruguay, defined by deaths, the routine uses of torture and violence, and the destruction of the opposition and of trade unions. In his closing speech, Michelini affirmed he was representing "those who could not be here because they have disappeared from the face of the earth . . . those that cannot be heard because their minds forever shut down as a result of the torments endured. Our voice is also that of all of those who, having suffered, cannot rebel, who cannot express their struggle. It is not simply a voice full of accusation and condemnation, but also of hope and faith, in our country and our people."[55]

Condemnation against the Uruguayan dictatorship from such an influential figure had significant reverberations internationally, but especially in Uruguay, making the senator a high-priority target. Returning to Buenos Aires in early June, Michelini initiated proceedings to obtain a permanent Argentine residency, but, behind the scenes, the Argentine Immigration Office notified Uruguayan authorities that they would not grant this.[56] Further, in late June the Uruguayan Ministry of the Interior canceled Michelini's passport and notified Argentine authorities and all relevant diplomatic representations in South America of this decision.[57]

The senator's son, Zelmar, who lived with his father at the time, clearly remembers the harassment they endured. Just three days after the senator's return from Rome, Michelini started receiving death threats.[58] A phone call warned him that "his eldest daughter Elisa [who was imprisoned in Uruguay] would be tortured if he delivered a similar speech in the future."[59] Moreover, Argentine and Uruguayan police were permanently stationed in the lobby of Hotel Liberty, where the senator lived, or just outside.[60] Michelini regularly cautioned his sons about the presence in Buenos Aires of Uruguayan commissioner Campos Hermida.[61]

This increasing persecution against exiles reflected the new system of re-pression: Uruguayan politicians were kept under constant surveillance and their movements curtailed, whether by canceling their passports (Michelini), or restricting their residence rights (Erro). The circle was slowly but surely closing in on all voices opposed to the Uruguayan dictatorship. And things were about to take a turn for the worse.

On June 1 the Argentine police arrested one hundred Uruguayans and one Argentine who had participated in a demonstration organized to repudiate the first anniversary of the Uruguayan dictatorship, held on the premises of the Box Federation in Buenos Aires. The detainees were all booked and some even sentenced to one-month imprisonment; Rubén Prieto, arrested on that occa-sion, later testified that Uruguayan officers had taken part in interrogations.[62] This episode, known as Operativo Gris,[63] was a turning point in three respects. First, the security forces collated and updated information about numerous Uruguayan exiles in Argentina, and this provided extremely useful data when persecution worsened later.[64] Second, the raid sent a stark message to the exile community in Buenos Aires, as Uruguayan national Nicasio Romero recalls: "After the act, we became aware the Uruguayan police was operating in Argen-tina, especially infamous commissioner Campos Hermida. Many people knew him because he was a renowned torturer in Uruguay, so they probably saw him when they were arrested or during detention. This recognition set alarm bells ringing."[65] Third, the communications channel for intelligence exchange, as advocated at the February meeting, was already operational as early as June 1974. In fact, a Uruguayan DNII memorandum from early June meticulously described Operativo Gris, distinguishing between detainees wanted by Uru-guayan authorities and those who possessed a criminal record; further, the list of the 101 detainees contained confidential information about each, including their home address, date of birth, immigration status, and date of entry to Argentina.[66] Similar documents, dated June 18, 1974, were found in the ar-chive of the Directorate of Intelligence of the Buenos Aires Provincial Police (Di-rección de Inteligencia de la Policía de la Provincia de Buenos Aires; DIPPBA), demonstrating how Argentine and Uruguayan intelligence agencies had quickly exchanged and disseminated information about this operation.[67]

During the austral winter of 1974, the Chilean and Uruguayan dictatorships consolidated their grips on power and secured the necessary resources to quash opposition. In Chile, Decree 521 of June 14 officially recognized the creation of the DINA, which had existed in practice since November 1973.[68] The DINA truly was General Pinochet's armed wing, enabling the dictator to destroy opposition and concurrently establishing his hegemony vis-à-vis other political and military actors.[69] This new body was extremely powerful, sui generis, and unlike anything ever seen before. As a technical and professional intelligence organ, it directly advised the military junta based on intelligence gathering and production.[70] Yet DINA's additional powers—to arrest people and conduct repressive raids—were hidden from sight.

In mid-1974 DINA expanded its range of actions in striving to locate prominent politicians who actively worked against the military government from abroad. Its Exterior Department (DINA Exterior), one of its six subdirectorates, which answered directly to National Director Manuel Contreras, carried out strategic intelligence and counterintelligence tasks, watched over the Ministry of Foreign Relations through delegates in diplomatic missions, and conducted operations abroad.[71] Contreras had personally set his sights on Carlos Altamirano, secretary general of the Socialist Party, and the DINA made several unsuccessful attempts on his life.[72] In August 1974 the chief of the Navy Mission of the Chilean Embassy in London, Raul López, met with naval reserve officers residing in Europe and ordered them to maintain a watch on Chilean leftists in their respective countries and to report any antijunta activities to London; any sighting of Altamirano had to be reported immediately and directly to López.[73]

A Violent September

September 1974 witnessed the DINA's first dramatic transnational operation, the assassination of Chilean general Carlos Prats González and his wife, Sofia Cuthbert, in Buenos Aires.[74] Prats had resigned as commander-in-chief of the Chilean Armed Forces in August 1973; soon after the military coup he had moved to Argentina, accepting an offer from President Perón. The exiled general was the most threatening rival for Pinochet and was writing a personal memoir, strongly condemning the military. The Chilean military junta meticulously tracked Prats throughout his exile and, in November 1973, entrusted General Arellano Stark, commander of the *caravana de la muerte*, with a special mission in Buenos Aires to discuss Prats's undertakings with the Argentines and convince them to maintain scrutiny over the general.[75]

With Perón's death on July 1, 1974, Prats lost his protector, and several assassination plots began to take shape. On September 26 Prats confided to Gladys Marín of the Chilean Communist Party that he had received numerous threats and that the Chilean services were working with the Argentines to kill him.[76]

He had received a visit from two alleged PFA agents whose credentials turned out to be fake and later an ominous phone call from a so-called Croat commando who warned him to leave Argentina or otherwise he would be murdered.[77] However, Prats proudly refused to travel without his Chilean passport, whose application for renewal had languished in the consulate for months.[78]

In the early hours of September 30, on Malabia Street in Buenos Aires's upscale Palermo neighborhood, American-born DINA agent Michael Townley and his wife Mariana Callejas set off a detonator, activating a bomb Townley had previously placed under the general's car. Prats and his wife died instantly. At the time, few doubted that this public murder was anything but the work of Chileans. The following day, the *Guardian* affirmed that the most likely explanation was that Chilean military intelligence had colluded with the Argentines to eliminate a man with a significant role to play in Chilean politics,[79] while Argentine government circles likewise blamed the Chileans, since "Prats had no importance on the Argentine political scene."[80]

Terror was now palpable in Buenos Aires. After Prats's shocking murder, Senator Michelini asserted that borders no longer deterred repression and that the security services of Chile, Argentina, and Uruguay were acting with absolute impunity.[81] Indeed, Uruguayan officers were also orchestrating deadly plans, and the next case illustrates a still relatively novel pattern at the time of clandestine arrest, torture, and murder of political activists, which would become systematic during the Argentine dictatorship (1976–83). The three victims—Daniel Banfi, Luis Latronica, and Guillermo Jabif—were rank-and-file militants, whose tortured and almost unrecognizable bullet-ridden bodies were found in the fields of San Antonio de Areco, over 100 kilometers away from Buenos Aires, after forty-five days of illegal detention. Like many of their compatriots, Banfi, Latronica, and Jabif, who all had links with the Tupamaros, had fled political persecution in Uruguay in the early 1970s and settled in Argentina.[82] Latronica had recently arrived from Chile and was living with the Banfis as he waited to travel to France under UNHCR auspices.[83]

In the early hours of September 13, the bell rang in the apartment of Aurora Meloni and Daniel Banfi in Haedo, on the outskirts of Buenos Aires. They lived with their two daughters, Leticia and Valeria; Aurora's mother and her husband; and Latronica. A family friend, Rivera Moreno, was spending the night there by chance. A group of about ten heavily armed men, in black civilian clothing and gloves, stormed the house, claiming to be police officers. Aurora and Daniel stared at each other; they had both recognized the man in charge: Uruguayan commissioner Campos Hermida, whom they knew from a brief arrest at Montevideo's police headquarters after a student protest in October 1969. They also identified a second Uruguayan, someone who had been involved in extreme right-wing groups during their university years, but failed to recall his name.

Daniel was locked up in the kitchen, from where Aurora could hear his screams as the men interrogated him about his relationship with the left in Argentina and with another Uruguayan, Andrés Correa. Unbeknownst to them, Correa had been detained in a similar operation on August 30. In the living room, the unidentified men asked Aurora and Latronica for their documents; upon seeing Latronica's refugee passport, one of them exclaimed, "Gol de media cancha" (Midfield goal). Aurora did not know much about football but understood it meant they had found someone important.[84] Banfi, Latronica, and Moreno were ordered to get dressed, as they had to be taken to the SSF. If they said all they knew, there was nothing to worry about, they were warned, but if they had unresolved issues with the Uruguayan police, they would be immediately sent to Uruguay. Aurora saw fear, bewilderment, and anguish in Daniel's eyes. She did not know that this would be the last time she would see him alive. Latronica, who had perceived the gravity of the situation, whispered to Aurora, "Vamos al estrellato," an expression meaning they would be killed.

A few hours earlier, another Uruguayan had been kidnapped: it was Nicasio Romero, a family friend, who worked at the same chain of music stores as Daniel Banfi. That day mysterious individuals had entered the store looking for Daniel, and Nicasio told them he worked in the Caballito neighborhood branch.[85] At midnight, as Nicasio ended his shift, several men violently attacked him, and he lost a shoe in the ensuing struggle; they then forced him into a car. Blindfolded and threatened with death, Nicasio was taken to an unidentified location, where he was beaten and interrogated about Daniel: he realized his captors were the same men who had visited the store earlier.[86] At lunchtime on September 13, an armed group of men broke into the Palermo flat where Guillermo Jabif, a longtime friend of Latronica, and his wife Alicia lived. The captors openly threatened Guillermo that he would not get away this time: "We will send you to Libertad," they said.[87]

Immediately after the overnight raid, Aurora started an agonizing journey that thousands of families would later repeat to discover the fate of the *desaparecidos*. Illicitly snatched from their homes in the middle of the night, or in broad daylight in public thoroughfares and workplaces, by armed men in civilian clothing, people were simply disappeared. Authorities continually denied their detention, pretending they had just vanished from the face of the earth as if they had never existed. In these unprecedented circumstances, Aurora turned for advice to Senator Michelini, who suggested filing a habeas corpus petition and holding a press conference,[88] which she did. At the press conference on September 19, she met the Jabif family; together they visited police stations, filed numerous judicial petitions, and denounced the kidnappings locally and internationally, including with Amnesty International, but to no avail. Frequently police officers refused to report allegations and sarcastically responded that the "men had gone fishing" or that Aurora's husband had "fled with a blonde." Aurora and Olga, Guillermo's mother, even sent a telegram to Argentine President María Estela Martínez de Perón, and were received at the Casa Rosada, the presidential palace, by a general who kept a revolver on his desk throughout the meeting, assuring the two women he would transmit their message. Pressured by the UNHCR, the Uruguayan Embassy investigated Latronica's disappearance, but neither the PFA nor the provincial police knew of his whereabouts.[89]

During their search, Aurora and Olga met commissioner Antonio Gettor in the SSF, who confirmed that Andrés Correa was being held in Devoto prison and provided the surname of the judge in charge, Luque. When Aurora mentioned that she had recognized Campos Hermida during the raid, Gettor confirmed that the Uruguayan police commissioner was in Buenos Aires: Campos Hermida had an office on the other side of the corridor, he asserted, and was the head of narcotics, but had nothing to do with their case.[90] Despite this denial, Gettor's response corroborated for Aurora and Olga that the commissioner was definitely collaborating with the PFA. At one point, a voice on Gettor's walkie-talkie suddenly asked, "What should we do with the Uruguayans?" Olga tried to get him to check if those Uruguayans were their missing loved ones, but Gettor vehemently denied this: those were other Uruguayans who had been detained for drug trafficking.

During the following weeks, Aurora regularly met with Judge Luque. He repeatedly asked her if Daniel had been involved in terrorist attacks in Argentina, but she fervently refuted this each time. In mid-October, two prisoners, Nicasio Romero and Rivera Moreno, were suddenly freed and reached Aurora's house in deplorable condition, with visible signs of torture and having lost half of their weight. Nicasio narrated how they had been imprisoned in different sites, always blindfolded, tortured, and kept almost starving. Argentine officers acted as guards, while the Uruguayans, who were obsessed with the Tupamaros, conducted interrogations and wanted to know if Daniel belonged to the group. Several nights later, the jailors picked up Nicasio, Rivera, and another Uruguayan prisoner, known only by his nickname "el viejo" (the old man), and drove them back to Buenos Aires. "Walk straight on, do not look back, and you must leave the country," they were admonished.[91] Aurora had previously made arrangements for asylum in Sweden, so Nicasio and Rivera immediately traveled there.

Their release generated expectations that the other three men would soon be released, but this hope was short-lived. On October 29 Aurora called Judge Luque for news, and he responded they should meet straightaway. Arriving at the café where Aurora, her mother-in-law, and Olga were waiting, the judge threw on the table a copy of *La Razón* newspaper, which reported the discovery of three bodies. "How do you know it is them?" Aurora begged. "I do," Luque responded irately.

The moon shone brightly that night when Aurora, Father José Carrol—a family friend—and Oscar Bonilla—Guillermo's brother-in-law—drove to the morgue of San Antonio de Areco to identify the bodies. Initially, they were sent to two wrong addresses, adding insult to injury.[92] Finally, at the morgue, they struggled to recognize the bodies—which had been partially buried in a field in the locality of Duggan, between San Nicolás and San Antonio de Areco—because the perpetrators had poured quicklime onto them to prevent identification.[93] At the local police station, officers repeatedly interrogated Aurora, Oscar, and the priest for no apparent reason, before they could return to Buenos Aires. After burying the three men together in San Antonio de Areco, Aurora and her two daughters left for Sweden. Before leaving, Aurora met with Michelini and brought some ground from the fields where the men had been discovered. "They were buried here, Zelmar," Aurora told the senator, who went pale, since he had never foreseen this tragic outcome.[94] She advised the senator to also secure asylum abroad, but he refused.

This episode, which profoundly shook the Uruguayan community in Buenos Aires, marked the beginning of the upsurge in their persecution that lasted for four more years, until late 1978. Throughout 1974 Argentina spiraled increasingly into further violence as its democracy crumbled once more: over 130 political killings occurred in the six months after Perón's death, including that of police chief Alberto Villar and his wife.

Kidnapped in Buenos Aires, Murdered in Soca

On December 20, 1974, the bodies of two men and three women, with their hands bound at their backs and bearing evidence of gunshot wounds, appeared on the roadside in Soca, Uruguay. The victims of these cold-blood executions were Héctor Brum, Floreal García, Graciela Estefanell, María de los Ángeles Corbo, and Mirta Yolanda Hernández, who had been illegally abducted in Buenos Aires on November 8. This episode, known as the Fusilados de Soca, was immediately interpreted as a retaliation for the assassination on December 19 of Colonel Ramón Trabal, the military attaché in the Uruguayan Embassy in Paris. However, as the US ambassador in Uruguay, Ernest Siracusa, observed in a cable, the fact the murder had happened so soon after Trabal's death suggested that the five victims had probably been in custody for some time.[95]

The victims belonged to the Tupamaros and had been exiled in Chile first and then in Argentina. In late 1974 they were not officially wanted by Uruguayan authorities, but intelligence files listed them as members of the Tupamaros' Buenos Aires branch.[96] For over thirty years, this episode remained shrouded in mystery until 2005, when Julio Abreu broke his silence to journalist Roger Rodríguez and admitted that he had also been detained with the five adults and little Amaral—Floreal and Mirta's three-year-old son.[97] Overcoming decades of fear, Julio's testimony helped reconstruct many missing pieces of this puzzle.

Julio, who had never been politically active beyond some sympathies for the Blanco party, had moved to Buenos Aires in August 1974 to work in the Ciba-Geigy laboratories.[98] Through his brother, Julio had met Floreal and Héctor, developing a friendship that was common among Uruguayans in Buenos Aires. On that fateful day in November, they were celebrating a friend's birthday, and Julio and Floreal had headed out to buy some roast chicken, not aware that the world as they knew it would end the moment they walked out the door.

"They will kill us!" Floreal suddenly screamed. They had barely reached the corner block when armed men attacked them, hitting and accusing them of stealing cars. Forced into unmarked Falcon cars by officers of the PFA and provincial police forces, they were then subjected to an ordeal that would last six weeks and span two countries. Julio remembered the extreme violence employed throughout, and even overheard one kidnapper say he had hit a woman so hard in her belly he "almost got her baby out of her mouth." Julio feared they were talking about his sister-in-law, who was eight months pregnant, but later discovered they were referring to six-months-pregnant María de los Ángeles. He endured mock executions, countless humiliations, and psychological torture, having to listen to his friends' torments.

The six adults and Amaral were confined in three different clandestine prisons in Argentina. Initially, Julio was kept in a minuscule room in a garage, from where he incessantly heard cars coming and going. One day an Argentine guard told him to close his eyes because "one of yours" was coming to identify him, probably referring to either a Uruguayan officer or a militant. The second imprisonment site resembled a jail, since Julio was held in a cell, and there were toilets to the left and a central staircase. Most likely, this was the police investigations brigade in San Justo, Buenos Aires province. Throughout all this little Amaral ran around playing, and guards told him "not to worry since his parents were having fun." The third site was a group of caravans, presumably located near an airport due to the continual noise of planes; Julio recalled that by then Amaral was no longer with them. In this makeshift location, Julio briefly talked to Floreal and Héctor, who showed him the extensive signs of torture they had endured and reassured him that he would not be killed. One night between November and December, a clandestine flight repatriated the six adults to Montevideo.

Upon arrival, officers mockingly greeted the prisoners saying, "Welcome to Uruguay," and, after loading them onto a truck, drove them to their fourth prison. In Montevideo they were kept in a house that had originally belonged to the Tupamaros, which the armed forces had turned into a secret jail known as La Casona or 300 Carlos R in Punta Gorda's outlying upmarket neighborhood, where Julio heard the sound of the River Plate. The fact he had to clean the bathroom every day enabled him to recognize years later the tiles and shower, when *Caras y Caretas* magazine published images of this clandestine site.

In La Casona there was a sense of calm before the storm. One day the two couples, Floreal and Mirtha, and Héctor and María de los Ángeles, were allowed to spend a few moments together to say goodbye. Julio spoke with Graciela, since she was alone. She had a message for him and one to deliver outside: "They will kill us, but they will not hurt you. When you get out, please reach out to the organization [Tupamaros], to say that we did not speak, that we did not give any information, this is the only thing I ask you."[99]

A few days after his companions had been taken away, on December 24, officers drove Julio to his godmother's house in the coastal town of Neptunia, where he was freed. In the car his jailers recurrently threatened him not to reveal what had happened, since otherwise he would be killed as well. Upon reaching his relatives' house, Julio learnt of his companions' execution and broke down, revealing everything to his relatives. Overwhelmed by fear, constantly watched, and mindful of innumerable intimidations, Julio remained silent and tried to rebuild his life, while battling an alcohol addiction that he eventually overcame to divulge the truth. In the meantime, Amaral had been illegally adopted by an Argentine intelligence agent and his family and was finally located in 1985 in Formosa, Argentina.

Uruguay's courts are still working to fully clarify the Fusilados de Soca case.[100] At the time, several theories were circulating; according to one, the security forces had wanted to execute nine Tupamaro leaders—kept as hostages since 1973—in revenge for Trabal's murder, but the five militants were chosen instead. In April 1975, as Floreal's relatives were attempting to locate Amaral, they met with President Bordaberry, who told them the "bloodshed could not be avoided," and he had only managed to lower the number of those killed.[101]

This episode exemplified existing practices but also reflected two new trends in cross-border operations: resorting to clandestine renditions and the inauguration of new secret prisons, namely the San Justo Brigade in Buenos Aires and La Casona in Montevideo, used for the first time.[102] The clandestine flight to Uruguay was the first of its kind and became known as *vuelo cero* (flight zero). Unlike Antonio, who had traveled on a regular commercial flight, this was instead a secret trip: the security forces transferred the prisoners overnight, after injecting them with tranquilizers to incapacitate them.

There were other victims of transnational repression in 1974. María Rosa Aguirre, a Paraguayan student activist, was detained in Uruguay in November and returned to Asunción, where she disappeared on December 31 after giving birth in the Rigoberto Caballero Police Hospital.[103] Also in November, Argentine security forces apprehended Chilean-British citizen Guillermo Beausire after he had landed at Buenos Aires's Ezeiza Airport.[104] Secretly repatriated to Chile, he was seen by several survivors, including his mother and sister, in various clandestine prisons in Santiago and disappeared after June 1975. The DINA persecuted his entire family to detain his other sister, Mary Ann, and her partner, Andrés Pascal Allende, Salvador Allende's nephew and a top MIR leader.

By December the situation for refugees in Argentina had significantly worsened. The UNHCR's Latin America representative repeatedly lamented violent attacks on refugee centers and death threats against personnel.[105] Refugees were also being refouled, as had happened to Chilean Jorge Valenzuela Soto and Sergio Quinteros Celis, who had been detained in Mendoza and expelled to Santiago, where Chile's Investigations Police detained them upon arrival.

The UNHCR expressly observed how refugees lacked protection in Argentina, since asylum seekers should never be returned to their country of origin if their lives were at risk.[106]

The disappearance of Uruguayan refugee and Tupamaro militant Natalio Dergan also illustrated how transnational repression was gradually becoming multilateral. Unidentified men illicitly detained Dergan on November 28 as he waited to travel to the United Kingdom. Dergan and his wife, Chilean refugee Ana Luisa Barraza, suffered repeated interrogations and beatings at the hands of several armed men, who broke into their home in Buenos Aires province.[107] The group, among which Barraza noticed at least two Chileans and two Uruguayans, spent hours at the house looking for arms and money and stealing property and the couple's blue refugee ID cards.[108] Barraza survived but was told not to report what had occurred and to leave Argentina within ten days, or otherwise she too would disappear. Dergan was never seen again.

Final Reflections

This chapter has explored several cases of victims in Argentina in 1974 to reveal the initial workings of the Interpol-inspired scheme of regional police coordination launched at the secret February 1974 meeting. Two exceptional features are worth reflecting further on.

First, the dedicated communications channel advocated for at the gathering quickly turned operational and enabled the region's police and intelligence forces to promptly exchange information about operations and sought or detained individuals. For instance, a September 1974 SID report assessed the Tupamaros' strength in Argentina by noting how, largely owing to the JCR, "they possessed large sums of money, weapons, ammunitions, and infrastructure."[109] A subsequent memo reported the arrest of Uruguayan citizens by Argentine security forces and included details on their criminal records and confidential information, also noting their previous detention following the Box Federation demonstration.[110] Similarly, the PFA rapidly notified the Uruguayan DNII that the bodies of Banfi, Latronica, and Jabif had been found.[111]

Second, the network of dedicated agents and detention centers gradually expanded. Clandestine centers functioned within the SSF and San Justo in Buenos Aires, Villa Grimaldi in Santiago, and La Casona in Montevideo. Agents involved in regional collaboration mainly came from the police forces in this period, but military intelligence agents such as Uruguayans Gavazzo and Cordero, and Chilean Jahn Barrera, were also involved. An innovative element was the permanent stationing in Buenos Aires of foreign agents, who were tasked with feeding information back to their home countries and participating in operations on the ground. The case of commissioner Campos Hermida is illustrative: he worked as an undercover narcotics agent in the SSF and was deeply feared by the Uruguayan exile community. During the February police meeting, Villar had proposed using "narcotics" as a code word to identify anti-subversive operations.

Similarly, Chilean DINA agent Enrique Arancibia Clavel began operating in Buenos Aires in late 1974. Coming from a traditional military family and linked to extreme right-wing groups, he worked at the Banco de Chile and subsequently became a DINA operative, allegedly being recruited by DINA head Contreras himself, owing to Aranciba Clavel's wide network of contacts in Argentina.[112] He regularly communicated via memos—the first dated October 10, 1974, and the last October 12, 1978—written under the pseudonym of Luis Felipe Alamparte Díaz and addressed to "Luis Gutiérrez," the alias of the head of DINA Exterior, who between 1974 and 1975 was Major Raúl Iturriaga Neumann.[113]

This network of agents progressively became more complex and varied. In 1974 there was already a clear division of tasks and responsibilities by nationality, since Uruguayan survivors concurred in affirming that Argentine officers conducted custodial functions, while Uruguayans dealt with interrogations.

During this second phase, whoever voiced dissent against dictatorial regimes in their home countries, whether or not they belonged to armed groups, was closely watched and permanently harassed, with high-profile figures and rank-and-file militants being equally targeted. Furthermore, the JCR's public appearance played into the hands of the security forces, which portrayed it as a "bogeyman" to justify subsequent broad repressive waves against all activists.[114]

The next chapter documents how, by early 1975, transnational repression had evolved once more: military intelligence officers increasingly took the lead in operations, and multilateral arrangements progressively complemented prior bilateral formats.

3 • Dynamics of Hybrid Cooperation

At the foot of the Andes, on Avenue José Arrieta 8200 (now 8401) on the outskirts of the Chilean capital, stood Villa Grimaldi, DINA's most important secret prison. Also known as the Cuartel Terranova, it housed the DINA's Metropolitan Intelligence Brigade, which was tasked with conducting repressive operations in Santiago.[1] Between late 1973 and 1978, approximately 2,000 to 2,500 individuals were held, tortured, and interrogated at this clandestine site.[2]

Jorge Fuentes Alarcón was one of Villa Grimaldi's 241 executed or disappeared prisoners. Numerous survivors remember how, in late 1975, a fellow detainee yelled on a daily basis: "I am Jorge Fuentes Alarcón, I was arrested in Paraguay." "El Trosko Fuentes"—so nicknamed for his aversion to Russian thinker Leon Trotsky—had studied sociology at the University of Concepción, 500 kilometers south of Santiago. In the early 1970s he had been the president of the students' federation and became a militant of the MIR, eventually forming part of its central committee.

Fuentes Alarcón was in Arica, a city near the northern Chilean-Peruvian border, the day of the 1973 coup. From there, he and three comrades—Mario Espinoza, Jorge Vercelotti, and Homero Tobar—fled to Peru and eventually to Cuba, where in 1974 the MIR assigned Fuentes Alarcón the task of establishing a base in Argentina to reorganize the struggle against the Chilean dictatorship.[3] By late 1976, however, the DINA would effectively quash most resistance efforts, assassinating numerous MIR militants in Argentina.

Little is known about the fates of Espinoza, Vercelotti, and Tobar, who disappeared in joint Argentine–Chilean operations between February and August 1976 in Buenos Aires.[4] In contrast, there are dozens of testimonies regarding Fuentes Alarcón's tribulations. Given his past as a national student leader, var-

ious survivors of Villa Grimaldi and Cuatro Alamos—another prison—easily
recognized him; many knew of his detention in May 1975 in Paraguay.[5]

At Villa Grimaldi, he was kept in deplorable conditions: he suffered from
scabies and other diseases, and was constantly tortured and punished. Guards
nicknamed him "el bicho" (the animal),[6] and held him in a small wooden shack
in the courtyard. Despite this, fellow prisoners remember Fuentes Alarcón sing-
ing every time he went to the bathroom, and recall his solidarity with other
detainees as he tried to cheer them up in such a harrowing environment.[7] Villa
Grimaldi survivor Sergio Requeña Rueda was the last person to see Fuentes
Alarcón alive on January 12, 1976: that day, DINA agents put him and another
prisoner in a van bound for Cuatro Alamos, but only the latter arrived.[8]

Fuentes Alarcón's arrest in Paraguay, while traveling on a JCR mission with
Amilcar Santucho of the PRT-ERP, constituted the first major multilateral operation in South America. The Paraguayan, Chilean, and Argentine security
forces jointly questioned Santucho and Fuentes Alarcón before the latter's secret rendition to Chile. This episode further showed the necessity, in the eyes
of South America's regimes, of creating a more sophisticated system and multilateral forum to counter subversive threats. The operation deployed existing
elements of the police coordination system, including the free movement of
agents and close information exchange, but it also marked a qualitative leap
forward, displaying two new elements: its multilateral nature, and the increasingly predominant role of military intelligence officers. In 2016 the Argentine
judiciary notably labeled the Fuentes Alarcón–Santucho case a "pilot test" for
the future Operation Condor.[9]

This chapter focuses on the third phase of transnational repression, *Hybrid
Cooperation,* which claimed 101 victims between February 1975 and February
1976. Throughout 1975, levels of persecution almost doubled compared to the
previous phase, and the repressive coordination displayed increasingly complex features, including the coexistence of bilateral and multilateral operations
and deepening collaboration between military and police agents. By late 1975,
Argentina, Bolivia, Chile, Paraguay, and Uruguay agreed that a more comprehensive and centralized structure, transcending all prior collaborative forms,
was required: Condor's founding meeting launched this new system that
would become fully operational by early 1976.

In this Hybrid Cooperation phase, extraterritorial repression incessantly targeted refugees, particularly militants of the JCR, the MIR, and the MLN in Argentina, but simultaneously became more ambitious, expanding its horizons
beyond the continent. In October 1975 exiled Chilean Christian Democratic

politician Bernardo Leighton and his wife barely survived an assassination attempt in Rome organized by the DINA in collaboration with the Italian extreme-right group Avanguardia Nazionale.

Spotlight on the JCR

In 1974 the JCR had developed some institutional autonomy separately from its founding organizations, as well as "a significant propaganda, logistics, and weapons infrastructure."[10] Consequently, it had consistently been on the radar of the Southern Cone's dictatorial regimes, as attested by numerous documents. A report dated November 1974 found in the Archives of Terror but most likely originating from the Argentine police analyzed intelligence information on the MIR, the JCR, and Chilean opposition networks in Argentina.[11] It described how, after Pinochet's coup, Fuentes Alarcón was in charge of the MIR in Argentina, and it discussed several Chilean resistance organizations and their connections with local revolutionary groups such as PRT-ERP, as well as foundations such as the Latin American Faculty of Social Sciences (FLACSO), which were apparently awarding scholarships to subversives.[12]

The wealth of detail about these organizations and their operations is remarkable: the report included their contacts in the Argentine National Directorate of Migration, helping obtaining residency permits; individual members' names, such as "Felipe," the MIR contact in Mendoza; and the locations of meetings in public squares or bars, normally in Palermo neighborhood. Around the same time, records from the Uruguayan SID exhibit a similar preoccupation with the MLN's strength and activities in Argentina, especially its connections with other revolutionary organizations and its ties to the JCR.[13] A 1974 SID memorandum delineated the MLN's collaboration with the PRT-ERP, and recurrent operations by Argentine security forces that resulted in the arrest of PRT-ERP members and the discovery in La Plata of its central printing house, which produced clandestine publications such as *El Combatiente* (the PRT-ERP's mouthpiece), the *Estrella Roja* newspaper, and *El Tupamaro*. The JCR was also at the heart of the Seventh Bilateral Intelligence Conference between Paraguay and Argentina in the second half of 1975, when the Paraguayan Army delegation spoke extensively about it, tracing its origins to the late 1960s, and outlining its current and upcoming activities in Europe and Latin America.[14]

In 1975 the Southern Cone intelligence agencies had, in fact, gathered abundant crucial information about the JCR, likely benefitting from the recurrent interrogations of both Fuentes Alarcón and Santucho. For instance, a Uruguayan memorandum,[15] signed by Major Gavazzo, the head of the SID's Third Department (plans, operations, and liaison), summarized comprehensive information, probably extracted through torture, on the JCR's activities from its creation in the early 1970s until the most recent developments.[16] The latter included the establishment of European headquarters in Paris and Lisbon, the creation of a press agency—the Latin American Press Agency (Agencia de Prensa América Latina) —and its clandestine bulletin to disseminate JCR activities, and collaborations with international bodies, particularly the International Commission of Jurists.[17]

Despite the JCR's ambition to unleash a revolution on a continental scale, this goal was never achieved. Intelligence gathered by regional security forces enabled them to conduct raids against the JCR so that the threat it posed was significantly reduced. Indeed, James Buchanan of the US State Department's Bureau of Intelligence and Research (INR) admitted in a September 1975 confidential memorandum that national security forces in Argentina had broken up the members of the JCR, and so the organization had not achieved much.[18] Buchanan also noted how the Southern Cone's security forces surpassed the terrorists in cooperation at the international level. This document clearly reveals that the US government knew that the Southern Cone countries were coordinating their policies of repression and that the JCR no longer posed a significant threat. This was further confirmed in an October report by the head of Paraguayan military intelligence, Benito Guanes Serrano, who explicitly recognized how the JCR had largely been "inactive since May 1975 as a result of the blows received."[19]

Notwithstanding the JCR's growing weakness, the Southern Cone's security forces intensified their efforts in regional collaboration in 1975. In August the US ambassador in Argentina, Robert Hill, cabled the State Department regarding a DINA operation with Argentine complicity to cover up the disappearance in Chile of 119 militants of the MIR, communist, and socialist parties between 1974 and 1975, known now as Operación Colombo. This document further noted that the police and military establishments of Argentina, Uruguay, Paraguay, and Chile were collaborating closely, and that these governments' security agencies had carried out assassination operations, although this was not considered proven back then.[20]

Refugees in the Crosshairs

Besides operations against the JCR, transnational repression targeted a series of political figures and activists in Argentina. The night between February

18 and 19, 1975, for instance, police officers from Buenos Aires's fiftieth precinct conducted raids at a UNHCR shelter on Fray Cayetano Rodríguez Street
in Flores, one of the capital's largest neighborhoods.[21] The shelter housed approximately sixty refugees and was one of six UNHCR sanctuaries in Buenos
Aires province at the time.[22] Four Uruguayans who lived there later recounted
how police officers searched the building twice that night, first at around 9:30
p.m. and then again at 4:30 a.m.[23] During the initial raid, three uniformed
armed officers, not wearing any identification nor exhibiting a search warrant,
inspected the ground floor for arms and repeatedly questioned residents regarding their means of subsistence, the reasons why they lived in the shelter,
and the countries where they were seeking exile.

After they left, the refugees set up a surveillance system around the property
and noticed that eight officers carrying large weapons had taken up positions
in nearby buildings and on rooftops. At dawn, more officers returned; this
time a refugee recognized a Uruguayan official, who rounded up all the Uruguayans on the premises. The men searched the ground floor for weapons a
second time and took away two Chileans and two Uruguayans. The latter two
were wanted by Uruguayan authorities, and fellow refugees feared they would
be deported to Uruguay or disappear. Before leaving, officers warned the remaining residents to stay inside the following day to avoid being caught in
a shootout, because an antisubversive operation would unfold in a building
nearby, where they had set up a *ratonera* (mousetrap).[24]

Several US declassified documents testify to the repeated persecution that
refugees suffered in Argentina. Numerous Chileans were forcibly repatriated
by local authorities or assassinated,[25] while UNHCR personnel working in
shelters faced daily attacks, threats, and kidnapping attempts.[26] The prolific
DINA agent Arancibia Clavel noted in an October 1975 memo to Santiago the
"preoccupation if not outright terror (*pánico*) among Chilean exiles because
of constant disappearances in Buenos Aires."[27] The raid at the Fray Cayetano
Rodríguez refuge was remarkable both because of the extent of the operation,
involving several men and vehicles, and the unmistakable evidence of regional
collaboration. Indeed, the police officers never disguised the presence of a
Uruguayan within their group and directly targeted Uruguayan and Chilean
exiles. Furthermore, the refugees' fear that their arrested companions could be
returned to their country of origin or disappeared shows how such practices
had become common knowledge.

Throughout 1975 the Argentine PFA continued to oversee the persecution
of refugees. Renowned Argentine journalist Rodolfo Walsh discovered in Au-

gust 1975 the existence of an AAA commando unit allegedly specializing in the elimination of exiles, whose mission had been established after the 1974 police meeting.[28] The unit, composed of seven police officers and two non-commissioned officers from SSF, operated out of a building in the central Buenos Aires Monserrat neighborhood at 700 San José Street, just four blocks from the SSF central building. This entity supposedly answered to Inspector Commissioner Juan Carlos Gattei, the head of the PFA's Department of Foreign Affairs, while Inspector Rolando Oscar Nerone was the unit's intelligence chief and Inspector Juan Batista Pietra, of the Department of Political Affairs, supervised operations.[29]

The PFA's leading role, especially its Department of Foreign Affairs, in the oppression of refugees in Argentina dates back to the early 1970s. It convened the February 1974 meeting and operated one of the earliest clandestine torture centers on the third floor of the SSF premises, where Argentine agents and their regional counterparts interrogated and tortured several foreign detainees, including Brazilian Jefferson Cardim in 1970 and Uruguayan Antonio Viana Acosta in 1974.

Alongside the PFA, diplomatic missions regularly and closely surveilled refugees and reported on their actions. The Uruguayan dictatorship was especially anxious about the intense political activities of exiled statesmen, who regularly exposed the crimes of the dictatorship through their international connections and endeavored to consolidate an organized resistance. In October 1974, for instance, Senator Enrique Erro had successfully established the Unión Artiguista de Liberación (Artiguist Liberation Union, UAL)—an alliance that brought together several Uruguayan opposition groups in Argentina, including the New Time (Nuevo Tiempo) faction of the Tupamaros and the Unifying Action Groups (Grupos de Acción Unificadora; GAU).[30] The historic leader of the Blanco party, Wilson Ferreira Aldunate, had also fled to Argentina after the Uruguayan coup and had become one of the dictatorship's harshest and most vocal critics.

Uruguayan diplomatic correspondence further corroborates the involvement of the PFA's Department of Foreign Affairs in monitoring and persecuting refugees. Commissioner Gattei was the embassy's contact point and main source in these matters, as diplomats strived to gather information about Erro and Zelmar Michelini.[31] In early March 1975 Argentine authorities arrested Erro for violating political asylum rules.[32] Initially the senator was imprisoned in Villa Devoto, but subsequently he was moved to prisons in Chaco, Formosa, and Rawson before his expulsion from Argentina in December 1976.[33] Commissioner Gattei also alerted the Uruguayan Embassy that Michelini was planning a trip to the US in response to an invitation from Senator Edward Kennedy; the embassy urgently collated any information it could obtain on Michelini's forthcoming travels.[34] The embassy soon established that the senator had not traveled to Miami and was still in his residence at the Hotel Liberty on Corrientes Avenue. Commissioner Gattei then summoned Michelini to his office so the senator could shed light on the contradictory reports regarding his trip.[35] Michelini confirmed his intention to travel to the US in the near future and promised to inform Argentine authorities once his dates had been set.

Beyond the PFA, the Ministry of Defense also watched over Michelini. The minister of defense himself, Adolfo Maria Savino, personally reassured the Uruguayan ambassador that inspectors were permanently controlling the senator and had clear instructions to arrest him if they detected any anomalies in his paperwork.[36] All Uruguayan missions thoroughly surveilled opposition politicians, especially when trips to the US were involved, since the latter offered a platform to internationally criticize the Uruguayan dictatorship. In December, the Uruguayan Embassy in the US confirmed Wilson Ferreira Aldunate's presence in Washington with his son, and his delivery of a talk on the Uruguayan human rights situation at the State Department.[37] Previously, while in Caracas, Senator Ferreira Aldunate had additionally voiced strong opposition to the Uruguayan dictatorship.[38]

Operation Dragon

Between March 24 and April 5, 1975, the PFA and the Buenos Aires Provincial Police, in collaboration with the Uruguayan SID, conducted one of the biggest and most successful operations against the JCR and the MLN. Operación Dragón—so code-named by Uruguayan security forces—encompassed various house raids in the Argentine capital and surrounding province, the arrest of thirty-four militants, and the seizing of money and weapons.[39] Consequently, the security forces successfully dismantled two of the JCR's main activities: the Plan Conejo, which related to the production of forged ID documents for JCR members, and Plan 500, which involved the manufacture of 500 JCR-1 submachine guns.[40]

SID Memorandum I-09/975 relates the details of the operation, which began on March 24 in Ituzaingó, a town 30 kilometers west of Buenos Aires, where Argentine security forces had discovered the location of an MLN building and arrested two female Tupamaro militants that night.[41] During subsequent raids, thirty-two more individuals were detained, including numerous Tupamaro and PRT-ERP activists, and three persons who were subsequently freed. Two Uruguayan militants, Julio Cesar Rodríguez Molinari and Eduardo Edison González Míguez, were murdered during a shootout with the security forces in a JCR site in Caseros, west of Buenos Aires. The memorandum's seven annexes contain additional information, including a list of detainees, the thirteen captured MLN and JCR sites, a record of confiscated weapons, prisoners' declarations, and an organizational diagram of the Buenos Aires MLN branch. The operation was also contextualized by recalling the MLN split in October 1974 into two factions:[42] the *peludos* (long hairs)[43] and the *burgueses* (bourgeois); the memo noted that the raids had effectively taken down the dominant *peludos* for the foreseeable future, arresting all the leaders and the majority of active militants and seizing their infrastructure, money, and weapons.

Major Gavazzo, who compiled the memorandum, never openly mentioned collaborating with Argentine agents. Their cooperation can be inferred, however, from the testimonies of MLN and other Uruguayan survivors, who were detained before, during, and after this operation. Andrés Cultelli, the Tupamaro representative for the JCR at the time, was arrested during Operación Dragón on March 31, and within two hours Argentine and Uruguayan agents were torturing and interrogating him on the premises of the San Justo Brigade. Cultelli unambiguously ascertained the presence of Uruguayan agents "by the tone and accent and by the type of certain questions—and because they simply did not hide it."[44] Uruguayan torturers recurrently interrogated other prisoners apprehended then. Furthermore, between February and March 1975, other MLN militants, namely María Asunción Artigas Nilo, Alfredo Moyano, and his mother, Enriqueta Santander, were held for a few days in San Justo. Enriqueta distinctly remembered that the arresting officer, whom she later identified as Gavazzo, was Uruguayan and he had used words like *botija,* a Uruguayan colloquialism for kid, when asking about her son.[45]

These testimonies validate the active presence of Uruguayan officers in Argentina in early 1975. Given the close interest of the Uruguayan security forces in MLN's extraterritorial activities, it is difficult to imagine that a large operation such as Operación Dragón would take place without their participation, particularly Gavazzo's. The major's *legajo* (personal military file) confirms his leading role and particular expertise in political repression. Since mid-July 1974 he had been the head of SID's operations and frequently informed his superiors about progress in the fight against subversion, including in December 1974 before the State Council—a body the Uruguayan dictatorship had created to replace Parliament—and in March 1975 before the president, state ministers, and the military command.[46]

Beyond the Tupamaros, militants of other Uruguayan groups that were linked to the anarchist movement, such as the FAU, ROE, and OPR-33, were brutally persecuted in Buenos Aires at this juncture. One emblematic leader, Hugo Cores—a journalist, trade unionist, and politician affiliated with the FAU and ROE—was abducted by the Argentine security forces in April 1975. In September 1973 Cores had escaped to Argentina after being arrested twice in Uruguay and participating in the two-week-long general strike that followed the 1973 coup. In Argentina he joined other figures including Gerardo Gatti, Alberto Mechoso, and Mario Julién to sustain a FAU leadership in exile and contributed to opposition efforts against the Uruguayan dictatorship.[47]

On April 14, 1975, just before his detention, Cores had met with Gerardo and Mauricio Gatti in a small square in Palermo to discuss recent developments in Uruguay, in particular a negotiation attempt by the armed forces, which wanted to recover the "Flag of the 33"—one of Uruguay's national symbols, in the hands of the OPR-33 since 1969—and were willing to reduce the sentences of several arrested members if the flag was returned. After this meeting, Cores headed to the central post office but saw officers waiting inside. He then fled, running along Paseo Colón Avenue in Buenos Aires's historical center, and got on a bus. Being chased by a car behind, Cores got off and entered a bar near the Casa Rosada. He started yelling, "I am Hugo Cores, they want to kidnap me," pleading with onlookers to contact Argentine Senator Hipólito Solari Yrigoyen about what was happening. The scene that Cores made likely saved his life: a transit police officer in fact intervened and took note of Cores's name, while undercover military officers grabbed the Uruguayan. A waiter then contacted the senator, who in turn notified Cores's family.

Initially Cores was kept incommunicado for twenty days, until Argentine authorities officially acknowledged his arrest in response to a habeas corpus writ. He was imprisoned alongside his Tupamaro compatriots in San Justo's secret prison, where Uruguayan officers frequently questioned and tortured Uruguayan prisoners. Juan Carlos Peré Bardier, a militant detained during Operación Dragón, was held there with Cores for two weeks. Eventually Cores and Operación Dragón's male detainees were transferred to the Sierra Chica prison in Buenos Aires province. Because of mounting international pressure, Cores was expelled from Argentina in December 1975 and continued his political activism from France first and then, starting in 1978, in Brazil. He remained

permanently in the crosshairs, surviving two other assassination and kidnapping attempts in Paris in 1976 and in Porto Alegre in 1978.[48]

Mission in Paraguay

In May 1975 the JCR attempted to broaden its revolutionary strategy by opening its doors to other South American organizations. Edgardo Enríquez, the
leader of the MIR from late 1974, proposed during a meeting of the JCR executive committee in Buenos Aires that two emissaries should undertake "a mission to spread the JCR's message of regional revolution" to other countries.[49]
The committee selected two second-ranking figures: Amilcar Santucho, the
brother of Mario Roberto (the PRT-ERP's founder and leader), and Jorge Fuentes Alarcón, the MIR's factotum in Buenos Aires.[50]

The men embarked on the almost eighteen-hour bus journey from Buenos
Aires to Asunción on May 15, using the false identities of "Juan Manuel Montenegro" for Santucho and "Ariel Nodarse Ledesma" for Fuentes Alarcón. The
latter's cover was as a Costa Rican sociologist who was undertaking field research sponsored by Professor Alain Touraine of the University of Paris. Arriving at the port of Itá Enramada in Asunción's southernmost neighborhood
facing the Paraguay River, the Paraguayan police, who had most likely been
tipped off, boarded the bus and arrested Santucho,[51] while Fuentes Alarcón continued his journey.[52] Paraguayan agents nonetheless closely monitored Fuentes Alarcón from the moment of his arrival: they tracked all his movements,
including his purchase on May 16 of tickets to travel onward to Peru, through
to the evening of May 17, when agents from the Capital Police's Investigations
Department arrested him at the Hotel España, where he was lodging in Asunción's old town.[53]

It took several days for Paraguayan agents to realize what a significant arrest
they had made.[54] Indeed, until May 23, Fuentes Alarcón was able to maintain
his cover as a Costa Rican sociologist.[55] By early June, however, his story had
crumbled, and everyone—including the FBI—knew who he really was. On
June 6 Robert Scherrer, the legal attaché in the US Embassy in Buenos Aires,
sent a letter to General Baeza Michelsen, the head of Chile's Investigations
Police, to inform him that one of the people arrested in Asunción was in fact
Fuentes Alarcón, who had admitted being a JCR courier.[56] Scherrer was a "one-
man intelligence station," whose sources in the Southern Cone both the CIA
and US military intelligence envied.[57] Concurrently, the FBI was conducting
investigations in the US at the request of Pastor Coronel, head of Paraguay's

Investigations Department, regarding three individuals whose names had been found in Fuentes Alarcón's address book.[58]

Upon Santucho's detention, a hidden compartment in his suitcase had been discovered, revealing several thousand US dollars, as well as briefings and progress reports on JCR activities.[59] Because of their direct knowledge of the JCR inner workings and its infrastructure in Latin America and Europe, as well as those of MIR and PRT-ERP, Fuentes Alarcón and Santucho were questioned repeatedly by the Paraguayan, Chilean, and Argentine security forces. Numerous long lists of questions for "Nene" (Fuentes Alarcón) and "Alicia" (Santucho), alongside their answers, were found in the Archives of Terror.[60] Over time, their interrogators became more precise and demanded information on specific JCR members,[61] their meeting places in Buenos Aires,[62] contacts in Santiago,[63] connections with Paraguayan resistance groups,[64] cash and arms flows from Argentina into Chile,[65] and the detailed objectives of the JCR mission across Latin America.[66] One such list of queries for "Alicia" starts off with a blatant warning: "This time without making stories up—until now he has consistently lied and delayed the investigation."[67] Colonel José Osvaldo Riveiro, alias "Rawson" or "Balita,"[68] an agent of the Argentine Army 601 Intelligence Battalion,[69] crafted several questionnaires for "Nene" and "Alicia." Rawson wanted to find out about other MIR agents operating in Buenos Aires, especially "David" (Edgardo Enríquez)[70] and Patricio Biedma,[71] as well as the role of various members of the Santucho family.[72]

In an interview given in Stockholm in October 1979, just a month after his deportation from Paraguay, Amilcar Santucho provided clear evidence about the modus operandi of the repressive coordination.[73] He narrated how, the second day after his arrest, he had been interrogated in Pastor Coronel's office, blindfolded, and tortured with electric shocks. That same night Argentine officers, likely from the embassy in Paraguay, joined in the interrogation: Santucho noticed how these agents were extremely well-informed about his family life and his connections in his native province of Santiago del Estero, northern Argentina. Two or three months later, Argentine and Uruguayan military officers questioned him again; the former probed him closely about the activities of the PRT-ERP and his brother in particular, while the latter asked about his connections to the MLN. Santucho also confirmed that Fuentes Alarcón had been handed over to a Chilean officer, possibly Air Force Colonel Edgard Cevallos Jones, who took him back to Chile outside all margins of the law.

The last entry on Fuentes Alarcón's Paraguayan police record is quite smudgy, but it can just about be read that he was expelled from Asunción on September 23, 1975, via President Stroessner Airport.[74] A letter found in the Archives of Terror corroborates that Fuentes Alarcón was turned over to Chilean agents in September. Manuel Contreras, head of DINA, wrote to Pastor Coronel on September 25, thanking him for the cooperation and help provided to his personnel during their mission in Paraguay. In what with hindsight reads as a foreboding sign of what was to come, Contreras asserted that "this mutual cooperation will only continue to increase so we can achieve the shared objectives of both services."[75]

Contreras's Master Plan

Throughout 1975 the Southern Cone intelligence agencies profited from the unprecedented and thorough information gathered on the JCR and the region's largest revolutionary groups through the interrogations of Fuentes Alarcón and Santucho. Meanwhile, exiles continued to face a tough situation in Argentina. MIR militants avoided mixing with other Chilean refugees, since they knew that DINA's agents closely monitored and permanently infiltrated those groups in Buenos Aires, operating with their Argentine counterparts to detain exiles; the activists also rarely socialized with Argentines, since their Chilean accents would be noticed immediately.[76]

In early August 1975 Contreras embarked on an ambitious mission to set up a system to facilitate regional collaboration against subversion, and his first stop was Washington, where he traveled under a false name and met with General Vernon Walters, the CIA's deputy director.[77] No information has ever been released on that meeting, but likely discussion matters included strengthening ties in intelligence collaboration and information exchange. By late August, Contreras and his DINA team were in Caracas, meeting with Rafael Rivas Vásquez, deputy director of the National Directorate of Intelligence and Prevention Services, and his colleagues. In June 1978 Rivas Vásquez would disclose details about that gathering to a US federal grand jury investigating the murder of Chilean exile Orlando Letelier in Washington in 1976; he declared that Contreras had "wished to obtain information about the activities of all the Chilean exiles living at that time in Venezuela."[78] Contreras had further outlined DINA's expansion plans to build a powerful service possessing worldwide information on subversive elements by placing agents in all Chilean embassies and involving the intelligence services of other Latin American countries.

Although the Venezuelan president eventually turned down Contreras's propositions, the DINA continued with its mission to recruit participants for this grand scheme, and Argentina, Bolivia, Paraguay, and Uruguay all enthusiastically signed up. During Contreras's trip, the DINA signed on August 21 an agreement with the Brazilian SNI to coordinate the persecution of opponents located in Europe: the SNI would target exiles in Portugal, while the DINA would do so in Spain. Ultimately, they planned to extend such efforts to other countries providing safe havens for subversives, including France, Italy, and Sweden.[79] Contreras's proposed plans were music to the ears of his Southern Cone counterparts, who were equally keen to eradicate subversion.

Starting in early 1975, official and clandestine cooperation networks had in fact been active in Buenos Aires, and Chilean Colonel Víctor Barría Barría began operating as the DINA attaché in the Chilean Embassy in March.[80] He closely collaborated with Argentine intelligence, particularly the State Information Secretariat (Secretaría de Informaciones de Estado; SIDE), and evaluated background records on Chileans wishing to settle in Argentina or Argentines wanting to conduct activities in Chile. Information was then transmitted to Santiago via diplomatic pouch.[81] Barría Barría's arrival in Buenos Aires was part of an exchange of officials between Argentina and Chile; indeed, a SIDE officer simultaneously worked with the DINA from the Argentine Embassy in Santiago. In Buenos Aires, the Colonel functioned as "the official representative" with intelligence services, while Arancibia Clavel was the "clandestine head of information."[82]

Argentine and Chilean officers closely traded information to fight subversion. In a memorandum from late August, Arancibia Clavel informed DINA Exterior that "Rawson" (José Osvaldo Riveiro) had offered to share the complete list of all Chilean citizens in Argentina since September 11, 1973. Significantly, according to Arancibia Clavel, Rawson had been the one who proposed "the idea of developing a coordinated intelligence headquarters among Chile, Argentina, Uruguay, and Paraguay."[83]

Close relations and operations in Buenos Aires endured between Argentine and Uruguayan officers as well. At dawn on September 17, a police–military task force arrested Uruguayan brothers Antonio, Mario, and Edén Echenique to return them to Uruguay by plane; but this mission had to be aborted when neighbors intervened, and the entire Echenique family was taken instead to the SSF.[84] The brothers were PCR militants who had left Uruguay in July 1973 but had remained politically active in Buenos Aires in the resistance against the Uruguayan dictatorship through the UAL. They were held in cells on the SSF's third floor, in the section called *tubos y leoneras* (pipes and lion cages), while the three women—one of whom was pregnant—and three children were released.

Uruguayan interrogators, including Campos Hermida and an army captain whom Edén personally knew because they had been classmates in their home city of Mercedes, tortured and questioned the men that night about their role and activities within the PCR. Edén noted that "they did not ask about the UAL, which likely indicated that they either did not know about our role in it or were waiting to gather more information." The thwarted transfer to Montevideo meant that the scope of the interrogations was significantly reduced.

An entry in Major Gavazzo's *legajo* on the same date confirms this arrest, noting how he had collaborated with the SIDE and facilitated the arrest of the Echenique brothers, thereby delivering "a heavy blow to that subversive organization [PCR]."[85] Argentine authorities later officially acknowledged the brothers' arrests: Antonio was jailed in Resistencia, Chaco province, and released in February 1977 in order to travel to Sweden, which had accepted him as a UNHCR refugee; Edén and Mario served time in Devoto prison after being prosecuted for possessing false documents and were freed in October 1978 to travel to Sweden.

Concomitantly, Paraguayan agents were also tightening their grip against opposition groups in Argentina. The Investigations Department in Asunción possessed lists of numerous political opponents such as the members of the Colorado Popular Movement (Movimiento Popular Colorado; MOPOCO), who lived in Argentine cities near the Paraguayan border such as Clorinda, Formosa, and Posadas, and in Foz do Iguaçu, Brazil.[86] Several of these individuals were later abducted and forcefully repatriated to Paraguay, where they disappeared.

Likewise, the DINA devoted much attention to silencing opposition voices that condemned the Chilean military junta in international spheres. Several prominent leaders from the socialist and communist parties, including Carlos Altamirano, Orlando Letelier, and Volodia Teitelboim, were among the individuals targeted for elimination. Teams of agents from DINA Exterior operated in 1975 in Mexico City, Frankfurt, Paris, Madrid, Rome, and Washington, DC.[87] Some targets were especially testing: Altamirano, for instance, had sought refuge in East Germany, and the strict control and protection local authorities provided there rendered any operation against him extremely risky.[88] The DINA thus shifted its attention to a more feasible target, Christian Democrat leader Bernardo Leighton in Rome.

The sixty-five-year-old Leighton had been endeavoring to unite Chilean exiles, including those of the Popular Unity, against Pinochet's dictatorship, while convincing European democrats to oppose South America's dictators more broadly.[89] Undoubtedly, he constituted a clear threat to Pinochet for undermining the junta's image in European circles, just as Carlos Prats had been doing a year earlier in Argentina. It has been widely documented how DINA agents Michael Townley and Mariana Callejas, along with Cuban exile and militant Virgilio Paz Romero, traveled to Rome in September 1975. Following orders from the head of DINA's Exterior, Townley and Callejas recruited Italian extreme right-wing terrorist Stefano Delle Chiaie, a long-standing DINA associate in Italy, for the murder mission.[90] Avanguardia Nazionale agreed to conduct the operation in return for weapons and money. Townley convinced the Italians of the desirability of such a mission, arguing that Leighton was not just a threat to the Chilean junta but to the Italian neofascist movement too.[91]

After several days of preparations, it was clear that Leighton and his wife, Anita Fresno, lived with no security. The evening of October 6, at around 8 p.m., Pierluigi Concutelli, a neofascist terrorist belonging to Ordine Nuovo group, shot both Leighton and Fresno in the back as they returned home on Via Aurelia, just behind the Vatican. Astonishingly, both survived but endured long-lasting injuries that left them severely debilitated. The attack against Leighton struck terror in the hearts of Chilean exiles everywhere, demonstrating the DINA's international reach and absolute mercilessness.[92] With the Pratses' assassination and the attempted murder of Leighton, the DINA unmistakably indicated that borders were no obstacle for Pinochet.

The success of the first multilateral operation in the Fuentes Alarcón–Santucho case confirmed for the DINA the necessity to press ahead with its grand plan of expansion; the next step was to establish an international headquarters for intelligence cooperation. To achieve that goal, the DINA organized the First Working Meeting on National Intelligence in Santiago between November 25 and December 1, all expenses paid by the DINA for up to three delegates per country. Contreras dispatched the DINA's second-ranked man, Colonel Mario Jahn Barrera, to personally deliver invitations in Paraguay, Argentina, Bolivia, Brazil, and Uruguay.[93]

Jahn Barrera was Contreras's "internationalization man:"[94] the colonel had participated in the February 1974 police chiefs meeting in Argentina as part of the Chilean delegation and was well-versed in the benefits of regional coordination. The Archives of Terror preserve the invitation that Jahn Barrera, accompanied by the military attaché of the Chilean Embassy, delivered on November 3 to Francisco Brítez, head of the Capital Police. In the invitation, Contreras expressed his hope that the meeting would form the basis "for excellent coordination and an improved action in the benefit of the national security of our respective countries."[95] In an internal report, it was noted that the Capital Police was not the appropriate recipient for such an invitation, since it did not operate on the national level, and recommended instead that the military attaché of the Paraguayan Embassy in Chile should be designated as an observer at the meeting.[96] In the end, a high-ranking military intelligence officer signed the Condor agreement on Paraguay's behalf. A similar modus operandi, whereby John Barrera and the local Chilean military attaché delivered the invitations, was likely followed in the other countries: indeed, the colonel admitted to the Chilean judiciary in 2003 that he had conveyed an invitation to General João Batista Figueiredo, the head of the SNI, in Brasilia.[97]

Closing the Net

By late 1975 Arancibia Clavel and "Rawson" were closing in on the MIR's main leader, Edgardo Enríquez. They strongly suspected that Enríquez was in Argentina and hoped to deal a fatal blow to both the MIR and the JCR by capturing him. Memos written by Arancibia Clavel from October 1975 illustrated progress in these operations in Argentina and referred to Fuentes Alarcón's rendition from Paraguay to Chile and the organization of the forthcoming intelligence conference in Chile.[98] Further, Arancibia Clavel informed DINA headquarters that Rawson was planning to travel to Santiago in early November to learn the latest news regarding the JCR and the MIR.[99] Rawson was, however, irritated with the Chileans, since he had not been consulted on the forthcoming intelligence meeting, to which a SIDE delegate had been invited instead. Finally, Arancibia Clavel reported that Edgardo Enríquez was likely to be in Buenos Aires or Mar del Plata, and requested photos to be urgently sent over for better identification.

By late October Argentine military intelligence was edging closer. On November 1 Jean Ives Claudet Fernández, a thirty-six-year-old Chilean-French chemical engineer, disappeared in Buenos Aires soon after checking into Hotel Liberty—also Senator Zelmar Michelini's place of residence; its owner, Benjamin Taub, ran a black market money exchange, handling money from both guerrilla groups and the security forces. The hotel permanently swarmed with undercover officers monitoring Michelini.[100] Claudet Fernández was a longtime MIR militant who had actively participated in the group's reorganization in Argentina as part of its intelligence team and had replaced Fuentes Alarcón as the MIR/JCR courier.[101] Upon Enríquez's instructions, Claudet Fernández had traveled to the JCR offices in Paris to report on the October 15 Malloco raid in Santiago, when the DINA had killed the MIR's military leader, Dagoberto Pérez, while several other figures, including Andrés Pascal Allende, had narrowly escaped.

In mid-November, after a meeting with Rawson, Arancibia Clavel conveyed to DINA Exterior that Enríquez was definitely in Buenos Aires and that Claudet Fernández had been murdered.[102] Rawson represented a crucial source of information for Arancibia Clavel, sharing vital intelligence details, and the DINA agent repeatedly insisted to his superiors that the confusion regarding the intelligence conference—to which Rawson had not been invited—should be resolved.

Preparations were unfolding in Santiago for Condor's founding meeting, referred to as the *coctel del 26* in Arancibia Clavel's memos.[103] Just a few days before this summit, a joint operation in Buenos Aires captured fourteen refugees, mainly militants of the Chilean Socialist Party, in a well-rehearsed modus operandi, whereby PFA officers detained activists in their homes and brought them to the SSF, where they were brutally interrogated about their political activities in both Chile and Argentina. Only after several days were the detentions officially acknowledged,[104] and subsequently the detainees spent months held in regular prisons, mainly Devoto and Resistencia, before later being expelled from Argentina.[105]

The operation began when the PFA detained Miguel Ángel Espinosa Machiavello, a MIR militant, and his wife, Elizabeth Rubio Farias, on November 22 at their home in Banfield, Buenos Aires province. At the SSF headquarters, both Argentine and Chileans agents subjected the couple to psychological and physical torture, including the *submarino* (similar to waterboarding) and electric shocks.[106] On November 25 Catalina Palma Herrera was arrested at home in the San Telmo neighborhood along with three of her Chilean companions and an Argentine comrade. Heavily armed and un-uniformed Argentine police officers told her they were "doing a *favorcito* (small favor) to Pinochet."[107] Inside the SSF, there were other captured Chilean exiles, including Roberto Pizarro, Juan Bustos, Alicia Gariazzo, and a British couple, Cristina and Richard Whitecross, who had sheltered Sergio Muñoz.[108] The Whitecrosses had been under surveillance for helping out several Chilean refugees in Argentina and were charged with having contacts with guerrilla groups; they only returned to the UK after spending months in Devoto prison. This jail had a dedicated block for political prisoners, which housed numerous Chilean, Brazilian, Paraguayan, Bolivian, and Uruguayan prisoners who had little or no connection to Argentine politics and had been arrested for political activities related to their home countries.[109]

Interrogators questioned the Chilean detainees about their organization and its structure, whether they possessed money and weapons, and their contacts with Argentine groups.[110] Several prisoners distinctly recalled being interrogated by individuals with strong Chilean accents, who had detailed knowledge of events taking place in Chile and who repeatedly threatened that they would be forcefully returned to their native country.[111] Argentine officers never hid the fact that they were collaborating with the Chileans, claiming this was part of a joint plan to eliminate all left-wing militants, no matter which country they came from.[112]

The Cocktail of November 26

Across the Andes, Colonel Contreras, the mastermind behind the First Working Meeting on National Intelligence, was waiting to receive his guests at the DINA-sponsored summit. Along with the invitations, Colonel Jahn Barrera had delivered a provisional agenda and background rationale for the gathering.[113] The region's heads of intelligence were being summoned to address the growing challenge of subversion, which was pervading all aspects of life and respected no borders. Additionally, the emergence of coordinated subversive action on a continental scale through bodies like the JCR was forcing threatened countries to respond in an analogous way. "Existing bilateral or gentlemen's agreements are no longer sufficient," read the conference's program, necessitating the creation of "an effective coordination [system] that would allow exchanging information and experiences, also counting on a certain level of personal acquaintance among the Heads of Security."[114]

Contreras's master plan was establishing an office of coordination and security (*oficina de coordinación y seguridad*) composed of three core elements. First, a *database* would centralize multinational information regarding people, organizations, and other activities directly or indirectly linked to subversion: "it would be similar to Interpol in Paris, but dedicated to subversion."[115] Second, a modern and swift *communications system,* using telex and cryptography, would allow the rapid and secure exchange of information. Third, *regular working meetings* would recurrently appraise the system's workings, solve specific problems, and generate closer knowledge and relationships; bilateral and extraordinary meetings, as appropriate, would complement this practice. The DINA offered Chile as the host country for the system but was open to considering alternatives.

On November 25, Pinochet's birthday, delegates arrived in Santiago and settled in for an intense week of meetings and social events, including a welcome
dinner hosted by Contreras on November 26 and a trip to and dinner at the
casino in Viña del Mar on the Pacific Ocean on November 29.[116] The conference took place in the War Academy on Alameda Avenue. After the DINA
opened the first working session by outlining the situation of subversion in
Chile, delegates from other countries presented their respective assessments
and responses on the afternoon of November 26 and the morning of the following day. Subsequently, on November 27 and 28, representatives debated the
design and format of the system of coordination and security, including its inner
workings, organization, personnel, expenses, and tasks allocated to each member. The final agreement was to be debated and approved on November 29.[117]

The composition of the country delegations can be partially reconstructed
from the minutes of the conclusions of the First Inter-American Meeting on
National Intelligence, which the National Security Archive (NSA) analyst Peter
Kornbluh obtained in the Chilean Ministry of Foreign Affairs archives.[118] The
head of each delegation signed the minutes. They were Army Colonel José A.
Fons, deputy director of the Uruguayan SID, who proposed calling the system
"Condor," honoring the host country and its national symbol, the Andes' majestic bird; Colonel Benito Guanes Serrano, head of Paraguayan military intelligence; Army Major Carlos Mena Burgos, deputy head of the Bolivian military
intelligence service; and Navy Captain Jorge Casas, subsecretary of the Argentine SIDE.[119] Contreras represented the Chilean delegation and was most likely
accompanied by Colonel Jahn Barrera and Major Iturriaga Neumann, among
others.

Brazilian investigative journalist Luiz Cláudio Cunha has uncovered that dictator Ernesto Geisel reduced the Brazilian delegation from three invited participants to two, under strict orders to "listen more than talk."[120] These observers—
who did not sign the final agreement—were military intelligence agents Flávio
de Marco and Thaumaturgo Sotero Vaz, veterans of counterinsurgency operations between 1972 and 1974 against the Araguaia guerrilla movement.[121]

The heads of the delegations signed the meeting's conclusions on November 28, one day earlier than planned, which suggests that common ground
already existed among the participants. Indeed, as previous chapters have
shown, intelligence sharing and joint operations had been unfolding since the
early 1970s, and the design of this novel scheme built upon a wealth of prior
experiences. Contreras's proposed system of coordination and security undoubt-

edly benefited from earlier practices but was exceptional in its transnational aspirations.

Records of what was discussed in this founding meeting are not available. However, several documents from Paraguayan, Argentine and Uruguayan archives demonstrate the shared agreement and common ground among the five countries. For example, an October 1975 Paraguayan military intelligence report recognized the value of intelligence collaboration against subversion, recommending the allocation of economic resources for intelligence liaison trips abroad to verify existing information within other countries' intelligence agencies [122] Similarly, Argentina was especially concerned with JCR operations in its territory, particularly after October 1975, when the military's antisubversive effort, initially concentrated in fighting the PRT-ERP guerrilla outbreak in Tucumán province (Operativo Independencia), was extended to the entire country [123]

In late October, just one month before the Santiago summit, the Eleventh Conference of American Armies unfolded in the Carrasco Casino Hotel in Montevideo, assembling eighty delegates from fifteen nations.[124] Records from this earlier conference help us appreciate the stances of the continent's security forces at the time. Predictably, this event largely focused on the armed, ideological, political, or economic manifestations of subversion, the menace of communist parties, and guerrilla activities.[125] Hosted by Uruguayan Commander-in-Chief General Julio Vadora, the conference aimed to construct the necessary instruments to face the aggression of international Marxism and to consolidate practices for exchanging information and methodologies in fighting subversion. But one of the subjects under discussion was the need for greater cohesion, which was required to develop more efficient responses to the shared challenges and dangers that guerrilla groups and communism represented for the continent.[126]

Contreras's thinking was thus very much in line with that of his neighbors, and his plan matched a shared desire to take existing arrangements one step further, leading to greater cohesion and centralization of antisubversive efforts. This is indeed what materialized after Argentina, Bolivia, Chile, Paraguay and Uruguay concluded the founding meeting in Santiago. The scheme possessed four main features: bilateral and multilateral exchanges of intelligence information; a coordinating office to centralize information on subversive individuals and organizations; a scheme of periodical contacts among the intelligence services; and the establishment of the coordination system in three steps. The initial phase encompassed the creation of a complete directory of intelligence agents to exchange information; swift and immediate contact when suspicious individuals were traveling, so as to alert services as appropriate; the use of cryptography systems; the posting of intelligence agents in embassies; and regular evaluatory meetings. The second comprised an evaluation of the results of the first phase and a feasibility project for the intelligence coordination system, as well as deepening the communications system to speed up both bilateral and multilateral information exchange; finally, the third phase related to the approval of the feasibility project and allocating funds for implementation.[127] The accord, to be ratified by each country, would become effective on January 30, 1976, and all the founding members had to approve the future inclusion of new members into the system.[128]

Final Reflections

By late 1975, conditions were ripe in South America for transnational repression to be further consolidated into the unified collaborative system proposed by Contreras. The Condor System built upon existing practices of transnational repression since the late 1960s, including intelligence exchange, joint cross-border operations, and prisoner renditions. But its core innovative elements related to the transnational nature of the latest scheme and the centralization of information and operations in dedicated headquarters located in Santiago and Buenos Aires, respectively. The next chapter demonstrates how, in a continent now dominated by criminal states, transnational repression reached its apex and particularly thrived in 1976.

4 • The Condor System

The penitentiary of Punta de Rieles in the outskirts of Montevideo stood out in 2019 as a model prison for the rehabilitation of offenders in Latin America.[1] Five decades earlier, however, it had served a much more sinister function; in January 1973 a dedicated prison for women guilty of subversive activities had been opened on this site, and throughout the Uruguayan dictatorship it held 651 female political prisoners.[2]

Sara Méndez was one of the women imprisoned in Punta de Rieles's red zone, which housed the most radical detainees.[3] On December 11, 1976, Sara was unexpectedly called to the prison's visitors' room, where she encountered her father and two sisters in the first family reunion since her disappearance in Buenos Aires five months earlier. Her brother was barred from entering the penitentiary because of his beard. Surprise, happiness, and tears characterized the short visit; Sara hoped her relatives would have news of her son Simón, but he was still missing.

Sara had fled political persecution in Uruguay in April 1973 and moved to Buenos Aires, where she became one of the founding members of the PVP in July 1975. On the evening of July 13, 1976, fifteen heavily armed Argentine and Uruguayan agents stormed into her house in Belgrano neighborhood, where she lived with her son and another Uruguayan PVP activist, Asilú Maceiro. The two women were immediately tortured, and afterward their captors took them to a secret prison across the city, later identified as Automotores Orletti. Sara was forced to leave twenty-one-day-old Simón behind. "This war is not against children," Major Gavazzo, who headed the operation, reassured her, "so don't worry about him."[4]

On Orletti's upper floor, Uruguayan officers repeatedly and brutally interrogated Sara while downstairs Argentine guards watched over numerous detainees. After ten days, a clandestine flight, known as the "first flight" (*primer vuelo*), copiloted by Uruguayan Air Force Lieutenant Enrique Bonelli, returned Sara and twenty-three other Uruguayans to Montevideo. There Uruguayan security forces incarcerated the prisoners in two secret sites: first La Casona and afterward the SID central building. After three months of clandestine imprisonment and torture, a fake operation was prepared to justify the militants' reappearance in Uruguay, which few observers were convinced by at the time.

Sara's tribulations illustrate the most systematic and lethal phase of transnational repression, when South America's security forces set up a borderless system of terror and impunity across the continent. This fourth phase, the *Condor System*, began in March 1976 and ended in December 1978, claiming 487 victims. The new scheme envisioned during Condor's founding meeting had quickly consolidated into reality, and terror was effectively internationalized throughout the region.

Three new elements distinguished the Condor System from the previous phases. First, a database located in Santiago centralized all intelligence information on subversion. Second, member countries used the dedicated encrypted communications channel Condortel to rapidly exchange intelligence and operational information. Finally, an operations command and coordinating office, Condoreje, was established in Buenos Aires, while the Teseo unit conducted special operations against targets in Europe. This multilateral and secretive arrangement integrated informational, communications, and operational tasks in an unprecedent manner. The same military and intelligence organs that had signed the Condor agreement were responsible for implementing operations: the Argentine SIDE, the Bolivian SIE, the Chilean DINA, Paraguayan military intelligence, and the Uruguayan SID.

Three sets of existing collaborative practices endured from the past. First, embassies still played a crucial role, helping coordinate Condor activities through designated representatives, often military attachés.[5] Brazilian colonel Carlos Alberto Ponzi, the former head of the Rio Grande do Sul's SNI office, later admitted that military attachés were "institutionalized spies."[6] Moreover, the dictatorial governments appointed military officers to cover other civilian administrative and secretarial functions within their diplomatic missions.[7] Further, evidence was found that an unusually large amount of weaponry—a dozen guns, machine guns, and respective ammunition—was kept in Buenos Aires's Uruguayan Embassy in mid-1976; these were assigned to seven military officers stationed there, a higher than normal number of military personnel for a diplomatic mission.[8] Second, various sets of operations coexisted: the Condor multilateral system overlapped with bilateral and unilateral repressive actions. Third, although the military was at the heart of the scheme, the police remained deeply involved. In Argentina PFA agents regularly contributed to operations undertaken by task force 5 (*grupo de tareas;* GT5), which the SIDE oversaw, mainly targeting the JCR and foreigners. In Uruguay, although the SID was primarily responsible for operations abroad, police officers such as Campos Hermida also formed part of the Orletti task force. Further, the SID habitually requested personal records of sought individuals from the Uruguayan police.[9]

This chapter unravels the intricate web of South American transnational repression in 1976. An analysis of emblematic cases, such as the murder of Uruguayan legislators Michelini and Gutiérrez-Ruiz, who were trying to generate democratic alternatives to the dictatorships, and recurrent operations against PVP activists and MIR militants in Argentina, elucidates the modus operandi of this period. In 1975 the security forces had dealt significant blows to the JCR in Argentina, with the arrest of over thirty Uruguayan and Argentine militants and the Fuentes Alarcón–Santucho operation. By late 1976 the JCR was forced to retreat to Europe, and all its leaders in Argentina had been eliminated, including Enríquez, Santucho, and Patricio Biedma.[10]

This chapter and the next employ the terms "Operation Condor" and "Condor System" interchangeably, but these have distinct origins. "Operation Condor" is most frequently used in Anglophone scholarship and investigative journalism; it originated from declassified US government documents, where it was employed when analyzing South America's secretive coordination. Conversely, evidence from South American archives demonstrates how "Condor System" (Sistema Cóndor), or simply Condor, was the predominant term.

A Hunting Ground

The military coup on March 24, 1976, removed any remnants of democracy in Argentina and marked a turning point in transnational repression: thousands of South American refugees who had considered Argentina their home since the 1960s found themselves fatally trapped. Surrounded by countries already under dictatorship, there was now nowhere for them to flee.

On the morning of the coup, a task force of the Argentine army, gendarmerie, and police arrested Paraguayan doctor Gladys Meilinger de Sannemann before her patients' eyes in her house-turned-clinic in Candelaria, Misiones province.[11] Gladys and her husband Rodolfo belonged to the MOPOCO, and their family had lived in Argentina for over a decade. After four months in detention, on the night of July 28 Gladys was conveyed—blindfolded and handcuffed—from the police headquarters in Posadas to the harbor on the Paraná River. Just across the river lay Paraguay, where Gladys was returned by the Argentine Navy Prefecture. Like Gladys, many other Paraguayans, including Domingo Rolón Centurión, Cástulo Vera Baéz, and Gladys's colleague and friend Dr. Agustín Goiburú, were apprehended during their exile in Argentina and subsequently handed over to Paraguayan authorities. Imprisoned in Asunción's infamous Police Investigations Department, they were all brutally interrogated and tortured. Eventually the Paraguayan regime officially incarcerated some detainees in the political prison of Emboscada, while others were disappeared.

A year later, in March 1977, pretending to release her, Paraguayan authorities instead put Gladys and her daughter Ruth Maria on an Argentine Air Force plane bound for Buenos Aires, and they were then confined at the Navy Mechanics School (Escuela de Mecánica de la Armada; ESMA). In a miraculous set of circumstances, helped by a guard whose mother's life Gladys had saved in the past, the doctor made a life-saving phone call to the German Embassy, which threatened to break relations with Argentina if Gladys and her daughter did not reappear alive.[12]

In April 1976 the DINA stepped up its operations in Argentina. On April 3 a joint Argentine–Chilean operation in Mendoza illegally detained three members of the Chilean Socialist Party, namely Juan Hernández Zazpe, Manuel Tamayo, and Luis Muñoz.[13] Persecuted by the Pinochet regime, the young men had fled Chile and worked to regroup party exiles abroad. They were just days away from requesting refugee status, since they also felt threatened in Mendoza, where the Argentine police and the DINA regularly harassed exiles.[14] The same night of the kidnapping, Chilean agents took them back to Santiago, where they were last seen, badly tortured, in the DINA's secret prisons of Cuatro Alamos and Villa Grimaldi.

In Buenos Aires the obsessive search for Edgardo Enríquez was nearing success. Wanted in Chile since late 1973, Enríquez had become by late 1974 the principal MIR leader and a key JCR figure.[15] By late 1975 Arancibia Clavel and agent "Rawson" were cornering him in Buenos Aires, and some of his closest collaborators, including Claudet Fernández, had disappeared. In December 1975 the head of DINA Exterior pushed for Enríquez's detention:[16] the Argentine Army had distributed Enríquez's photos across the country and Rawson was on the lookout for another MIR/JCR member, Brazilian intellectual Ruy Mauro Marini, who could lead them to Enríquez.[17]

The net was closing. On March 29, 1976, the owner of La Pastoril farmhouse in Moreno, west of Buenos Aires, alerted the security forces to a possible extremist gathering.[18] The intervening military–police task force interrupted a meeting of the PRT-ERP central committee, in which several MIR delegates, including Enríquez, were participating. Enríquez successfully fled from the back of the farmhouse and hid in the fields, but several militants were killed while others were detained. One Chilean survivor later recounted how he was repeatedly interrogated about Enríquez on that occasion.[19]

Just days after his lucky escape, on April 10, Enríquez was murdered in Buenos Aires during coordinated sets of operations against the MIR, in which eight other militants and a six-month-old baby were also detained or disappeared.[20] The US Embassy in Santiago confirmed Enríquez's assassination through "an impeccable Chilean Navy source,"[21] while in Argentina, Enríquez's fate was discussed in an internal PFA report, which detailed the campaigns undertaken against foreign groups. In September 1976 Inspector Alberto Obregón, head of the PFA Department of Foreign Affairs, requested the promotion of forty-three of his men involved in operations conducted against foreign citizens in 1976, which had led to "the fall of the MIR's most important man" and his principal collaborators in Argentina.[22] Although Obregón never mentioned Enríquez by name, he was undoubtedly pointing to the MIR's leader, whose murder was a major blow to the organization and its exiled militants.

A Death Trap[23]

Besides guerrilla leaders, the repressive coordination also silenced prominent political figures who denounced human rights violations and strived to nurture democratic alternatives to the dictatorships. This was what occurred with Uruguayan legislators Zelmar Michelini and Héctor Gutiérrez-Ruiz, and former Tupamaros William Whitelaw and Rosario Barredo. Senator Wilson Ferreira narrowly avoided capture in the same operation. Their fate in Argentina had been sealed back in November 1975, when the Uruguayan Ministry of Foreign Affairs canceled the politicians' passports.[24]

At 2:30 a.m. on May 18, 1976, armed men, allegedly belonging to the PFA, broke into Gutiérrez-Ruiz's fourth-floor apartment, where he slept with his wife, Matilde, and their five children, in the Retiro neighborhood of Buenos Aires.[25] Acting with complete impunity, the task force ransacked the house for an hour, stealing anything valuable, including silverware and children's toys, and filling up seven of the family's suitcases, which were then loaded into Ford Falcon cars parked outside. Matilde and her son Juan Pablo later identified two of the men: Aníbal Gordon and Osvaldo Forese,[26] former AAA members. Gutiérrez-Ruiz told his wife the names of several Argentines and Uruguayans she could turn to for help; upon hearing Michelini's name, one captor affirmed, "We will get that communist too."[27] Gutiérrez-Ruiz was taken away, half-dressed in light-blue pajamas and hooded.[28] Before leaving, the men cut the phone line and threatened Matilde "not to contact any Uruguayans until midday, otherwise her husband would be killed."[29]

Three hours later, at 5:30 a.m., three unmarked Ford Falcons reached Hotel Liberty on Buenos Aires's central Corrientes Avenue. Ten to fifteen heavily armed men, purportedly commanded by Major Cordero,[30] emerged and, after intimidating the night porter, seized the keys to Michelini's room.[31] Screaming "Zelmar, your hour has come," they stormed into room 75, where Michelini lodged with two of his sons.[32] There too, documents and personal possessions were stolen before the senator was dragged away.[33] The men acted with no fear of interference, telling hotel employees they belonged to the security forces and were conducting an antisubversive operation.[34]

Days earlier, in the early hours of May 13, Whitelaw, Barredo, their two children, and Rosario's oldest daughter, Gabriela, had been apprehended at their home in the Caballito neighborhood in a similar operation. The task force had looted their belongings, trashed the house, and interrogated neighbors about what they labeled "the extremist couple."[35] Vicious inscriptions were left on the walls; one said, "Death to the sons of bitches of the Tupamaros."[36]

Relatives of Michelini and Gutiérrez-Ruiz attempted to denounce the overnight kidnappings, but police officers turned them away, affirming that they had been official operations.[37] "Don't waste time, ma'am," a police commissioner told Matilde Rodríguez. "You can file a habeas corpus if you want, but it will be a waste of paper."[38] Wilson Ferreira, who barely escaped abduction that fateful night, owing to his location at his farmhouse in Buenos Aires province, denounced the captures from a safe refuge before seeking exile at the Austrian Embassy.[39] Family members sent telegrams to Argentine President Jorge Videla and other government ministers, pleading for the politicians' release, but to no avail. Neither the police nor judicial authorities showed any interest in what was unfolding: they never inspected the legislators' homes nor talked with their loved ones to clarify the circumstances.[40] Uruguayan journalist Julio Traibel, who had connections in the Casa Rosada, informed Ferreira that the two men were being held in a military unit known as "DF"; "the Argentines were not responsible," he said, and "they needed to look outside (*bus-car afuera*)."[41] On May 20 Argentine Defense Minister Brigadier José María Klix affirmed that "this was a Uruguayan operation," but he did not know "if it was official or not."[42]

The tragic outcome is well-known. On May 21 the bullet-ridden bodies of Michelini, Gutiérrez-Ruiz, Barredo, and Whitelaw were discovered in a red Torino car parked under a tunnel on the outskirts of Buenos Aires, covered in leaflets alleging a PRT-ERP execution.[43] No one believed in the culpability of the guerrillas, and most observers considered that the security forces were responsible.[44] The PRT-ERP immediately rejected the accusations and blamed the Argentine and Uruguayan regimes.[45] The US quickly reached the same conclusion, given speculations that the Argentine government was rounding up important Uruguayan exiles and considering Michelini's "symbolic significance."[46] Robert Hill, the US ambassador in Argentina, concurred that the kidnappings could not have been accomplished without the acquiescence of the Argentine government,[47] and later noted that, according to the local press, the modus operandi was "typical of Triple A operations."[48] The US State Department, generally cautious in its assessments, agreed that the murders "could not have been carried out without the tacit support of at least some Argentine officials."[49]

In the days before the abductions, surveillance of the two politicians and threats against them had significantly increased. On the evening of May 17, Juan Raúl Ferreira, Wilson's son, had seen two Ford Falcon cars stationed outside Gutiérrez-Ruiz's house.[50] Afterward, on May 23, *La Opinión*, where Michelini had worked as a journalist, published a posthumous letter in which the senator revealed his fears of being captured and forcefully returned to Uruguay.[51] At the time, Gutiérrez-Ruiz, Ferreira, and Michelini had been working to encourage a political rapprochement in Uruguay, collaborating with the dictatorship's economy minister Alejandro Végh Villegas.[52] Michelini, who had met with Végh Villegas at the Richmond Café in Buenos Aires just days earlier,[53] was the ideal person to generate a dialogue with all political groups in searching for a democratic solution.[54]

It remains unclear where the prisoners were held prior to their executions. Barredo and Whitelaw, along with their children (who eventually were released and reunited with their paternal grandfather in late May), were possibly imprisoned in Orletti.[55] Juan Azarola Saint, a Uruguayan survivor, heard the voice of a young child playing during his imprisonment there.[56] Two Uruguayan former militants imprisoned inside Orletti in July 1976 also recognized Whitelaw's boxer dog there.[57] Michelini and Gutiérrez-Ruiz were probably confined in the central SSF building or the secret prison known as Bacacay, located in the same block as Orletti. Recent judicial investigations corroborated that police officers from the fortieth precinct participated in covering up the murders.[58]

Automotores Orletti

The clandestine Orletti prison (fig. 3), situated in Venancio Flores 3.519/21, in the western neighborhood of Floresta, facing the Sarmiento railway, was the heart of Condor in Buenos Aires between May 11 and November 3, 1976. Approximately three hundred prisoners passed through its walls, and the large majority were foreigners, mainly Uruguayans, Chileans, and Cubans, many of whom eventually disappeared.[59]

At the time, agents called the site *el jardín* (the garden), *el taller* (the garage), or *la cueva de la vía* (the railway cave).[60] The "Automotores Orletti" name originated only after the center closed down when, on November 3, PRT-ERP militants José Ramón Morales and Graciela Vidaillac successfully escaped after a gunfight with their captors. As they frantically ran outside, they saw a poorly maintained sign, which read at the top "Automotores S.A." and underneath "Cortell, Cortell, Cortell."[61] Automotores Orletti originated from the misreading of this sign during the breakout. Santiago Ernesto Cortell was the owner of this two-floor car workshop, which he had rented out starting June 1, but the provisional tenancy had begun on May 11.[62]

Inside Orletti, prisoners were kept in inhuman conditions on the ground floor, where the old car workshop had been located. Upstairs, task force leaders used one room as an office (where a portrait of Hitler hung), while others functioned as cells; at the back, a vast salon was employed for torture and interrogation sessions. Survivors recall the constant noise of trains, the keyword *operación sésamo* to open the metallic entrance shutter door, the wooden staircase up which prisoners were dragged to torture sessions, and the sound of children playing during recess in a nearby school.[63]

The site belonged to the Department of Tactical Operations I of SIDE's Subsecretariat A and was known as OT 18 (for *Operaciones Tácticas*).[64] It also had connections to Campo de Mayo, one of Argentina's largest military bases, and its 601 Intelligence Battalion. The Orletti task force (*patota*) reflected this mixed composition, comprising SIDE agents such as Eduardo Ruffo, officers of the 601 Intelligence Battalion such as Raúl Guglielminetti, and former AAA mem-

Figure 3. Exterior façade of Automotores Orletti secret prison in Buenos Aires, Argentina.

bers including Gordon and Forese.[65] Foreign agents, mainly from Uruguay and Chile, regularly participated in certain operations.

By June 1976 the harrowing killing of the four Uruguayans had terrified the exile community in Buenos Aires and reverberated internationally. According to the UNHCR, many Uruguayans were now anxious to leave Argentina and sought asylum in embassies.[66] Buenos Aires was no longer a sanctuary for refugees: armed groups of civilians, known to belong to the security forces, freely roamed the city, alarming Uruguayans enormously.[67] On June 2 the exile community was shaken again when the Argentine police discovered the body of former Bolivian President Juan José Torres, who had been living in Buenos Aires since 1973 and had disappeared two days earlier.[68] Blindfolded and shot three times, he was found near San Andrés de Giles, about 100 kilometers from the capital. Argentine authorities attempted again to hide their involvement. Initially, Interior Minister General Albano Harguindeguy hinted that Torres's disappearance might have been voluntary and linked to "a very well-orchestrated campaign to discredit" Argentina's new leaders.[69] Subsequently, Economy Minister José Martínez de Hoz accused leftist extremists of killing "one of their own," while letting blame fall onto Argentine authorities.[70]

Conversely, the US Embassy voiced the widely held belief that the Argentine security forces had been involved in Torres's killing, with the government's tacit approval.[71] The connection with the murder of the Uruguayans was inescapable: like the Uruguayans, Torres too had been consolidating political opposition against the Banzer dictatorship in Bolivia.[72] The anxious exile community was at nervous breaking point, and evidence pointed to a campaign "to eliminate leftist exile leadership in Argentina and probably intimidate exile communities."[73]

The dramatic situation of refugees in Argentina produced different reactions. Uruguayan authorities acted ambiguously. On one hand, the Ministry of Foreign Affairs directed the embassy in Buenos Aires to offer "all the assistance and protection within reach to Uruguayans in need."[74] On the other, the same instructions stipulated that for those individuals whose arrest had been legally requested by Uruguayan authorities, "their transfer to the Republic will be provided for."[75] This latter statement seemed to approve the return of exiles wanted back home.

The US government sought to understand the dynamics on the ground in South America, particularly why so many people were being persecuted and "whether this was the result of a conspiracy to murder opponents."[76] Thus, in early June, Secretary of State Henry Kissinger requested that embassy staff in Argentina, Uruguay, Paraguay, Chile, Brazil, and Bolivia provide information on the role of local governments in the deaths of refugees, potential international arrangements behind these executions, and the forceful return of refugees to countries of origin.[77]

Simultaneously, the State Department's INR analyzed the killing spate, probing the degree of cooperation among the Southern Cone's security forces, and gauging whether they were actively participating or passively acquiescing in murdering exiles.[78] The INR concluded that the cooperation among local security forces was justified in tackling leftist subversion and the JCR, albeit admitting that the latter had never conducted any major operations. It found no evidence that governments were cooperating to kill political exiles and instead blamed the murders of prominent political exiles on unique circumstances in Argentina and the victims' association with extremist groups.

Information coming in from the region in response to Kissinger's request, however, partially contradicted this assessment. David Popper, the US ambassador in Santiago, noted that the region's security forces were collaborating to some extent, but the specific degree depended on each country's national interests.[79] Despite lacking corroborating evidence, the ambassador believed that international killing arrangements, with the participation of Chilean agents, were quite possibly in place, as well as potential cooperation in returning refugees. Ambassador Hill in Argentina was rather direct in his response, raising three crucial points.[80] First, circumstantial evidence suggested that elements of local security forces were involved in the murders, which were approved and tolerated by higher ranks. Second, collaboration between Argentine security officers and their regional counterparts was likely, particularly since Uruguayan agents were known to operate in Buenos Aires "in identifying Uruguayan exiles of interest."[81] Third, the murder of the Uruguayan legislators had presumably been a warning "against any '*apertura*' [opening]," thereby eliminating any potential opposition to the Uruguayan dictatorship.[82] The assassinations had probably been a favor to the Uruguayans, since the politicians were of limited interest to Argentina. Hill also observed that Chilean officers apparently operated in Mendoza, while Brazilians did the same in Buenos Aires.

Neither ambassador was in a position to confirm the existence of a murder conspiracy, but both asserted it was a possibility because of long-standing regional cooperation. Conversely, Ernest Siracusa, the US ambassador in Uruguay, downplayed the role of the Uruguayan dictatorship, contending that there was no evidence that the recent murders of Uruguayan exiles had resulted from the action, desire, or arrangement of the local government.[83] Nevertheless, he conceded that Uruguayan officials were traveling to Argentina and occasionally to Chile to interrogate Uruguayan prisoners or obtain the results of interrogations.

Exchanges between the State Department and its diplomatic missions on the possible collusion among South American dictatorships to murder opponents lasted for months until August, when Washington concluded that a conspiracy was indeed taking place.[84] Consequently, on August 23, Kissinger urgently cabled embassies in Argentina, Uruguay, Chile, Bolivia, Brazil, and Paraguay to unequivocally notify ambassadors that, while the US understood the need for "coordination of security and intelligence information," "government planned and directed assassinations within and outside the territory of Condor members" had most serious implications, constituting a serious moral and political problem.[85] Immediate action was required, and ambassadors were directed to arrange meetings as soon as possible at the highest levels in each country. This *démarche*—if delivered—would have clearly signaled to the Condor countries that the US strongly opposed their deadly operations.[86]

In practice, however, only Ambassador George Landau transmitted the message to President Alfredo Stroessner in Asunción; no warnings were communicated elsewhere. A month later, on September 20, Harry Shlaudeman, the chief of the Bureau of Inter-American Affairs, directed ambassadors "not to take further action," remarking that there had not been a report in weeks that indicated any intention to activate the Condor scheme.[87] Tragically, the following day Condor hit in the very heart of Washington. A bomb, placed by DINA agent Michael Townley and anti-Castro Cuban militants, killed exiled Chilean politician Orlando Letelier and Ronni Moffitt, his colleague at the Institute for Policy Studies, as they drove to work; Ronni's husband Michael survived.[88]

No Respite

In Buenos Aires the situation had quickly deteriorated since mid-1976. On June 9 armed men stole records—including the names and addresses of thousands of political refugees—from the offices of the Catholic International Migration Committee. The committee, sponsored by the Roman Catholic Church, was one of Argentina's largest organizations working with the UNHCR. Although authorities attempted to reassure refugees, affirming they "were not in any danger,"[89] everyone feared that "whoever stole the lists meant to do something with them."[90] That was indeed the case.

That same day at dawn, a twelve-man task force, which also included Uruguayan officers, abducted Uruguayan exiles and former Tupamaro militants Brenda Falero and José Luis Muñoz from their apartment in Buenos Aires, where they had lived since December 1974.[91] The prisoners later identified Aníbal Gordon and SIDE agent Miguel Ángel Furci, as well as Uruguayans Campos Hermida and Cordero, among their captors. Taken to Orletti, they were interrogated by Uruguayan agents about their connections to Michelini and Gutiérrez-Ruiz, the PVP, other Uruguayans in Argentina, and Argentine political groups. Their interrogators knew precise details from their past militancy in Uruguay. They wanted Brenda to single out other sought Uruguayans from a photo album, where she noticed that a cross and "R.I.P." were written on pictures of Michelini, Gutiérrez-Ruiz, Barredo, and Whitelaw.[92]

In the early hours of June 11, two groups of twenty armed men forced entry into two refugee shelters, Hotel Pinot and Hotel Ilton, in the Villa Crespo neighborhood.[93] The men, dressed in civilian clothing, arrived in unlicensed cars and forced the entrance doors open; they then proceeded to inspect all the rooms and steal personal belongings, documents, and money. They drove away, taking all male residents, including two minors, to an unknown destination. At Hotel Ilton, they also threatened the owner's wife that they would burn down the building if she contacted the police. In total, twenty-three Chileans, one Uruguayan, and one Paraguayan—the proprietor of Hotel Ilton—were captured. According to reports, the officers had lists and photos of the people they sought, and they claimed to be from the army's security superintendency, a unit that did not exist.[94]

The twenty-five refugees were taken to Orletti, and the abduction of this large group likely saved the lives of Brenda and José Luis: their relatives successfully added their names and that of another Uruguayan, Luis Muniz, to the list of refugees that had been seized from Hotel Pinot. Eventually bowing to international pressure, dictator Videla himself allegedly ordered that the refugees had to reappear. Just before her liberation, the task force leader told Brenda, "You were lucky, madam, you won the lottery today."[95]

Another Uruguayan Orletti survivor, who was just sixteen and had traveled to Argentina to try to join the Quilmes football team, remembered how, soon after a large contingent of people had arrived, the task force received urgent counterorders to free everyone. One captor said, "What a mess, we filled up the place with people and now we have to let them go."[96] Another, who had realized the youngster was not involved in politics, released him out of pity, but gave him a stark warning: "Look, you remind me of my son; if you are Uruguayan, you need to leave, because they are looking for anyone who is Uruguayan, so flee and don't return."[97] All the prisoners were released between June 12 and 13 and reported to the UNHCR that Chilean and Uruguayan security officers had taken part in abductions and interrogations; the kidnappers possessed information previously stolen from the Catholic migration committee, along with files brought from Chile and Uruguay.[98]

Simultaneously with this unfolding ordeal, Argentine Foreign Minister Admiral Cesar Guzzetti met with Kissinger in Santiago and discussed the troubles allegedly caused by refugees in Argentina, complaining that up to ten thousand were potentially engaged in illegal activities.[99] While Argentine government officials accused refugees of supporting guerrillas, Ambassador Hill painted a different picture and spoke of the extreme fear they lived in, referring to the recent episode of the UNHCR refugee group who had all received death threats during their detention.[100] By that point, it was irrefutable that the kidnapping of exiles relied on the direct involvement and cooperation of the Argentine security forces, as it would otherwise be unthinkable for task forces to raid refugee hotels undisturbed.[101]

The Uruguayan Embassy in Buenos Aires knew of the refugees' plight but tried to shift culpability away from the top, contending that Argentine security officers operated and acted with impunity because the higher ranks could not control them.[102] The embassy estimated that many more Uruguayans than officially documented could have been targeted, since the local press only reported a minority of deaths and disappearances.[103]

Persecuting the PVP

The kidnapping at dawn on June 9 from an apartment in the exclusive Núñez neighborhood in Buenos Aires of Gerardo Gatti—a prominent Uruguayan political and trade union leader who had been among the founders of the FAU, the ROE, and OPR-33—marked the start of the first repressive wave against PVP militants in 1976. Exiled in Argentina since 1973, Gatti became in 1975 the PVP's first secretary general.[104] His secretary Pilar Nores was seized later that day from the same flat.

Previously, PVP activists had been apprehended in seemingly isolated incidents, such as the detention on March 28 in the harbor at Colonia by the Uruguayan Navy Prefecture of Ricardo Gil Iribarne, Luis Ferreira, and Elida Álvarez, who had been traveling in a caravan full of PVP propaganda against the Uruguayan dictatorship. Subsequently they were imprisoned in clandestine centers within the premises of the Uruguayan Naval Fusiliers Corps (Fusileros Navales; FUSNA)[105] and the 300 Carlos[106] in Montevideo. At that point, Uruguayan security forces did not possess much information on the PVP. Gil Iribarne recalled first being questioned broadly by Cordero about activities in Buenos Aires and individuals captured there.[107] But by June, Cordero increasingly asked him specific questions about the PVP and its structures, aiming to garner useful information to destroy the party.[108] Cordero also regularly went to Buenos Aires and returned with concrete elements for questioning. By late June the SID had acquired significant intelligence from interrogating prisoners in Argentina and had discovered details regarding PVP operations in Uruguay, Argentina and Europe.[109]

The first wave of detentions of PVP militants occurred between early June and mid-July 1976, when joint Argentine–Uruguayan task forces kidnapped thirty-nine Uruguayans. In some cases the PFA initially apprehended the militants, such as with Gatti and Nores, and imprisoned them in the SSF headquarters or other police precincts. After their nationality was determined, however, they were handed over to the "Uruguayan specialists" in Orletti.[110] The night of June 13, a task force in Morón, Buenos Aires province, picked up Uruguayan trade union leader Washington Pérez, who was no longer politically active in Buenos Aires and worked as a news vendor but was a close friend of Gatti.[111] For weeks until mid-July, Pérez was repeatedly taken to Orletti to act as an intermediary between the PVP and the patota, negotiating first Gatti's freedom and subsequently that of León Duarte, another PVP leader. The patota knew the PVP possessed large sums of money—the result of a successful ransom paid in 1974—and began negotiations to obtain $2 million in exchange for Gatti's freedom and that of other militants held in Uruguay.[112]

By mid-July Orletti was bursting with Uruguayan prisoners kidnapped in successive large-scale operations since early June—largely against the PVP but also including some activists of the MLN, Hugo Méndez of the GAU, and Francisco Candia of the PCU. Simultaneously, relatives of the PRT-ERP leader Mario Roberto Santucho, namely his brother Carlos, sister Manuela, and his sister-in-law Cristina, were also imprisoned there and later disappeared. On July 19, the day Santucho was killed in an ambush on a PRT-ERP safehouse in Villa Martelli, the patota cruelly murdered his brother Carlos, drowning him in Orletti in front of his relatives and other Uruguayan prisoners.[113]

The Argentine–Uruguayan task force followed the same modus operandi in all its operations. They violently broke into victims' flats, usually at night, stealing virtually all their belongings, including furniture and cars. On July 24, the night of the clandestine flight to Montevideo, Uruguayan officers loaded the plane with all their stolen items, including car engines, and were labeled *cirujas* (rubbish collectors) by their Argentine colleagues.[114]

Chaos and confusion defined prisoners' lives inside Orletti, where they were viciously tortured to rapidly gather information.[115] Their captors blatantly disregarded basic human needs: survivors recalled eating only a couple of times within a ten-day period, and prisoners with serious injuries such as Gatti lacked adequate medical attention for days. Orletti's detainees were treated with extreme sadism,[116] and the site housed a much larger number of individuals than initially planned.[117] Survivors called Orletti "the house of torments and crimes,"[118] where people permanently moaned from the pain of brutal tortures and were kept in freezing conditions on the lower-floor garage in the midst of winter. Loud music at night attempted to cover the screams of those interrogated.[119] In this Dantesque hell,[120] Sara Méndez's pleas for her baby Simón went unanswered.[121]

Aníbal Gordon, nicknamed *el jefe,* the boss—a SIDE agent since 1968 and formerly the AAA leader—ran Orletti.[122] There was a clear division of labor within the task force: Argentine agents oversaw the logistics of operations, while soldiers covered guard duties; SID officers interrogated Uruguayan prisoners about their militancy and connections with other exiles in Argentina.[123] Relations among Argentines and Uruguayans were strained, and they frequently fought over the *botín de guerra* (war booty).[124] Argentine officers also questioned detainees about the PVP money,[125] since they did not trust the Uruguayans and thought they were being lied to (*los estaban mejicaneando*) to avoid sharing the money as previously agreed.[126] Survivors identified several Uruguayan officers, whom they knew from previous detentions in Montevideo, including Captain Ricardo Arab, Captain Gilberto Vázquez, and a soldier dubbed "Dracula," namely Ernesto Soca.[127]

Uruguayan officers did not hide their identities and felt "invincible and proud of what they were doing."[128] Cordero, for instance, introduced himself to prisoner Ana Salvo, affirming "they were old acquaintances," since he had interrogated her in Montevideo.[129] Likewise, José Nino Gavazzo asked Sara Méndez if she knew him; when she answered negatively, he told her his name and who he was.[130] Most survivors concur that while Gavazzo overall commanded the Uruguayans, Cordero was the PVP specialist, since he obsessively interrogated prisoners to reconstruct *la sabana* (the bedsheet), a large PVP organizational diagram on which Cordero placed all the militants.[131]

Just a few of Orletti's prisoners were liberated; the majority were murdered or disappeared, including Gatti and Duarte, while twenty-five (mostly PVP militants) were secretly transferred to Montevideo in late July. Detention in Uruguay in La Casona secret prison (also known as 300 Carlos R or *infierno chico*)[132] was a significant improvement. After suffering the cold and near starvation in Orletti, the ability to shower and use a blanket seemed astonishing: "We were eating properly for the first time in days," Sara Méndez recalled. "I will never forget that, and even a soup felt like a blessing [*manjar de la vida*]."[133] In August the detainees were moved to the SID headquarters in Montevideo's central Boulevard Artigas; a clandestine center functioned in its basement, where most of the prisoners were kept, handcuffed and blindfolded. At night torture and interrogation sessions continued.[134]

In Buenos Aires, meanwhile, the disappearance of the large group of Uruguayans had caused turmoil. Daily requests by victims' relatives to locate their missing loved ones overwhelmed the Uruguayan Embassy.[135] Diplomatic staff had their hands tied and could not obtain information from local authorities that merely responded, "The disappeared were not located in their dependencies."[136] The remaining PVP militants lived in absolute fear, as one remembered: "You felt so powerless before your comrades' disappearance. Ford Falcon cars symbolized terror, driving around the city slowly, observing, and with machine guns peeking through the windows. Each time, I thought, that's it, it's my turn, and yet it wasn't. You could touch the fear."[137]

The situation had degenerated so completely in Buenos Aires that terror had reached the stage of "psychosis."[138] Since the March coup, hundreds of refugees had been kidnapped, tortured, and murdered.[139] Declassified US documents have revealed that the CIA was aware of the Uruguayans' fate and the modus operandi used in these operations. A July 26 secret cable affirmed that Argentine SIDE and Uruguayan SID were responsible for capturing the exiles, who would not be returned to Uruguay but would "be handled in accordance with current Argentine procedures regarding subversives: they will probably be killed."[140] Further, the cable admitted that the group's leaders, Gatti and Duarte, had been assassinated.[141]

Liquidating the MIR

Throughout 1976 at least twenty MIR militants were disappeared or murdered in Argentina. After Enríquez's murder in April, Patricio Biedma became the MIR leader and its representative before the JCR.[142] Biedma was Argentine but had joined the MIR when he lived in Chile;[143] owing to relentless harassment by the Pinochet dictatorship since late 1973, he had returned to Argentina in 1974. As the situation worsened in 1975, Fuentes Alarcón (before his capture) had advised Biedma's wife and children to travel to Cuba for safety, which they did.[144] The Argentine security forces were indeed closing in on Biedma, and agents were keen to establish his activities in helping Chilean exiles and his MIR and JCR functions.[145] The house where he lived with his parents in Buenos Aires was raided, but he was not found.

Biedma was responsible for arranging the escape of the remaining MIR militants from Argentina, as well as the transfer of money and messages for the JCR between Argentina and Chile.[146] He was accidentally captured in late July 1976 in an *operativo rastrillo*, a "razor operation," in which agents randomly checked large numbers of people on public transport or the street. Biedma maintained his cover story for a while but eventually broke under torture, admitting his real identity.[147] In Orletti Biedma also disclosed to José Luis Bertazzo, an Argentine prisoner captured in late August, that earlier that month he had perceived the presence of two Cuban prisoners, distinguishing their accent and the unusual use of words such as *caballero* (gentleman).[148]

Indeed, on August 9, Orletti's task force had kidnapped two young Cuban diplomats, Jesús Cejas Arias and Crescencio Galañena Hernández, who were tortured for forty-eight hours and then killed.[149] DINA agents, probably including Townley, who regularly collaborated with anti-Castro Cubans for the DINA, traveled from Chile to question the Cubans and Biedma.[150] The bodies of Cejas Arias and Galañena Hernández were later hidden in "fifty-five-gallon drums, which were dumped in the Paraná River"[151] near Puente Colorado in San Fernando, a location the SIDE used to dispose of prisoners' bodies. Subsequently, a fabricated story was disseminated to the local press, alleging that they had defected to another country.[152]

Biedma and Mario Espinoza, another seized MIR militant, both admitted that the Cuban Embassy regularly funded revolutionary groups in Argentina, including the JCR, Montoneros, and PRT-ERP.[153] Biedma himself had received $75,000 to support MIR activities in Argentina.[154] For the security forces, cutting the funding channels that supported political groups and armed organizations was a priority objective. Indeed, the lack of economic resources weakened the strength of political resistance and threatened militants' very survival, thereby facilitating their capture and elimination.[155]

The Argentine PFA actively participated in operations against members of the MIR and the PVP in Argentina, including the detention of Biedma and Espinoza,[156] the arrest or disappearance of 95 percent of MIR militants, and the capture of thirty-four PVP activists.[157]

The Informer

In mid-September 1976 Carlos Goessens, a PVP militant in Buenos Aires nicknamed *el karateka* because he was a martial arts expert, phoned the First Army Division in Montevideo proposing a deal.[158] In return for sparing his life,[159] Goessens offered to hand over militants of the PVP operational arm that he belonged to, whose leader was Alberto Mechoso.[160] Major Gavazzo immediately traveled to speak to Goessens in person.[161] Goessens's betrayal accelerated the ongoing efforts by the Uruguayan security services to eliminate the PVP in both Argentina and Uruguay.[162] Since late August Cordero had resumed efforts to locate militants "who possessed a significant amount of PVP money."[163] Uruguayan officers knew they had to find those funds, beyond simply tracking activists, if they wanted to entirely disband the PVP.[164]

From September 23 to October 5, Uruguayan agents were back in Buenos Aires collaborating with the Orletti patota to undertake a second wave of operations during which thirty-seven Uruguayans were seized, including twenty-seven PVP members, Adalberto Soba's and Mechoso's wives, and eight children

of various couples. Everyone except Mechoso's wife and children was imprisoned in Orletti, where Goessens was seen behaving "as if he were a Uruguayan
Army officer."[165]

On September 26 three major operations occurred to target the PVP leadership. In the early afternoon in Villa Lugano, south of Buenos Aires, Gavazzo
led twenty to thirty Uruguayan and Argentine agents in a raid on the house of
Mechoso, who had been captured earlier that day.[166] The men ransacked the
property until they found the money they were after, approximately $1.5 mil-
lion.[167] Afterward, Mechoso's wife, Beatriz Castellonese, and the couple's two
children were imprisoned in the former house of Sara Méndez, which the
SIDE had transformed into an intelligence base.[168]

In Haedo, west of Buenos Aires, a similar operation unfolded at Soba's
home. His wife, Elena Laguna, their three children, and two PVP activists (Juan
Pablo Errandonea and Raúl Tejera) working at a printing press located within
the property were detained.[169] Earlier that day Soba had been seized and brutally tortured. Finally, in the late afternoon another operation by a GT5 team
comprising SIDE and PFA agents with Uruguayan agents occurred in San
Martín, northwest of Buenos Aires, targeting Mario Julién's family.[170] As this
book's introduction recounts, Mario was murdered, and Victoria and their two
children were taken to Orletti.

On September 27 a task force involving Uruguayan officers and Argentine
agents from the 601 Intelligence Battalion and the SIDE kidnapped María
Emilia Islas, Jorge Zaffaroni, and their eighteen-month-old daughter Mariana
from their apartment in Vicente López, north of Buenos Aires.[171] Afterward,
SIDE agent Miguel Ángel Furci illegally adopted Mariana, who recovered her
identity only in 1992.[172] That same day the wives and children of Soba and
Mechoso were forced to travel on a commercial flight to Montevideo with Gavazzo and Ricardo Arab, who, posing as their husbands, carried the stolen PVP
money to Montevideo. Laguna recounted how, at one point, Arab opened a
wooden box snatched from her house and began to stash dollars into his pockets, saying that "he could not have enough."[173] The women and children were
later freed.

Similar operations continued in Buenos Aires throughout late September.
Beatriz Barboza and Francisco Javier Peralta are among the few survivors of
this second wave; in Orletti, Barboza briefly spoke with María Emilia Islas, who
told her how her husband was being viciously tortured to reveal information
about other Uruguayans.[174] The evening of their abduction, Barboza and Peralta were put on a commercial flight back to Uruguay, escorted by two guards.

Peralta's Spanish nationality and the fact that his employer had called the Campo de Mayo military base to inquire about his detention likely contributed toward saving their lives.[175] In Montevideo they were initially kept in the infamous 300 Carlos secret prison; subsequently Barboza was incarcerated in Punta de Rieles, and Peralta in Libertad.[176]

By early October this second wave was winding down, with Washington Queiro being the last militant to be detained on October 4. But unlike the first wave in June–July, it remains unclear whether all the prisoners were transferred to Montevideo. Survivor Álvaro Nores, who was taken to Uruguay by plane on October 5, recalled how Gavazzo told him that prisoners' transfers had been suspended and only the heads of the SID and SIDE could authorize those operations, but that an exception was being made for him.[177] Likewise, Cordero repeatedly mentioned to Gil Iribarne that his friend Juan Pablo Recagno had been captured in Buenos Aires, but the major was unsure whether *el Colorado* (ginger head, Recagno's nickname), could be brought to Uruguay.[178]

By October 7 only Biedma and Espinoza were left in Orletti, while all the Uruguayans had gone.[179] The fate of this second group of PVP activists has never been entirely determined. One likely hypothesis by journalist Roger Rodríguez is that they were flown to Montevideo on the "second flight" (*segundo vuelo*) on the night of October 5, in a C-47 Uruguayan Air Force plane piloted by Major Walter Pintos, Major José Pedro Malquín, Captain Daniel Muñoz, and Major Walter Dopazzo, which landed at Carrasco Airport with twenty-two prisoners. Likely incarcerated in 300 Carlos, the detainees were subsequently murdered, and their bodies buried on military grounds.[180]

Another clandestine flight from Buenos Aires to Montevideo, possibly on October 6 or 7, carried Anatole and Victoria Julién, together with seven-months-pregnant Argentine national María Claudia García, who had been captured in August with her husband Marcelo, son of renowned Argentine poet Juan Gelman, and incarcerated in Orletti.[181] In a set of still not fully clarified circumstances, María Claudia was confined with the Julién siblings in a ground-floor room in the SID building,[182] where many prisoners remember seeing a pregnant woman and hearing the noise of children playing on the floor above theirs.[183] After María Claudia gave birth to a baby girl in early November in Montevideo's Central Military Hospital, Captain Arab and Colonel Juan Antonio Rodríguez Buratti removed her and the child from the SID in December; that day a soldier overheard Arab say that sometimes one had to do "tricky things" (*cosas embromadas*).[184]

María Claudia was later assassinated at Base Valparaíso, another secret prison in Montevideo, whose premises had been purchased with the appropriated PVP money.[185] According to Captain Gilberto Vázquez, the funds, estimated between $1 million and $6 million, were split among the SID, the Army Command, and the First Army Division, and were employed for institutional expenses.[186] The Argentines retained a portion too, which became a bone of contention.[187] To resolve this matter, four Argentine Orletti agents, including Gordon and Osvaldo Forese, visited the SID in early December.[188] Most likely, Argentine and Uruguayan agents also discussed the fate of María Claudia and the other *segundo vuelo* prisoners on that occasion.

Charade at Shangrilá

Just before the start of the second repressive wave against PVP militants, Gavazzo had begun negotiations with the *primer vuelo* prisoners in Montevideo in late August. According to the major, the Uruguayan security forces had saved their lives and rescued them "from the Argentine murderers, who had wanted to send them up to play the harp with Saint Peter."[189] To justify their presence in Uruguay, Gavazzo continued, they had to collaborate in simulating a fake guerrilla invasion—a proposal that the detainees unanimously rejected. Amid threats, negotiations continued for a month until another plan was agreed upon. The farce began on October 23, when some agents, standing in for the prisoners, were arrested in various hotels in Montevideo and in a house, Chalet Suzy, in the coastal town of Shangrilá. Special communiqués, which Gavazzo had previously redacted, informed the Uruguayan population of the detention of sixty-two PVP members in Uruguay.[190] In late November fourteen of the twenty-six Uruguayan prisoners transferred from Argentina were prosecuted by the military justice system and later transferred to the Libertad and Punta de Rieles jails.[191] By December 22 all the remaining detainees had left the SID: six more were incarcerated, while another six were released.

Few believed the story of Chalet Suzy at the time, and the unexpected reappearance of the Uruguayans raised many questions. In Montevideo, US Ambassador Siracusa welcomed the news of their forced repatriation from Argentina, given earlier reports indicating their summary execution. The situation, however, clearly demonstrated cooperation between the two dictatorships, including the attempts to cover up what had happened.[192] In Buenos Aires, Ambassador Hill forcefully challenged the Uruguayan version of events and squarely attributed the kidnappings to the Argentine and Uruguayan security forces. He declared that no one in Argentina or abroad would believe the cover story, and pointed out that numerous refugees remained still unaccounted for.[193]

Many PVP activists kidnapped in the first wave inexplicably lived to tell their tales, while the majority of those seized in the second were murdered. One potential explanation relates to efforts by the Uruguayan dictatorship to convince the US that guerrilla groups threatened the country, thus warranting continued American economic and military support.[194] On October 1 the US Congress had signed into law an amendment—proposed months earlier by Democratic Congressman Edward Koch—that halted $3 million of military aid going to Uruguay in 1977, because of its abysmal human rights record.[195] The Shangrilá charade possibly aimed to demonstrate to the US that Uruguay was still under attack. The US government knew, however, that the PVP had been decimated by coordinated operations in Argentina conducted by Argentine and Uruguayan intelligence officers.[196]

Throughout 1976 Argentina was irrefutably the main theater of Condor operations, but exiles were also pursued in neighboring countries, with prominent cases in Bolivia and Uruguay. Several ELN leaders, especially Argentine Luis Stamponi and Uruguayan Enrique Lucas López, were targeted in operations unleashed by the Bolivian security forces. Between April and September 1976 numerous militants were captured in the cities of Oruro, Cochabamba, Llallagua, and Santa Cruz and subsequently interrogated by police agents from the Department of Political Order (Departamento de Orden Político; DOP).[197] Argentine PFA officers also traveled to La Paz to question Stamponi and Graciela Rutila Artes, the wife of Lucas López.[198] On September 17 the Bolivian State Intelligence Service (Servicio de Inteligencia del Estado; SIE)[199] notified Uruguay through encrypted Condortel cable no. 707/76 that DOP agents had murdered Lucas López during a raid in Cochabamba.[200]

Just a few weeks earlier, after a lengthy detention in Bolivia, Rutila, her one-year-old daughter Carla, and another Argentine prisoner had been handed over to the Argentine police on August 29 at the border towns of Villazón, Bolivia, and La Quiaca, Argentina.[201] Subsequently flown to Buenos Aires, they were straightaway imprisoned in Orletti, where they disappeared.[202] In a similar manner, on October 15 Stamponi and prisoner Oscar González were delivered at the same boundary. Stamponi's mother, Mafalda Corinaldesi, who went to Bolivia to investigate her son's whereabouts and unearthed evidence of his illegal rendition to Argentina, was herself disappeared upon returning to Buenos Aires in November. Out of this group, only baby Carla survived; she was illegally appropriated by Orletti agent Eduardo Ruffo but recovered her biological identity in 1985.

Argentines were also targeted in Uruguay. In early November Argentine siblings Claudio and Lila Epelbaum of the communist organization Poder Obrero were unlawfully seized in a joint operation in Punta del Este. Returned to Argentina by plane, they were held in the secret prison known as Protobanco or Brigada Güemes, southwest of Buenos Aires, and later disappeared.[203]

Condor in Action

Unquestionably, 1976 was the year of Condor. On January 30 the Condor agreement had come into effect, and the new system began to materialize and consolidate. Several core features of the Condor System are now clear. First, the leadership of the Condor organization rotated annually among member countries and fell first upon Argentina, which was represented by SIDE Director General Otto Paladino.[204] Second, meetings of Condor countries were regularly held; the second gathering occurred between May 31 and June 2, 1976, in Santiago.[205] On that occasion Chilean, Argentine, Bolivian, Paraguayan, and Uruguayan intelligence chiefs mainly discussed long-range cooperation, while Brazil sent an observer. For Uruguay, the head of the SID, General Amauri Prantl, attended with Major José Nino Gavazzo, who was the SID's "representative of the area of operations"[206] and thereby managed Condor operations for Uruguay.[207] Gavazzo permanently coordinated with the intelligence services of other member countries, ensuring "a perpetual exchange of information to enable better action in the struggle against subversion."[208]

Three crucial decisions were taken at this second Condor conference. First, Brazil formally joined the organization.[209] Second, "a basic computerized data bank," collating copies of all intelligence cards and files from participating countries, would be created and physically located in Santiago.[210] Finally, through a separate accord but still in line with "Condor cooperative thinking," Argentina, Chile, and Uruguay decided to send teams to operate covertly in Paris to liquidate top-level JCR and leftists targets.[211] The logistics of these operations were extensively debated during a separate Condor summit on July 2 in Buenos Aires.[212]

The Condor System rested overall on two main pillars: Condortel and Condoreje.[213] Already by April 1976, if not earlier, the secret and encrypted communications channel Condortel was operational, and this secure system enabled exchanging data on sought individuals and prisoners, tracking the movement of people across borders, transmitting orders to operational teams, and exchanging intelligence across South America.[214] A cryptography system was initially made available to member countries by late December 1975, later replaced by cryptographic machines.[215] By early 1977 Brazil had provided all Condor countries with a manual Swiss-made cipher system machine that was similar to an old cash register, with numbers, slide handles, and a manually operated dial on the side.[216] By late 1977 Argentina had supplied Hagelin Crypto H-4605 equipment to enhance Condortel's security.[217] The Condor Editing Center would also be hosted in Buenos Aires, "to handle limited edition publication of intelligence documents required by Condor members."[218]

Condortel confidential cables found in the Uruguayan Ministry of Defense provide an example of how it worked. On April 9, for instance, Condor 1 (Argentina) requested from Condor 5 (Uruguay) "the ideological record of [name blacked out], Uruguayan, born on July 10, 1955, single, son of [name blacked out] and [name blacked out]. He entered our country on January 20, 1976. The person in question is in detention."[219] Similarly, on April 21 Condor 1 (Argentina) asked Condor 4 (Paraguay) to transmit the criminal records of two Paraguayans accused of subversive activities who were residing in Corrientes city; one had been arrested.[220] Declassified US government documents confirmed in 2019 hypotheses that Condortel followed a simple alphabetical order for the original five Condor states:[221] Condor 1 was Argentina, 2 Bolivia, 3 Chile, 4 Paraguay, 5 Uruguay, while Brazil maintained observer status.[222] Supposedly the CIA also helped establish computerized links among the Condor states' intelligence and operative units. The Paraguayan chief of staff Alejandro Fretes Davalos disclosed in a 1978 meeting with US Ambassador Robert White how South American countries kept in touch and coordinated confidential intelligence information through a US communications installation in the Panama Canal Zone.[223]

Condoreje oversaw operational activities. Each Condor country sent "two officers to Buenos Aires to man this forward command and coordinating office," which was distinct from Santiago's "central archives office of Condor."[224] John Dinges contends that the Condoreje office was located in a SIDE building in Recoleta neighborhood, on Billinghurst 2457 (fig. 4).[225] Officers stationed there processed incoming intelligence, including information and requests transmitted by Condortel, into orders for raids and kidnappings, and operational teams were dispatched to execute the orders.[226] Military officers openly remarked that colleagues were out of country because they were "flying like a condor."[227]

Figure 4. Exterior façade of Condoreje operative base at Billinghurst 2457 in Buenos Aires, Argentina.

DINA Army Brigadier Cristoph Willeke Floel further explained Condor's operational logistics.[228] He had been designated by Manuel Contreras as the Chilean representative to the Condor organization in Buenos Aires between September 1976 and January 1978 under the false name of Georg Wegner Stapf. Other permanent representatives included an Argentine civilian called Enrique Domínguez (potentially a cover name), and an unnamed Uruguayan officer (possibly Ricardo Arab). Paraguayan and Bolivian delegates only traveled to Buenos Aires when needed, and thus varied.

In his later testimony to the Chilean judiciary, Willeke Floel declared that between October 1976 and April 1977 he was the liaison officer between the DINA and the SIDE, facilitating the transmission of information between Chile and Argentina. Further, he closely and regularly collaborated with Colonel Barría Barría, based at the Chilean Embassy, who remitted documentation to Santiago via diplomatic pouch to the head of DINA Exterior. Willeke Floel's superior in Argentina was Colonel Juan Ramón Nieto Moreno, the head of GT5. The Chilean brigadier also provided assistance to what he labeled the "chasing unit,"[229] whose agents traveled from Chile to Argentina at various intervals and in diverse compositions; he helped them coordinate meetings with Colonel Nieto and facilitated various other tasks.

Argentina, Uruguay, and Chile were Condor's most enthusiastic members and engaged in operations against targets primarily in Argentina.[230] Willeke Floel admitted that once sought individuals were detained, requesting countries could collect them, and, although there were different handover procedures, "usually there would be no records left" (*no quedaba registro de ello*).[231] Allegedly, Brazil's participation in Condor was limited to information exchange, including providing communications equipment for Condortel, training foreign agents, and monitoring subversives; its involvement fell short of murder operations.[232]

The 2019 declassification of US documents revealed for the first time the existence of the so-called Teseo unit,[233] which primarily targeted JCR members in France.[234] Teseo was a distinct initiative but still reflected Condor's collaborative philosophy. Previously to this latest round of declassification, operations conducted by special teams against targets outside South America were known as the "Third Phase."[235] Teseo was a top-secret operation, whose true nature was known by only a few high-ranking officials; these included, in Uruguay, Army Commander-in-Chief General Julio Vadora and, in Chile, Contreras, who coordinated details and target lists with Pinochet.[236] Although Brazil, Bolivia, and Paraguay initially tentatively adhered to this new unit, none of them eventually followed up. Paraguay feared that Teseo would bring "nothing but problems" and assisted by only providing information.[237] Bolivia also withdrew because of a lack of funds, the fact that its principal targets were located in Peru, and potential adverse international reactions if Teseo activities were linked back to Condor countries.[238] Ultimately, only the three Southern Cone countries moved ahead, since they already had agents on the ground in France,[239] where the largest concentration of Latin American exiles, including JCR leaders, resided.[240] According to the CIA, the Teseo operations center was located within the 601 Intelligence Battalion in Buenos Aires.[241]

Targets for Teseo included both alleged terrorists and political figures, such as Uruguayan PVP activist Hugo Cores, Senator Ferreira, leaders of Amnesty International (possibly Edy Kaufman),[242] US Congressman Koch (the sponsor of the amendment cutting military aid to Uruguay), international terrorist Ilich "Carlos" Ramirez, the JCR/MIR leader René "Gato" Valenzuela and his partner, and Carlos Altamirano.[243] Each Condor country participating in Teseo had to provide financial contributions for the unit and send two representatives for two months of training in Argentina before teams would be dispatched to France.[244] A single list of targets would be approved:[245] interested parties proposed their choices, and the final selection was by simple majority vote.[246] Subsequently, operations would proceed in two steps. First, an intelligence team would locate, identify, and monitor the target(s), transmitting information to the Condoreje operations center. The latter would use Condortel in its communications with each participating service, while those from abroad would use telephones or cable "in a previously agreed upon language."[247] Second, an operational team would be dispatched "to carry out the actual sanction against the target" and then escape.[248] For security, members of these teams did not know each other, except for the team leaders.[249] Teams were reportedly composed of members of different nationalities, and structured like a US Army Special Forces team.[250]

Between September and early December 1976, Argentine and Chilean officials dictated the training course for Condor officers from Argentina, Chile, and Uruguay to operate in France,[251] which included urban search-and-destroy techniques for surveillance operations and the subsequent elimination of targeted persons.[252] Assassinations were planned for approximately twenty intended victims, but all European missions were aborted after the CIA presumably alerted the French intelligence services.[253] Indeed, in early December 1976 a Condor team of Uruguayans and Argentines was on the ground in Paris to operate against three Uruguayans, including Cores.[254] But the mission was unsuccessful; the team was convinced its operational plan had been leaked and thus returned to Argentina.[255]

These failed European missions closed out Condor's first and deadliest year. The next chapter considers its evolution and changes in 1977 and 1978 before explaining the waning of transnational repression in South America between 1979 and 1981.

5 • Condor's Demise

Back in January 1974 the Elgueta Díaz family had fled political persecution in Pinochet's Chile and settled in Buenos Aires. Life there was, however, far from serene.[1] In January 1975 PFA officers led by Commissioner Juan Carlos Gattei raided the family house in the San Cristóbal neighborhood. Luis Segundo Elgueta Estevan was arrested for one day and questioned about his sons, Luis and Carlos, who were MIR militants. Eighteen months later, on the night of July 27, 1976, security forces abducted Luis, who had recently arrived from Santiago, from his house in Buenos Aires, together with his Argentine wife Clara Fernández and her sister Cecilia; they were never seen again. After this episode, Carlos and his wife Sonia immediately left Argentina for Mexico, while the rest of the family moved to a different house within Buenos Aires. A year later, on the night of July 12, 1977, a joint Argentine–Chilean task force, commanded by PFA Commissioner Antonio Benito Fioravanti, and with the participation of DINA agent Arancibia Clavel, targeted the family a third time: this time Laura Elgueta Díaz and her sister-in-law Sonia, who was visiting from Mexico to introduce six-month-old Jaina to her grandparents, were apprehended.

Agents took the two women to a clandestine prison known as El Club Atlético in the nearby San Telmo district. Upon arrival, Laura and Sonia noticed that various Chilean officers were drinking and socializing with the Argentines. When they expressed surprise at their presence, one agent hit Sonia and responded, "Because Pinochet wants it so" (*así lo quiere*). Argentine PFA officers and DINA agents brutally tortured both women for hours. Laura's interrogator asked about her brother Luis and his participation in the MIR, to check "whether or not she was a liar."[2] Laura learned then that, after cruel interrogations in Argentina, Luis had been sent back to Chile "because he had too much to pay back for there" (*porque allí tenía muchas cuentas por pagar*).[3]

Commissioner Fioravanti repeatedly threatened the women that they would also be transferred to Chile, implying that this was common practice at the time. Eight hours later Laura and Sonia were released, but were warned not to report what had happened and to stop looking for Luis. The following day Commissioner Fioravanti called the family house to tell Laura's mother that Laura and Sonia had been spared Luis's fate, but they had to depart Argentina immediately, which they did, heading for Mexico days later.[4] In February 1978 Laura's parents also had to abandon Argentina, because of the repeated threats and arrests her mother endured as she continued searching for Luis.

The story of the Elgueta Díazes vividly illustrates the repeated harassment that hundreds of South American families experienced in Argentina at the hands of the security forces. The family's relocations did not lessen the political persecution they endured first from the Pinochet regime and later in Buenos Aires. Indeed, the Condor System continued to thrive throughout 1977 and 1978: in this period, operations by agents from the SIDE, SID, DINA, and Paraguayan military intelligence in close collaboration with the police persisted in Argentina, where exiled activists of the Chilean, Paraguayan, and Argentine communist parties, as well as Uruguayan PVP and GAU militants, were relentlessly pursued. Refugee agencies were repeatedly ransacked, and their resettlement case files and technological equipment were stolen.[5]

Increasingly, operations were conducted in nearby countries too. The violent repression unleashed in Argentina since early 1976 meant that thousands of Argentine militants from political and armed groups, including the Montoneros and the PRT-ERP, were fleeing all across the region. By April 1977 at least a thousand Argentines had sought asylum in Brazil.[6] The Argentine security forces aggressively pursued exiled activists abroad: Bolivia was asked, for instance, to return any Argentine wanted citizens found on its territory.[7] Furthermore, in collaboration with their Uruguayan, Brazilian, and Peruvian counterparts, Argentine agents abducted and subsequently transported back to Argentina numerous Montoneros militants.

As 1977 drew to a close, significant shifts occurred inside the three core Condor countries. In Argentina, officers of the ESMA and the 601 Intelligence Battalion took on a proactive role in conducting extraterritorial operations. In Chile, the negative international repercussions and pressure from Orlando Letelier's assassination led to the closure of the DINA and Contreras's fall from grace. In Uruguay, the FUSNA assumed a central role in transnational operations and progressively displaced the SID. Furthermore, relations between Argentine SIDE and Uruguayan SID agents, which had represented a fundamental axis of repressive coordination in 1976, had grown increasingly sour, most likely because of conflicts over stolen PVP funds and because numerous Uruguayan detainees meant to disappear had actually survived.

Tensions also heightened within the military in both Argentina and Uruguay: the case of captured Montoneros leader De Gregorio, discussed later in this chapter, exposed internal competition and struggles for power—particularly between the Argentine Army and Navy. Finally, power disparities between member states, which had characterized the Condor organization from the start, and previous tensions intensified and contributed toward its eventual downfall: Brazil withdrew in late 1977, while territorial disputes between Argentina and Chile spelled the scheme's end in late 1978.

By the late 1970s, the threat posed by the JCR had also so drastically diminished[8] that the CIA now labeled it "a paper tiger" and observed that it had been "reduced to a European-based publishing enterprise serving a continually decreasing readership."[9] The JCR had been an ambitious and extremely well-funded organization in 1974, but the heavy blows it received, especially the assassination of its main leaders in Argentina during 1976, meant that its activities in South America and Europe had significantly decreased.[10]

This chapter ends by focusing on the final phase of transnational repression, *Post-Condor Dynamics*. Between January 1979 and February 1981, extraterritorial operations targeted 112 victims and predominantly unfolded on a bilateral basis, comprising a clear set of actors: Argentine military intelligence agents were the main perpetrators, and Montoneros activists involved in the Contraofensiva campaign constituted the largest set of activists seized in Brazil, Paraguay, Peru, and Argentina.

Clouds on the Horizon

One year after the founding meeting, the Condor countries met in Buenos Aires between December 13 and 16, 1976, for the third conference, reviewing past activities and discussing future plans. Delegations were composed of specialized officers in communications intelligence and psychological operations,[11] who largely deliberated on strategies for coordinated psychological warfare operations.[12] Since August 1976, the Condor countries had indeed endorsed the development of a propaganda program, and by April 1977 both Argentina and

Chile had used it extensively in attempts to refute international criticism and instill a new sense of pride in the population.[13]

Between late 1976 and early 1977, the Condor System faced two daunting challenges: externally, repercussions from the Letelier murder and the failed European operations, and internally, rising problems and tensions. In late 1976 the termination of European operations because of suspected security leaks resulted in multiple consequences: Uruguayan authorities reconsidered the wisdom of such activities,[14] while the security of Condor's operations center in Buenos Aires was strengthened and compartmentalization increased. All matters were handled with maximum caution, given that both European and US intelligence agencies had by then learnt of Condor's existence.[15] By June 1977 the CIA noted that Condor "was an increasingly tough target" due to tightened security measures, with fewer people let into the action.[16] At the December 1976 meeting, General Carlos Laidlaw, who had replaced General Otto Paladino as head of SIDE upon the latter's retirement, was named the new chief for Operation Condor. This position served to manage and coordinate Condor matters and mediate major meetings.[17] For the second year in a row, an Argentine general would preside over Condor.

By early 1977, Condor activities outside South America had been confined solely to intelligence gathering. A team might be sent to verify a target's presence in a country, but no physical action was authorized.[18] The security services of foreign countries could be contacted if additional measures were required. Further, assassinations were possible only in the territories of some Condor countries and were no longer routine given the international spotlight on human rights.[19] In December 1976 even US Ambassador Siracusa, who had repeatedly defended the Uruguayan regime, had declared his discontent regarding murder operations after discovering the plans by Uruguayan officers Gavazzo and José Fons to eliminate Congressman Koch and various Uruguayans in Paris.[20] Siracusa voiced the uncomfortable moral issues raised by inaction in the face of premeditated assassinations and questioned whether the US was becoming a passive collaborator in this scenario.[21]

As long as Condor operations were confined to South America, the US contentedly looked the other way. But it was certainly shaken up by Letelier's murder in Washington, which marked a turning point. According to the CIA, repercussions from this case showed that "political assassinations of extremists abroad had definite detrimental effects on Condor countries," with the Chilean DINA being blamed for that assassination.[22] In August 1977 the once all-powerful DINA was in fact forced to close down and was replaced by a much weaker body, the National Information Center (Central Nacional de Informaciones; CNI).[23] In April 1978 General Odlanier Mena replaced Contreras—until then one of Chile's most powerful men and the mastermind behind Condor—as the head of the CNI.

By early 1977 it had become evident that the Condor System was not working as smoothly as originally envisioned. Disparities in financial and human resources among participating countries meant that some members sent significantly more personnel abroad to where sought activists operated. Thus, states with better resources primarily pursued their own targets, disregarding "those of interest to other members."[24] Consequently, the overall expansion of the Condor organization was hindered.[25] Further, once a country refused to participate in a Condor program, it would no longer be included in additional discussions about it.[26] Some declassified CIA cables from early to mid-1977 note how Condor members lacked coordination and had achieved few practical undertakings beyond holding numerous meetings,[27] while others argued that while Condor suffered from some organizational inefficiency, this factor had not inhibited its overall effectiveness.[28]

While Condor's success had been starkly evident in 1976,[29] divisions and tensions had nonetheless permeated the organization throughout its existence and rose throughout 1977. Member countries did not always follow through on what was agreed to at gatherings, which served primarily as social occasions and were constantly canceled or postponed. By April 1977 bilateral information exchanges, largely between Chile and Argentina, seemed to constitute Condor's principal activity; the psychological warfare department was rather active too, but it was equally limited to information interchange and lacked operational capacity. Indeed, the US State Department affirmed how in early 1977 Condor was likely "shifting more to non-violent activities" and making extensive use of the media in carrying out a psychological warfare program.[30]

Escaping Argentina

Despite the increasing fragmentation within Condor, operations against exiles in South America continued unabated. In early 1977 a multilateral action, which closely resembled the Fuentes Alarcón–Santucho episode (see chapter 3), unfolded in Paraguay. On March 29 the Capital Police in Asunción detained, in the context of an operation probing the sale of forged documents to foreigners, two Uruguayan and three Argentine refugees who had arrived in Paraguay earlier that year.[31] Gustavo Inzaurralde and Nelson Santana were Uruguayan

PVP militants who were trying to obtain documentation for themselves and other activists to flee to Europe.[32] Inzaurralde was the PVP's last leader in South America at the time, after consecutive operations in 1976 in Argentina and Uruguay had dismantled the party.[33] Alejandro Logoluso and Marta Landi were members of the Argentine Peronist Youth,[34] and Argentine José Nell was a friend of Inzaurralde, who habitually sheltered exiles in his house in Buenos Aires and helped them secure false documents to leave Argentina.[35] In Paraguay Nell similarly had assisted militants who were escaping from Argentina to reach Brazil, where UNHCR protection to travel to Europe could be obtained.

One week after the arrests, personnel from the Argentine SIDE, the PFA, and the Uruguayan SID traveled to Asunción to question the prisoners, bringing along relevant documents, including PVP organizational diagrams drawn up by the Uruguayan Army that illustrated the party's structure and a list of sixty-three wanted OPR-33 members.[36] Between April 5 and 7 this international task force, composed of Colonel Benito Guanes Serrano and Lieutenant Colonel Galo Escobar of Paraguayan military intelligence, Lieutenant Ángel Spada and Sergeant Juan Carlos Camicha from Argentine Formosa province, SIDE agents José Montenegro and Alejandro Estrada, and Uruguayan SID Major Carlos Calcagno, conducted interrogations. No new information supposedly emerged, beyond confirmation that Inzaurralde was indeed the highest-ranking PVP leader left in South America.[37]

At this time the Investigations Department also held numerous Paraguayan prisoners who had been unlawfully transferred there after arrest in Argentina. In early 1977 Paraguayan security officers operated aggressively on Argentine soil, and this activity generated much preoccupation within the exile community.[38] Refugees knew that Paraguayan police officers constantly snooped around in Buenos Aires and other cities, looking for people in public places such as bus stations, which exiles avoided at all costs.[39] President Stroessner also counted on an irregular army of informants, known as *pyragüés* ("feet of feather" in Guaraní).[40] At this juncture, Paraguayan agents targeted individuals perceived as potential threats to the dictatorship, including some who had been living in Argentina for decades.[41]

In January 1977 Argentine authorities had seized various members of the Paraguayan Communist Party (Partido Comunista Paraguayo) in Puerto Iguazú, Misiones province, including Lidia Cabrera, her husband Eduardo Sotero Franco, and her brother Esteban, all of whom were later illegally returned to Paraguay. Subsequently, acting at the Paraguayans' request, Puerto Iguazú's local authorities abducted and handed over Juan José Penayo, the leader of Puerto Iguazú's Paraguayan Communist Party Committee, and Cástulo Vera Baéz, who were last seen alive in Asunción.[42] An Investigations Department document, the "List of prisoners in these headquarters that do not appear" (whose title unmistakably indicated the clandestine nature of these imprisonments), included the five Argentine and Uruguayan detainees, and seven Paraguayan prisoners secretly returned from Argentina.[43]

Inside the Investigations Department, Lidia Cabrera shared her cell with Marta Landi, who confided that the Paraguayan person who had promised to sell them the counterfeit passports had instead betrayed them to the police.[44] Marta was frequently and viciously tortured, including by Argentine PFA officers, who on one occasion gave her a pill to force her to speak and left her completely disoriented.[45] Marta was terrified that Paraguayan police officers would hand her and her boyfriend over to the Argentines, and she pleaded with them not to do so. "If they send us to Argentina, we will not survive," she repeated to Lidia.[46] Alejandro Logoluso likewise voiced similar fears to Esteban Cabrera.[47]

Marta's worst suspicions materialized when Argentine dictator Jorge Videla visited Paraguay in mid-May. On May 16 the Paraguayan police delivered the foreign prisoners to SIDE agents José Montenegro and Juan Manuel Berret, and an Argentine Navy plane piloted by a Captain José Abdala (Navy Captain Luis D'Imperio's cover name) took them all back to Buenos Aires.[48] That day Lidia overheard the Argentines say the detainees would die along the way.[49]

Only one of the five was later seen in Buenos Aires. Ricardo Peidró, a survivor of El Club Atlético, briefly spoke with Gustavo Inzaurralde on May 26, 1977. The latter recounted his PVP militancy and arrest in Paraguay as he attempted to join his pregnant wife in Sweden. Inzaurralde further recalled how the flight crew had admitted that he was being taken to Argentina so that Uruguayan officers could interrogate him.[50]

Geographies of Terror

In 1976 Automotores Orletti had physically embodied the terror of Condor. But after its closure numerous other sites in Buenos Aires—city and province— continued to be used to clandestinely imprison exiled militants in Argentina. The Buenos Aires Provincial Police, for instance, managed at least twenty-nine secret prisons that composed the so-called Camps Circuit (Circuito Camps), named after General Ramón Camps, the head of the force.[51] Four of these centers—COT1 Martínez, Pozo de Banfield, Pozo de Quilmes and the San Justo Brigade—secretly incarcerated foreign prisoners and Argentines who had been kidnapped abroad. The PFA also ran a circuit of three *pozos* (literally, wells, black sites), as agents called them—namely, El Club Atlético, El Banco, and El Olimpo—collectively known as "ABO" from each center's initials.

El Club Atlético—where Gustavo Inzaurralde was detained in the San Telmo neighborhood—operated between February and December 1977 in the basement of the PFA's Administrative Division building, where up to 1,500 people were held overall. In March 1977, Uruguayan Isabel Tejera, the sister of a PVP militant who had disappeared in September 1976, and her husband were interrogated there by Uruguayan officers.[52] Uruguayan Army intelligence officers, including Major Calcagno and Captain Eduardo Ferro, purportedly interrogated Uruguayan prisoners at this site.[53]

In late 1977 the building where El Club Atlético was located had to be demolished to make space for a new motorway. Its agents and one hundred prisoners then moved to a new location, El Banco, which functioned between December 1977 and August 1978 in an area called Puentes 12 in Buenos Aires's southwestern outskirts.[54] Another *pozo,* known as Brigada Güemes or Protobanco, had previously operated there between 1974 and 1977 and was also associated with transnational operations, including the case of Argentine siblings Lila and Claudio Epelbaum. Foreign agents and prisoners were seen at El Banco; in March 1978 Uruguayan intelligence officers interrogated eight Uruguayan prisoners and took them away upon leaving.[55] In mid-1978, Uruguayans Edison Cantero, Raúl Olivera, and Fernando Díaz and Chilean Cristina Carreño were all detained there; the latter, a young militant of the PCC, was subsequently transferred to El Olimpo and later murdered.

This third site, situated a few blocks away from Orletti, functioned between mid-August 1978 and late January 1979 in a garage, which had originally been built as a tramway terminal but which now housed the PFA's Automotive Division in the Floresta area. Approximately five hundred detainees were incarcerated in this prison, which had been outfitted by reusing installations from El Club Atlético, including cell doors.[56] The officer in charge, Army Major Guillermo Minicucci, named it El Olimpo (Olympus), since the staff had the power to decide which prisoners lived and which died. The agents who operated in this three-prison circuit often were redeployed from one site to the next over time: for instance, 601 Intelligence Battalion agent Raúl Guglielminetti and SIDE officer Eduardo Ruffo operated at Brigada Güemes, then Orletti, and finally within the ABO circuit.[57]

Trans-Andean Operations

In possibly one of its last major extraterritorial operations, the DINA, supported by Argentine agents, pursued nineteen members of the PCC and the Argentine Communist Party (Partido Comunista de la Argentina; PCA) in Argentina and Chile between May and June 1977. Uruguayan officers also participated, helping to cover up the fate of one victim.[58]

After brutal persecutions in 1976, the PCC was attempting to regroup in Argentina, where financial resources could be received and then brought into Chile.[59] Consequently, PCC leaders Ricardo Ramírez and Héctor Velázquez left their exile in Hungary and worked to establish a new PCC base in Buenos Aires,[60] where they contacted PCA members who frequently assisted recently arrived Chileans with finding work and accommodation.[61] Meanwhile, leader Américo Zorrilla entrusted Swiss-Chilean Alexei Jaccard with the mission of traveling from Geneva to Buenos Aires to deliver a significant amount of money. Jaccard was a perfect choice: he was a Swiss national, was not an official party member, and had not been to Chile since 1974.[62]

On May 15 Jaccard landed in Buenos Aires, where he planned to deliver the funds to Ramírez and Velázquez before continuing to Santiago.[63] Allegedly disobeying security protocols, Jaccard briefly visited his mother, sister, and brother-in-law; he confided in the latter that "people looking for him were very close and he would be unable to dodge them."[64] The next day, in fact, Jaccard, Ramírez, and Velázquez all disappeared in Buenos Aires, and on May 17 police officers collected Jaccard's belongings from the Hotel Bristol, where he had been lodging.[65]

Immediately after these abductions, PFA and military officers also seized twelve PCA members, some of whom had closely assisted the Chileans; only three survived.[66] The operation continued on May 29, when Argentine security forces detained Chilean Jacobo Stoulman and his wife Matilde Pessa upon arrival at Ezeiza Airport. Stoulman, who owned money exchange houses in Chile and Argentina, had been tasked with collecting the funds destined for the PCC.[67] Concurrently, related kidnappings took place in Santiago. On May 27 DINA agents seized Ruiter Enrique Correa, who was responsible for receiving the PCC money; his badly tortured body appeared near the Mapocho River the following morning.[68] On June 7 Hernán Soto, another participant in the PCC operation, was forced into a car and never seen again.[69]

Subsequently, a complex cover-up campaign was implemented to stave off international pressure, especially from Swiss authorities who were inquiring about Jaccard. Forged documents and a paper trail were assembled to suggest that Jaccard had arrived in Santiago on May 26 and then left on June 12 for Montevideo.[70] Meanwhile, the Stoulman family hired lawyer Ambrosio Rodríguez, a man close to the Chilean dictatorship, to investigate the couple's fate. In Buenos Aires Rodríguez met with First Army Corps officials, who confirmed the couple "had been handed over to DINA agents."[71] The lawyer gave the family a different version, however, claiming that their relatives had been involved in funding guerrilla uprisings in Argentina; subsequently, all attempts to elucidate the truth were paralyzed.[72]

The victims' final fate was shrouded in mystery for decades. Contreras placed the blame on the Argentine intelligence services,[73] but relatives firmly believed that their loved ones had been transported to Chile, and they were proved right.[74] In 2007 three former agents of the DINA Lautaro Brigade admitted that Captain Germán Barriga and his men from the elite Grupo Delfín had brought Jaccard, Ramírez, and Velázquez to the Cuartel Simón Bolívar secret prison in Santiago's La Reina neighborhood.[75] It appears that after two or three months, the prisoners were killed with sarin gas by DINA agent Eugenio Berríos. In 2015 human remains discovered in the Cuesta Barriga mine on the outskirts of Santiago, where the DINA regularly disposed of victims' bodies, were identified as belonging to the Stoulmans and Ricardo Ramírez; this find unquestionably corroborated that these prisoners originally apprehended in Argentina had ultimately been murdered in Chile.

In 1977 no South American country offered a truly safe refuge for militants. At the time Brazil had become a temporary haven for fleeing Argentines, from where they could travel to safer exile destinations.[76] But Brazil was too close for comfort, given that Argentine security services could easily reach refugees there. Moreover, despite official commitments to the contrary, Brazil habitually engaged in the refoulement of refugees, which was especially likely when caught militants did not hold official refugee status. In August 1977 the UNHCR representative in Rio de Janeiro, Belela Herrera, publicly denounced the increasing harassment levels and the heightened potential for refoulement.[77]

The federal police forces of both countries had a long history of cooperation, which included prisoner renditions. Starting in late 1976, Brazilian security forces began looking for approximately 150 wanted Argentine citizens: Argentines who resided legally in Brazil would be located and kept under close surveillance, but those who lived clandestinely risked immediate arrest.[78] The Argentine consulate in São Paulo also contributed to this collaboration. For instance, on April 15, 1977, Consul Julio Alfredo Freixas helped two Argentine

PFA officers, who wanted two Argentine nationals arrested in São Paulo and returned to Buenos Aires, arrange a meeting with Brazilian Federal Police Colonel Benedito Felix de Souza. Just four days later, the mission had been accomplished.[79]

A similar fate awaited Argentine refugees across Brazil, although such operations unfolded more easily in the south, because of the long porous border of Rio Grande do Sul state.[80] Episodes of unlawful detention and torture nevertheless also occurred in Rio de Janeiro and São Paulo. In June Argentine legal residents in Brazil Miguel Ricci and Elsa Brega were picked up in a general police sweep of illegal aliens in São Paulo. Ricci was tortured and interrogated by DOPS agents,[81] who also checked his criminal record and passport's validity with the Argentine consulate.[82] The couple left Brazil upon being released weeks later.[83] The Brazilian Army regularly turned suspected Montoneros militants detained in southern Brazil over to Argentine military authorities,[84] while Brazilian and Argentine federal police officers jointly harassed and questioned Argentine exiles who lived in Rio de Janeiro.[85]

The Beginning of the End

Significant changes took place within Condor during 1977. First, the organization expanded when, in September, the Argentine SIDE invited the Peruvian and Ecuadorian intelligence services to join, and both accepted.[86] This addition was meant to strengthen the system and potentially turn it into a large intelligence community, encompassing both the internal affairs of Condor countries and also hemispheric and global questions.[87] In early 1978 Peru thus became Condor 6, while Ecuador became Condor 7. The Ecuadorian Armed Forces allocated Condor responsibilities as follows: the army oversaw intelligence reporting and information exchange, the navy managed telecommunications, and the air force tackled psychological warfare.[88] Chile then funded four scholarships for Ecuadorean officers to attend the intelligence school in Santiago.[89] Finally, the chief of Condortel, Argentine Lieutenant Colonel Luis Francisco Nigra, supervised the installation of the telecommunications system within the Ministry of Defense in Quito.[90]

Second, power disparities and conflicts among Condor members worsened. Paraguay resisted joining Teseo, despite increasing pressure from Argentina and the latter's accusations that Paraguay feared the US reaction.[91] President Stroessner had previously expressed his opposition to the unit, because it employed underworld tactics and crossed international borders. Paraguay only collaborated in Teseo by exchanging information; allegedly, Stroessner objected to Condor meetings even taking place in Paraguay if Teseo-related matters might be discussed.[92] Conversely, Brazil adopted an aggressive posture and continually tried to usurp the organization's leadership.[93] When other fellow Condor countries apparently resisted its domineering attempts,[94] Brazil determined to return to the periphery as an observer. When no Brazilian representatives were sent to the Condor conference in Buenos Aires between October 3 and 6, 1977, Brazil was considered to have effectively withdrawn from the scheme.[95]

Montoneros in Uruguay

Significant transformations also unfolded beyond the Condor organization itself in 1977. The Argentine and Uruguayan navies particularly took on a more prominent role in extraterritorial operations than in the past, when intelligence organs linked to the armies, such as the Uruguayan OCOA and SID and the Argentine SIDE, had dominated. Discontent generated by some of the operations in Buenos Aires in 1976 most likely caused this readjustment in Uruguay.[96] Furthermore, shifting power relations and internal conflicts within the armed forces inside each country likely played a role.[97]

Collaboration between the Argentine and Uruguayan navies in intelligence exchange and the fight against subversion dated back to mid-1974, and was especially close between the two prefectures,[98] as well as the ESMA and the FUSNA.[99] In late 1977 cooperation intensified and border patrol security was especially strengthened, because the Montoneros were planning to use Uruguay as an operative base from which to launch operations that would disrupt the 1978 World Cup in Argentina.[100] A former Uruguayan Navy commander later admitted that Argentine and Uruguayan Prefecture officers at that time regularly patrolled the *Vapor de la Carrera* ferry, which connected Buenos Aires and Montevideo, and investigated various passengers.[101]

Between November 1977 and May 1978, the ESMA and FUSNA collaborated in three large operations against Montoneros members in Uruguay and against Uruguayan opposition groups in Argentina. First, twelve Montoneros and five children were apprehended in Montevideo between mid-November and mid-December 1977. Second, twenty-six Uruguayans linked to the GAU, PCR, and MLN (along with three babies) were detained in Buenos Aires between late December and early January 1978 and subsequently disappeared.[102]

Linked to these operations, the FUSNA simultaneously detained and tortured over thirty GAU militants or sympathizers in Montevideo. Finally, in April 1978 Argentine and Uruguayan officers kidnapped another fourteen Uruguayans in Buenos Aires who had been previously linked to the MLN; nine were freed, but five disappeared, including teenager Carlos Severo.

The detention of high-ranking Montoneros leader Oscar De Gregorio on November 16, 1977, by the Uruguayan Prefecture in Colonia's harbor kicked off this set of interlinked operations.[103] He had just returned from one of his regular trips to Buenos Aires, traveling under the false identity of a businessman, and was carrying two grenades and a revolver hidden in a *yerba mate* packet and a thermos.[104] His partner, Rosario Quiroga, witnessed his arrest from a distance.[105] De Gregorio, Quiroga, and her three daughters had fled Argentina months earlier, seeking refuge first in Brazil and then in Uruguay since October.[106] She realized their security had been compromised, and she immediately abandoned her apartment and contacted De Gregorio's mother, who reported her son's kidnapping to Uruguayan authorities.[107] Quiroga also sought help from other Argentine exiles who lived in Montevideo, including the celebrated pianist Miguel Ángel Estrella.[108] Together they decided that she would rent a house in Lagomar, just outside Montevideo, to live with another Argentine exiled family.

Meanwhile, the day after the arrest, the Uruguayan Navy commander decided that De Gregorio should be transferred from Colonia to the FUSNA in Montevideo, since he was potentially a Montoneros member. Having been notified by the Uruguayans, ESMA Lieutenant Antonio Pernias immediately traveled to Uruguay.[109] After his first torture sessions, De Gregorio had convinced his FUSNA captors, most likely Navy Lieutenant Jorge Néstor Troccoli, head of intelligence, and his right-hand man Juan Carlos Larcebeau, to let him attend a meeting in Montevideo's old town.[110] When De Gregorio then tried to escape, he was shot at; Lieutenant Pernias arrived on the scene just in time and shouted "We need him alive," thus preventing a FUSNA officer from firing the coup de grâce.[111] De Gregorio subsequently underwent life-saving surgery at Montevideo's Central Military Hospital. During his convalescence, ESMA officers, who had traveled with prisoners brought from Argentina, interrogated him.[112]

As events unfolded, the Uruguayan Army, which had identified De Gregorio as a Montoneros big shot (*pez gordo*), agreed to hand him over to the Argentine Army.[113] This decision by the Uruguayans stretched preexisting Argentine intrabranch rivalries to a breaking point: upon finding out, the Argentine Navy began planning a military action to capture De Gregorio from the hospital in Montevideo. To avoid this warlike scenario, the Argentine Army and Navy eventually arranged that De Gregorio would be handed over first to the Navy, who would later transfer him to the Army.[114] Apparently, a second agreement known as the Conclave de Solis was also sealed by the two navy commanders and Uruguayan President Aparicio Méndez. Supposedly, the Uruguayans would deliver De Gregorio in return for three cars, the helicopter the Argentines had come in, and control of Uruguayan nationals abducted in Argentina.[115] This arrangement also covered other Argentine prisoners that had been captured.

Between December 15 and 16, several successive operations targeted more Argentine exiles in Montevideo. On the morning of December 15, Quiroga and Rolando Pisarello were attacked at a bus stop near their house in Lagomar. Forced into a car, they were taken to a nearby secret prison known as the Castillito de Carrasco, named as such because it looked like a medieval castle.[116] In its basement, Argentine and Uruguayan officers savagely interrogated Quiroga and threatened that her daughters would also be tortured.[117] That afternoon security forces intercepted the car in which Montoneros militants Jaime Dri and Alejandro Barry were traveling. Dri was in Montevideo to meet Barry, the Montoneros' political secretary.[118] The two men ran away in different directions: agents shot Barry dead, while Dri was wounded.[119] Also taken to the Castillito, Dri was subjected to long torture sessions and interrogated about his political activities. Argentine officers, whom Dri later identified as Army official Julio César Coronel, Navy Prefect Héctor Febres, and Navy officer Raúl Scheller, told him he would be transferred to Argentina. The third operation that day targeted the house of pianist Estrella, where he lived with three other Argentines. Uruguayan agents menaced Estrella, saying that although they were not murderers like their Argentine counterparts, they would destroy him by keeping him in prison.[120]

In the early hours of December 16, Rosario Quiroga's house in Lagomar, where María Milesi was staying with her baby and Rosario's three daughters, was raided. Another Montoneros militant, Susana Matta—the wife of Alejandro Barry—had sought refuge there with her four-year-old daughter Alejandrina after her husband had failed to return home the previous day. The security forces detained Milesi and the five girls, but Matta killed herself by ingesting a cyanide pill.[121] The following day, another Montoneros perished in the same way upon being identified by the Uruguayan Immigration Police in Carrasco Airport.

After these arrests, nine prisoners were illegally transferred to the ESMA via clandestine flights: on December 17 a helicopter carrying De Gregorio took off from Montevideo's harbor, while Quiroga and her daughters traveled by plane, escorted by Navy Prefect Febres; Dri and the Pisarello family were repatriated to Argentina on December 18.[122] At the ESMA, Quiroga was finally reunited with De Gregorio, whom she barely recognized after the torture he had endured.[123] ESMA officers then took Quiroga's three daughters to a nearby convent, where a family relative lived. In complying with the accords, De Gregorio was sent to the army base in Campo de Mayo for interrogation; in April 1978 he died of heart failure inside the ESMA, before Quiroga's eyes. Dri was also temporarily moved to another Army secret prison called Quinta de Funes; back at the ESMA, he successfully convinced his jailors to take him to Asunción, where he offered to identify other militants. But Dri was planning to escape instead, which he did in July 1978.[124] Quiroga, Pisarello, and Milesi were freed in 1979.

In Uruguay, international pressure forced the dictatorship to officially acknowledge the arrest of pianist Estrella and his housemates. After being prosecuted by the military justice system, they were incarcerated in mid-January 1978.[125] The clandestine transfer of the other detainees remained a secret, however; indeed, the story of toddler Alejandrina Barry was used in psychological operations to demoralize Montoneros militants, alleging that her family had abandoned her.[126]

Despite the secrecy surrounding this operation, by early January 1978 the US Embassy in Montevideo was aware of De Gregorio's arrest and interrogation at the FUSNA, as well as the succeeding cover-up operations by local authorities.[127] One cable from the embassy to Washington observed that De Gregorio had been "quietly turned over to Argentine authorities in keeping with the close cooperation" between the security forces of the two countries.[128]

This operation clearly illustrated Condor's capabilities. De Gregorio's rapid identification and the swift arrival of Argentine Navy officers in Montevideo revealed the existence of well-oiled and tested cooperation mechanisms that facilitated the quick movement of officers between countries that would otherwise have been difficult without preexisting agreements.[129] The collaboration between the Argentine and Uruguayan navies became even closer when, in early 1978, Jorge Néstor Troccoli was designated as a liaison officer based in Buenos Aires.[130] Throughout 1978 he operated in various locations, including navy bases in Puerto Belgrano and Mar del Plata, and the ESMA, where he participated in its infamous task force between May and December 1979.[131]

Operation Gringo

Throughout 1978, exiled Argentine Montoneros activists across South America remained in the crosshairs. The Argentine family of Claudio Logares, his wife Mónica Grinspón, and their twenty-three-month-old daughter Paula was abducted in Montevideo on May 18, 1978, and later transferred to Argentina, where Claudio and Mónica disappeared. Paula was illegally appropriated by a Buenos Aires provincial police subinspector.[132]

Besides Uruguay, Argentine security forces actively pursued Montoneros militants in Brazil. In the late 1970s Brazilian authorities were deeply preoccupied with refugees, and cooperation unfolded at the highest levels between Brazilian and Argentine intelligence services.[133] In Brazil the activities of Argentine resistance groups were constantly watched, and officers stayed on the alert for the potential entry of Montoneros militants,[134] while the Argentine police operated on the ground.[135] Between 1977 and 1978, Brazil was in fact the most important base in South America for Montoneros: several leaders, including Raúl Yager and Horacio Mendizábal, lived in Rio, while others were located in São Paulo.[136]

The kidnapping of journalist Norberto Habegger clarifies the sophisticated coordinated mechanisms at play. For years Argentine agents had been pursuing Habegger, who was in 1978 the Montoneros' political secretary.[137] His wife, Florinda Castro, and brother, Gustavo, had been imprisoned in El Club Atlético in 1977.[138] Subsequently Florinda and their son, Andrés, had moved to Mexico City.[139] It was from there that, on July 31, 1978, using the name of Héctor Esteban Cuello, Habegger traveled to Rio de Janeiro, where he planned to meet two Montoneros members to begin planning the *contraofensiva* campaign, a series of political and military actions meant to undermine the Argentine dictatorship.[140] Afterward Habegger intended to travel to Spain.[141] But at an unknown date between August 1 and 9, agents from the Brazilian CIE, the Argentine 601 Intelligence Battalion, and the PFA unlawfully abducted Habegger and transported him back to Buenos Aires, where he was likely held in Campo de Mayo until late November or early December 1978, when he was executed.[142]

This operation was carefully assembled by Argentine Army officers Adolfo Feito, Enrique Del Pino, and Guillermo Cardozo from El Banco.[143] They learned of the planned *contraofensiva* gathering after the capture in Buenos Aires of the two militants that Habegger was scheduled to meet in Rio.[144] The Argentines told the Brazilians that Habegger was carrying a lot of money as an additional incentive.[145] This kidnapping happened as part of a preexisting collaborative scheme between the Argentines and Brazilians known as Operacão Gringo, which targeted Argentine suspected militants in Brazil and was assigned to Brazilian CIE Colonel Paulo Malhães.[146]

Ostensibly, Argentina financed Operacão Gringo with $20,000 a month, and an Argentine agent infiltrated local activists and groups.[147] Colonel Malhães collaborated with agents in the Argentine consulate, informants at Rio's UNHCR office, and his long-standing police contacts; gradually he assembled an album containing photos of numerous Argentines in Rio.[148] This "tacit persecution," as Malhães called it, enabled him to learn the routines of Argentine suspects so that when kidnapping orders came through, everything was already in place for action.[149] The colonel later admitted receiving the order to kidnap an important Argentine national in Rio (most likely Habegger), given his ability to conduct the operation without mistakes or attracting the public's attention. The Argentines wanted the prisoner alive: a doctor thus gave the detainee an injection to weaken him, and he was then wrapped like a mummy to facilitate his transfer to Argentina.[150]

Broken Shoe

In parallel to the persecution against the Montoneros, operations against PVP militants in South America persisted, and a third attempt to seize PVP leader Hugo Cores was carried out in 1978. On November 17 the head of *Veja* magazine in Porto Alegre, Brazil, journalist Luiz Cláudio Cunha, received a frantic phone call from an anonymous caller who pleaded with him to rush to a flat on Botafogo Street to check on a Uruguayan couple, Lilián Celiberti and Universindo Rodríguez, and Lilián's children, Camilo and Francesca, who had not been heard from for several days.[151] The caller was Cores himself, who had moved with his wife Mariela Salaberry and their daughter from France to São Paulo earlier that year to resume denunciations of human rights violations in Uruguay.[152]

Lilián and Universindo were PVP activists, and Lilián's silence since November 12 had set alarm bells ringing for Cores, since she was supposed to be in daily contact with him prior to their meeting in Porto Alegre on November 17. That day Cores and Salaberry also sought help from the São Paulo–based human rights NGO Clamor; journalist Jan Rocha, a Clamor member, asked her friend Omar Ferri, a lawyer in Porto Alegre, to pass by Lilián's flat as soon as possible.[153] Ferri went to the apartment several times that day and the next but never found anyone. The family had in fact already been seized days earlier.

The operation had begun in early November, when an unidentified caller had tipped off the Uruguayan Army Command that someone wanted by the security forces could be found at a specific address in Montevideo. On November 2 the army's Counter-Information Company (Compañía de Contrainformaciones, hereafter Counter-Information Branch) investigated the lead and detained one individual.[154] Subsequently, seven more PVP activists were arrested and accused of distributing the clandestine PVP magazine *Compañero* in Uruguay. Brutal interrogations then determined that Celiberti and Rodríguez were living in Porto Alegre, while other PVP militants, including Cores, were also based in Brazil.[155] Cores was again within the grasp of Uruguayan security officers, and failure was no longer an option.

A plan was accordingly devised and meticulously prepared, code-named *zapato roto* (broken shoe), referring to Cores's habit of using the same old, worn-out shoes.[156] Unilateral action was too risky, and thus Colonel Calixto de Armas, the Army General Staff's head of intelligence, contacted his Brazilian counterpart and sent to Porto Alegre Major José Bassani, chief of the Counter-Information Branch, and Captain Eduardo Ramos, head of operations; later on, Major Carlos Rossel traveled to finalize the details. The operation began in the second week of November when three vehicles left Montevideo: a truck carried four blindfolded and hooded PVP prisoners escorted by soldiers, while SID Captain Eduardo Ferro and the Counter-Information Branch's Captain Glauco Yannone followed in a Fiat 128; Hugo García Rivas and another soldier drove a yellow minivan.[157] At the border in Chuy, captains Ferro and Yannone and three prisoners continued to Porto Alegre in two vehicles with Brazilian Federal Police officers who had come to collect them, while the others waited behind in Uruguay.[158]

The morning of November 12, men in civilian clothes, claiming to be police officers, detained Lilián at the bus station in Porto Alegre and took her to the Rio Grande do Sul DOPS office.[159] Hours later, Universindo, Camilo, and Francesca were apprehended as they left their flat to watch the Inter vs. Caxias football match that Sunday. At the DOPS, officers including Uruguayans Ferro and Yannone interrogated and tortured Lilián and Universindo, and that evening DOPS chief Pedro Seelig informed them that they would be immediately transferred to Montevideo. After traveling all night by car, they reached the border at dawn.[160] In the nearby army premises in Santa Teresa, Captain Ferro continued to interrogate Universindo and Lilián about other PVP activists in Brazil and Europe.[161] On the afternoon of November 13, Universindo and the children were transported to Montevideo, while Lilián returned to Porto Alegre with two Brazilian police officers and Captain Ferro. In exchange for her children's safety, she had disclosed her forthcoming meeting with a high-ranking PVP figure, and a *ratonera* was accordingly set up at Lilián's flat in Porto Alegre.[162] Afterward, under the watchful eyes of Uruguayan and Brazilian agents, she called her contact in Paris to confirm the 5 p.m. meeting; unbeknownst to them, however, "5 p.m." was the agreed code word to alert that something was wrong.[163] Since receiving that coded message, Cores had looked for ways to help Lilián.

Journalist Cunha and photographer João Baptista Scalco reached Lilián's flat around 5:30 p.m. on November 17. As soon as they knocked on the door, they were pulled into the flat and held at gunpoint. The task force waiting inside mistakenly assumed they were the PVP activists Lilián was meeting. But as soon as Cunha started speaking Portuguese and said they were journalists, the security agents were perplexed.[164] Lilián's call for help had succeeded. Indeed, by checking on the flat, the journalists had exposed the operation. Cunha and Scalco were eventually freed after agents assured them that this was a case of foreigners residing illegally in Brazil, but both sensed something else was going on, since they had spotted Didi Pedalada, a former Inter player turned DOPS agent.[165]

Cunha embarked on a tireless campaign to denounce the operation on Brazilian media, which in the long run saved Lilián and Universindo's lives.[166] Lilián's mother, Lilia, had also traveled to Porto Alegre to look for her daughter, and lawyer Ferri assisted her.[167] During a press conference, Lilia pleaded that at least her grandchildren be returned, which occurred on November 25 when security officers brought Camilo and Francesca to their grandparents' house in Montevideo.[168] In December Cunha traveled to Montevideo to investigate the case and spoke with Camilo, who,[169] despite being just eight years old, identified without hesitation the DOPS building where he had been kept, and precisely recalled the car trip to Uruguay as well as the participation of Uruguayan officers, affirming how two agents "spoke Spanish like we do," meaning they were Uruguayans.[170]

The abduction of the Uruguayans put the exile community in Porto Alegre on high alert.[171] In late November the Uruguayan dictatorship ineffectually attempted to defuse the negative media campaign and associated international repercussions by releasing two public communiqués claiming that the family had been detained upon illegally entering into Uruguay carrying subversive materials, fake documents, and weapons.[172]

The detention of PVP and Montoneros activists in Brazil showed how bilateral operations were persisting into late 1978, despite Brazil's withdrawal from Condor. Operations in Rio and Porto Alegre revealed careful planning and close working relations between the region's security forces, within and beyond Condor structures. The *zapato roto* operation, with its careful orchestration of men and resources, could have been the perfect crime. Yet the brave actions of Brazilian activists, journalists, and lawyers protected Lilián and Uni versindo's lives. Despite being held incommunicado and tortured at the notorious Thirteenth Infantry Battalion in Montevideo, they were spared being disappeared, which was their original projected fate.[173]

Condor Undone?

The year 1978 marked the beginning of Condor's downfall. By the late 1970s the brutal repression unleashed against political activists had been rather successful in significantly weakening opposition to South America's dictatorships. Paraguayan Chief of Staff General Alejandro Fretes Davalos admitted during a meeting in Asunción with US Ambassador Robert White in October 1978 that collaboration and regular country meetings among the chiefs of South American intelligence services were no longer particularly useful, since the main threat from militants in Argentina had been eliminated.[174]

Moreover, disagreements and tensions, which had always underlain Condor, significantly worsened: throughout 1978 the return of traditional territorial conflicts gradually shifted attention away from the counterinsurgency preoccupations that had united the Condor countries until then. Divisions were evident during what likely was the last meeting of Condor countries, held between September 11 and 14, 1978, in Asunción. The intelligence chiefs of Argentina, Chile, Uruguay, Paraguay, and Bolivia gathered, at Chile's request, to discuss the Letelier case and adopt a common position. But feelings were running so high that the meetings had to be structured so that "the representatives of Argentina and Chile were never present at the same session."[175] Supposedly, the summit ended badly when the Argentine representative attempted to influence other countries regarding his government's point of view on the Beagle Channel—the main issue of contention between the two countries.

By late 1978 the deep-rooted animosity in Argentine–Chilean relations had been reignited after the temporary parenthesis of the Condor years, and the

Argentine–Chilean axis, which had been the motor behind Condor until then, broke apart. The long-standing territorial dispute regarding the exact demarcation of the border across the Beagle Channel, in the southernmost Tierra del Fuego, brought the two countries to the brink of war once more, with all settlement attempts having failed.[176] By November both armed forces were on high alert, and an armed confrontation loomed on the horizon. Argentine commanders adopted increasingly fiery language;[177] for instance, First Army Corps Commander General Carlos Suárez Mason threatened that if the Beagle matter was not resolved by a meeting between the countries' foreign ministers in December, Argentina would occupy the three contested islands and fight Chile until the bitter end.[178] Hostilities were eventually and narrowly averted, and the dispute was submitted to papal mediation.[179]

But in Argentina, preparations for a possible conflict with Chile had redirected the dictatorship's energies back toward traditional warfare and away from the fight against subversion.[180] An Argentine colonel told the US Embassy's political officer in Buenos Aires that the Beagle dispute "had dramatically changed the Army's professional focus."[181] Indeed, whereas previously participation in the war against subversion helped advance one's career, by this point regular professional assignments had become the most sought-after jobs within the army. The return of traditional sovereignty concerns and territorial-based conflicts displaced the focus on counterinsurgency and internal enemies among the Condor countries. This shift in policy and practice, which reflected ideological stances but also internal developments and divisions inside the Chilean and Argentine militaries, had positive effects on the human rights situation, since disappearances started to drop significantly in 1978 compared with previous years.

Post-Condor Dynamics

During the last phase of transnational repression between early 1979 and early 1981, repressive coordination lost its centralized and systematic format and reverted to its previous ad hoc nature, which had characterized the *Embryonic Interaction* phase in the late 1960s and early 1970s. This change resulted from the rupture of the Argentine–Chilean axis in 1978, coupled with Brazil's withdrawal in 1977, and an overall lessening of repression given the preceding dismantling of opposition organizations. From 1979 onward, South American countries resorted to transnational repression mechanisms to pursue specific activists in dedicated operations, in a modus operandi that mirrored practices seen at the start of the decade. In this phase the main targets were Montoneros militants attempting to return to Argentina, and these bilateral operations were conducted by Argentine agents, mainly from the 601 Intelligence Battalion, in collaboration with their counterparts in Brazil, Paraguay, and Peru.

In late 1978 Montoneros leaders in exile, including Roberto Perdía and Miguel Bonasso, believed that the balance of forces was finally shifting, and conditions were ripe for accelerating the downfall of the Argentine dictatorship. They thus launched the *contraofensiva* campaign, which was meant to deepen the Videla regime's increasing internal divisions and spur on the worker-class mobilizations that they expected to happen.[182] Over 450 militants were involved in this campaign: half were already in Argentina, and the others planned to return from exile.[183] Militants, some of whom had received training in Lebanon, Libya, and Spain, were divided into two groups.[184] The Special Infantry Troops (TEI), which reported to the Military Secretariat, were "organized into groups of approximately five men" who would "carry out selective terrorist activities" targeting the dictatorship's economic advisors.[185] The Special Activist Troops (TEA), answering to the Secretariat of Agitation, Press, Propaganda, and Indoctrination, would implement political activities and transmit antidictatorship messages by hijacking radio and TV signals. The *contraofensiva* unfolded in two phases in 1979 and in 1980, but both were crushed by Argentine security forces: forty militants died or disappeared in 1979 alone.

Argentine state agents were in fact always a step ahead. They strategically used existing regional collaborative mechanisms to alert neighboring countries about militants' movements, or to request collaboration in carrying out operations on their territories. In April 1979, for instance, the Argentine Navy's intelligence service informed the Paraguayan military intelligence that Montoneros top leaders Mario Firmenich and Fernando Vaca Narvaja would be attempting to enter Argentina via Paraguay; police authorities at Asunción's international airport and in the border city of Encarnación were alerted.[186] In July 1980 Navy Lieutenant Orlando Ruiz requested permission for an Argentine team with one Montoneros prisoner to enter Paraguay and collaborate with local military authorities to potentially identify and detain a TEI couple coming to Asunción from abroad.[187] The triple Argentine–Brazilian–Paraguayan border was especially permeable yet risky: two Montoneros, Liliana Goldenberg and Eduardo Escabosa, killed themselves in August 1980 with cyanide pills when they noticed Argentine police officers on the boat they were traveling on from Brazil into Argentina.[188]

On March 12, 1980, following a similar modus operandi to Habegger's kidnapping, the Argentine 601 Intelligence Battalion and Brazilian CIE agents abducted Horacio Campiglia, a high-ranking Montoneros leader overseeing *contraofensiva* operations, and Monica Pinus, a militant from the same group, when they landed at Rio International Airport. A Montoneros base was being set up in Rio so that leaders such as Campiglia could be physically closer to Argentina; Edgardo Binstock, Monica's husband, had been there for one month already making preparations for their arrival.[189] The capture operation had been planned after a Montoneros militant detained in Buenos Aires began to cooperate under torture. Argentine intelligence officers then requested permission from their Brazilian colleagues to capture Campiglia and Pinus.[190] Accordingly, agents traveled to Rio aboard a C130 plane and, after the kidnapping, returned to Campo de Mayo with the two detainees, who were confined with another twelve TEI members, who had also tried reentering Argentina from Paraguay, Uruguay, and Brazil.[191]

Three months later an analogous operation unfolded in Peru after careful preparation. In early May a Montoneros militant detained in Buenos Aires had confessed to a scheduled meeting in Lima.[192] Argentine Army Commander Leopoldo Galtieri reached out to his Peruvian counterpart, General Pedro Richter, so that an Argentine task force could detain and transfer several Argentine exiles to Buenos Aires.[193] On June 5 Argentine Colonel Ronald Rocha arrived in Lima with eight army officers and the Montoneros prisoner who would pinpoint the militants. Peru contributed to the mission by providing logistical support, vehicles, officers, and rooms in a military holiday center, Playa Hondable, which was converted into a secret prison. The prisoner unsuccessfully attempted to flee while in Lima and was then forced to attend the afternoon encounter on June 12 with Maria Inés Raverta, who was overseeing *contraofensiva* logistics in Peru. After her capture Raverta withstood cruel torture for hours and divulged the location of the two Montoneros bases only late that evening, when she knew they would be empty. Security protocols dictated that militants had to abandon their premises within two hours of someone failing to return from a meeting.

Underestimating the risks in Lima, Montoneros leader Roberto Perdía decided to leave with his wife, but told Julio César Ramírez, Noemí Gianetti and her eighteen-year-old son Gustavo Molfino to stay put in the two houses. That evening Gustavo repeatedly called, from a public phone across the street, two Peruvian politicians to update them about Raverta's disappearance. At 11 p.m., during one call, he witnessed military men surround the house and immediately called his mother, who advised him to abscond. Days later, on June 17, prisoners Raverta, Gianetti, and Ramírez were expelled from Peru into Bolivia; from there they were handed over to Argentina.[194] By late June the Peruvian and international press had extensively denounced the incident and strongly criticized Peruvian authorities for collaborating with Argentina.[195] General Richter unsuccessfully tried to justify his actions, arguing that the Argentines had been "legally expelled and delivered to a Bolivian immigration official in accordance with long-standing practice."[196] But he was forced to concede that although "the Peruvians had made no agreement to have the three turned over to Argentines," the Bolivian military did just that.[197]

One month later, on July 21, Gianetti's body was found in an apartment in Madrid.[198] Gustavo Molfino and his sister Alejandra later identified her and came to the conclusion that their mother had recently been in Argentina, since they found a new pair of shoes, towels, and cosmetic products with "made in Argentina" labels among her belongings. There seemed little doubt that Argentine security officers had murdered Gianetti in Spain after a period of time she spent in Argentina, probably in Campo de Mayo.[199]

As we have seen, border areas facilitated abduction operations. The border cities of Paso de los Libres, Argentina, and Uruguaiana, Brazil, provided such settings.[200] On June 26, 1980, two Argentine militants traveling to Brazil on different buses were apprehended there: Priest Jorge Adur, the Montoneros' chaplain, and Lorenzo Viñas. Both had seat number 11, which was apparently reserved for suspicious travelers targeted for detention.[201] Adur, using the false name of Pedro Ramon Altamirano, was going to Porto Alegre to meet members of the Madres de Plaza de Mayo, who were in Brazil to see Pope John Paul II during his visit, while Viñas was fleeing to Rio de Janeiro under the identity of Néstor Ayala. In both instances, upon reaching the frontier some passengers were asked to step down from the bus for further checks; all later continued their journeys except for Adur and Viñas.[202]

Marcadores—militants who had agreed under torture to recognize other activists at border locations—had likely spotted them.[203] A ranch turned into a torture center called La Polaca was located just 15 kilometers from Paso de los Libres; there Argentine officers including the notorious torturer Julio Simón initially interrogated detainees before they were transported to Buenos Aires.[204] Montoneros militant Silvia Tolchinsky, detained at the Argentine–Chilean border in Mendoza in September 1980, saw Adur and Viñas during her detention in Campo de Mayo before they disappeared.[205]

In 2007 General Agnaldo Del Nero Augusto—the former head of the Brazilian CIE's operations branch in the early 1980s—admitted that when Brazil

received information from an allied country about a suspected foreigner that
would be entering the country, the target would be arrested and handed over
to the requesting state, and that this modus operandi had been followed regarding the two Italo-Argentine victims Campiglia and Viñas.[206]

Final Reflections

While November 28, 1975—the day in which the founding agreement was
signed—has been taken as Condor's start date, disagreements abound regarding when it effectively stopped operating. The last explicit mention of "Operation Condor" in South American archival records was found by investigative
journalist John Dinges in an April 1981 report by the Paraguayan police on the
activities of exiled opposition groups in South America.[207] Some researchers
include under the Condor umbrella several later events, such as the murder
of Chilean DINA agent Eugenio Berríos in the early 1990s in Uruguay, while
others, predominantly Paraguayan lawyer Martín Almada, contend that Condor never ceased operating. Conversely, NSA analyst Carlos Osorio argues that
by the late 1970s Condor only functioned as a framework for intelligence
coordination,[208] while Argentine historian Melisa Slatman notes how Condor
entered a period of crisis in 1978, during which coordination practices became
looser and psychological operations prevailed.[209] According to the periodization
outlined in chapter 1, I claim that Condor—understood as a multilateral, centralized, and institutionalized coordinated scheme—stopped functioning by
early 1979, and there was subsequently a return to bilateral operations against
a limited set of targets, mirroring phase one of transnational repression.

Correspondingly, this first part of this book, by adopting the concept of transnational repression and outlining a five-phase periodization, has revealed three
distinctive and crucial features of extraterritorial violence in the 1970s in South
America. First, the Condor System phase took place from March 1976 to December 1978, which matches with just one of the five phases of South America's
transnational repression. Second, continuities and discontinuities regarding
the main actors equally typified each phase, and their roles shifted depending
on differing amounts of power at specific time junctures; in the early days the
police led transnational repressive operations against largely guerrilla groups,
while later on military intelligence actors spearheaded actions targeting both
armed and peaceful opposition groups. Third, transnational collaboration was
defined by a complex web of overlapping and intersecting modes of cooperation of a unilateral, bilateral, and multilateral nature. This kaleidoscopic sce-

nario of violence reflected South America's long-lasting trajectories of regional collaboration in police and security matters that dated back to the early twentieth century.

My analysis so far has only tangentially touched on the role of the US. Undoubtedly the US supported many right-wing authoritarian regimes in South America starting in the mid-1950s, ideologically through the National Security Doctrine, technologically through access to communications infrastructure, and financially through military aid and economic assistance. Nonetheless, the extent of the US's specific involvement in Condor remains controversial, and several authors, including Patrice McSherry, Dinges, and Stella Calloni, have put forward diverse arguments. Future research and additional rounds of declassification of US government documents may provide deeper and more complete insights on this question.

PART II
JUSTICE FOR
TRANSNATIONAL CRIMES

6 · Justice Seekers

An Analytical Framework

During the 1970s transnational repression sowed terror in all corners of South America and instilled fear and impunity beyond borders. Rather than being paralyzed by this horror, however, survivors, victims' relatives, legal professionals, and journalists promptly began seeking justice and denouncing the atrocities they had witnessed. They have not stopped since. The second part of this book now turns to revealing and analyzing these long-lasting efforts.

South America has been the cradle of transitional justice since democratization processes began in Bolivia and Argentina, in 1982 and 1983, respectively, which marked the start of the "third wave" of transitions in this region.[1] In the following years, the other dictatorial regimes relinquished power too: Uruguay and Brazil in 1985, Paraguay in 1989, and finally Chile in 1990. As part of transitional negotiations and bargains, countries had to strike a difficult balance between consolidating democratic governance and investigating the unspeakable crimes of the recent past. Both advances and setbacks have defined transitional justice processes over time. Gradually, Argentina and Chile adopted policies to redress atrocities, combining the interrelated objectives of truth, criminal accountability, and reparations. Uruguay conducted a few emblematic trials, including of high-ranking military and civilian figures of the dictatorship, but the majority of its human rights violations still remain shrouded in the unknown. Bolivia, Brazil, and Paraguay have undertaken only timid steps toward shedding light on their dictatorial pasts, and impunity remains the norm.

Scholars and practitioners have examined these diverse justice pathways with reference to various factors, including the mode of transition, the balance of power, the influence of international norms, leadership preferences, and the role of the judiciary, civil society, and veto players. Building on the extant literature, this chapter proposes an analytical framework anchored in the notion of justice seekers to illuminate the role that individuals play within transitional justice and how they navigate these complex processes both at the domestic and the international level.

The proposed approach overcomes two prevalent dichotomous framings in the scholarship: the tension between governments and civil society, and that between the national and the international arenas. The concept of "justice seekers" essentially denotes individuals who are deeply dedicated to obtaining justice and denouncing human rights violations, and who frequently embark on especially complicated and risky commitments. They usually operate within overlapping and intersecting settings: at the domestic level, these comprise civil society, the judiciary, the executive, and other institutions such as parliament or the attorney general's office; at the international level, they include relevant international and regional human rights bodies such as the UN and the Inter-American Commission on Human Rights (hereafter Inter-American Commission),[2] international NGOs such as Amnesty International, and other organizations and agencies.

There is no agreed-upon definition of justice in the literature, and Dustin Sharp usefully distinguishes between narrow and holistic understandings of justice. The narrow view is usually associated with human rights legalism and "legal and atrocity justice,"[3] and focuses on individual accountability and rights; accordingly, justice can mainly be achieved through legal mechanisms and reforms. Conversely, a more holistic perspective contends that justice is multifaceted and encompasses social, political, economic, and legal elements; consequently, justice seeking involves a wide spectrum of efforts comprising retributive, restorative, and distributive justice. This latter understanding is also endorsed by scholars promoting transformative justice, who have observed that transitional justice should entail the just pursuit of societal transformation by dealing with past wrongdoing, and by tackling deep-seated and structural socioeconomic causes of violence to firmly establish guarantees of nonrepetition.[4] In this book I follow the narrow vision of justice, specifically referring to accountability processes through truth telling and criminal proceedings, since these mechanisms have prevailed in South America.

Justice seekers typically comprise human rights activists, victims' relatives, and lawyers, but also journalists, judges, prosecutors, policymakers, and other leaders. Searching for justice is an uphill struggle and requires proactive, strategic, and often pioneering efforts. Justice seekers mobilize and catalyze accountability demands; without their persistent endeavors, transitional justice policies are unlikely to emerge and be sustained over time. Functioning inside and beyond states, these actors endeavor in every possible way to obtain justice for past atrocities, challenging the dominant culture of impunity and silence. They constantly act as a force for change in spite of the adversities and obstacles that exist within the intricate political contexts of dictatorship or conflict, the immediate post-transition years, and decades later, as accountability processes stretch over time. Strong pro-impunity pressures from the cronies of old regimes and their sympathizers, as well as weak or appeasing new democratic regimes and political leaders, frequently define the years following a transition from dictatorship to elected civilian government. Later on, other challenges persist, including the residual power of former perpetrators, the predominance of passive judiciaries and public prosecutors, and the lack of political will to probe a contested past.

During my fieldwork, I witnessed the obstinate work that justice seekers conduct daily. Their resilience and courage inspired me to develop this notion and better capture their efforts. To substantiate my ideas on a theoretical level, I drew upon several bodies of literature, including sociology, international relations, and public policy, and different iterations of "entrepreneurs" in these disciplines. I discarded the term "entrepreneurs," however, because of its usual association with business and economic profit, which is unsuitable to the context of human rights. The idea of justice seekers improves our understanding of variance in transitional justice and compels us to look in more depth at the role of specific individuals within these dynamics.

The chapter is divided into four sections. The first outlines dominant explanations behind diverse transitional justice pathways, while the second unpacks the notion of justice seekers. The third provides a typology of these actors. Finally, the four sets of functions that justice seekers carry out are described with reference to examples from South America.

Justice Paths

Transitional justice as a field of practice and academic discipline has progressively grown into a global phenomenon since the 1980s.[5] One of the main challenges for scholars and practitioners has been elucidating variation in transitional justice responses and divergent outcomes across time and space. Numerous arguments have been proposed in this regard.

Initially, in the 1980s and 1990s, the *mode of transition*, namely how a country transitioned from dictatorship or conflict to democracy or peace, was considered a crucial factor in explaining whether or not transitional justice policies had occurred. Depending on the type of transition—whether it was a collapse, negotiation, or transformation—diverse balances of power ensued between the outgoing and incoming regimes, and these in turn shaped the contours of the emerging democracy and directly affected the possibility and scope of transitional justice initiatives.

Situations of *collapse* or *rupture,* whereby an old regime significantly weakens or even implodes (e.g., Argentina and Czechoslovakia), are perceived as those theoretically most favorable to accountability, since a clean break with the past and a fresh start are possible.[6] In instances of *negotiation,* by contrast, formal or informal pacts or peace agreements control the timing and speed of democratization. This was the most common type of transition in the 1980s and 1990s in countries including El Salvador and South Africa. In these cases there was a roughly even balance of forces: both the outgoing and incoming regimes retained significant power, and they thus met at the negotiating table to find a mutually convenient way out. This precarious equilibrium often places severe constraints onto the nascent regime and frequently diminishes opportunities for accountability. Indeed, successor governments have to contend with still-powerful elites and former incumbents, including potential spoilers, who can hypothetically constrain the transition process and introduce setbacks.[7] Transitions by *transformation* unfold instead when regimes gradually open up and turn into democracies (e.g., Brazil and Bulgaria): slow political change is usually orchestrated from above, and the outgoing regime remains a central actor throughout the process. Transitional justice prospects are restricted here too, because outgoing and incoming officeholders have to collaborate and find common ground on numerous thorny issues.

For transitologists, the mode of transition and ensuing power balance constituted decisive explanatory variables in their analysis of nascent democracies and the resulting chances for transitional justice. Power dynamics are continually changing, however, and policy reversals can subsequently ensue.[8] Indeed, new balances of power among different actors are likely to emerge and can trigger more, or less, favorable conditions for accountability. Accountability processes habitually last for years if not decades, and the term "post-transitional justice" well depicts the enduring nature of such efforts far beyond the immediate transitional period.[9]

While the mode of transition is useful in understanding initial dynamics during democratization, this variable is less illuminating as time progresses, given the emergence of new actors and gradually shifting power balances. Power balance arguments elucidate some interactions within transitional societies and the different abilities of various actors to shape accountability outcomes. Nonetheless, these perspectives only provide partial explanations, since they do not pay sufficient attention to the role of specific individuals and often treat concepts such as civil society or the judiciary as homogenous, when instead substantial differences characterize each category. This is why focusing on justice seekers provides a more comprehensive account of the multifaceted dynamics: justice often results from the patient and persistent efforts carried out by specific victims, human rights activists, and lawyers. Even when the right structural conditions exist, justice may not necessarily follow unless justice seekers make proactive and specific efforts in that respect.

Given that accountability dilemmas are rarely resolved within the initial transitional period, scholars have considered other factors and actors to account for change over time. Political scientist David Pion-Berlin has explained diverse outcomes in the Southern Cone by assessing six potential influences over human rights policy, namely the legacy of human rights abuses, the balance of power, elite preferences, organized and interest group pressures, strategic calculations, and the contagion effect, and concluded that the two most relevant factors were elite preferences and strategic calculations.[10] Executive leadership is especially relevant in South America, where presidential systems dominate and power is concentrated at the top.[11]

Since the mid-1990s, scholars have more closely probed the role of civil society and the judiciary. Civil society actors stand at the heart of transitional justice because of the tireless efforts by human rights activists and victims' groups.[12] They denounce atrocities when violence occurs, persistently lobby governments to investigate past horrors, and conduct parallel investigations when confronted with state inaction.[13] Similarly, the existence or absence of reforms to the judiciary and of judicial leadership have critical implications in transitional justice contexts: key variables, such as high levels of judicial independence[14] and the judiciary's institutional structure and ideology,[15] help explain judges' diverse attitudes regarding past atrocities and the likelihood of criminal trials. Further, judges themselves can become agents of justice when targeted pedagogical interventions promoted by human rights activists effectively alter norms and shape judges' legal preferences, thinking, and capabilities in favor of toppling impunity.[16]

Undeniably, although transitional justice processes often primarily depend on and are shaped by domestic factors, international dynamics and institutions play an important part.[17] International relations scholar Kathryn Sikkink has particularly examined the implications of international human rights norms and dynamics, producing leading theories to explain change, including the "boomerang effect," "the spiral model," and the "justice cascade." The boomerang effect illustrates the role of domestic NGOs in bringing pressure to bear on a repressive state from the outside by developing strategic transnational advocacy networks.[18] Subsequently, the spiral model incorporates four levels (international/transnational interactions, domestic society, societal opposition and transnational networks, and national government) within a single framework to reveal different degrees of governments' compliance with human rights.[19] Sikkink later critiqued both models, since they begin from a premise of state repression and only address change in authoritarian regimes.[20]

Finally, the justice cascade reflects a new trend in world politics toward holding individual state officials accountable for human rights violations, and the materialization, since 1948, of a system of global accountability built on international, domestic, and foreign prosecutions and a streambed of international law norms.[21] The justice cascade acknowledges the unfolding of unprecedented numbers of trials for serious crimes, but likely overemphasizes the importance of their occurrence and potentially underestimates the intricacies of local contexts, especially the obstacles that still delay prosecutions on the ground. The normative shift captured by Sikkink does not mean that trials will necessarily happen, and even when they do, innumerable difficulties continue to hamper judicial proceedings, including a lack of access to relevant archives, inadequate specialization and training in human rights of legal professionals, and inefficient judicial bureaucracies. Factual manifestations of impunity remain a lasting threat. Focusing on justice seekers sheds light on the persistent challenges that actors navigating transitional justice continue to face, locally and internationally.

Scholars remain divided on the comparative influence of national and international factors. Cath Collins challenges the predominant effect of international dynamics, pointing out instead how in the Southern Cone the "strategic action by legally literate, domestic, pro-accountability actors, plus domestic judicial change over time" mainly triggered the renaissance of domestic accountability since the late 1990s.[22] Other scholars have called for more nuanced understandings and a closer examination of the interactions between domestic actors and international dynamics.[23] The notion of justice seekers bridges this dichotomy, since it reveals the close and vibrant interfaces between different

factors that function on the national and international spheres, and their mutually reinforcing contributions to obtaining justice outcomes.

Over the past decade, a prevailing consensus has been reached that multiple variables, rather than a single factor, best explain diversity in transitional
justice processes.[24] For instance, the *multidimensional approach* by Oxford
scholars Leigh Payne, Francesca Lessa, and Gabriel Pereira identifies four pro-
accountability factors: civil society demand, international pressure, judicial
leadership, and the absence of veto players.[25] When all four factors are strong,
accountability is possible, but when they are all weak, impunity likely results.
In between these extremes there are both opportunities and challenges for
impunity and justice. While each factor plays a functional role in overcoming
impunity, no single one is sufficient to bring about a pathway to accountability,
and only their combined strength predicts whether impunity can be overcome.

This brief review has summarized the complex dynamics driving transitional justice and the myriad of actors involved in shaping these processes.
Multidimensional approaches are best placed to account for the intricate and
multifaceted scenarios transitional societies experience, but more attention
needs to be dedicated to the role of specific individuals. Centering on justice
seekers provides this missing piece of the puzzle.

The Framework

In developing the concept of justice seekers, I have drawn upon my earlier
notion of "advocates of change," which identified political leaders, human rights
activists, and committed individuals who assiduously worked to surmount hin-
drances that obstructed justice.[26] Further, I have incorporated the scholarship
on social movements, and especially the definition of activists as "people who
care enough about some issue that they are prepared to incur significant costs
and act to achieve their goals."[27] Similarly, justice seekers go against the tide,
undertake risky endeavors, and defy unfavorable circumstances in striving to
fulfill their objectives.

The notion of justice seekers builds on prior scholarly work within sociology, international relations, and public policy concerning key actors working
to transform society. The term *moral entrepreneurs*, coined by US sociologist
Howard Becker in 1963, identifies individuals who are profoundly devoted to
a particular cause and marshal their efforts to achieve that goal.[28] These resourceful actors take the initiative and work hard to create new rules, norms,

and values. Likewise, the category of *memory entrepreneurs,* which Argentine sociologist Elizabeth Jelin generated—drawing upon Becker—to examine memory struggles in the Southern Cone, similarly points to how people mobilize
energies for the sake of a cause they strongly believe in and seek social recognition for. Energy and perseverance are required to sustain such endeavors
over time, as well as "someone who initiates, who promotes and devotes her
or his energies to the desired end."[29]

Constructivist international relations scholars have generated other useful
categories to explain social and political mobilization, as well as the emergence
of new norms. US academics Martha Finnemore and Kathryn Sikkink pio-
neeringly studied the influence of norms at the international level and defined
norm entrepreneurs as "agents having strong notions about appropriate or desir-
able behavior in their community," who play a crucial role in actively building
new norms through persuasion.[30] Norm entrepreneurs "call attention to issues
or even 'create' issues by using language that names, interprets, and drama-
tizes them"; in this process they are often motivated by empathy, altruism, and
ideational commitment.[31]

Further, the concept of *political entrepreneurs* has been used to refer to activists who drive international mobilization around a specific issue that is important to them, marshaling resources and identifying new political opportunities
within the context in which they operate.[32] These actors "identify under-studied
causes and begin to work through their social networks to rally other influential individuals to their cause."[33] More recently, the idea of *communicative entrepreneurs* conveys how a large community of stakeholders often participates
in the process of developing new norms through multidirectional, consensual,
and horizontal participatory dynamics.[34] Finally, *policy entrepreneurs* denotes
agents of change who promote innovation: these actors are "ambitious in pursuit of a cause," draw on past successes and their specialized knowledge, are
obstinate, and resort to diverse strategies and tools to fulfill their objectives.[35]

Justice seekers blend many characteristics of these various types of entrepreneurs, since they are likewise profoundly dedicated to the cause of justice
and are frequently moved by empathy and altruism toward victims of human
rights violations. Very often their actions challenge the status quo and aim to
significantly alter it: this requires energy, perseverance, and proactive mobilization, and the ability to identify windows of opportunities for progress, by
developing and sustaining social networks of actors to accomplish these goals.
In realizing their goals, justice seekers are creative and innovative, developing

new strategies and tools based on their acquired expertise and maintaining an obstinate attitude in the face of adversity.

Further, justice seekers defy existing patterns of action and are agents of change: this requires courage, ambition, and determination. Their ventures are likely to take a significant amount of time and demand proactive steps in replacing preexisting practices, rules, norms, or behaviors, whether these are displayed by states at the international level or by local actors in the domestic sphere. Following Becker, justice seekers have a double function as both rule creators and rule enforcers, who take proactive steps to change both normative discourses and the actual practices of human rights, being involved in multi-directional and participatory processes.

My framework for considering justice seekers builds on the "boomerang effect" and the "spiral model" of human rights change but takes them further, since it is not limited to periods of authoritarian rule or repression but also encompasses democratic contexts. It is actually within these latter circum-stances that justice seekers may have more scope to attain accountability, once systematic crimes have subsided and a transition of political actors has un-folded. Furthermore, in this model, neither the international sphere nor the domestic sphere is privileged. Instead justice seekers permanently and con-stantly interact on both levels, generating networks of actors pushing for change and action at the intersection of the national and international. Their exchange is multidirectional: pressures from the international sphere can strategically be brought to bear on negative domestic policies in order to modify them. But practices and norms generated inside countries can in turn be used to enact further change in the international arena as well.

Closely probing the role of justice seekers enables us to more fully unpack the convoluted and manifold dynamics leading to transitional justice processes and move away from prevailing dichotomies, understanding instead how in-dividuals, domestically and internationally, and within civil society and govern-ment, can work together in strategic ways to achieve shared goals. For years many governments across the globe imposed top-down policies of impunity and silence. Consequently, a tendency emerged to sideline state actors from transitional justice analyses. As Argentine sociologist Lorena Balardini has highlighted, too little attention is paid to the tangible work that state institu-tions carry out, once they shift away from their role as perpetrators of atrocities and transform into "agents of accountability."[36]

Justice seekers operate at both the domestic and international spheres through energetic interactions and multifaceted dynamics. These actors often initially mobilize at home and then expand their strategic networks beyond national borders when needed. Justice seekers within civil society usually identify counterparts that may exist within the judiciary, the executive, and other state institutions. They later also detect potential justice seekers operating within other states, as well as international organizations and NGOs, building strategic alliances cutting across state borders and enabling them to fulfill their objectives in a mutually productive exchange and interaction.

A Typology of Justice Seekers

How do justice seekers emerge, and what motivates them to take action?[37] The activities undertaken by individuals are undeniably driven by different rationales, and therefore I draw a distinction between *impunity challengers* and *strategic facilitators,* in attempting to capture the variety of reasons behind the actions of justice seekers. If placed on an imaginary continuum, drivers for action can range from unconditional commitment to human rights at one extreme to gaining political capital and personal prestige at the other. Notwithstanding various incentives, both impunity challengers and strategic facilitators should still be considered as justice seekers, because their activities contribute to ultimately advancing justice.

A clear dedication to human rights compels impunity challengers. Impunity as a concept lacks a shared definition but generally refers to the absence of judicial accountability or appropriate investigation of the facts surrounding crimes. Diverse individuals, but most often victims of human rights violations and their relatives, can be considered impunity challengers. The experience of having one's rights infringed upon or having witnessed such an occurrence in the lives of loved ones, combined with the profound implications for personal and family life, is what frequently triggers these people's transformation into justice seekers. Human rights violations shatter a person's life, marking a definitive before and after. While not all victims automatically and necessarily become justice seekers, a large number do. Victims and relatives frequently coalesce around NGOs and other organizations to amplify their demands and increase the impact achieved by joint activism. Plentiful examples exist for this category, including Emilio Mignone, Vera Jarach, the NGOs Mothers of May Square (Madres de Plaza de Mayo) and the Grandmothers of May Square (Abuelas de Plaza de Mayo, hereafter Abuelas) in Argentina; Nila Heredia and the NGO Asociación de Familiares de Detenidos, Desaparecidos y Mártires por la Liberación Nacional in Bolivia; Carmen Hertz and the NGO Agrupación de Familiares de Ejecutados Políticos in Chile; and Father Luis Pérez Aguirre and the NGO Mothers and Relatives of Uruguayan Disappeared Detainees (Madres y Familiares de Uruguayos Detenidos Desaparecidos, hereafter Madres y Familiares) in Uruguay.

Impunity challengers further include individuals who possess specific training and expertise in human rights, which they use to advance the cause of justice. Judicial actors, journalists, academics, historians, and archivists can also become justice seekers when they permanently and proactively generate actions to challenge impunity. Dedication to human rights among these professionals may have developed from a direct personal experience or the professional training they received. Their placement in strategic posts within state or international institutions is what often enables them to directly influence and shape justice goals. These experts often operate collectively within human rights groups and NGOs, but can also be found inside relevant state bodies including the judiciary, public prosecutors, and various ministries. Pertinent examples include NGOs such as the Uruguayan Luz Ibarburu Observatory, the Argentine Center for Legal and Social Studies (Centro de Estudios Legales y Sociales; CELS), and Chilean Londres 38. Specialized government agencies include the Prosecutor's Office for Crimes against Humanity in Argentina, the Human Rights Program in the Ministry of Justice and Human Rights in Chile, and the Directorate of Memory and Reparations in Paraguay. There are also international and regional human rights bodies such as UN-related agencies and committees and the Inter-American system, as well as international human rights NGOs.

Strategic facilitators are individuals such as politicians, parliamentarians, judges, and prosecutors who may not necessarily be motivated solely by a commitment to human rights but may have other rationales. They are improbable justice seekers in a sense, since they may be driven by reasons including political gain, prestige, and career progression. In this category I also include former perpetrators who defect from the repressive apparatus and provide crucial evidence of the atrocities committed. Notwithstanding their incentives, strategic facilitators are important actors in this framework, since their actions may provide crucial contributions to advancing accountability. Strategic facilitators are often instrumental to obtaining justice outcomes because they create useful mechanisms, possess information, or remove obstacles that had until then blocked justice. Therefore they constitute essential partners for impunity challengers.

These categories are ideal types; in practice, the same individual can be motivated by various reasons simultaneously. Furthermore, being a justice seeker does not constitute a permanent and static state, and the most committed impunity challengers can also stop acting as such: owing to a variety of motives, the strength of their commitment and activism can be diluted or lost entirely.

A diversity of lived experiences can transform individuals into justice seekers. The stories of Judge Mariana Mota and President Raúl Alfonsín (1983–89) provide useful examples. Alfonsín's experience especially demonstrates how individuals can be moved by human rights dedication and also political goals at different junctures.

In the early 1980s, presidential candidate Alfonsín marked a rupture with Argentina's tradition of impunity when he decided to call on the courts to prosecute dictatorship-era human rights violations if he became president. While Peronist candidate Ítalo Luder endorsed the military's self-amnesty, Alfonsín promised instead that independent investigations would take place.[38] Alfonsín believed that the foundations of Argentina's nascent democracy had to be built upon truth and justice, and his justice path was truly innovative but also by far the most difficult and controversial option.

Alfonsín's commitment derived from his personal trajectory. As a lawyer, he had defended political prisoners and filed numerous habeas corpus writs during the dictatorship. He was also one of the founders of the Permanent Assembly of Human Rights (Asamblea Permanente por los Derechos Humanos; APDH), which had been established in 1975 to respond to escalating violence before the military coup of 1976. Just days after becoming president in December 1983, Alfonsín ordered the creation of the first truth commission and the prosecution of nine military commanders, aiming to prevent future atrocities by "internalizing in the collective conscience the idea that no group, however powerful it might be, is beyond the law."[39]

By the late 1980s, nonetheless, the occurrence of various military uprisings in opposition to human rights trials pushed Alfonsín's government to change its course: Parliament enacted two laws, the December 1986 Full Stop Law and the June 1987 Due Obedience Law, which ended the possibility of criminal investigations for past atrocities.[40] Despite these noteworthy setbacks, Alfonsín's actions were unprecedented, setting Argentina onto a path as a transitional justice leader globally. Its 1984 truth commission and 1985 Trial of the Juntas are still remembered decades later as historic milestones in the global fight against impunity.

In Uruguay Judge Mota actively fought against the seemingly unbreakable system of impunity that for decades had forestalled tribunals from properly scrutinizing allegations of dictatorship-era crimes. In February 2010 she sentenced, in a historic decision, former dictator Bordaberry to thirty years' imprisonment for leading the 1973 coup against democracy and for several instances of disappearances.[41] As a law student initially and later as a judge, Mota was always moved by the search for the truth, and she firmly believed that "the truth, at least the one that can be achieved through a serious investigation, could contribute to resolving conflict and reestablishing relationships, by attributing responsibility to the wrongdoer(s) when appropriate."[42]

In early 2013, when Mota was probing over fifty allegations of past atrocities, the Supreme Court suddenly removed her from her post and transferred her to a civil court without reasonable justification, which she unsuccessfully appealed. Although it was never explicitly admitted, Mota was being reprimanded for conducting serious investigations regarding the crimes of the dictatorship and reacting against the Uruguayan judiciary's inaction on this matter.[43] Nevertheless, she had effectively removed some of the obstacles standing in the way of justice, and her innovative jurisprudence, which actively drew on international law provisions, stood in clear contrast to her colleagues' persistent delays in resolving existing allegations of atrocities. She knew that negative consequences would result. In the late 1990s and early 2000s, three other judges (Alberto Reyes, Estela Jubette, and Alejandro Recarey) had been transferred or suspended after similarly attempting to probe past atrocities.[44] Justice seekers often suffer threats and intimidation, censorship and defamation, removal from their jobs, and, in the worst cases, personal injury. Since 2017 Mota has continued working for justice, having been elected one of the directors of Uruguay's National Institute of Human Rights, after being nominated by numerous feminist, trade union, and human rights groups.

Striving for Justice

This final section provides a typology of four actions that justice seekers carry out, and these can take place simultaneously or independently of each other. They encompass generating new opportunities and mechanisms; engaging in tactical action and developing innovative arguments; investigating atrocities; and removing specific obstacles to justice.

Justice seekers often *create new opportunities and mechanisms* to counter situations of injustice. The establishment of the "truth trials" in Argentina exemplified this first type of action. In May 1995, relatives of four victims, some of whom were closely linked to the CELS, namely its president, Emilio Mignone, and another member, Carmen Aguiar de Lapacó, filed lawsuits before the Federal Appeals Courts in Buenos Aires grounded in the emerging notion of the right to truth in order to clarify the circumstances surrounding the fate of their disappeared loved ones, including Monica Mignone and Alejandra Lapacó, their respective daughters.

In October 1998, after Argentine courts refused to conduct further investigations, Aguiar de Lapacó then presented a petition before the Inter-American Commission, and a friendly settlement was reached in November 1999, through which Argentina committed to guaranteeing the right to truth and obtaining information on the *desaparecidos*.[45] Accordingly, federal courts were granted exclusive jurisdiction to compile information to help determine the truth about the victims, and special assisting prosecutors were also designated to aid the truth-seeking process.[46] Consequently, these hybrid mechanisms, which combined features of criminal trials and truth commissions to elucidate the desaparecidos' fate, were established in numerous jurisdictions throughout the country. This innovative tool consolidated the evolving right to truth and aided the process of chipping away at the prevailing impunity, providing an alternative tool for victims to achieve accountability despite the amnesty laws.[47] In this case, justice seekers, comprising victims' relatives and CELS's lawyers, strategically resorted to the Inter-American Commission to produce a notable shift at the domestic level. The new evidence gathered as part of these truth-seeking exercises in the early 2000s has been regularly employed in subsequent judicial investigations since 2006.

Justice seekers also can *engage in tactical actions* at the national, regional, and international levels to challenge a context of impunity and silence. Most frequently, this happens through strategic litigation for human rights, attempting to put pressure on various state institutions and often to shake judges and prosecutors out of operational apathy and passivity. Frequently justice seekers develop inventive arguments to question the status quo and find ways to achieve justice. In some cases, judges and prosecutors function as justice seekers themselves by producing or endorsing pioneering legal solutions or arguments. Starting in the late 1990s, justice seekers in the Southern Cone were especially prolific in defying outright the validity of amnesty laws and were ultimately successful in numerous instances.[48]

In Chile, lawsuits regarding human rights violations by the Pinochet regime grew exponentially after the filing of the first allegation in January 1998 (see chapter 8). The argument that disappearances constituted a permanent crime was a fundamental legal strategy employed to bypass Chile's 1978 amnesty decree. This thesis, known in Spanish as *secuestro permanente* (permanent kidnapping), presumably originated from the work of the lawyers of the Vicariate of Solidarity NGO in the 1970s. It posited that if a person "disappeared before 1978 but remained missing after that date, the post-1978 'portion' of the disappearance could still be prosecuted under the charge of kidnapping."[49] The amnesty decree only covered acts committed up until March 10, 1978, and, since most desaparecidos had actually been kidnapped prior to that date but their bodies never found, the crime could therefore be classed as being continually perpetrated until the victims' remains were located. This argument enabled judges and lawyers to exploit the loophole in the strict application of the amnesty, and in 2004 Chile's Supreme Court of Justice sanctioned the *secuestro permanente* thesis as the main basis for conviction.[50] As of June 2021, 190 verdicts relating to 412 victims of enforced disappearance had been handed down following this jurisprudential line.[51]

Internationally, justice seekers have conducted strategic litigation efforts in two additional ways when opportunities for judicial accountability were blocked domestically. On one hand, they resorted to so-called "foreign trials," namely prosecutions "conducted in a single country for human rights abuses committed in *another* country";[52] on the other, they presented claims before regional or international systems for the protection of human rights, putting pressure on domestic legal justice processes and catalyzing anti-impunity efforts.[53]

Justice seekers also *undertake investigations* into human rights violations, either by unearthing relevant evidence such as archival records or specific witnesses, or by conducting pioneering unofficial inquiries when faced with state inertia. The 1985 *Brazil: Never Again* report (*Brasil: Nunca Mais*) is emblematic of this type of action. In the late 1970s the archbishop of São Paulo, Cardinal Paulo Evaristo Arns, Presbyterian Rev. Jaime Wright, and a team of over thirty collaborators embarked on an unprecedented investigation of the dictatorship's atrocities in Brazil, with the support of the World Council of Churches. The sanctioning of the 1979 amnesty law, which allowed lawyers to temporarily gain access to military archives to prepare petitions on behalf of their clients, activated this investigative project, which offered an unprecedented chance to consult state archives that had been off-limits until that point. In 1980 twelve lawyers began to take out files that could be checked out for twenty-four hours from the archives of the Supreme Military Court in Brasilia, which included information on 707 lawsuits regarding approximately seven thousand defendants.[54] Originals were later returned, but photocopies were immediately transported for security reasons to São Paulo, where they were processed and stored.

By 1983 the entire archive had successfully been photocopied, totaling 1 million paper copies and 543 microfilm rolls. A twelve-volume index organized the data, which provided information on the number of prisoners who had passed through military courts, allegations of torture, and victims of disappearances.[55] In late 1983 the archdiocese team asked two journalists to develop a summarized version of the investigation for publication, combining victims' testimonies with the historical background and context of the violence. This publication was released on July 15, 1985, just a few months after the nation's democratic transition, and quickly became a bestseller. In November a list of 444 torturers was also disseminated. Although this initiative lacked the official nature of a state-sponsored truth commission, it was nonetheless a remarkable achievement, since it convincingly demonstrated how torture had been an essential part of the military justice system, and that judicial authorities had had explicit knowledge of its use to extract confessions.[56] Furthermore, it broke the dominant silence by using irrefutable evidence taken from the military regime's own records, which had never been "intended to be read by the public at large."[57]

Finally, justice seekers *actively remove obstacles* that prevent justice. This is often accomplished by generating successful strategic alliances with sympathetic justice seekers within domestic institutions and international bodies. In Uruguay, impunity challengers worked relentlessly for over two decades to remove the nation's 1986 impunity law, thus enabling the judiciary to investigate past atrocities. The repeated challenges to the law's validity included a referendum in 1989, a plebiscite in 2009, and numerous unconstitutionality appeals filed before the Supreme Court of Justice.[58] Between 2010 and 2011 a broad coalition of justice seekers, including victims and their relatives, lawyers, trade unionists, and student activists, coalesced around efforts to repeal the law and prevent the stalling of judicial proceedings.[59] Urgent action was required then, since the statute of limitations for murder (the category that judges had employed in the few cases in which dictatorship-era crimes had been probed) was due to set in on November 1, 2011, potentially spelling the end of all future investigations.

Justice seekers launched a public awareness campaign and identified sympathetic allies holding strategic posts in the executive, legislative, and judicial branches, whose collaboration was needed to develop legislation to derogate the impunity law and ensure the continuity of judicial proceedings. In particular, impunity challengers identified strategic facilitators within Uruguay's Parliament, such as legislators Felipe Michelini, Jorge Orrico, and Luis Puig, who were sympathetic to human rights. By developing these strategic networks, justice seekers worked side by side and produced eight draft bills that were discussed between September and October 2011. Eventually, on October 27, Parliament approved Law 18.831, which effectively repealed the impunity law almost twenty-five years after its sanctioning. The joint efforts of impunity challengers and strategic facilitators also benefited from the international pressure generated by the *Gelman v. Uruguay* sentence dictated just a few months earlier by the Inter-American Court of Human Rights.[60] This historic derogation of the impunity law took place at a moment when veto players, mainly the armed forces, were also relatively weak.[61]

Conversely, despite repeated efforts by justice seekers, the probing of dictatorship-era atrocities has recurrently stalled in Brazil. Even the simultaneous pressures brought to bear by challenges against the amnesty law domestically and internationally in 2010 were insufficient. In 2008 lawyers of the Brazilian Bar Association had presented a petition against the amnesty law before the Federal Supreme Court (Supremo Tribunal Federal; STF). In April 2010, however, the STF declared that the amnesty law had been a political decision, and accordingly it stood outside the remit of the judicial branch to review.[62] In November 2010 the Inter-American Court condemned Brazil in *Gomes Lund et al. (Guerrilha do Araguaia) v. Brazil*, contending that its 1979 amnesty was incompatible with the American Convention on Human Rights and thus lacked legal effect.[63] Brazil was ordered to conduct an investigation to reveal the truth regarding enforced disappearances in the Araguaia region. While the government afterward complied with some elements of the judgment regarding economic compensation and official acknowledgment, the amnesty law remains in place and represents the main obstacle preventing criminal investigations at present.[64]

Final Reflections

Justice seekers play a decisive role in shaping transitional justice outcomes across time and space. Success is not always part of the picture, and negative cases must also be accounted for. The enduring impunity in Brazil shows how, despite relentless endeavors, justice seekers may sometimes fail in their attempts. In this case, despite strong pressure from the Inter-American system, the existence of powerful veto players within the armed forces and the political establishment, combined with a conservative judiciary functioning in a context of weak civil society and a lack of allies within the executive and congress, hampered the justice seekers' success.

The presence of a strong civil society and the existence of international pressure can help facilitate the progress achieved by justice seekers. But the ability of justice seekers to create strategic partnerships with their counterparts within the executive, judiciary, and legislative bodies, as well as on the international sphere, is a critical factor for progress. When such alliances cannot be generated, as in Brazil, progress is impeded or more difficult to achieve.

The examples discussed in this chapter were taken mainly from South American countries, where transitional justice struggles have largely been associated with the removal of amnesty laws from the legal system and the possibility of obtaining justice through criminal trials. The framework can, however, also be applied outside of South America, since justice seekers are not unique to this region.

By focusing on justice seekers, the next four chapters identify the main actors involved in the search for truth and justice regarding the Southern Cone's transnational atrocities, beginning with the 1970s and 1980s, when such crimes were still being perpetrated, and then exploring the emblematic trials that occurred in Argentina, Chile, Uruguay, and Italy starting in the late 1990s. None of these extraordinary achievements would have been possible without the actions of justice seekers.

7 · Condor Unveiled

Breaking Silence in the Midst of Transnational Terror

The abduction of Uruguayan exiled militants in Argentina and Brazil prompted international human rights bodies to begin considering allegations of serious crimes in the late 1970s and early 1980s.[1] On July 29, 1981, the UN Human Rights Committee released a particularly pioneering decision in the case of *Celiberti de Casariego v. Uruguay*,[2] and addressed for the first time the thorny question of the extraterritorial application of the provisions of the International Covenant on Civil and Political Rights.[3]

In its groundbreaking resolution, the committee contended that human rights obligations applied extraterritorially and deliberated that the heart of the discussion was not the geographical location where the alleged violations had occurred but, instead, "the relationship between the individual and the State" wherever the crimes had occurred.[4] That same day the committee also released a second, nearly identical decision in *López Burgos v. Uruguay*.[5] In both, the committee crucially observed how Uruguayan state agents had perpetrated crimes on foreign soil. In the early 1980s this pronouncement that states' human rights obligations extended beyond their borders in some circumstances was revolutionary, and it reinforced the universal moral and philosophical foundations of human rights.[6] At the time the committee significantly sparked a necessary and overdue debate on the question of the extraterritorial applicability of human rights guarantees.[7]

In the early 1980s human rights protections struggled to be asserted within the geopolitical context of the late Cold War. Denunciations by relatives and victims of South America's transnational repression helped place states' human rights responsibilities, both inside and outside geographical boundaries, under international scrutiny. The *Celiberti* and *López Burgos* cases were two of many initiatives that justice seekers undertook at the time, finding ways to denounce the unprecedented human rights atrocities committed throughout the region.

Understanding state-sponsored extraterritorial abuses, however, raised noteworthy difficulties: states are considered the cornerstone of the human rights system and thereby the core entities tasked with protecting human rights within their territories. But what happens when human rights are violated across geographical frontiers? Who is responsible in those circumstances, under a state-centric framework?

This chapter provides a concise overview of the different tools and strategies that justice seekers deployed starting in the late 1970s to break the silence and impunity surrounding South America's transnational terror. Initially, in the late 1970s and early 1980s when dictatorships still governed the region, justice seekers focused their efforts on the international sphere: survivors narrated their ordeals to Amnesty International and other human rights NGOs, and presented petitions to the UN and the Inter-American Commission. Inside South America, limited windows of opportunities existed in Brazil and Argentina in the early 1980s. Afterward, since the mid-1980s, impunity challengers took advantage of additional openings offered by redemocratization processes and pushed for official investigations to take place, with differing degrees of success.

Voices against Impunity

On June 4, 1976, two days after the murder of former Bolivian president Juan José Torres in Buenos Aires, Richard Gott pondered in the *Guardian* whether the recent wave of assassinations of Latin American nationalist officers and politicians was attributable to something akin to "Operation Phoenix," that is, a "CIA-funded assassination programme during the Vietnam War, designed to eliminated the Viet Cong leaders."[8] Gott was the first to indirectly point the finger at Operation Condor and its role in eliminating South America's moderate political figures, pushing many others into seeking asylum overseas.

At the time, numerous human rights NGOs and governments were closely scrutinizing the dire situation in South America. The Washington Office on Latin America (WOLA) openly blamed the assassination of Uruguayan legislators Zelmar Michelini and Héctor Gutiérrez-Ruiz on the Argentine dictatorship and contended that the latter had colluded with its Uruguayan counterpart, which had "ordered the assassination of its principal adversaries."[9] Other similar episodes were denounced, including the abduction of twenty-five Chilean and Uruguayan refugees in Buenos Aires and the breaching of the premises of the Venezuelan Embassy in Montevideo, where security officers had violently kidnapped an asylum seeker, PVP militant Elena Quinteros.

The US Congress was equally preoccupied with the worsening scenario, and its Subcommittee on International Organizations, headed by Congressman Donald Fraser, received important witnesses, including Uruguayan Senator Wilson Ferreira, who testified in June 1976 on his miraculous escape, when he had narrowly avoided being kidnapped with Michelini and Gutiérrez-Ruiz.[10] Ferreira was the only Uruguayan able to travel to the US to decry the crimes of the Uruguayan dictatorship before the Congress. In September 1976 Argentine labor lawyer Lucio Garzón Maceda also spoke at length before the same subcommittee and particularly corroborated how South American police forces had been cooperatively harassing political exiles since 1974, pointing to the close collaboration that existed especially between Argentina and Uruguay.[11]

It was Uruguayan trade unionist Washington Pérez who provided first-hand details on this unfolding cooperation between Argentines and Uruguayans. Speaking in early September 1976 to Amnesty International representatives in Alvesta, Sweden, Pérez recounted how, in the early hours of June 14, 1976, armed men had forcefully snatched him from his house in Buenos Aires's outskirts and brought him to the secret prison later identified as Automotores Orletti.[12] There an Argentine–Uruguayan task force had forced him to act as an intermediary in negotiations with the PVP to trade the life of leader Gerardo Gatti for a large amount of money (see chapter 4).[13] Inside Orletti, Pérez recognized Uruguayan police commissioner Hugo Campos Hermida, whom he knew from a previous arrest in Montevideo. Pérez also briefly spoke alone with Gatti and noticed the brutal torture he had sustained.

Negotiations proceeded for a month, during which Pérez was repeatedly taken to Orletti. The kidnappers gradually grew frustrated, and once they threatened to kill a large number of prisoners out of irritation with the PVP leadership, who were "messing about."[14] On July 17 Pérez was suddenly told that "Gatti's problem had been liquidated,"[15] but he would now have to negotiate the release of Uruguayan PVP leader León Duarte. Duarte, who had been viciously tortured and had not eaten since his kidnapping days earlier, advised Pérez to flee, warning him that his jailers "were murderers."[16] Following Duarte's advice, Pérez sought protection with the UNHCR and left Argentina with his family.

Pérez's thorough declarations validated for the first time the rumors regard-

ing the alarming practices that had been occurring for some time in Argentina, including the systematic use of torture and clandestine prisons, and especially the presence of Uruguayan police and military officers freely operating
in Argentina. Pérez had moreover spotted several other Argentine and Uruguayan officers, including Argentine Aníbal Gordon and Uruguayans José Gavazzo and Manuel Cordero.[17]

Pérez's declarations were part of Amnesty International's efforts to name
and shame South American dictatorships for their abysmal human rights records and thereby generate pressure to ameliorate the situation on the ground.
Six months later, on March 23, 1977, Amnesty arranged a press conference
at its London headquarters to launch a report on the first anniversary of the
Argentine coup and release the testimony of Uruguayan Enrique Rodríguez
Larreta, who had survived illegal imprisonment and torture in both Argentina
and Uruguay.[18] His ordeal provided additional proof of the terror coordination
and the persecution refugees suffered in Argentina at the hands of local paramilitary groups and agents from their countries of origin. Rodríguez Larreta
disseminated this testimony at great personal risk, since his family still lived
in Uruguay.

Back in July 1976, fifty-five-year-old Rodríguez Larreta had traveled from
Montevideo to Buenos Aires after his daughter-in-law had informed him that
his son, also called Enrique, had disappeared. Together they incessantly denounced the disappearance before local judicial, governmental, and police
authorities, the media, and church officials, until the night of July 13 and 14,
when armed men broke into his daughter-in-law's house and seized both of
them.[19] During his imprisonment in Orletti, Rodríguez Larreta was cruelly
tortured and endured merciless detention conditions alongside thirty other
Uruguayans, including prominent trade unionists Gatti and Duarte.[20] Ten days
later, Rodríguez Larreta, his son, daughter-in-law, and twenty-one other Uruguayans were secretly flown to Montevideo at night.[21]

After spending another five months imprisoned in two different clandestine
centers in Montevideo,[22] Rodríguez Larreta was released just before Christmas,[23] and soon afterward began investigating the ordeal he had endured. He
successfully confirmed the exact location of the La Casona secret prison in
Montevideo and further retraced the steps of his abduction in Buenos Aires,
where, helped by the community of Uruguayan exiles, he located Orletti, which
seemed abandoned by then.[24]

At a time when allegations of human rights violations were often accused of
partiality, Rodríguez Larreta's career as a journalist at the conservative news-

paper *El País* and his lack of political activism granted additional legitimacy to his words. His testimony complemented Pérez's declarations with supplementary information he had collated during his six-month-long disappearance, including details on the division of labor in Orletti, where Argentine army soldiers carried out custodial functions while intelligence and paramilitary agents led kidnapping operations.[25] Moreover, Uruguayan officers oversaw Uruguayan prisoners' interrogation and torture sessions. These officers used code names to conceal their identities: OCOA officers were known as "Oscar" followed by a number from 1 to 10, where "Oscar 1" was the highest-ranking official. Conversely, SID officers from the 300 Division only used numbers as aliases: "302" was Gavazzo, and "303" was Cordero.[26] Moreover, Rodríguez Larreta's tale of the secret flight constituted a crucial discovery, which undeniably proved the institutional support behind transnational practices. The fabricated cover-up story concocted to justify the prisoners' reappearance in Uruguay was fully exposed.

After London, Rodríguez Larreta embarked on an international dissemination campaign in Europe, the US, and Latin America.[27] His case was presented to the Inter-American Commission[28] and was reproduced in major newspapers and magazines, including the *Times, Le Monde,* the *New York Times, La Stampa,* and *Cambio16.*[29] During his trip to Mexico City, refugees from other South American countries stated that they had similarly sustained persecution and kidnapping attempts by individuals associated with their countries' embassies in Mexico.[30] Rodríguez Larreta's declarations were quoted by US Congressman Edward Koch, who had secured a ban on military aid to Uruguay months earlier, in his May 1977 denunciation of Argentina and Uruguay's "internationalization of terror."[31] This case was also included in the Inter-American Commission's momentous *Report on the Situation of Human Rights in Argentina,* released after its groundbreaking visit in September 1979.[32]

Meanwhile, two other Uruguayan survivors who had been imprisoned with Rodríguez Larreta—Eduardo Dean Bermúdez and Alicia Cadenas—escaped to Sweden in 1979 and testified to Amnesty International on the horrors they had suffered. Dean Bermúdez noted the persecution that Uruguayan PVP militants continued to face at the time in both Uruguay and Brazil.[33] Cadenas narrated that during her detention she had perceived the presence of a pregnant woman, a newborn baby, and children playing in the SID's secret prison. One day in November 1976, the guards had asked female prisoners to help them prepare baby bottles to feed the newborn, and afterward a soldier had asked Alicia for the teddy bear she had been making so that he could give it to "a little boy upstairs who had no toys."[34] Years later, the newborn was identified as Macarena Gelman and the little boy as Anatole Julién.

Simultaneously, the Swiss section of Amnesty International released one of the few testimonies given by former military officers; these statements critically supplemented victims' accounts, which were necessarily limited since survivors were always imprisoned blindfolded and in unknown locations. Former Uruguayan Army Lieutenant Julio César Cooper, who had been forced to retire in 1977 because of his refusal to torture prisoners, appeared at a news conference in Geneva and divulged that 90 percent of Uruguay's officer corps had tortured political prisoners, and no one had ever been punished.[35] In earlier declarations before the International Secretariat of Jurists for Amnesty in Uruguay (Secretariado Internacional de Juristas por la Amnistia en Uruguay; SIJAU), Cooper admitted to the existence of an intense and permanent coordination between South America's military forces.[36] He asserted that Uruguayan OCOA and SID officers—explicitly mentioning Gavazzo and Cordero—regularly carried out missions that included prisoner renditions in neighboring countries, while regional counterparts undertook similar operations in Uruguay.

Another Uruguayan military officer provided further essential pieces to help reassemble the puzzle of transnational terror. In May 1980 Hugo García Rivas, a former soldier of the army's Counter-Information Branch between 1977 and 1979, defected and abandoned Uruguay with his family, hoping to move to Europe for a better life.[37] In Brazil he gave detailed statements, first in Porto Alegre before the recently created human rights NGO Justice and Human Rights Movement (Movimento de Justiça e Diretos Humanos; MJDH),[38] and later before SIJAU in São Paulo,[39] which elucidated the fate of several PVP activists apprehended in late 1978. García Rivas's testimony precisely reconstructed the *zapato roto* operation, launched by the Uruguayan Army in November 1978 to apprehend PVP leader Hugo Cores (see chapter 5). The soldier's account matched victims' allegations filed before the Inter-American Commission[40] and the lived experiences of activists and journalists in Porto Alegre.[41] But García Rivas possessed insider information that no one else had, since he had participated firsthand in the operation and knew the names of the involved Uruguayan and Brazilian military officers. His tale painstakingly described how high-ranking Uruguayan Counter-Information Branch officials had methodically planned each step of the operation and ironed out all the details in collaboration with officers from the Brazilian DOPS. Subsequently, Brazilian and Uruguayan officers had jointly apprehended Lilián Celiberti's family in Porto Alegre and set up a trap in her flat to seize Cores. In Montevideo, officers permanently monitored and constantly intimidated Lilián's parents, and moreover had spied on any Brazilian activists who traveled there to investigate the case further.

While victims and some perpetrators had begun in 1976 to disclose critical fragments of evidence regarding the repressive coordination's modus operandi, the term "Condor" was publicly employed for the first time in January 1979 by FBI agent Robert Scherrer.[42] During his testimony at the Letelier murder trial in Washington, DC, Scherrer confirmed the existence of "the long-suspected continental arrangement."[43] On August 2, 1979, *Washington Post* journalist Jack Anderson published an article, "'Condor': South American Assassins," which further revealed the activities of this criminal network.[44] In this piece, Anderson—who had accessed secret US government documents, including an FBI report that he extensively quoted—contemplated the possibility that Letelier's assassination had been a so-called phase three operation, referring to secret missions undertaken by special teams of Condor agents to target opponents anywhere in the world.[45]

Anderson's exposé was momentous. Two days later, US Secretary of State Cyrus Vance sent confidential instructions to the US embassies in Chile, Argentina, Bolivia, Brazil, Paraguay, and Uruguay on how to respond to potential questions regarding these countries' participation in Condor.[46] The guidelines significantly downplayed Condor's scope and its role in the Letelier case: the embassies were instructed to state that assassinations had never been committed and that Condor's activities were limited to intelligence exchanges.[47] The US continued to send mixed signals: on one hand, it investigated allegations of human rights violations in Congress and prosecuted individuals responsible for Letelier's murder, while on the other, it tried to deflect attention away from Condor and cover up the fact that Pinochet had ordered Letelier's assassination.

As transnational repression peaked in 1976 and 1977, justice seekers largely operated in the international sphere and took advantage of the available opportunities to unravel Condor's secrets. Survivors, human rights NGOs—prominently Amnesty International—and journalists acted as impunity challengers to disseminate victims' experiences and to dismantle the propaganda and cover-up stories that South American regimes contrived to hide their systematic atrocities. Strategic facilitators such as former military officers contributed to exposing the truth, unearthing the responsibility of agents involved in operations and uncovering the repressive coordination's inner workings. Their declarations effectively corroborated victims' statements with decisive details that only officers from inside Condor itself knew.

After January 1977, when it began to function, the UN Human Rights Committee constituted an additional tool justice seekers could turn to for denouncing crimes and generating external pressure on the military regimes. Its reach was limited, however. Out of the Condor countries, only Uruguay had ratified the First Optional Protocol to the International Covenant on Civil and Political Rights, which allowed the committee to consider communications by victims on alleged human rights violations committed by the Protocol's states. Uruguayans presented numerous complaints, and between 1977 and 1985 the committee resolved forty-one accusations regarding Uruguay, which included arbitrary detentions and lack of a fair trial; five allegations specifically concerned Uruguay's extraterritorial operations.[48]

Windows of Opportunity

Inside South America, justice seekers faced extremely challenging contexts of silence and impunity, since the dictatorships held on to power well into the 1980s. Yet impunity challengers tried to pursue justice, disclose the truth, and divulge information about atrocities, often at very high personal risk.

Unexpected opportunities for accountability emerged in Brazil in 1974, when the country embarked on a top-down, long, and gradual process of political liberalization, known as *aberdura*, which eventually culminated in a democratic transition in 1985.[49] Consequently, from the mid-1970s onward, the political and social context in Brazil significantly improved: political persecution progressively lessened, some political parties acceptable to the dictatorship started functioning, and an amnesty law benefiting regime opponents and political prisoners was sanctioned in 1979 in response to public mobilization.[50] Many South American exiles settled in Brazil at the time to reorganize political activities and resistance to the remaining dictatorships.

The backdrop of Brazil's prolonged transition offered justice seekers some unexpected avenues. In the immediate aftermath of the kidnapping of the Uruguayans in Porto Alegre in late 1978, impunity challengers including journalist Luiz Cláudio Cunha, lawyer Omar Ferri, and activist Jair Krischke crucially exposed this transnational operation through an unrelenting media campaign with international repercussions that, in the long run, forced the Uruguayan regime to spare the victims (see chapter 5). Indeed, these impunity challengers achieved two unparalleled and noteworthy accomplishments in 1979, namely the holding of a parliamentary commission of inquiry and a criminal investigation into the 1978 abduction. Building on rising discontent with the violent methods of the security forces, twenty-six opposition members of the legislative assembly of Rio Grande do Sul demanded the establishment of a Parliamentary Investigative Commission (Comissão Parlamentar de Inquérito; CPI), which was inaugurated on March 24, 1979. Commissions of this kind had not been created for over a decade, with the last one in 1966.[51] Politicians, the media, representatives of state and federal institutions, and lawyer Ferri participated in the CPI, which functioned for six months in a tense environment, gathered 700 pages of documentation, involved 450 people, and listened to thirty-nine depositions, including those of journalists Cunha and João Baptista Scalco and former state governor Sinval Guazzelli.[52]

Jarbas Lima, a politician from the pro-regime Social Democratic Party, produced on September 17 the first report that concluded that no crime had been committed and that the accusations against police officers were unfounded. The CPI rejected this report and tasked Ivo Mainardi, a member from the opposition Brazilian Democratic Movement party, with submitting a new one by October 10. Mainardi conversely determined that the events under investigation had effectively occurred as alleged, and his conclusions received the CPI's majority approval.[53]

At the same time, a criminal investigation into the victims' fate, originally requested by lawyer Ferri in late 1978 as part of his attempts to locate the family members and in his allegations before local DOPS and the federal police, also finally began.[54] On March 3, 1979, Porto Alegre's public prosecutor Dirceu Pinto charged DOPS delegate Pedro Carlos Seelig and police inspector Orandir Portassi Lucas with abuse of authority. Two other defendants, inspectors Janito Keppler and João da Rosa, were later added to the proceedings. As historian and activist Krischke has explained, the Brazilian Criminal Code did not recognize the crime of torture at that point, and hence the charge of abuse of authority was used.[55] On March 5 the case was assigned to Porto Alegre's Third Criminal Court, first in the hands of Judge Antônio Carlos Netto Mangabeira and then, in May 1980, of Moacir Danilo Rodrígues.[56] The court heard numerous testimonies, including those of French jurist Jean Louis Weil and Porto Alegre's DOPS Director Marco Aurélio Reis, and also received García Rivas's groundbreaking declarations, which the MJDH transmitted, to directly prove the high-level planning and collaboration between Brazilian and Uruguayan authorities.[57]

On July 21, 1980, Judge Rodrígues released a condemnatory verdict, in which he corroborated the capture and imprisonment of the Uruguayans in Porto Alegre and their subsequent transfer to Montevideo.[58] Two of the accused, Portassi Lucas and da Rosa, were sentenced to six months and received a two-year prohibition from exercising police functions, while Seelig and Kepler were absolved due to lack of evidence. The judge condemned the two police officers for whom he possessed irrefutable proof of culpability, but the two higher-ranking defendants were possibly acquitted to avoid the risk of jeopardizing the entire verdict on appeal.[59] In April 1981 the Rio Grande do Sul's Appeals Court partially upheld the sentence, confirming only Portassi Lucas's guilt.[60]

This verdict, despite its limited scope, was nonetheless exceptional, it being the only one handed down during the dictatorship by a Brazilian criminal court for crimes committed by state agents. It was also the sole verdict in South America to disclose state-sponsored transnational abduction operations at the time. In the trial prosecutor Pinto had strategically employed the charge of abuse of authority to secure a conviction, given the lower threshold of proof required: if kidnapping had been used, all defendants would have probably been acquitted.[61] Personally and professionally, Pinto paid a high price. He was continually harassed for uncovering the responsibility of the DOPS in the abduction,[62] and at one point he was nearly removed from his post as the public prosecutor. This was only averted because of intense protests by his colleagues, lawyers, and the press. Judge Rodrígues subsequently revealed how he too had withstood continual pressure during the trial.[63]

Breaking the Silence

Elsewhere in the Southern Cone, impunity remained near absolute. But justice seekers were fully mobilized, and numerous associations began spontaneously emerging out of relatives' necessity to ascertain the fate of their loved ones.[64] Scope for action varied in each country. In Chile the Catholic Church initially led opposition to political repression by the Pinochet dictatorship,[65] and in October 1973 the Committee of Cooperation for Peace in Chile (Comité de Cooperación para la Paz en Chile) was created, composed of representatives of the Catholic and Evangelical churches and the Jewish community. It provided legal, economic, psychological, and social support to victims, particularly assisting between 1973 and 1975 over eight thousand relatives of the desaparecidos.[66] Novel groupings were also created in 1975, including those of relatives of political prisoners and families of victims of disappearances. After the committee's closure by the regime, Cardinal Raúl Silva Henríquez, the archbishop of Santiago, established the Vicariate of Solidarity in January 1976.[67] The vicariate resumed the committee's work and ceaselessly supported victims' families; its lawyers filed thousands of petitions of habeas corpus and of presumed misfortune (*presunta disgracia*) to pressure the judiciary into probing victims' fate. The fact that many Chileans had been abducted in Argentina generated further challenges that complicated the chances of discovering their fate, thus curbing the vicariate's ability to help their families.[68]

In Argentina, relatives of victims of both domestic and transnational repression routinely filed habeas corpus writs to denounce disappearances, but courts only seriously investigated a handful of allegations during the dictatorship.[69] Nevertheless, Argentina's human rights activism stood out in the region and significantly predated the dictatorship:[70] indeed, the Argentine League for the Rights of Men (Liga Argentina por los Derechos del Hombre)—founded in December 1937—had been the first organization of its kind in the country. Other associations emerged in 1977, including the Madres de Plaza de Mayo that was established by women looking for their abducted sons and daughters, as well as the Abuelas, formed by grandmothers striving to locate their missing grandchildren. In 1979 eight victims' relatives, survivors, and lawyers, including Emilio Mignone and Augusto Conte, founded the CELS, which immediately acted as an impunity challenger, vigorously gathering information and disseminating reports to prove state-sponsored atrocities.

In an early human rights report covering the period October 1979 to October 1980, the CELS included the cases of eight Argentine citizens abducted abroad and clearly noted the responsibility of Argentine state agents in their disappearance, observing how the extraterritorial action of these officers had likely been possible because of the complicity of local counterparts.[71] As the dictatorship imploded, the CELS released in August 1983 its *Uruguay/Argentina: Repressive Coordination* report, which squarely concentrated on transnational terror.[72] This investigation focused on the Argentina–Uruguay axis and explored the cases of 120 citizens who had fled Uruguay only to later disappear in Argentina. Despite this limited framing, the report began disentangling the broader modus operandi of the region's repressive coordination.

Significantly, the early origins of the terror collaboration were traced to 1974 and 1975, when paramilitary groups murdered ten Uruguayans. After the 1976 military coup, the persecution against Uruguayan refugees in Argentina significantly increased, and several emblematic cases, including the murders of Michelini and Gutiérrez-Ruiz, were discussed extensively in the CELS report.

The report also mentioned that similar collaborative practices were in place with the armed forces of Chile and Paraguay and claimed that approximately thirty Chilean refugees apprehended in Argentina had afterward reappeared in secret prisons across the Andes. A list of Uruguayans disappeared in Argentina, including their detention dates, closed out this pioneering report. At a time when available information on cross-border repression was still fragmented, the CELS raised several central points regarding the extraterritorial application of the National Security Doctrine, the practice of baby kidnappings, and the simultaneous violation of the human rights of victims with the theft of their possessions, properties, and money.[73] The report notably acknowledged how repressive coordination had begun to fade after 1978 and noted that the last recorded case of a disappeared Uruguayan was in March 1979.

In contrast to Argentina, there was no prior tradition of human rights activism in Uruguay, and organizations there would not emerge until the late 1970s. Abroad, however, Uruguayan exiles were extremely active, innovatively employing the language of human rights to denounce state repression before the UN and the US government.[74] Several human rights campaigns kept Uruguay under constant international scrutiny.[75] In 1976, for example, the first report of the Paris-based Defense Committee for Political Prisoners in Uruguay (Comité de Defensa por los Prisioneros Políticos del Uruguay) had openly blamed the Uruguayan regime for murdering Michelini and Gutiérrez-Ruiz, and it emphasized the dangerous security situation of many refugees in Argentina.[76]

Inside Uruguay, relatives looked for information from local churches or the archbishop's office in Montevideo, but with limited success.[77] The fact that neither Argentina nor Uruguay officially recognized the detention of Uruguayans in Argentina rendered their inquiries even more difficult.[78] In Montevideo, relatives of Uruguayan victims of disappearances in Argentina were the first to mobilize, following in the footsteps of the Argentine Madres. The UNHCR representative in Argentina, Guy Prim, helped catalyze this activism by putting several Uruguayan women, including Luz Ibarburu, Violeta Malugani, Elisa Delle Piane, Hortensia Pereira, and Irma Hernández, in contact with each other in 1977.[79] This first association, called Mothers of Uruguayans Disappeared in Argentina (Madres de Uruguayos Desaparecidos en Argentina), formally emerged in September 1979 and was the sole human rights group in Uruguay at the time.[80] The 1979 historic visit of the Inter-American Commission to Argentina had triggered its emergence, and members of the newly formed association traveled to Buenos Aires to denounce the disappearance of their loved ones in Argentina before the commission. In the early 1980s other groups were established, including the Peace and Justice Service (Servicio Paz y Justicia; SERPAJ) in 1981 and Madres y Familiares in 1983, which merged three preexisting relatives' associations.[81]

Justice seekers had little scope for action under Paraguay's long-standing dictatorship (1954–89) and its unrelenting repression. Although relatives had sought to determine the fate of their loved ones since the early 1960s, it was mainly in the mid- to late 1970s that activism consolidated in Paraguay. Two new human rights NGOs emerged: in 1976 the Committee of Churches for Emergency Assistance (Comité de Iglesias para Ayudas de Emergencia), led by Pastor Armin Ilhe, aided relatives of Paraguayan victims of disappearance in both Paraguay and Argentina, and in 1978 an association of relatives of the disappeared and politically executed was created in Asunción.[82] The Paraguayan Commission for the Defense of Human Rights (Comisión de Defensa de los Derechos Humanos del Paraguay), the first human rights commission to be established in Paraguay in 1967, was also active, presided over by legislator Carmen De Lara Castro.[83]

Between 1976 and 1977, several Paraguayan relatives began mobilizing in Buenos Aires, gathering in churches and bars and collaborating with Argentine groups. Victims' relatives in both Paraguay and Argentina jointly compiled lists of victims of disappearance and detention for dissemination in Europe and the US, with Amnesty International's support. The testimonies of several direct survivors, especially physician Gladys Meilinger and Colorado Party politician Epifanio Méndez Fleitas, especially helped raise awareness of the repressive coordination within the exiled Paraguayan community.[84]

Valentín Cabrera, the brother of Lidia Cabrera, who had been seized with her family in 1977 in the Argentine border town of Puerto Iguazú and returned to Paraguay, also energetically denounced his sister's ordeal. From Switzerland, where he had been forced to seek exile after also being threatened with arrest in Argentina as he tried to locate his sister, Valentín filed a petition in April 1977 before the Inter-American Commission with the support of Paraguayan lawyer Arturo Acosta Mena.[85] In 1979 the commission acknowledged the violations of the victims' rights and recommended the punishment of those responsible.[86] (In July 1978 Lidia had been released from Emboscada's prison in Paraguay, owing to pressure from Amnesty International and the International Red Cross. She also moved with her family to Switzerland, from where they participated in international campaigns.)[87]

The 1979 visit by the Inter-American Commission also spearheaded in 1980 the formation in Buenos Aires of the Commission of Relatives of Paraguayans

Disappeared in Argentina (Comisión de Familiares de Paraguayos Detenidos-Desaparecidos en la Argentina), which comprised Idalina Radice, María Gastón, Alberto Bogado, and many others.[88] This commission brought together victims' relatives and aimed to shed light on instances of disappearances, to support judicial investigations, and to push for the creation of a parliamentary commission to investigate the dictatorship's crimes.[89] These associations of Uruguayan and Paraguayan relatives in Buenos Aires often collaborated in the early 1980s and strived to generate additional impact by running denunciation campaigns that revolved around the desaparecidos' professions or nationalities.[90]

Unexpected Openings

The democratization processes in South America in the early 1980s significantly enhanced the possibilities for obtaining truth and justice, and consequently justice seekers redoubled their efforts. But they still faced diverse challenges in each country and had to adjust their strategies accordingly.

In Argentina the chaotic defeat in the 1982 Falklands War exacerbated a preexisting explosive mix of economic downturn, unparalleled accusations of atrocities, and mounting demands from politicians, labor unions, the press, and the judiciary. In late 1983 the dictatorship's collapse, combined with the election to the presidency of radical party candidate Raúl Alfonsín (see chapter 6) engendered an advantageous scenario for justice. Conversely, the negotiated transitions of Uruguay and Chile, in 1985 and 1990 respectively, drastically reduced chances for accountability there.

President Alfonsín took unprecedented steps to promote the investigation of the crimes of the dictatorship in Argentina.[91] He established by executive decree in late 1983 the groundbreaking National Commission on the Disappearance of Persons (Comisión Nacional sobre la Desaparición de Personas; CONADEP) and the Trial of the Juntas. As part of their proceedings, both mechanisms also touched on transnational repression.

The CONADEP's innovative *Never Again* (*Nunca Más*) report, released in September 1984, contained a dedicated section on "The Repressive Coordination in Latin America" ("La coordinación represiva en Latinoamérica"), which described the inner workings of South America's regional terror and its four defining features.[92] First, the repressive coordination had encompassed the security, police, and intelligence organs of various countries. Second, this collaboration had accelerated the detention of individuals outside all the margins of the law and their clandestine rendition to the country of origin; this had occurred with complete disregard for geographical borders and international law protections safeguarding asylum seekers and refugees. Third, Uruguayan, Paraguayan, Chilean, and Bolivian citizens had all been apprehended in Argentina, but Uruguayans represented the largest number of victims by nationality. Lastly, the interaction between Argentine officers and their foreign counterparts had been so close that they had "worked together as if they formed part of the same organ," composing a "'multinational' repressive apparatus."[93] This report by a state body offered the first official acknowledgment of the transnational terror machinery and particularly its operations in Argentina, where the majority of these cross-border atrocities had been perpetrated.

Besides the CONADEP, impunity challengers took advantage of other opportunities provided by this democratic spring and filed cases before the Argentine judiciary. One of these focused specifically on the coordination between the Argentine and Uruguayan dictatorships. On February 22, 1984, Uruguayan journalist Rodríguez Larreta and CELS lawyers Mignone, Octavio Carsen, and Jorge Baños presented a lawsuit in Buenos Aires before Judge Alicia Baumgartner of Investigating Court No. 22.[94] The complaint addressed the crimes committed against Rodríguez Larreta in Orletti and contended that these had constituted violations of human rights and refugee protections. Further, it directly accused twenty-four top Argentine and Uruguayan civilian and military figures, such as former Argentine dictators Jorge Videla and Eduardo Massera, Uruguayan Army Commander Julio Vadora, Defense Minister Walter Ravenna, and lower-ranking officers.[95]

The lawsuit drew upon Rodríguez Larreta's Amnesty International declarations but incorporated additional evidence in four respects. First, supplementary information was provided on Argentine and Uruguayan officers, including their full names and military grades or unique identifying physical characteristics and cover names, to help authorities with identification.[96] Second, the complaint specifically referred to "the tight coordination that existed between the Uruguayan and Argentine military governments in exchanging information and unlawfully capturing prisoners."[97] Third, crimes that materially occurred outside of Orletti but were nevertheless connected to it, such as the illegal appropriation by the Argentine Army of the flat belonging to Rodríguez Larreta's daughter-in-law, were also included. Finally, a photo taken in 1979, which showed an army vehicle exiting Orletti, corroborated how the site had been used at least up until that point.[98] The complainants asked the judge to also probe other connected offenses, including the disappearances of Uruguayan leaders Gatti, Méndez, and Duarte, of Uruguayan newborn Simón Riquelo, and of three members of the Argentine Santucho family.[99]

Months later, in April, the judge requested the testimony of Uruguayan survivors Gastón Zina, Sara Méndez, and Ana Inés Quadros. After some initial fear and uncertainty, since the three were still under probation and could not leave Montevideo, they resolved to travel together to Buenos Aires.[100] After delivering their testimonies on April 2, the judge asked them if they would take part the following day in an inspection of Orletti, to which they agreed. Lawyers Baños and Carsen participated, along with Rodríguez Larreta. This first inspection of the site occurred within a very delicate political context, as Argentine society was slowly coming to terms with the full extent of the atrocities perpetrated, through daily reports on the discovery of mass graves and former secret prisons.

Outside Orletti, journalists swooped in to take photos when the metallic shutter entrance door began rolling up, and the police had to restrain them to stop them from entering. Some reporters threw themselves onto the pavement in an attempt to capture interior images as the door lowered down. Inside, everything matched the survivors' recollections from their imprisonment in 1976. The ground floor housed the car workshop. Two safes were found in the guardroom near the main entrance, and the judge decided to force them open: one contained two guns and the other a cylindrical glass container half full of wedding rings and small golden jewels. Upstairs a room still stored shoes and clothes while another, next door, was filled with furniture and other items stolen from victims' houses, where Zina found his gingham fabric suitcase. Upon exiting Orletti, the survivors were bombarded with journalists' questions, while neighbors began sharing their reminiscences, recalling the constant noise of cars coming and going and people's screams. Relatives of the desaparecidos had also gathered and showed the Uruguayan survivors photos of their missing loved ones in the hope that they had seen them.

The trip to Buenos Aires was a powerful experience for the survivors. Testifying before a judge stood in stark contrast to the situation in Uruguay, where the dictatorship still ruled, albeit much weakened, and the on-site inspection of Orletti constituted a fundamental step in the search for truth and justice. After returning to Montevideo, the three witnesses were summoned by military authorities, and intelligence officers in the Third Infantry Battalion interrogated Zina and Méndez at length as to why they had traveled to Argentina, holding them for a few hours.

In Buenos Aires pressure from CELS's lawyer Baños ensured that the investigation progressed significantly. Arrest orders were issued against nine Uruguayan military and police officers, including Cordero and Campos Hermida, if they were to enter Argentina.[101] In 1986 Judge Néstor Blondi of Buenos Aires's Federal Tribunal No. 3 took charge of the investigation, which continued expanding owing to Baños's unremitting efforts in gathering evidence regarding Orletti's officers, including Aníbal Gordon, whom several survivors had identified as the site's chief.[102] Others had also mentioned four Uruguayan officers who had operated in Buenos Aires, and Baños petitioned the judge to request their extradition.[103] Former soldier Julio César Barboza, a guard in two secret jails in Montevideo, provided further essential information on Uruguayan military structures, individual officers, and their roles within this system, and confirmed that numerous agents had operated in Argentina.[104]

In late July 1986 Judge Blondi formally charged Gavazzo, Cordero, Silveira, and Campos Hermida, and extradition requests then followed. The magistrate also subpoenaed four other Uruguayan officers. This indictment was a landmark step and the first decision of its kind: never before, in fact, had high-ranking officials of the armed and security forces of another country been accused in Argentina of human rights violations.[105]

Concurrently, Alfonsín's administration also promoted the criminal prosecution of nine heads of the military juntas, in what became known as the Trial of the Juntas that occurred before Buenos Aires's Federal Criminal Appeals Court between April and December 1985. Never before had military commanders been called to account for their actions while in power in Argentina or elsewhere in South America. The verdict, handed down on December 9 and upheld on appeal in 1986, confirmed the systematic nature of the atrocities perpetrated and acknowledged the repressive coordination. In a short section of the sentence, the judges discussed the collaboration between Argentine and Uruguayan security officers in Orletti and noted how it also encompassed the clandestine rendition of prisoners to Montevideo.[106]

Several Uruguayan survivors, including Washington Pérez, Ana Inés Quadros, and Asilú Maceiro, provided crucial testimony in this extraordinary trial.[107] Survivor Elba Rama recalled this experience in a positive light, noting that she felt that the Argentine judges were protecting her and that the president of the tribunal repeatedly challenged questions raised by the commanders' defense attorneys each time they overstepped the line.[108] In the mid-1980s a negative bias against political activism still dominated, and witnesses feared that their militant past could adversely compromise the veracity of their declarations.

Another former activist, for instance, told the Argentine judges that she had met PVP leaders Gatti and Duarte because they were her father's friends, but she never mentioned that she also knew them from being a militant herself.[109]

Undeniably, the witnesses' past lives as exiled activists in Argentina could generate potentially harmful consequences in the trial. Sara Méndez faced this dilemma most profoundly. During her testimony, she wanted to mention her missing son Simón, because the trial's publicity might help with his ongoing search. But consequently, she had to admit that when registering his birth in June 1976, she had used an ID card that she had borrowed from her friend Stella Maris Riquelo. She had had no choice at the time, since Simón was born less than two weeks after the disappearance of her brother-in-law, Gerardo Gatti, and unknown individuals had been asking for her at the hospital where she had first planned to give birth. Hence, she went to a different hospital and registered the baby as Simón Riquelo. After the hearing, Videla's lawyer, Carlos Tavares, threatened to file a complaint against Sara for falsifying a public document.[110] But the trial prosecutor, Julio Strassera, defended her: not only had Sara's actions been driven by absolute necessity to protect her life and her son's, but she willingly disclosed the full truth to the judges, risking legal consequences and self-incrimination.[111]

Just months after the conclusion of the Trial of the Juntas, the Argentine government enacted two amnesty laws in 1986 and in 1987 to halt all criminal investigations into past atrocities, because of military resistance and increasing discontent with trials. Later, Decree 1003 of October 6, 1989, signed by President Carlos Menem (1989–99), exonerated from criminal accountability the four Uruguayan officers indicted in 1986. This pardon, however, indirectly confirmed that the activities of foreign security agents in Argentina had become a well-established fact by then.

An Uphill Struggle

Between 1983 and 1984, as Argentina was setting the foundations for its new democracy, negotiations between representatives of the armed forces and some political parties began to pave the way for a political transition in Uruguay. As the military slowly retreated to the barracks, justice seekers exploited minuscule windows of opportunity. In this scenario, the first criminal lawsuit alleging human rights violations was filed in Montevideo when Lilián Celiberti and Universindo Rodríguez denounced on February 23, 1984, their ordeal before Montevideo's Criminal Judge of the Sixth Circuit.[112] Hugo Batalla, a well-

Figure 5. Jair Krischke (middle), Universindo Rodríguez (left), and Lilián Celiberti (right), on the day that the latter two were released from prison on November 19, 1983, in Montevideo, Uruguay. Image courtesy of Jair Krischke and Movimento de Justiça e Direitos Humanos.

known attorney for political prisoners, and lawyer Mario Jaso accompanied them, along with Jair Krischke, the MJDH's president, who had traveled from Porto Alegre for the occasion.[113]

Months earlier, on November 19, 1983, when Lilián and Universindo had finally been released from prison (fig. 5), numerous Brazilian journalists had listened to their testimonies at Lilián's parents' house.[114]

From some photographs Lilián had identified without hesitation Brazilian officers Pedro Seelig and Marco Aurélio Reis, Uruguayan Captain Eduardo Ferro and soldier Hugo García Rivas.[115] Lilián and Universindo learned that day of the extensive international campaign, undertaken largely from Porto Alegre, to protect their lives. They therefore decided to file a case before Uruguayan authorities, and, with the help of Lilián's father, they searched for lawyers willing to take it on.[116] The lawsuit clearly articulated the ethical imperative that motivated their action, affirming that "we would behave dishonestly with all those people who showed solidarity, with our own country, and ourselves, if we stayed silent, for fear or indifference. . . . More than repairing what happened, we present this complaint driven by the absolute conviction that such acts should never be repeated."[117] The efforts of various justice seekers had rendered the filing of this allegation possible, ranging from journalists who had denounced the victims' abduction in Brazil to García Rivas's testimony, which had disclosed the participating Uruguayan officers who were hence included in the case.[118] Other survivors and victims' relatives soon followed suit. In mid-April 1984 Enrique Rodríguez, accompanied by CELS lawyers Baños and Marcelo Parrilli, presented to Montevideo's Criminal Judge of the Seventh Circuit essentially the same case he had filed two months earlier in Buenos Aires.[119] On July 1, 1984, the final complaint to be filed while still under dictatorship concerned a PCR militant who had disappeared in Uruguay but in connection with operations in Argentina.[120]

On March 1, 1985, Uruguay returned to democracy when Julio María Sanguinetti was officially inaugurated as president. Nonetheless, possibilities for truth and justice were significantly limited compared with Argentina because the Colorado Party, to which Sanguinetti belonged, maintained close relations with the armed forces. The diametric opposite to Alfonsín's truth-and-justice approach, Sanguinetti never sponsored any official truth seeking or judicial investigations to elucidate the dictatorship's atrocities. Instead, his famous slogan "No hay que tener los ojos en la nuca" (You should not have eyes at the back of your head) urged Uruguayans to look forward and leave the past behind, depicting it as a dark period best left in historians' hands.[121]

Impunity challengers, mainly comprising victims, relatives, lawyers, activists, and opposition politicians, had instead to shoulder the burden of conducting investigations without government support. Against all odds, their persistent efforts obtained noteworthy results. During Sanguinetti's first term (1985–90), forty-six criminal cases regarding dictatorship-era crimes, including atrocities perpetrated jointly by Argentine and Uruguayan agents, were presented to the courts.[122]

In April 1985 Uruguayan and Argentine lawyers together filed two interrelated cases concerning disappeared PVP militants in Buenos Aires. Lawyers Helios Sarthou, Rosa Chiachio, Cecilia Anandez, and Graciela Borrat presented a first case regarding trade union leaders Gatti, Méndez, and Duarte before Montevideo's Criminal Judge of the Fourth Circuit on behalf of their close relatives.[123] The same four lawyers, together with Anuar Frances, Luis Guerrero, Maria Piazza, and Mireya Argelaguet, then filed a second complaint regarding twenty-five other PVP activists before the Fifth Circuit's Criminal Judge, representing seven relatives, namely Violeta Malugani, Milka González, Esther Gatti, Irma Hernández, Luz Ibarburu, Ademar Recagno, and Asunción González.[124]

The filing of these parallel lawsuits represented the culmination of collaborative endeavors by justice seekers in Argentina and Uruguay.[125] A month earlier, Argentine lawyers Eduardo Luis Duhalde and Carlos González Gartland from SIJAU and Baños from the CELS had agreed on a plan of action with counterparts in Montevideo to present these complaints. On April 17, 1985, a press conference was held to disseminate the news, with the participation of Duhalde and Baños, Uruguayan lawyers, relatives of Uruguayan victims, SERPAJ's Father Luis Pérez Aguirre, and delegates from the union confederation, the Inter-Union Workers and National Workers Convention (Plenario Intersindical de Trabajadores and Convención Nacional de Trabajadores; PIT-CNT)

Owing to the Sanguinetti government's lack of interest in truth seeking, opposition politicians from the Blanco and Frente Amplio parties were the ones who placed the question of past crimes on the parliamentary agenda on February 15, 1985, the first day the Uruguayan Parliament reopened after twelve years of inaction. These legislators proactively pushed for the creation of three investigative commissions to probe emblematic political murders and disappearances. Two commissions focused on extraterritorial atrocities: the Investigative Commission on the Situation of Disappeared People and Its Causes, and the Investigative Commission on the Kidnapping and Assassination of National Representatives Michelini and Gutiérrez-Ruiz.[126]

In early November 1985 the commission on disappearances presented its final report to Parliament and confirmed 164 disappearances, recording that 32 had taken place in Uruguay but the majority had unfolded abroad—mainly in Argentina, where 127 Uruguayans had disappeared. The report officially acknowledged that the disappearance of nationals abroad was directly connected to the Uruguayan dictatorship, and that Uruguayan officers had operated in Buenos Aires.[127]

The commission on Michelini and Gutiérrez-Ruiz in contrast worked until 1987, when in mid-August two final reports were submitted to Parliament, reflecting the profound party-line divisions that had underpinned the commission's work and the convoluted political environment of the time. The majority report, drafted by commissioners from opposition parties, examined the close relationship between the Argentine and Uruguayan regimes and confirmed the participation of Uruguayan personnel in operations in Argentina near the time of the assassinations. It concluded that criminals reporting to the Argentine Army had murdered the legislators and could not find any evidence of direct Uruguayan participation. Notwithstanding, it notably affirmed that Uruguayan authorities had left the legislators exposed to lethal danger in Buenos Aires by canceling their passports, and that they had never helped with investigations into their murder. The minority report by Colorado MPs claimed that the results obtained were of little significance and did not clarify the case.[128]

These parliamentary commissions had a necessarily limited impact given their lack of real power and resources: commissioners, for example, had to fund trips to Buenos Aires out of their own pockets. Moreover, Sanguinetti's government never officially acknowledged the final reports and openly discredited their findings.[129] The commissioners' efforts were nevertheless important in resisting top-down governmental policies of silence and impunity, and gathered much new information and direct testimonies that were later used in judicial proceedings. Further, they positioned the question of disappearances and murders on the parliamentary agenda from the first day of democracy.

SERPAJ also embarked on an ambitious truth project to reveal the dictatorship's atrocities. In March 1989 the report *Uruguay: Never Again* (*Uruguay: Nunca Más*), written by a team of individuals working under the supervision of Professor Francisco Bustamante, was released. Drawing on a nationwide survey of 313 former political prisoners between 1972 and 1985 as well as other sources, it addressed numerous themes, including the historical background, the repressive methodology, and societal impacts of state terror.[130]

The report devoted a section to considering the large number of Uruguayan citizens disappeared in Argentina, and a chapter was dedicated to the repressive coordination. Two notable elements of this investigation are worth emphasizing. First, transnational terror operations conducted against Uruguayan refugees in Argentina were closely connected to the dismantling of political opposition concurrently taking place in Uruguay: indeed, the report observed how militants of the same political group were often detained in simultaneous operations in Buenos Aires and Montevideo. Second, the report transcended the prevailing focus on Argentina and Uruguay and addressed the regional geographical scope of repression, showing how Uruguayan security officers had also operated in Chile, Brazil, and Paraguay.[131] Since the 1960s successive military coups had furthered "the creation of an enormous borderless space, where law and human dignity were suspended and innumerable abuses were committed."[132] The report identified early manifestations of regional cooperation against Uruguayans in the immediate aftermath of Pinochet's coup in Chile in late 1973. Bustamante recalled how the report's authors wanted to show "how the repressive coordination had sought to render exile in bordering countries ineffective" and that "the human rights violations perpetrated against the citizens of neighboring countries could not have occurred without complicity of all of the region's dictatorial regimes."[133]

Unlike Argentina's situation, top-down policies of impunity defined Uruguay's early years of democracy and silenced discussions of human rights violations, claiming these had been isolated excesses. Progress in judicial accountability was quickly forestalled too. Responding to increasing military threats and discontent with attempts to judicially probe past crimes, Parliament approved the Ley de Caducidad de la Pretensión Punitiva del Estado (Law on the Expiry of the State's Punitive Claims, hereafter Ley de Caducidad) on December 22, 1986, which granted the executive branch the sole power of deciding whether allegations should be investigated or shelved. Between 1986 and 2000, all complaints filed were systematically archived.[134]

Final Reflections

In the midst of South America's terror and impunity in the 1970s, justice seekers strived to reveal the truth about the atrocities perpetrated and to find ways to achieve justice. At a time of unparalleled political repression, impunity challengers faced extraordinary difficulties in denouncing crimes in South America, gripped by military dictatorships. Relatives of victims of transnational repression were especially confronted with further obstacles, since their loved ones had disappeared outside their country of origin, which especially complicated any attempts to find out their whereabouts. These cases were partially different from local repressive dynamics, but also deeply interrelated to them:[135] these victims had been targeted abroad, but because of political activism that was linked to their home country.

Throughout the 1970s justice seekers progressively collated crucial fragments of evidence to piece together the puzzle of transnational repression. The international sphere was initially more conducive to such endeavors vis-à-vis the extremely closed scenario in South America. Survivors' testimonies, such as those compiled by Amnesty International, began to unveil aspects of transnational repression's inner workings and enabled victims' families to begin to comprehend the potential fate of their loved ones. Further, impunity challengers strategically used available international and regional mechanisms, including the UN Human Rights Committee and the Inter-American Commission, to keep the South American human rights situation in the international spotlight. Journalists, including Jack Anderson and John Dinges, contributed to defying impunity and untangling some of these complex cases, such as the Letelier assassination.[136]

Impunity challengers faced diverse scenarios. In Brazil human rights activists, lawyers, and journalists effectively pushed for investigations into the 1978 abduction of the Uruguayans and found strategic facilitators for their cause in Prosecutor Pinto and Judge Rodrígues. Their unrelenting efforts produced unprecedented achievements given the overall dominant context of impunity: the 1979 CPI and the 1980 criminal verdict officially admitted the perpetration of the transnational operation and uncovered the collaboration between Brazilian and Uruguayan agents, one of whom was found guilty.

In Argentina impunity challengers repeatedly filed habeas corpus writs throughout the dictatorship, albeit with little success. High-profile events such as the 1978 Football World Cup and the 1979 visit by the Inter-American Commission helped buttress their work, since these occasions generated broader international awareness about unfolding horrors in Argentina, and multiplied mobilization opportunities by local activists.[137] In late 1983 the CELS released the first report on the repressive coordination between Argentina and Uruguay, and presented in early 1984 the first lawsuit to investigate the crimes committed in Orletti. In 1986 the first-ever indictment of foreign military officers in Argentina took place just before all investigations were frozen because of military insubordination. Justice seekers also functioned within the Argentine state, including President Alfonsín, who spearheaded the creation of justice and truth-seeking bodies that formally documented the crimes of the repressive coordination. Exceptional justice results were achieved.

In contrast, justice opportunities were significantly constrained in Uruguay, Chile, and Paraguay. In Chile and Paraguay, Pinochet and Stroessner governed with iron fists throughout the 1980s. In Uruguay the democratic government instated in 1985 never endorsed accountability demands, advancing impunity instead. Justice seekers, however, actively resisted state-sponsored impunity and silence. In Parliament, opposition politicians effectively created several investigative commissions to shed light onto egregious crimes, including the disappearance of over one hundred Uruguayan citizens abroad. Furthermore, victims, survivors, and their lawyers began filing criminal lawsuits in early 1984, when the military retreated to their barracks, while SERPAJ released a landmark investigation into past atrocities to compensate for the government's idleness. The next chapter discusses the continuing efforts by justice seekers who launched Condor investigations in Chile and Uruguay in the late 1990s.

8 · Eluding Amnesty

Condor Trials in Chile and Uruguay

No se mueve ninguna hoja en este país si yo no la estoy moviendo.[1]
—*General Augusto Pinochet*

In the late 1990s Juan Guzmán Tapia was an unexpected justice seeker. Son of a poet and diplomat of Chilean high society, he was born in El Salvador in 1939 and later studied law in Santiago and Paris. In 1970 he began his career as a judge in Chile. On September 11, 1973, Guzmán Tapia and his family welcomed the military coup with relief and famously toasted to it with a glass of champagne.[2] Twenty-five years later in January 1998, in an unpredictable turn of events, a judicial draw (*sorteo*) assigned to the judge the first criminal complaint that indicated former dictator Pinochet as the principal party responsible for numerous human rights violations.[3] After years of inquiries, in December 2004 Guzmán Tapia deemed Pinochet sufficiently fit to stand trial and charged him with nine counts of kidnappings and one of murder committed during Operation Condor.[4] The judge's prior attempt to prosecute the former dictator had previously been reversed.

In the early 2000s Guzmán Tapia's indictments against Pinochet were truly revolutionary, given the judge's conservative background and the general's continuing power as a lifetime senator, with powerful allies in the Supreme Court of Justice and Chile's political establishment. The transformative power of human rights and of the truth regarding the crimes probed profoundly affected Guzmán Tapia, turning him into a radically different person and an unanticipated human rights champion.[5] He thoroughly examined all allegations and traveled the length of Chile to piece together the evidence required to prove the materiality of the atrocities committed and thus dismantle the official cover stories. Ostracized by his colleagues, putting his career at risk, and living permanently with bodyguards because of unrelenting threats,[6] Guzmán Tapia courageously went against the tide and, by indicting Pinochet, simultaneously implicated large sectors of Chilean society that remained supportive of the dictatorship period.

Prosecuting Pinochet was unthinkable in the early 1990s. Whereas in Argentina a clear commitment to accountability had defined democratization, the scenario in Chile and Uruguay stood at the opposite end of the spectrum. In Uruguay President Sanguinetti had implemented since 1985 a top-down policy of impunity, which rested on the notion of "peaceful change" (*cambio en paz*) and prioritized democratic consolidation. Accordingly, truth and justice efforts were portrayed as dangerous, since they could potentially cause institutional destabilization and provoke the armed forces. The central legal pillar of this institutionalized impunity was the Ley de Caducidad, which had halted all judicial investigations of dictatorship-era atrocities in 1986.

In Chile newly elected President Patricio Aylwin Azócar (1990–94), who headed the coalition of center-left parties Concertación de Partidos por la Democracia, initially achieved substantial progress in truth seeking and reparations. In April 1990 the National Commission for Truth and Reconciliation (Comisión Nacional de Verdad y Reconciliación, also known as Rettig Commission) was established to scrutinize politically motivated murders and disappearances committed between 1973 and 1990, and it presented its final report in February 1991. The scope for judicial investigations, however, was extremely narrow. Aylwin Azócar famously asserted that justice could only be achieved *en la medida de lo possible* (to the extent possible): his words well captured the obstacles faced in the immediate post-dictatorship years.[7]

By the mid-2000s, both Chile and Uruguay had commenced criminal proceedings against high-ranking military and civilian figures of their dictatorships. Justice seekers unrelentingly pushed to achieve judicial accountability and developed creative strategies to bypass judicial and institutional obstacles, and these prosecutions represented the culmination of decades of attempts dating back to South America's dark days of dictatorship. Transnational human rights violations served a critical function within these strategic litigation efforts. While in the 1970s and 1980s extraterritorial crimes had generated additional difficulties for victims' families in determining the fate of their desaparecidos, the cross-border element later opened some of the first cracks in the seemingly indestructible walls of impunity. The facts that these atrocities had taken place outside the national territory and had often involved foreign

state agents offered additional arguments, combined with that of disappearances as permanent crimes, to claim that the amnesty laws were inapplicable.

There is an extensive literature that thoroughly analyzes Chile's and Uruguay's transitional justice policies.[8] This chapter focuses particularly on the significance of transnational crimes and how their litigation tactically buttressed
the search for truth and justice. Indeed, criminal investigations into Condor
atrocities, originally filed by Chilean and Uruguayan impunity challengers in
the 1990s, generated new opportunities in these countries' transitional justice
trajectories and led to unprecedented accomplishments, including the indictment and house arrest of Pinochet in 2004–5 and the first conviction of Uruguayan security officers for human rights violations in 2009.

(Im)possible Justice?

In the late 1980s Chile's transition to democracy was a top-down affair: the
armed forces, which retained significant power and legitimacy, effectively acted
as the arbiters of this process. In October 1988 Pinochet lost the plebiscite on
whether he would remain in power for another eight years, which opened the
way for presidential elections in December 1989. Nevertheless, the military
still oversaw a "step-by-step passage to a protected democracy."[9] Further, last-
minute tying-up laws (leyes de amarre), sanctioned in the dictatorship's dying
days between December 1989 and March 1990, restricted the powers of the
nascent democracy.[10] Among other things, they granted security of tenure to
civil servants, created nine appointed senatorial positions filled by Pinochet
supporters, and increased the numbers of pro-Pinochet judges in the Constitutional Tribunal and the Supreme Court of Justice. Moreover, the general would
remain as commander-in-chief of the army until early 1998, when he would
then take on a lifetime senatorial seat.

Throughout the twentieth century, Chile had habitually embedded forget-
fulness and impunity "as the basis for social peace."[11] In line with this tradition, the military junta had enacted Decree Law 2191 on April 18, 1978, which
ensured immunity from prosecution for all individuals involved in crimes perpetrated between September 11, 1973, and March 10, 1978, whether as authors,
accomplices, or accessories, and without distinguishing between common
crimes and politically motivated wrongs. This time frame matched the years
of DINA's operations, the most brutal period of political repression in Chile.

Upon democratization, these institutional and judicial obstacles significantly
constrained prospects for justice, and impunity appeared unbreakable. Indeed,

on August 28, 1990, Chile's Supreme Court ruled that the amnesty decree was constitutional and of compulsory application.[12] During the 1990s, criminal courts only dictated four sentences, mostly in cases not covered by the amnesty, "either because they had been committed after the 1978 enactment date or through specific exemption."[13] For instance, the October 1995 Supreme Court conviction of fifteen police officers in the so-called *degollados* (the beheaded) case, involving the kidnapping, torture, and murder of three PCC members in Santiago, fell outside the amnesty's temporal remit, having been committed in 1985. The argument of *secuestro permanente* (permanent kidnapping), described in chapter 6, also helped activists to press ahead. This was used in September 1993 in the first criminal verdict regarding dictatorship crimes since the transition. In a ruling that rejected the application of amnesty and statutory limitations, a court in Lautaro, southern Chile, determined that unsolved disappearances should be considered as crimes that were still being perpetrated. The Supreme Court endorsed this stance in 1995.[14]

A momentous step forward occurred in this period during investigations into the murder of Orlando Letelier and his colleague Ronni Moffitt, an emblematic Condor crime. The 1978 amnesty decree (article 4) had expressly excluded from its remit criminal acts in this case, because of strong pressure from the US.[15] In March 1978 Santiago's Second Military Court had opened an investigation into the forged passports used by DINA agents,[16] which could have potentially implicated both former DINA head Manuel Contreras and Pinochet. But little immediate progress was made: on one hand, in 1979 Chile's Supreme Court denied US extradition requests regarding Contreras, his right-hand man Pedro Espinoza Bravo, and agent Armando Fernández Larios, and on the other, the military justice system dismissed the passports case in 1980 because of direct Pinochet intervention.[17] Nonetheless, lawyer Fabiola Letelier, the victim's sister, and her colleagues Jaime Castillo Velasco and Andrés Aylwin, repeatedly appealed to both the military and civil court systems to prevent the permanent closure of the passports case. Eventually they achieved decisions in 1982 and 1987 that characterized the dismissal as one of "temporary status," which meant that the investigations could possibly be reopened in the future.[18]

Indeed, in 1990, Fabiola Letelier and her allied human rights lawyers successfully convinced the Supreme Court to reopen proceedings after new evidence surfaced, and to also transfer the case from the military justice sphere to the civilian.[19] The presiding judge in the reopened investigation was Supreme Court Justice Adolfo Bañados, who in 1991 accused Contreras and Espinoza

Bravo as being the murder's intellectual authors.[20] In November 1993 Bañados condemned the defendants to seven and six years, respectively, and in May
1995 the Supreme Court upheld the verdicts, thereby rendering the sentences
final.[21]

The convictions of Contreras and Espinoza, who reported directly to Pinochet, were groundbreaking events: the first time two DINA high-ranking military officers were convicted for abhorrent crimes in Chile. Lawyer Nelson Caucoto observed how the relatively short sentences could be perceived as "absurd
and laughable," given the gravity of the crimes.[22] But the verdicts were extremely significant nonetheless, particularly considering that never before had
high-ranking military officers been sentenced for perpetrating extraterritorial
crimes.[23] Lawyer Cristian Cruz remarked how Contreras's condemnation was
a momentous step forward with vast symbolic impact, since he was "the most
visible face of the harshest phase of repression in the 1970s" and was finally
serving time for one of the DINA's numerous atrocities.[24] Letelier's murder recurrently haunted the Chilean military: the case had led in 1977 to the DINA's
replacement by the CNI and to Contreras's fall from grace. Twenty years later
the verdict shook Chile up again. Contreras and Espinoza resisted incarceration
for months, helped by the connivance of the armed forces; they were ultimately
imprisoned in the special prison in Punta Peuco, which had been built to imprison individuals convicted of crimes against humanity in the mid-1990s.[25]

Meanwhile, in Uruguay, Sanguinetti's policy of impunity was strengthened
when, in May 1988, the Supreme Court of Justice confirmed the constitution-
ality of the Ley de Caducidad and later when the citizenry endorsed the law in
an April 1989 referendum.[26] The government of President Luis Lacalle (1990–
95) of the Blanco Party and a second term by Sanguinetti (1995–2000) perpet-
uated this scenario.[27] Yet throughout the 1990s justice seekers countered this
dominant willful silence through various initiatives that included the holding
of the first March of Silence on May 20, 1996, to remember victims of disappearance on the twentieth anniversary of Michelini's and Gutiérrez-Ruiz's
murders, and the filing of four criminal complaints in 1990, 1994, and 1997.[28]

Two of these cases progressively became emblematic of Uruguay's struggles
against impunity. The first, related to the disappearance of teacher and PVP
militant Elena Quinteros, was initiated in 1990 when opposition senators presented a lawsuit before Montevideo's Criminal Judge of the First Circuit against
four high-ranking civilian officials of the Ministry of Foreign Affairs, including former foreign minister Juan Carlos Blanco (1972–76), who had become
a senator in 1990. The Quinteros case was a high-profile disappearance that

had, in 1976, led to the rupture of diplomatic relations between Uruguay and Venezuela.

The second case was filed in March 1997 by Senator Rafael Michelini, son of the slain senator, before Montevideo's Criminal Judge of the Twentieth Circuit regarding the so-called Operación Zanahoria (Carrot Operation). Michelini requested the judiciary to investigate General Alberto Ballestrino's claims in *Posdata* magazine in 1996 about an alleged operation between 1985 and 1986 to remove the bodies of victims who had died under torture and had been secretly buried on military grounds in the Thirteenth Infantry Battalion in Montevideo and the Fourteenth Infantry Battalion in Toledo.[29]

In an unprecedented and unanticipated decision, on April 15, 1997, Judge Alberto Reyes ruled that sufficient evidence existed to warrant the opening of a judicial investigation into the fate of over 150 desaparecidos. For the first time since the Ley de Caducidad's enactment, a judicial authority ordered the start of investigations into past violations.[30] But progress was short-lived, and impunity structures instantaneously fought back. Two months later, on June 14, the Appeals Court accepted the petition filed by the case prosecutor and halted Reyes's investigation, contending that the Ley de Caducidad "forbad any intervention by the judiciary in the clarification of human rights crimes during the dictatorship."[31] In August Sanguinetti applied the Ley de Caducidad to completely shelve the investigation.

Judge Reyes acted as a strategic facilitator for justice demands and defied institutionalized impunity at this juncture, also innovatively drawing upon regional human rights provisions in the Inter-American Convention on Forced Disappearance of Persons, which Uruguay had recently ratified.[32] But he paid a high price for his stand: the Supreme Court transferred him to a different tribunal that dealt with civil law matters. This move was a clear sanction against his willingness to investigate.[33]

Turning Points

Meanwhile, in Chile Pinochet was scheduled to retire as army commander-in-chief in March 1998 and take on his lifetime senator seat.[34] On January 12 Gladys Marín, the PCC's secretary general, and her lawyer Eduardo Contreras filed the first complaint directly accusing the general of human rights violations, specifically the 1976 disappearance of Marín's husband.[35] The main objective of this attempt was to express discontent at the prospect of the former dictator becoming a senator under democracy,[36] while a broader and interrelated goal was to try to confront the prevailing impunity.[37] The political context of the late 1990s did not leave much room for optimism that the case would be suitably investigated. Nor did assignment of the case to Judge Guzmán Tapia bode well, given the magistrate's notoriously old-fashioned views.[38]

Guzmán Tapia would never forget the exact moment when the Appeals Court's acting president informed him, with "an almost malicious grin," that the lawsuit against Pinochet had been allocated to him and wished him luck; undoubtedly, that investigation posed an extremely delicate issue for the Chilean judiciary (*"pupu caliente más importante"*).[39] After mulling over the complaint for the weekend, Guzmán Tapia met with lawyer Contreras the following Monday: "Rest assured" he told him, "I will conduct a serious inquiry."[40] Contreras was left speechless upon learning of the judge's willingness to begin investigations: he had never imagined such a response, given Guzmán Tapia's reputation as "the most conservative of judges."[41]

Seeing the magistrate begin conducting meticulous investigations, victims and activists exploited this window of opportunity and soon started filing additional criminal complaints against Pinochet, which were all collated under the first lawsuit, no. 2182-98. This case file especially mushroomed after the general's detention in London in October 1998.[42] The criminal case in Spain that led to Pinochet's arrest encompassed charges of genocide, terrorism, and torture against ninety-four victims, and Condor stood at its very heart: indeed, Judge Baltasar Garzón noted in his second arrest warrant how the Chilean and Argentine militaries had carried out coordinated criminal actions in various countries to physically eliminate, torture, kidnap, and disappear both Chilean and foreign nationals.[43] At that moment, Guzmán Tapia's investigations in Chile acquired critical importance, since they enabled the Chilean government to claim that European courts did not need to prosecute Pinochet, because a local judge "was perfectly able to put on trial the military leader in his own country."[44]

By December 1998 over sixty criminal complaints had been filed in Chile owing to justice seekers' strategic actions, which had generated momentum to press ahead with judicial investigations.[45] Back in June, Guzmán Tapia had begun differentiating separate episodes (*episodios*)[46] to better manage such a large investigation, and he formalized this division in January 1999.[47] Later, in October 2002, the Supreme Court nominated five judges to work exclusively on the by then ninety-nine episodes, and Guzmán Tapia continued investigating the *episodio* Condor, among others.

The early origins of this episode date to the writ of *amparo*,[48] which Elba

Alarcón had filed before Santiago's Criminal Appeals Court in early October 1975 after learning that her son, Jorge Fuentes Alarcón, was being held incommunicado in the DINA secret prison of Cuatro Alamos. She requested information on her son's exact whereabouts and asked that the authorities officially acknowledge his arrest.[49] After democratization, in May 1992 lawyer Sergio Concha filed another complaint regarding Fuentes Alarcón's disappearance.[50] This case was especially emblematic of Condor, given the voluminous and concrete evidence that the victim had been detained in 1975 in Paraguay and later secretly taken to Chile, where various detainees had seen him alive for months.[51]

Guzmán Tapia formally created the Condor episode on September 7, 1999,[52] and between January and August 2000 relatives of other Condor victims, including Greite Weinman Hernández (Edgardo Enríquez's wife) and Ana Tamayo Martínez, Edith Muñoz Velásquez, and Flor Hernández Zazpe (sisters of three disappeared members of the Socialist Party) subsequently presented additional complaints.[53] Lawyer Karinna Fernández Neira remarked how this episode materialized as a result of spontaneous and discrete lawsuits that victims' relatives progressively presented, rather than as part of a preplanned framing around Operation Condor.[54] Indeed, unlike other episodes, which were often framed around a detention center or the persecution of a discrete political group, the Condor investigation encompassed victims from different time periods and diverse political affiliations, who were disengaged from each other both geographically and temporally, but these distinct cases were later merged under the Condor umbrella, which was the common element they all shared.[55]

In December 2003, acting on a petition by lawyers Contreras, Concha, and Francisco Bravo, Guzmán Tapia initiated proceedings to strip Pinochet of his senatorial immunity before the Appeals Court in the Condor episode.[56] The removal of immunity was a prerequisite step before initiating criminal proceedings. This was the judge's second attempt to prosecute the dictator, after the Supreme Court had closed down proceedings in July 2002 against Pinochet in the Caravan of Death *episodio* on health grounds.[57] In May and August 2004 the Appeals Court and the Supreme Court unexpectedly endorsed the judge's petition and decided that Pinochet could face trial for crimes against nineteen Chilean Condor victims.[58] Notably, the Supreme Court's ruling inverted its previous stance (in place since 2001) of regularly blocking all efforts to investigate the general, by "finding Pinochet 'preemptively' immune from prosecution on medical grounds," and recommended instead new medical tests to assess if Pinochet's ability to face trial had changed.[59]

Eventually, Judge Guzmán Tapia, after carefully considering reports by various medical experts on Pinochet's physical and mental health, resolved on December 13, 2004, to indict the former dictator on nine counts of abduction and one murder.[60] These Chilean Condor victims had disappeared between 1975 and 1977 in Paraguay, Bolivia, and Argentina, and there was sufficient evidence of the involvement of the DINA's Exterior Department in these operations, including that seized individuals had been returned to Chile, where they disappeared. Pinochet's defense attorneys presented an *amparo* writ, but in early January 2005 the Supreme Court surprisingly confirmed both the indictment and the arrest order in a historic decision.[61] Consequently, the dictator spent several days under effective house arrest. His lawyers then opened dismissal proceedings before the Appeals Court to prevent the trial from taking place. In line with previous jurisprudence, the Appeals Court annulled the Condor indictment on health grounds,[62] while the Supreme Court later effectively closed proceedings in September 2005.[63]

In the late 1990s many Chileans had little hope that Guzmán Tapia's investigations would go very far. But within a few years, the formerly untouchable and powerful dictator Pinochet faced the real prospect of sitting in the dock to account for atrocious crimes. By resorting to the *secuestro permanente* thesis, the magistrate acted as a strategic facilitator of victims' justice demands and repeatedly bypassed the amnesty, thus initiating criminal proceedings in several episodes. Following the steps of other brave Chilean judges, including Carlos Cerda Fernández, who had attempted to investigate atrocities during the dictatorship,[64] Guzmán Tapia similarly met with victims' relatives, began serious investigations into past horrors, and ordered excavations in searching for the desaparecidos. His efforts "opened a door" and effectively enabled investigations to move forward.[65]

Despite the closure of the case against Pinochet, the accusation against the former general in the *episodio* Condor constituted a crucial step ahead. Until then, judicial authorities had been unable to establish a direct link between Pinochet and the DINA, but the Condor investigation, given the organization's nature as a multicountry framework to coordinate political persecution, successfully showed that the general had to have been aware of extraterritorial operations.[66] Journalist John Dinges has noted how the international atrocities of Condor provided the keystone in building the case against Pinochet personally since, before then, it had been extremely difficult to tie the general directly to specific crimes.[67] Guzmán Tapia intentionally based his indictment in the Condor episode on a sophisticated yet ambiguous argument: the accusation acknowledged for the first time how South American intelligence services had established Operation Condor to "combat and repress the supposed enemies of their respective governments" and included the role of the DINA's top echelons within this regional scheme.[68] The magistrate indirectly hinted that Pinochet was the ultimate head of the DINA but never specifically asserted this.[69] Guzmán Tapia knew he was running out of time and operating in a tense political context, since rumors had reached him that his investigations were again displeasing judicial officials, and he wanted to submit the Condor indictment before retiring.[70]

The Pinochet Effect

Indictments against Pinochet in Chile and Spain resonated powerfully across the Southern Cone, where justice seekers were continually looking for ways to undermine the prevalent impunity in their own countries. Undoubtedly, the proceedings against Pinochet marked the "start of the downfall of the model of juridical impunity" which had previously dominated.[71] Further, the disintegration of Pinochet's aura as an untouchable dictator inspired impunity challengers beyond South America: the fact that someone as powerful as the former Chilean general was close to seeing his day in court reenergized existing efforts to achieve justice across the world.

In Uruguay, despite the shelving of the 1997 Operación Zanahoria investigation, justice seekers continued to explore different pathways to achieve justice, both domestically and internationally. In 1998 lawyer Javier Miranda, the son of a disappeared member of the PCU, began contending that if the Ley de Caducidad prevented the judiciary from investigating, the executive branch could at least be compelled to probe disappearances. This objective required a complex undertaking that began with a petition to the executive branch to open an investigation; when the petition was rejected, an appeal was filed before the Contentious Administrative Court (Tribunal de lo Contencioso Administrativo; TCA). In mid-1999 the TCA dictated a provisional yet encouraging decision which overruled the executive's contention that the Ley de Caducidad should render proceedings ineffective.[72] In parallel, Uruguayan human rights and trade union activists keenly resorted to opportunities in the international sphere. In March 1998 a delegation traveled to Madrid with Argentine counterparts to discuss Operation Condor with Spanish Judge Baltasar Garzón.[73] Subsequently they transmitted a list of twenty-two Uruguayan police and military officers to the judge.[74] In June 1999 a group of Uruguayan and Argentine victims' relatives also filed a criminal case in Rome relating to Condor operations (see chapter 10).

In Montevideo, lawyer Pablo Chargoñia and María Almeida de Quinteros, known as Tota, were also endeavoring to force the government to start a new investigation into Elena Quinteros's disappearance. In December 1999 Chargoñia presented to the TCA an *amparo* writ, grounded on Tota's right to know the truth about her daughter's fate, to prompt the government to reopen proceedings in light of new available witnesses. Chargoñia, originally a labor lawyer, was linked to the central trade union PIT-CNT, which also functioned as an impunity challenger that consistently activated justice demands in Uruguay. In February 2000 civil judge Estela Jubette decided that enough legal grounds existed for the *amparo;* three months later, her ruling forcefully criticized the executive branch for failing to investigate Elena's abduction and ordered the Ministry of Defense to carry out an administrative inquiry.[75] Despite suffering intense political pressure, neither the judge nor the PIT-CNT backed down, and their tenacity was vindicated when the Appeals Court surprisingly ratified Jubette's verdict in late May, concurring that national and international law required the government to investigate.

Jubette's decision was remarkable given the backdrop of impunity in Uruguay, and its subsequent ratification on appeal was completely unforeseen given the notorious conservative stance of higher judges. As with Judge Reyes in 1997, Jubette risked being sanctioned; the Supreme Court eventually did not transfer her, but the judge took a lengthy sick leave due to the stress she suffered as a result of political pressures and ostracism by her colleagues.[76]

Starting in the late 1990s, a small group of Uruguayan impunity challengers comprising victims' relatives, their lawyers, and the PIT-CNT obstinately strived to obtain justice, firmly believing that it "was necessary under all circumstances."[77] At this time, investigations into the Elena Quinteros and María Claudia García de Gelman cases attempted to upset the applecart vis-à-vis dominant judicial impunity. The public identification of Macarena Gelman in April 2000 profoundly moved the Uruguayan public. Macarena, born after her mother's clandestine rendition from Argentina (see chapter 4), had been illegally adopted in January 1977 by Uruguayan police commissioner Ángel Tauriño and his wife, who had raised her as their daughter.[78] Only in early 2000 did Macarena's adoptive mother admit that she was not her biological daughter, and the youngster learned from Bishop Pablo Galimberti, the intermediary between the biological and adoptive families, of her grandfather's persistent search for her.

Argentine poet Juan Gelman had, since 1976, tirelessly tried to locate his daughter-in-law and her newborn. After corroborating that María Claudia García had given birth in Montevideo's Military Hospital, Gelman had traveled to Uruguay in 1999 to continue his search, but local authorities never cooperated.[79] Gelman then sent an open letter to President Sanguinetti in October 1999 and launched an international campaign openly accusing the Uruguayan government. Over twenty thousand people, including 115 poets from seventy-one countries and Nobel laureates such as José Saramago, Adolfo Pérez Esquivel, and Dario Fo, endorsed Gelman's demand for thorough investigations. But Sanguinetti never budged. In January 2000 he unapologetically declared that "no child had disappeared on Uruguayan soil," in a response to German novelist Günter Grass.[80] Macarena's identification only weeks later unmistakably revealed Sanguinetti's duplicity. In contrast, President Jorge Batlle, of the same Colorado Party, who had taken over in early March, took a small yet significant step forward by publicly announcing Macarena's identification.[81]

Concurrently, the administrative investigation into Quinteros's disappearance did not produce significant findings. During *amparo* proceedings, however, activist Raúl Olivera discovered that a criminal complaint on the case, previously filed in 1990, had been archived incorrectly in 1995.[82] Building on Olivera's finding, Tota Quinteros and lawyer Chargoñia requested in November 2000 that the criminal investigation be reopened, based on a two-fold contention that disappearances constituted a permanent crime and that the Ley de Caducidad did not shield civilians. Former prosecutor Mirtha Guianze observed that this was a pioneering stance, since those two concepts had been discussed theoretically, but not a single case had made it to court on those grounds until then.[83]

As a result, and rather unexpectedly, in October 2002 Judge Eduardo Cavalli of Montevideo's First Circuit Criminal Court endorsed the complainants' request and formally charged and ordered the arrest of former foreign minister Juan Carlos Blanco for Elena's illegal deprivation of liberty.[84] For the first time since democratization, a prosecution for dictatorship-era crimes went ahead. Chargoñia's juridical elaboration represented a pivotal turning point, for it clearly demonstrated that criminal proceedings could begin despite decades of impunity.[85] This historic verdict validated the "utopian lawyering" (*abogacía utópica*) of some impunity challengers, who had continued pursuing the reopening of criminal proceedings against all odds.[86]

Separately, lawyer José Luis González, representing the Gelmans, had also filed a case before Montevideo's Second Circuit Criminal Court in July 2002 for the abduction and murder of María Claudia García, her daughter's kidnapping, and the concealment of the newborn's identity.[87] This second high-profile case put further pressure on Batlle's government, which in August 2000 had timidly and reluctantly started addressing dictatorship-era crimes by establishing the Peace Commission to collate information on the disappeared.

Simultaneously, another case of transnational repression contributed to undermining the enduring impunity. In March 2002 an independent investigation by Senator Rafael Michelini and journalist Roger Rodríguez had led to the identification in Buenos Aires of Simón Riquelo, Sara Méndez's long-lost son, whom a police commissioner had illegally adopted the same night of his mother's kidnapping in 1976.[88] After Macarena's case, Simón's location in Argentina exposed yet again the passivity and inaction of the Uruguayan government. Indeed, just a year earlier in March 2001, a member of the Peace Commission had told Sara during a private meeting that Simón could be dead.[89] Sara's instinct kept telling her that Simón was alive, and her unfaltering international campaigns to find him since 1981 eventually succeeded.

Justice, at Last

In the early 2000s, justice seekers' efforts finally began to effectively break through the dominant impunity in Uruguay, and these successes were bolstered by similar advances in neighboring Argentina and Chile. The swearing in of the first left-wing Uruguayan government by the Frente Amplio coalition on March 1, 2005, raised hope for a turning point in human rights.[90] In his inaugural speech, President Tabaré Vázquez affirmed that his government would allow the investigation of disappearances and that the Ley de Caducidad did not cover the cases of Gelman, Michelini, and Gutiérrez-Ruiz.[91] Vázquez's words signaled an important change of direction from all prior executives. Yet the government's stance remained problematic, since it only contemplated the elucidation of a few emblematic atrocities while impunity would continue to shield other violations, including thousands of arbitrary detentions and torture.[92] This ambiguous policy mirrored internal Frente Amplio divisions regarding how to proceed with the Ley de Caducidad; eventually the coalition had decided to keep the law in place but to apply it to the letter, thus permitting only a limited number of investigations.[93]

Human rights organizations also diverged on how to move forward at this juncture. Some lawyers believed that the strategy of evading the Ley de Caducidad by indicting civilians or higher-ranked officers—followed since the early 2000s—should continue, and that direct confrontations with the Vázquez administration should be avoided. Others, principally lawyer Chargoñia, believed instead that the window of opportunity offered by the first left-wing executive should be exploited and more ambitious approaches should be attempted than in the past. His proposed tactic focused on demanding the inapplicability of the Ley de Caducidad by resorting to international law, the argument that disappearances constituted permanent crimes, and the necessity of indicting both high-ranking and subordinate officers.[94] He argued that the prior limited focus on only the higher ranks could potentially backfire in the long term, since most potential defendants had already passed away, and accusing only the top echelons would reinforce the impunity of the subordinate officers.

On September 19, 2005, Chargoñia filed the first case based on this strategy: the 1974 disappearance in Argentina of Tupamaros militant Washington Barrios, on behalf of the victim's mother and sister; six middle-ranking agents and their commanding officers were accused.[95] Further, Barrios's kidnapping was expressly framed as a crime against humanity and a wrongdoing that "continues in time until the person appears or there exists judicial proofs of his/her death."[96] The complaint relied on the innovative 2001 Inter-American Court's judgment in *Barrios Altos v. Peru* on the inapplicability of amnesty laws to serious human rights violations.[97] The litigants claimed first that the Ley de Caducidad lacked legal effect as it contradicted provisions in the American Convention on Human Rights (which Uruguay had ratified in 1985) that required states to punish human rights violations, and second that the law's specific time frame only related to offenses perpetrated until March 1985, while the victim's disappearance still endured in 2005.[98] According to Chargoñia, these tactical litigation efforts aimed to "install the idea that crimes against humanity are not subject to prescription and promote litigation on that point, so that Uruguayan judges would engage with these considerations."[99]

The following day, Montevideo's criminal judge of the Nineteenth Circuit, Luis Charles, consulted the government on whether or not an investigation could be opened regarding Barrios's disappearance. Weeks later, on October 31, the administration approved the beginning of proceedings, marking the first time in which the Uruguayan government had authorized the judiciary to open an investigation by identifying specific exceptions to the application of the Ley de Caducidad.[100]

Since the first breach of this law through the 2002 *Quinteros* indictment, victims' relatives and their lawyers had presented several criminal complaints, and this trend particularly intensified during the Frente Amplio government, when seventeen of twenty-one new cases filed between 2002 and 2009 were lodged during Vázquez's first term (2005–10).[101] At this time the atrocities of South America's repressive coordination played a key role, and eight of the seventeen complaints filed post-2005 comprised crimes perpetrated against Uruguayan exiles in the region. These impunity challengers relentlessly pressured the legal system, and consequently a new policy effectively surfaced. When the government received a request from a judge regarding the Ley de Caducidad's applicability, it responded positively in some cases and so allowed several investigations to begin.[102] The main architect behind this shift was Gonzalo Fernández, the president's principal advisor, and it represented an ad hoc response to justice seekers' persistent demands.[103]

Fernández's approach, colloquially referred to as the "cheese holes theory" (la teoría de los agujeros del queso), derived from a literal reading of the text of the Ley de Caducidad, according to which two sets of wrongdoings fell outside the law's scope. Article 1, which explicitly shielded military and police personnel who were fulfilling their functions and obeying orders, was interpreted to exclude civilian officers and high-ranking military/police commanders, while article 2(b) expressly excluded crimes carried out to obtain economic benefits. Moreover, crimes committed outside of Uruguay were exempted from the amnesty on the basis of the principle of territoriality of criminal law.[104] Some lawyers questioned the latter exception and pointed to the Uruguayan Criminal Code (article 10.4), which provides that Uruguayan law applies to crimes abroad in cases of state officials who abuse their functions or violate the duties inherent to their posts.[105]

Nevertheless, the government proceeded with this strategy of literally interpreting the Ley de Caducidad based on these three exceptions, and thus superseded its original approach not to touch the Ley de Caducidad beyond emblematic cases.[106] Fernández's tactic attempted to reconcile the internal divisions within the government coalition and potential military resistance with renewed pressures by impunity challengers who had resumed filing lawsuits. The cheese holes theory undoubtedly produced positive effects in belatedly opening up numerous judicial investigations and generating important results.[107] Yet from the perspective of human rights lawyers and activists, this policy was far from an acceptable solution, since it failed to embrace consolidated international and regional jurisprudence on the invalidity of amnesties and the imprescriptible nature of crimes against humanity.[108]

In early April 2006 Chargoñia presented a second case on behalf of the wife and three children of PVP leader Adalberto Soba, who had disappeared in

Argentina in 1976; the PIT-CNT also formally participated. Criminal judge Charles and public prosecutor Mirtha Guianze were in charge of both this and the 2005 complaint. On September 11, 2006, the judge indicted retired military and police officers José Gavazzo, Jorge Silveira, Ernesto Ramas, Ricardo Medina, José Arab, Gilberto Vázquez, Luis Maurente, and José Sande for Soba's illegal deprivation of liberty and a charge of criminal conspiracy.[109] This resolution was groundbreaking in Uruguay in three respects: for the first time, military and police officers were indicted for dictatorship-era atrocities; second, the Ley de Caducidad was bypassed by endorsing the claimants' argument on disappearances as permanent crimes;[110] and the victim's detention was explicitly framed within Condor.

This case eventually led to the first sentences delivered in Uruguay for dictatorship-era atrocities: on March 26, 2009, Judge Charles condemned the eight officers for the 1976 murder of twenty-eight PVP activists abducted in Buenos Aires.[111] Gavazzo, Arab, Silveira, Ramas, and Vázquez were sentenced to twenty-five-year terms, and Maurente, Medina, and Sande to twenty years. The verdict, which placed these crimes within the backdrop of Operation Condor, noted how the accused had served functions within the SID and the OCOA, and had acted "in accordance with a common plan of intelligence and operational tasks" in Argentina.[112] Accordingly, they "constantly traveled to Argentina, exchanged information, interrogated prisoners under psychological and physical duress, conducted abductions and clandestine prisoner renditions, mainly against militants of the PVP, but also other organizations."[113] In particular, the defendants had carried out "operations that disregarded all borders and victims' nationalities, with unlimited powers, since they were unbound by substantive laws, nor moral or ethical ones."[114] Remarkably, Charles underlined the importance of the right to truth, which pertained not only to victims' relatives but to society as a whole, and affirmed that Uruguayan state terror amounted to crimes against humanity that were imprescriptible.[115]

Additional Condor Cases

Throughout the 2000s, Uruguayan impunity challengers tactically used other allegations of Condor atrocities to push ahead for the successful reopening of criminal investigations. On May 16, 2007, lawyer Oscar López Goldaracena presented a complaint on behalf of the relatives of another fifteen Uruguayan exiles before Judge Charles, given the shared context of Operation Condor be-

tween these and the murders the tribunal was already scrutinizing.[116] Two
weeks later, relatives of two PVP victims disappeared in Paraguay, supported
by the PIT-CNT's Human Rights Secretariat and lawyer Chargoñia, appeared
before Montevideo's criminal judge of the Seventh Circuit to request the start
of criminal investigations against sixteen Paraguayan, Argentine, and Uruguayan officers, including former dictator Gregorio Álvarez and SID Major
Carlos Calcagno.[117]

This case relied on the same arguments Chargoñia had previously made
that disappearances affected an interrelated set of core guarantees, such as the
rights to life and due process. Further, such atrocities had an impact beyond
the direct victims, generating terror, uncertainty, and anxiety in their relatives
and society too, producing "fear and impunity that undermined public security."[118] This criminal investigation proved particularly significant in Uruguay's
transitional justice efforts. In September 2010 Judge Mariana Mota was the
first magistrate to accept the request by prosecutor Guianze to charge Major
Calcagno with the international law category of enforced disappearance, which
had been codified in Uruguay through Law 18.026 of 2006, which ratified the
Rome Statute of the International Criminal Court (ICC).[119] Until then judges
had applied the legal figure of homicide even in cases of disappearances.[120]

Judge Mota contended instead that international law norms regarding serious human rights violations and crimes against humanity were already manda-
tory for Uruguay at the time the crimes were committed.[121] Further, in another
remarkable rupture in Uruguayan jurisprudence, the Appeals Court ratified
Mota's indictment in July 2011 and validated the position that "enforced disappearances are and should be treated as *permanent crimes*."[122] Appeals magistrates Judges Alberto Reyes and Anabella Damasco extensively cited international jurisprudence to support their stance, including the recent *Gelman*
verdict and sentences dictated in Mexico, Colombia, and Peru.[123] This was the
first time a Uruguayan appeals court had ratified an indictment using the
classification of enforced disappearance. Previously, higher courts had always
modified into murder charges all previous attempts by prosecutor Guianze to
frame the persecution of Uruguayan exiles as enforced disappearances.

Judge Mota acted as an impunity challenger at this juncture, since she enabled victims' justice demands and defied the broader scenario of impunity:
she was the only first-instance judge who applied international law categories
while investigating past crimes. Her efforts were buttressed by Judges Reyes
and Damasco, who likewise favored the application of international law provi-

sions in domestic criminal proceedings.[124] Mota's stance remained exceptional; in particular, the Supreme Court of Justice has consistently displayed a conservative position, which sets it apart as a laggard in South America.[125] The high magistrates—except Judge Lesley Van Rompaey—have repeatedly maintained since May 2011 that the crime of enforced disappearance was created in Uruguayan law only in 2006 and that, accordingly, this category cannot be applied retroactively to crimes committed prior to that time.[126]

Beyond domestic efforts, impunity challengers operated internationally to bring further pressure to bear, and once again a Condor lawsuit catalyzed important policy changes in Uruguay. In May 2006 the continued denial of justice experienced in Uruguay pushed Macarena and Juan Gelman to file a petition before the Inter-American Commission with the support of the Center for Justice and International Law (CEJIL) and their Uruguayan lawyer.[127] Since the *Gelman* complaint had originally been filed in 2002, the Gelmans and lawyer José Luis González had confronted "a juridical route full of recurrent stumbling blocks": judges, prosecutors, and the executive branch had all obstructed its progress at different junctures, and the plaintiffs had to request the reopening of investigations in 2005 and 2008.[128] The petition to the Inter-American Commission eventually resulted in the first sentence pronounced against Uruguay by the Inter-American Court in February 2011. In *Gelman,* the court resoundingly condemned Uruguay for its responsibility in the disappearance of María Claudia García and Macarena Gelman, and for the violation of several of Juan Gelman's rights. In line with its preexisting jurisprudence on amnesties,[129] the court affirmed that the Ley de Caducidad was incompatible with the American Convention, since it hampered the punishment of serious crimes and thereby lacked legal effect.[130] The combined pressure of this first regional verdict and existing domestic anti-impunity efforts produced the parliamentary derogation in October 2011 of the Ley de Caducidad, twenty-five years after its enactment.[131]

Chilean Condor Episode

Investigations into the *episodio* Condor continued in Chile after proceedings closed against Pinochet in 2005; the legal strategy since then has focused on establishing the responsibility of other high- and middle-ranking DINA officials. After Guzmán Tapia's retirement, the case was assigned first to Judge Víctor Montiglio Rezzio and subsequently to Judge Mario Carroza Espinosa. Between 2005 and 2010 Montiglio Rezzio surprised human rights activists as he moved away from his original posture of applying the amnesty decree and began to investigate human rights violations in depth.[132] He notably widened the scope of the initial Condor inquiry to include as new defendants additional DINA agents who had operated in the Villa Grimaldi and Simón Bolívar secret prisons; he wished to carefully examine the entire repressive structure and the role of each agent.[133]

The Chilean Condor investigation lasted well over a decade. Only in February 2016 did Carroza Espinosa finally close pretrial investigations and open trial proceedings, indicting fifty-five DINA agents on seven counts of kidnappings involving Héctor Heraldo Velásquez Mardones, Alexei Jaccard Siegler, Jorge Fuentes Alarcón, Manuel Tamayo Martínez, Luis Muñoz Velásquez, Juan Hernández Zazpe, and Julio Valladares Caroca, and five assassinations of Ricardo Ignacio Ramírez Herrera, Ruiter Enrique Arce Correa, Jacobo Stoulman Bortnik, Matilde Pessa Mois, and Hernán Soto Gálvez.[134]

During this long investigation, the Condor episode was first divided into two separate dossiers; in November 2015 a third file was added. The two criminal cases were Rol 2182–98 "Cóndor"—which was the main case in the trial phase—and Rol 2182–98 "Cóndor BIS," which comprised eleven Chilean victims who disappeared in Argentina but for which limited evidence of their transfer to Chile existed.[135] Investigations for this second dossier have remained at the pretrial phase, and as yet no one has been formally prosecuted.[136] The third file is administrative, relating to investigations seeking to locate and identify victims' bodies, thus satisfying the right to truth. Carroza Espinosa opened this dossier after the remains of Ramírez Herrera, Stoulman Bortnik, and Pessa Mois were identified in May 2015.[137] This discovery was, in the words of a human rights lawyer, a "completely unanticipated" development.[138] Indeed, none of the investigations had previously provided any hint that the Stoulman–Pessa couple had been taken to Chile after their disappearance in Argentina.

On September 21, 2018, almost twenty years after the start of the investigations, Carroza Espinosa sentenced twenty former DINA members for abductions and murders committed against twelve Condor victims, and acquitted thirty-two agents.[139] The condemned officers included emblematic DINA figures such as Director of Operations Pedro Espinoza Bravo, who was sentenced to fifteen years and a day regarding eleven victims, and Juan Morales Salgado, who faced the same penalty for five victims. The latter had commanded the dreaded DINA Lautaro Brigade, which had originally been created to protect DINA chief Contreras and his family but also exterminated the PCC leadership. High-ranking officers of the DINA Exterior Department, such as its chief

Raúl Iturriaga Neumann and the liaison officer in Buenos Aires, Cristoph Willeke Floel, were sentenced to seventeen years for all twelve victims. Other officers sentenced to ten years and a day included Carlos López Tapia, the director of Villa Grimaldi, and Gladys Calderón Carreño, a DINA nurse known as "the cyanide angel" (el ángel del cianuro).[140] The sentence also included a civil element, whereby the state had to compensate victims' relatives for moral damages, with amounts ranging from 20 to 90 million Chilean pesos ($25,000 to $115,000).[141]

The verdict significantly acknowledged the role that the DINA Exterior Department had played in monitoring, detaining, torturing, murdering, and disappearing Chilean opponents to the Pinochet dictatorship who were located abroad.[142] In order to fulfill these objectives, the DINA had in 1974 set up the department and the intelligence and operational Mulchén Brigade that, headed by Major Iturriaga Neumann, comprised several operational groups. One of these, code-named "the Sharks" (los Tiburones) undertook operations abroad. Its agents included Christoph Willeke Floel, Ingrid Olderock, Michael Townley, and Armando Fernández Larios, among others.[143] Willeke Floel in particular had operated as the coordinator of the DINA network in Buenos Aires between 1976 and 1978, the time frame in which many victims had been kidnapped and murdered.[144] According to Sandro Gaete of the Investigations Police Human Rights Brigade, the DINA Exterior successfully operated outside of Chile through Condor, originally to hunt down JCR members but in practice to attempt eliminating all political opponents, wherever they lived.[145]

The judgment illuminated new details regarding the fates of some victims. For instance, former Socialist Party militant turned DINA collaborator Luz Arce Sandoval recounted how in 1975 she had overheard agent Miguel Krassnoff Martchenko, head of the DINA Caupolicán Brigade's Hawks groups (Halcones 1 y 2), which particularly pursued the MIR, make arrangements to pick up Fuentes Alarcón from Paraguay.[146] Krassnoff Martchenko and agent Osvaldo Pincetti Gac, who would hypnotize the victim to bring him back without problems, traveled to Asunción. Arce Sandoval corroborated the victim's subsequent presence at Villa Grimaldi, where he was imprisoned in a wooden shack and mistreated.

Two former Lautaro Brigade defendants positively identified Alexei Jaccard and provided details about his detention in Santiago's Simón Bolívar extermination camp. One agent recognized Jaccard from photos and narrated how he sometimes ate with some guards, that they had played ping pong or soccer together, and how he had told them about his studies and life in Switzerland, where his wife awaited him.[147] Another officer recounted the precise moments in which Jaccard and Héctor Velásquez Mardones had arrived at Simón Bolívar, escorted by Argentine officials who collaborated with agent Fernández Larios. The two prisoners were held for approximately two months before being murdered.[148] These revelations by former agents were crucial in clarifying these cases, given that there was until then no evidence that the two victims, who had disappeared in Argentina, had been transferred to Chile. The absence of any survivors from Simón Bolívar meant that information about it must necessarily come from the perpetrators.[149]

The Condor case in Chile focused largely on elucidating the victims' murders or abductions, only indirectly touching upon the structures of regional coordination. The investigative strategy reflected the dominant approach in most Chilean human rights trials: namely, to first validate that a victim was held in a specific detention center, and then to prosecute the agents who operated there and their superiors.[150] This framing, when applied to Operation Condor, was rather limited, and the proceedings missed the opportunity for probing notable aspects of the repressive coordination. The investigative logic remained squarely focused on the Chilean network of secret prisons and perpetrators in each case, as well as on the need to bypass amnesty protections, rather than attempting to understand the coordination's inner workings by using, for instance, the charge of *asociación ilícita* (criminal enterprise).[151]

Investigating Condor from Chile was no easy feat given that DINA's crossborder operations had mainly taken place outside national territory, which complicated attempts by lawyers and judges to compile information. Lawyer Karinna Fernández Neira recalled that many efforts had long focused on finding traces of Edgardo Enríquez, who was rumored to have been transferred to Chile, only later to discover that he had been clandestinely buried in Argentina. Conversely, the bodies of the Stoulmans, although all leads indicated they had been murdered in Argentina, were later found in Chile. The lack of evidence and misleading clues meant that many Chilean relatives faced solitary struggles in trying to determine the fate of their loved ones: "If they disappeared in Argentina," Chilean authorities conveniently told them, "what can we do here?"[152]

The Condor investigations and sentences were critically important in ascertaining the DINA Exterior Department's modus operandi and confirming that targeted victims had been returned to Chile to be interrogated and ultimately disappeared.[153] Indeed, agents' revelations on the presence of Jaccard and Velásquez in Santiago gave their families "the first precise information in years:

DINA's officers not only identified them from photos, but also provided specific details, which exactly matched the victims' personalities."[154] The families' decades-long struggles were thus vindicated: a close relative of Alexei had always thought that if he had passed by Chile and been seen, someone would speak out sooner or later, "since Alexei was an impossible person to forget" (*una persona muy difícil de olvidar*).[155]

The *episodio* Condor constructed a juridical truth which firmly established that the Chilean dictatorship—through the DINA—had closely participated in the regional terror network and that, owing to this system, its agents and associates had operated both regionally and beyond the continent to murder South American exiled opponents from the organized left.[156] These cases exceptionally illuminated the overlapping set of domestic and international operations that DINA had conducted, since victims—originally abducted abroad—were returned to clandestine prisons in Chile to be tortured and assassinated.[157]

As is often the case, the verdicts caused mixed feelings for victims' relatives. On one hand, they welcomed the sentences, which constituted an official acknowledgment by the Chilean state of the outrageous crimes the victims had suffered and ratified the information the families had been gathering over the years through significant challenges. On the other, the convictions—and especially the reduced prison terms—could not repair the loss of a loved one and the pain caused to their families for decades.[158] Some activists, lawyers, and family members considered that the sentences were insufficient in light of the unspeakable atrocities committed; Espinoza Bravo, for instance, received only fifteen years and one day for his role in abducting and murdering eleven victims.[159] Human rights lawyer Francisco Bustos believed that life imprisonment sentences could have been contemplated for some high-ranking defendants, such as Iturriaga Neumann, since they had taken advantage of their role as public officers to perpetrate transnational crimes and guarantee their own impunity.[160] Ultimately the judge condemned the defendants on charges of abduction and murder. The charge of *asociación ilícita* was not incorporated, which could have resulted in higher prison terms.[161] On this point, lawyer Magdalena Garcés noted how Chilean judges reluctantly apply *asociación ilícita* in human rights trials and prefer to sentence defendants for individual crimes (*delito único*)—generally either murder, kidnapping, or torture—rather than multiple wrongdoings, despite the fact that generally several offenses happened concurrently.[162] Appeals proceedings took place in July 2021, and a verdict was expected by late 2021.[163]

Probing Condor

Investigations in Chile and Uruguay into Operation Condor faced three main sets of difficulties and challenges. First, only limited information was initially available on the repressive bodies involved in the regional coordination. In Chile much secrecy surrounded the DINA, particularly its Exterior Department, and its covert network of military attachés in embassies and its interactions with other DINA departments.[164] The Human Rights Brigade, officially created in 2007 as a specialized unit of the Investigations Police but operating in practice since 1991, had a fundamental role in illuminating several of these unknown aspects of Chile's repressive structures in the Condor episode and many others.[165] Further, the Vicariate of Solidarity's archives and those of the Rettig Commission were instrumental in supporting judges with these complex criminal investigations given the lack of access to military records.[166] Likewise, in Uruguay, access to information from state archives, especially of the Ministries of Defense and Interior, was extremely reduced in the early and mid-2000s.[167] Furthermore, public prosecutors could not directly investigate but had to request judges to officially demand specific documentation to be rendered available in the proceedings.[168]

Second, investigations were especially protracted due to their complexity: they not only passed through the hands of several judges, but defense lawyers also pursued all possible appeals to delay their resolution. In Chile three different judges were involved in the *episodio* Condor, and each magistrate followed a distinct vision as to how to move forward.[169] Once proceedings finally entered the trial phase, one defense attorney submitted an appeal to the Constitutional Court in October 2017, claiming the violation of fundamental rights. The appeal was ultimately rejected in July 2018, but this nonetheless generated a delay of approximately one year, during which time trial proceedings were completely suspended for seven months.[170] In Uruguay all judicial rulings were constantly appealed before higher courts, and some historic Condor lawsuits that were filed in 1984 still remain in the pretrial phase over thirty-seven years later, amounting to a denial of justice for victims.

Third, relevant evidence, both archival and testimonial, had to be requested from neighboring countries, especially from Argentina and Paraguay, which contributed to the slowing down of proceedings. This was particularly the case in the initial investigative phases; more recently, cooperation mechanisms have become smoother: the digitization of archival and testimonies evidence, combined with the use of videoconferencing, has helped reduce delays.[171] Having to resort to diplomatic channels for judicial cooperation nonetheless meant that each request on average took six to eight months, which has been a significant obstacle in the smooth progress of the proceedings.[172] In Uruguay, petitioners sometimes had to resort to personal connections—when available—to ensure that such requests were followed up and were ultimately successful.[173]

The Chilean and Uruguayan investigations into the crimes of South America's repressive coordination have been scattered across many criminal cases, which have generally depended on the efforts of the impunity challengers who proactively filed them.[174] In Chile sentences have been delivered in six other lawsuits beyond the landmark 1995 Letelier case and the 2018 Condor episode.[175] Significantly, in June 2008 Judge Alejandro Solís condemned nine high-ranking DINA officials, including Contreras, for the 1974 murder of General Carlos Prats and his wife in Argentina; six high-ranking defendants were also sentenced for the first time on the charge of *asociación ilícita*, a verdict later ratified in 2010 by the Supreme Court.[176] As Chilean journalist Mónica González observed, nothing would have likely happened in Chile in the Prats case had it not been for the actions of the Argentine judiciary in the late 1990s, especially the investigation by Judge María Servini de Cubría into the general's murder and her extradition requests. These triggered the opening of a similar criminal case in Chile in January 2003 and the conviction years later of Contreras himself.[177] Additional investigations related to Condor probed the disappearance of three Chilean citizens in Argentina and of five Uruguayans in Chile in late 1973.[178]

In Uruguay fourteen criminal proceedings have specifically dealt with transnational atrocities and are at various stages of the judicial processes: so far, five sentences have been delivered, one was archived due to the defendant's death, one is at the trial stage, and seven remain in pretrial phases. Key figures of the dictatorship have been condemned in some of these cases. In October 2009 Judge Charles found former military dictator Gregorio Álvarez guilty of the homicide of thirty-seven Uruguayan and Argentine exiles,[179] while in June 2011, Montevideo's Criminal Judge of the Eleventh Circuit, Roberto Timbal, sentenced former civilian dictator Juan María Bordaberry and foreign minister Juan Carlos Blanco to thirty years for the assassination of Zelmar Michelini, Héctor Gutiérrez-Ruiz, William Whitelaw, and Rosario Barredo.[180] The ruling clearly stated that the Uruguayan politicians had no "involvement whatsoever in Argentine politics" and that their kidnappings and murders indisputably "had been determined by decisions taken at the highest levels of the Uruguayan government."[181] Finally, in September 2020 Uruguay's Supreme Court confirmed the thirty-year sentence against five military and police officers, including José Gavazzo, for the murder of María Claudia García.[182]

Final Reflections

Beginning in the late 1990s, the atrocities of South America's transnational repression became strategic tools in the hands of justice seekers who had been attempting for years to breach the prevalent impunity across the region. The Condor episode, which Judge Guzmán Tapia formally initiated in September 1999, contributed to undermining Pinochet's enduring power in democratic Chile. The investigation not only helped reverse a trend by which the country's higher courts systematically halted all criminal investigations against the general, but also established for the first time a direct connection between Pinochet and the DINA. Indeed, while Pinochet had repeatedly maintained he was unaware of his subordinates' actions, Chile's participation in "Condor, as a framework for repression among several countries, in fact demonstrated that Pinochet had to possess firsthand knowledge about it."[183] Similarly, in Uruguay the endurance of the Ley de Caducidad forced justice seekers "to look outside the country's borders and ground criminal lawsuits on Operation Condor atrocities."[184] Indeed, the crimes' transnational nature constituted a decisive factor in enabling Uruguayan courts to begin investigating and prosecuting these human rights violations; undoubtedly, most of the progress was achieved initially in Condor-related criminal investigations.[185]

In both Chile and Uruguay, the verdicts in Condor cases only touched upon the transnational terror network and devoted more attention to the particular roles and responsibilities of individual agents in the crimes probed. Nonetheless, the investigations substantially validated the role of domestic repressive structures and the participation of agents from the Chilean DINA and the Uruguayan SID, OCOA, and FUSNA in collaborative operations abroad. Lawyer Chargoñia observed how the Condor lawsuits exposed the real nature of state terror in South America; the fact that security agents could operate with "absolute freedom on foreign territories" to hunt down political exiles demonstrated their unchecked power.[186] The transnational network demonstrated the macrocriminality of South American dictatorships. These revelations enabled other justice seekers to file additional lawsuits in Uruguay to probe domestic human rights repression, increasingly grounded on the notion that all these crimes, both national and transnational, constituted crimes against humanity.

On both sides of the Andes, justice seekers catalyzed the shift from judicial impunity toward accountability. In Chile impunity challengers comprised numerous victims, their relatives, and their lawyers. For example, Gladys Marín and her lawyer Eduardo Contreras crucially filed the historic first complaint against Pinochet in January 1998, and their justice demands were reinforced by strategic facilitators including Judge Guzmán Tapia, who, against all odds and predictions, accepted the case and began a formal investigation against the still powerful former dictator. Pinochet's subsequent arrest in London, a result of the efforts of a transnational coalition of impunity challengers, generated additional pressure on Chile to begin criminal proceedings at home. Similarly, in Uruguay victims and their lawyers were the force behind the disintegration of a seemingly unbreakable policy of impunity in place since the mid-1980s. Relatives including Tota Quinteros and the families of Gelman, Washington Barrios, and Adalberto Soba, supported by lawyers such as Pablo Chargoñia and José Luis González, provided some of the early cases used for strategic litigation that eventually undermined impunity in Uruguay. Activists linked to the PIT-CNT's Human Rights Secretariat bolstered these efforts and also contributed to filing criminal cases regarding disappeared Uruguayan citizens in Spain, Italy, and Argentina.[187] A handful of justice seekers existed also within the Uruguayan state, namely criminal prosecutor Guianze and Judges Mota, Reyes, and Jubette, who willingly defied institutionalized impunity and facilitated victims' justice demands but paid high personal costs as a result of their actions. Last but not least, impunity challengers within the international sphere, including CEJIL and the Inter-American system, decisively sustained domestic efforts to challenge impunity in the *Gelman* case, which resulted in the crucial derogation of the Ley de Caducidad.

The next two chapters turn to a detailed consideration of two historic *mega-causas* in the courts of Argentina and Italy.

9 • Against Impunity
The Condor Trial in Argentina

On May 27, 2016, Federal Criminal Court No. 1 (Tribunal Oral en lo Criminal Federal No. 1; TOF1) in Buenos Aires delivered an unprecedented verdict in the struggle for justice for transnational atrocities in South America. Concluding a landmark trial, which had lasted three years, two months, and twenty-two days, presiding Judge Oscar Ricardo Amirante announced the resolution that condemned one Uruguayan and fourteen Argentine defendants for the abductions and torture of Uruguayan, Chilean, Argentine, Paraguayan, Bolivian, and Peruvian victims.[1] The accused were also sentenced for forming an *asociación ilícita* dedicated to committing extraterritorial human rights violations in South America.

May 27 was a typical autumn day, with gray skies and drizzling rain, similar to the weather I had left behind in Oxford two years earlier, when I had moved to Buenos Aires to monitor proceedings in this trial. The usual hustle and bustle of the downtown Comodoro Py's courthouses felt more intense on verdict day, in expectation of this long-awaited moment. Hundreds of people had registered to attend this historic occurrence, and the large audience filled four rooms, two of which had to be prepared for the occasion. I had never seen the courthouses so packed. Electric anticipation filled the air.

The conclusion of this extraordinary proceeding was a testament of the unyielding and inspirational endeavors of victims' relatives, survivors, and human rights lawyers in challenging the prevailing impunity in Argentina since the 1990s. In particular, the Argentine Condor trial broke new ground in human rights in two respects. First, it prosecuted for the first time atrocities of a transnational nature, both in terms of the nationality of victims and perpetrators and the location of the crimes. Second, it punished state officials for committing cross-border atrocities. This prosecution was the latest demonstration of Latin America's cutting-edge role in transitional justice innovations.

The trial exemplified a new kind of strategic litigation for human rights violations conducted in domestic tribunals discussed in this book. In this case, impunity challengers identified sets of crimes and defendants that the amnesty laws did not cover, filing lawsuits deliberately calculated to bypass them. Consequently, judges were compelled to begin investigations. This chapter retraces the origins of the trial and its ensuing progress at critical moments throughout its twenty-year history. It also outlines its main characteristics regarding victims and defendants, their nationalities, and the charges. The analysis primarily focuses on the first-instance phase, which I monitored in person and constituted the trial's most significant part, unfolding orally and publicly. Efforts by justice seekers are discussed, revealing the web of actors that supported the trial and noting the difficulties encountered; finally, the verdict's relevance nationally and internationally is evaluated.

Justice in Times of Impunity

Argentina's search for justice dates back to the mid-1980s, when the CONADEP and the Trial of the Juntas broke away with the country's past tradition of impunity and also began unraveling some of the features of the regional repressive coordination (see chapter 7). By the early 1990s, however, the sanctioning of amnesty laws and presidential decrees reduced the chances of justice, and, despite strong social protests opposing these measures, criminal investigations into dictatorship-era crimes were eventually closed.

Throughout the 1990s, only lawsuits probing instances of baby kidnapping progressed, since that crime was explicitly excluded in the amnesties. These litigation efforts were relatively successful. Between 1988 and 2005, Argentine courts sentenced twenty-three individuals for the illegal appropriation of children.[2] The potential group of perpetrators was significantly larger, however, given that approximately five hundred babies are estimated to have been stolen. Pitted against this difficult scenario of "absolute closure at the institutional level,"[3] activists and lawyers ingeniously sought ways to obtain justice on a larger scale. According to the Condor trial prosecutors, "human rights groups and victim associations absolutely galvanized all investigations occurring after the enactment of the impunity laws. Without them, nothing would have happened."[4]

These impunity challengers were active on four complementary fronts.[5] First, on the international sphere, justice seekers had attempted—beginning in the early 1980s—to initiate criminal proceedings to probe dictatorship-era crimes in foreign courts.[6] Since many Argentines were descended from European immigrants, relatives could file lawsuits in countries such as Spain, Germany, and Italy. Such efforts began to succeed in 1990, when a Parisian court sentenced in absentia infamous ESMA officer Alfredo Astiz to life imprisonment for the 1977 kidnapping and murder of French nuns Alice Domon and Léonie Duquet.[7] Several other officers, including former dictators Jorge Videla and Eduardo Massera, were successively indicted throughout the 1990s and 2000s. The reverberations from these trials conducted in European courts were felt strongly in Argentina and directly contributed to reactivating local accountability efforts. According to former CELS lawyer Marcos Kotlik, those proceedings "hurt the pride of Argentine judges," and pushed them to investigate dictatorship crimes at home.[8]

Second, on the domestic front, a group of relatives closely connected to the CELS successfully pushed for the right to truth and established the truth trials in the early 2000s, which crucially aided the process of chipping away at impunity and provided an alternative path for victims and relatives to achieve some accountability (see chapter 6).

Third, existing prosecutions for baby kidnapping were taken one step further. On December 30, 1996, lawyers Alberto Pedroncini and David Baigún, with Julio Maier and Ramón Torres Molina, filed the first of two strategic court cases directly challenging impunity, presented on behalf of six members of the Abuelas NGO, namely Estela Carlotto, María Isabel Chorobik, Cecilia Fernández, Elsa Pavón, Rosa Tarlovsky, and Rosaria Valenzi.[9] The complaint on the systematic plan to appropriate minors (*plan sistemático de apropiación de menores*) alleged that families loyal to the dictatorship had unlawfully adopted babies born to women in clandestine detention, and that this had amounted to a systematic plan. Back in 1985, the Trial of the Juntas had documented the occurrence of child kidnappings but could not demonstrate that it had unfolded in an organized format.[10] As investigations advanced, several emblematic dictatorship figures were indicted in the late 1990s for baby theft, abduction, and forgery.[11] Eventually, in July 2012 Buenos Aires's Federal Criminal Court No. 6 condemned Videla to fifty years in prison and another ten defendants to lesser sentences—from five to forty years—for the plight of thirty-four stolen babies, further acknowledging the systematic nature of this practice.[12]

Fourth, a criminal investigation was opened into Operation Condor as a result of the second case that Pedroncini and Baigún had presented before the courts in 1999, with the support of Albor Ungar, Carlos Zamorano, and the APDH. The Condor and the *plan sistemático* cases were the keystones of this resourceful strategic litigation that eventually undermined judicial paralysis in Argentina.[13] According to Judge Daniel Rafecas, the struggles of human rights and victim groups gradually produced "cracks and holes in the wall of impunity" (*muralla de impunidad*).[14]

The Condor Trial

The original complaint (*querella*) was presented to the federal courts in Buenos Aires on November 8, 1999, on behalf of six women who were relatives of Condor victims—Chilean Dora Carreño, Paraguayan Idalina Radice, Uruguayan Sara Méndez, and Argentines Elsa Pavón and Claudia and Ana María Careaga. The crime of *desaparición forzada* (enforced disappearance), categorized as aggravated deprivation of liberty in the Argentine Criminal Code (article 144), stood at the heart of the lawsuit, but other charges, including *asociación ilícita*, were also included.[15] The querella encompassed seven desaparecidos, namely Chilean Cristina Carreño, Paraguayans Federico Tatter and María Esther Ballestrino, twenty-one-day-old Uruguayan Simón Riquelo, and Argentines Mónica Grinspón and Claudio Logares with their two-year-old daughter, Paula. These victims had vanished between 1976 and 1978 in Argentina and Uruguay, and their disappearances shared two elements: they had unfolded in more than one country and were all partially committed on Argentine territory. Pedroncini deliberately chose victims from different countries and the charge of deprivation of liberty for strategic purposes, given that notwithstanding amnesties and pardons, the judiciary had to investigate these kidnappings as ongoing crimes.[16] An Argentine prosecutor noted how this stratagem was irrefutable, because the state had the ethical and constitutional obligation to investigate before potentially applying an amnesty or pardon to the crimes alleged.[17]

The second main charge of *asociación ilícita*, which is similar to the crime of conspiracy under UK and US laws, penalizes under the Argentine Criminal Code (article 210 and 210 bis) participation in a criminal group, irrespective of whether a crime is eventually committed. It constitutes a particularly serious crime that carries severe penalties ranging from three to ten years, and up to twenty in its aggravated form.[18] Pedroncini used *asociación ilícita* intentionally, as he strived to identify the wrongdoings that the amnesties did not cover. Because of its gravity, he hoped that judges would not shut down the investigation as rapidly as they normally did when other types of accusations were employed.[19]

The original querella explicitly named seventeen high-ranking South American officers as responsible for establishing a criminal organization devoted to carrying out unlawful cross-border detentions, using state apparatuses and resources. They included former Argentine dictator Jorge Videla and First Army Corps General Carlos Suárez Mason; Chilean former dictator Pinochet and the former head of DINA Manuel Contreras; Paraguayan former dictator Alfredo Stroessner, the head of the Capital Police Francisco Brítez, and the head of the Investigations Department Pastor Coronel; and from Uruguay, the head of the armed forces Julio Vadora and six agents who had operated on Argentine territory, including José Gavazzo, Manuel Cordero, and Hugo Campos Hermida.[20] The deliberate inclusion of foreign officials also permitted a circumvention of the amnesties, since "those laws could by no means shield foreign accused."[21]

Overall, the querella had three main goals. First, on a personal level, the families wanted to have the judiciary investigate the fate of their missing loved ones.[22] Second, the lawyers wished to demonstrate the existence of an agreement among South America's dictatorships to persecute political opponents, and particularly to document Argentina's role within it. Third, they aimed to contribute to the larger process of defying impunity;[23] Paraguayan Federico Tatter, son of one of the victims, recalled "Pedroncini and Baigún's brilliant minds" and their daily attempts to develop ideas to outsmart the amnesties, including by using the charge of *asociación ilícita*.[24] During the 1990s, South America's darkest years of impunity, the Condor investigation represented an *estrellita en la noche* (a little star in the night).[25]

The End of Amnesty

Between 2000 and 2003, the querella proceeded slowly in the *etapa de instrucción* (pretrial phase) before Buenos Aires's Seventh Federal Court for Criminal and Correctional Matters.[26] The prevailing impunity, combined with the complex economic and social crisis that overtook Argentina in 2001 and 2002, created a generally adverse scenario. Against this backdrop, investigative Judge Adolfo Bagnasco focused on gathering testimonies and archival documents so that these would be readily available when proceedings could progress under more advantageous future circumstances.[27]

Change was looming on the horizon. The 1998 derogation of the amnesties by Argentina's Congress meant that these laws could no longer be applied, but their effects remained vis-à-vis cases already filed. In an attempt to remove this lingering obstacle, the CELS developed an innovative legal argument in a case regarding stolen baby Claudia Poblete, which the Abuelas had originally filed in 1998. In late 2000 the CELS requested that judges investigate the torture and disappearance of Claudia's parents, José Poblete and Gertrudis Hlaczik, soliciting a declaration that the amnesties were unconstitutional on the basis of a fundamental contradiction these laws generated: namely, that courts could prosecute individuals responsible for baby kidnapping and identity alteration, but not for the initial crime of the parents' disappearance.[28] In March 2001 first-instance Federal Judge Gabriel Cavallo accepted this contention and unprecedentedly declared the amnesties unconstitutional, further affirming that they violated international law; his verdict was ratified on appeal in November 2001.[29] At this juncture, Judge Cavallo acted as a strategic facilitator, buttressing the efforts of the activists and lawyers who had filed the claim and contributing to achieving justice in this specific case and to broadly undermining impunity in the long term. This declaration of unconstitutionality, however, only applied to the *Poblete/Simón* case and lacked broader applicability to other proceedings.

In the early 2000s, the Condor investigation took only small steps forward. Former CELS lawyer Luz Palmás Zaldua noted that "there was never a judicial resolution nor prosecutor statement affirming the Condor lawsuit should not continue because of the impunity laws. And this is the particularity of this case, that it was not archived. It did not progress as quickly as we wished, but the strategy of focusing on disappearances as permanent crimes allowed the lawsuit to move forward. This was the juridical bet [of Pedroncini], to begin generating fissures at a time when judicial proceedings were still closed."[30]

After Judge Bagnasco's retirement in January 2001, Judge Rodolfo Canicoba Corral took on the investigation.[31] Significant progress occurred in April 2001 when the judge indicted defendants for *asociación ilícita*,[32] while in July he also requested the extradition of various high-ranking accused, including Stroessner and Vadora.[33] The investigation largely centered on the high command: the crime of conspiracy covers the agreement to commit unspecific crimes, and each Condor country's top officials were deemed responsible.

In September Videla was further charged with seventy-two enforced disappearances.[34] Judge Canicoba Corral contended that the disappearances violated both national and international law, and he resorted to the Inter-American Convention on Forced Disappearances to argue that "no barriers to prosecution, such as statute of limitations, applied because disappearances are continuing crimes."[35] The judge also demanded the arrest and extradition of the Uruguayan officers accused of kidnapping and disappearing Uruguayans in Argentina.

Under President Néstor Kirchner (2003–7), the political context significantly shifted toward accountability. In August 2003 the Congress passed Law 25.779, which annulled the amnesties. A year later, the investigation into the murder of General Prats further consolidated positive progress. In this case, the Supreme Court of Justice established for the first time in Argentine jurisprudence that statutory limitations should not apply to crimes against humanity, and thus opened the door to additional investigations into dictatorship crimes.[36] In June 2005 the Supreme Court moreover ruled on the unconstitutionality of the amnesties in the *Poblete/Simón* case and thereby signaled that, after two decades of impunity, judicial proceedings could finally reopen.[37]

Opportunities for Justice

As Argentina's structure of impunity began to disintegrate, the Condor investigation witnessed a "qualitative jump."[38] Between 2003 and 2007 it mushroomed, with the addition of numerous victims and defendants. Yet there were continuing significant delays.[39] The restart of criminal trials in 2006 saw the judiciary handling hundreds of intricate proceedings that tribunals were initially ill-prepared to manage. Ordinary criminal judges, normally used to tackling isolated crimes such as murders and robberies, suddenly had to confront multifaceted investigations that often encompassed hundreds of victims and perpetrators, involving multiple overlapping and systematic atrocities.[40] Basic logistical issues also needed to be resolved. For example, only a few courtrooms were initially available to hold hearings in Buenos Aires, and the lack of suitable venues generated a backlog of cases and the postponement of many trials. This remained a problem until 2010.[41] Other delays resulted from procedural matters. TOF1 was scheduled to hear proceedings in two separate cases: the first regarded the crimes committed in Orletti, and the second involved various Condor atrocities. The judges eventually prioritized the Orletti trial to safeguard due process guarantees and the defendants' rights, since they were all in preventive detention, unlike the Condor defendants.[42]

Obstacles in the international sphere complicated these national-level difficulties. The multicountry search for evidence inevitably slowed down proceedings. The transnational nature of Condor meant that prosecutors and judges had to compile relevant evidence, both testimonial and archival, not only in

Argentina but in neighboring countries too.[43] Official international requests for information through ministries of foreign affairs took on average at least a year to be processed; upon receipt, many documents had to be translated into Spanish for incorporation into the case.[44]

Finally, extradition requests generated resistance in the receiving countries, especially Brazil. Of the eight requests issued in 2001, only one—that of former Uruguayan army intelligence agent Manuel Cordero—was ultimately successful, largely owing to the determination of impunity challengers. Uruguayan journalist Roger Rodríguez and Brazilian activist Jair Krischke located Cordero, who was living in the Brazilian border city of Santana do Livramento. After several twists and turns, he was finally apprehended in 2005 when he went to the Uruguayan consulate to sign a proxy that would enable his brother-in-law to collect his pension.[45] After a lengthy judicial process, his extradition to Argentina finally went ahead in January 2010.[46]

In November 2007 a major step forward was taken when Judge Sergio Torres, by then investigating the case, concluded pretrial investigations in the first Condor dossier and submitted it for trial proceedings. *Condor I,* as it is known, included thirteen defendants, who stood accused of *asociación ilícita* and 108 disappearances.[47] This was the biggest case file, and the remaining portions—*Condor II* and *III,* begun in 2008 and 2011, respectively—would be submitted for trial in August 2011 and May 2012.[48] Chief Prosecutor Pablo Ouviña contended that the Condor investigation could be compared "to a jug of water that fills several glasses: each glass contains a separate portion of the investigation, but the jug remains the same, so all the glasses tap into the same source."[49]

Meanwhile, criminal investigations regarding Orletti reached the trial phase in June 2010. The Orletti and Condor investigations were tightly interrelated, since Orletti was the secret prison where the largest number of Condor victims was imprisoned in Argentina. Proceedings evolved in parallel, in the hands of two judges: Judge Rafecas oversaw the Orletti investigations as part of the broader case probing the crimes of the First Army Corps (Primer Cuerpo del Ejército), while Judge Torres dealt instead with other *mega-causas* such as the Condor and ESMA proceedings.[50] The Condor case was unique in that it only comprised disappearances, while Orletti encompassed a broader set of crimes, including torture and executions.[51] On April 1, 2011, Buenos Aires's TOF1 condemned four defendants in *Orletti I,* namely former General Eduardo Cabanillas, former AAA and SIDE intelligence agents Eduardo Ruffo and Honorio Martínez, and civilian intelligence agent Raúl Guglielminetti, for the unlawful detention of sixty-five prisoners, with sentences ranging from twenty-five years to life imprisonment.[52] Afterward, the court turned to the Condor proceedings.

The Trial

On March 5, 2013, well over a decade after the filing of the original querella, the Condor trial finally started in Buenos Aires before Judges Oscar Ricardo Amirante, Adrián Federico Grünberg, Pablo Gustavo Laufer, and Substitute Judge Ricardo Ángel Basílico. Since 1999 the court case had grown exponentially, encompassing three Condor dossiers and one for Orletti; the initial seven victims and seventeen defendants had increased to 173 and twenty-seven, respectively. The accused included one Uruguayan defendant and twenty-six Argentine officers, of which twenty-four had belonged to the army and one to the navy; the remaining officer was the only individual indicted in the *Orletti II* dossier, namely SIDE agent Miguel Ángel Furci.[53] Among the defendants were symbolic figures of the Argentine dictatorship, including former dictator Reynaldo Benito Bignone (1982–83) and Fourth Army Corps Commander Santiago Omar Riveros. The trial also included other high-ranking officers who had overseen the implementation of repression, including Carlos Caggiano Tedesco, in charge of Misiones province, and Enrique Olea, for the Neuquén and Río Negro provinces.

The trial retained the original focus on high-ranking defendants. This reflected the decision by activists, lawyers, and prosecutors to target the *asociación ilícita*'s intellectual authors, and also the fact that the crimes' direct perpetrators were often unidentified.[54] Consequently, twenty-five defendants were prosecuted as *autores mediatos* (perpetrators by means) for occupying decision-making posts and giving orders, and were tried for illegal kidnappings and *asociación ilícita*. Conversely, Cordero and Furci were indicted as *autores materiales* (material authors) for directly committing abductions and torture,[55] and they faced different charges.[56] Cordero, because of his extradition's terms, could only be prosecuted for kidnappings; the Brazilian Supremo Tribunal Federal (Federal Supreme Court) had in fact dropped the *asociación ilícita* accusation by applying statutory limitations under Brazilian law. Furci was the only person accused of illegal detentions and torture against the *Orletti II* victims. Overall, there were 173 victims: 106 victims in the three Condor dossiers and 67 victims in *Orletti II*. When broken down by nationality, the 106 Condor victims comprised forty-seven Uruguayans, twenty-one Chileans, seventeen Argentines, eleven Paraguayans, nine Bolivians, and one Peruvian.[57]

Much anticipation marked the beginning of the trial, both in Argentina and abroad. Prosecutor Ouviña asserted how trials for crimes against humanity "transcend individual interest, concerning not only victims and relatives, but the entire society."[58] The focus on the repressive coordination made the case highly relevant across South America, since victims in neighboring countries had long been waiting for answers. "Not only were our fellow [Argentine] nationals watching us, but *all our neighbors were too*," Ouviña noted.[59]

Two months into the trial, in May 2013, Videla died. The death amounted, for prosecutors Ouviña and Mercedes Moguilansky, to "the worst of our nightmares," since Videla had been one of the most significant heads of the *asociación ilícita*, charged exclusively with the disappearance of forty-four victims.[60] His passing had major procedural consequences beyond its powerful symbolic impact. Eventually investigations into all the crimes attributed to Videla continued, in order to satisfy the victims' right to truth and given that the *asociación ilícita* involved a series of interconnected crimes. The downside was that ultimately no one was sentenced for numerous disappearances.[61]

The oral and public phase of the proceedings unfolded in two stages. The first, the *recepción de prueba* (admission of evidence), was the longest, lasting from May 2013 to April 2015. For almost two years, the prosecution and defense probed hundreds of testimonies and several types of evidence. Owing to the large number of countries and victims, the court structured this phase in *binomios* (dyads of two countries), combining the countries to discuss testimonies, evidence, and documents.[62] Proceedings started with the Argentina–Uruguay dyad, which constituted the biggest group of victims, followed by the remaining countries. The *recepción de prueba* played an indispensable role in piecing together the Condor puzzle, reconstructing the circumstances regarding each disappearance and simultaneously assembling the elements needed to demonstrate the terror network's modus operandi. The court received over two hundred testimonies from survivors, victims' relatives, document analysts, and other experts. Witnesses traveled to Buenos Aires from nearby countries or, in many cases, testified from the premises of Argentine consulates abroad. The tribunal was especially conscious of the needs of survivors and relatives; for some individuals, giving testimony constituted a form of reparation and catharsis, while others might experience health-related or psychological conditions that prevented them from testifying.[63] Therefore, several testimonies already given in previous trials, especially *Orletti I*, were incorporated into the proceedings without having to call the same witnesses to declare again.

A large amount of documentary evidence, including academic books, jour-nalistic investigations, and thousands of archival records from Argentina, Bra-zil, Uruguay, Chile, the United States, and Paraguay, was also scrutinized. The testimonies of Carlos Osorio of the NSA, Rosa Palau of Paraguay's Archives of Terror, Veronica Almada from the Argentine Ministry of Defense, and Claudia Bellingeri of the DIPPBA were instrumental in helping the judges appreciate the documentary evidence that corroborated Condor's inner workings. This first stage was fundamental in demonstrating that the 106 Condor victims did not constitute isolated incidents but were part of a systematic and coordinated pattern of transnational crimes.

The second phase, the *alegatos* (prosecution and defense arguments), pro-ceeded between June 2015 and April 2016. Jaime Nuguer, the lawyer for the original querella after Pedroncini's retirement, appeared first before the judges and argued that "the accusations presented back in 1999 had been entirely proven, through the extraordinary wealth of high-quality proof."[64] Other pri-vate prosecutors followed afterward.[65] Martín Rico, a lawyer for Argentina's Secretaría de Derechos Humanos y Pluralismo Cultural (Human Rights and Cultural Pluralism Secretariat), reiterated "Argentina's firm and unwavering commitment to investigate dictatorship crimes," distancing the state from its previous role as a perpetrator of human rights violations.[66] Lastly, the *querella unificada* (joint pleas by CELS, Kaos, and the Argentine League of Human Rights) observed that the cases under scrutiny provided only a narrow window into a much larger universe of victims, but they sufficiently demonstrated the participation of all Condor states. Lawyer Palmás Zaldua reflected how "South America's criminal states created a truly transnational criminal pact to coordi-nate their individual projects of repression, with Operation Condor constituting the apex of this collaboration."[67]

The public prosecution outlined its argument for four months. The prose-cutors stressed that Condor had constituted "a criminal organization by illegit-imate states, which coordinated their structures and resources to commit the most serious crimes against humanity."[68] They further contended that Condor had standardized preexisting regional coordination practices, taking them to the next level and setting up a new framework and structure to facilitate re-gional collaboration, whether bilateral or multilateral.[69] The prosecution had three goals in the trial: "first, to discover the truth . . . , second for the perpe-trators to face criminal responsibility for their crimes in court and third, but profoundly interconnected [with the first two goals], to give answers to the victims."[70] This trial constituted the first judicial response specifically focusing on Condor and was therefore unprecedented in the region.

Between December 2015 and April 2016, private and public defense lawyers presented their arguments. Lawyer Eduardo San Emeterio, defending Cordero, was the first of the private attorneys to appear. He asked to show a video he and other lawyers had prepared, immediately provoking a storm of opposition.[71] Public and private prosecutors vehemently resisted its screening, contending that the admission-of-evidence phase had ended months previously, and that San Emeterio had had ample previous opportunities to request the video's incorporation as evidence. The tribunal concurred, noting that it had always accepted relevant evidence throughout the trial and that the defense should have filed it earlier. In his subsequent presentation, San Emeterio claimed that all trials post-2005 violated constitutional norms protecting defendants. All the private lawyers carried out a largely ideological defense for their six accused clients,[72] drawing upon traditional discourses of war and asserting that the actions of guerrilla groups had provoked the reaction of the armed forces. Next the four public defense lawyers, who represented eleven accused officers,[73] put forward more technical arguments in their pleas. Chief Attorney Pamela Bisserier contended that their position rested on two key unconstitutionality claims regarding the charge of *asociación ilícita,* because of its normative uncertainty, and the imposition of severe prison sentences against elderly defendants.[74]

The Ruling

After thirty-eight months of public hearings, survivors and victims' relatives packed the courtroom in Buenos Aires on sentence day, as well as the Argentine consulates in Santiago, Asunción, La Paz, and Montevideo, where it was livestreamed. Journalists from major international outlets including the *New York Times,* the *Washington Post,* and the BBC attended too.

By 2016 only seventeen of the initial twenty-seven defendants remained; ten had either passed away or been deemed unfit to stand trial due to poor health. The judges found fifteen defendants guilty and sentenced them to prison terms ranging from eight to twenty-five years.[75] Three defendants were condemned to the highest permitted penalty of twenty-five years: Santiago Riveros (the commander of the Institutos Militares in the Campo de Mayo military base), Furci, and Cordero. Former dictator Bignone received twenty years, as did Rodolfo Feroglio, director of the Campo de Mayo's Infantry School. Federico Minicucci, head of the Third "Gral. Belgrano" Infantry Battalion in Buenos

Aires province, received the most lenient sentence of eight years. The two former directors of Mendoza's Military Lyceum, Juan Rodríguez and Carlos Tragant, were acquitted.

The verdicts reverberated outside Argentina, making headlines in numerous international newspapers,[76] with Spain's *El País* noting that Argentina had been the first country to condemn the leaders of Operation Condor.[77] Such widespread international repercussions are quite unusual for human rights trials.[78] Certainly never before had a court of law handed down verdicts regarding crimes against humanity perpetrated by "a transnational *asociación ilícita*, dedicated to illegally exchanging information and intelligence, and persecuting, kidnapping, forcefully repatriating, torturing and murdering political activists in the Southern Cone."[79] This was in fact the first time a tribunal had acknowledged such a conspiracy had taken place internationally.

In their verdicts, the judges linked Condor's origins to the geopolitical context of the Cold War, devoting significant attention to the influence of the National Security and French School doctrines.[80] The magistrates especially noted that unofficial mechanisms of information exchange and prisoner deportations had existed in the early 1970s and were implemented through "gentlemen's pacts."[81] These prior practices facilitated the formalization of Condor in November 1975. The tribunal outlined how the system had constituted a platform that "homogenized practices of coordinated repression already existing in the region and [that] involved the provision of human, material, and technical resources . . . to enable the annihilation or eradication of political opponents—actual or potential—whether they were individuals or organizations."[82] In the judges' opinion, there was no doubt that Condor operated as an institutionalized and enduring transnational network.

Furthermore, the justices observed that Condor member states had efficiently and deliberately suspended traditional norms of international relations, including national sovereignty and territorial integrity. The states also repeatedly breached the internationally accepted right to asylum and a long tradition of protecting refugees. Instead, all Condor countries had coordinated the politically motivated harassment of both nationals and foreign citizens, many of whom were under UNHCR protection. Indeed, starting in the late 1950s, thousands of exiles had fled the dictatorships in Paraguay, Brazil, Bolivia, Uruguay, and Chile. A large number settled in Argentina, which by 1973 had been the only country left in the region under relatively democratic rule. After 1976, most Condor crimes unsurprisingly happened in Argentina, as the magistrates remarked: "Being the stronghold where activists and opponents to different dictatorships were situated, this country was dialectically converted from a sanctuary into a hunting ground in which they [the exiles] were trapped."[83]

The court observed how the transnational terror network operated outside of any jurisdictional control. Condor had disregarded all borders and unleashed a systematic campaign of atrocities encompassing kidnappings, torture, sexual violence, executions, illegal raids, thefts, baby kidnapping, extortion, and threats across the territories of its members and beyond. The judges emphasized that the armed forces, together with security and intelligence agencies, played a primary role in executing the Condor agreement, but that civilian structures, including the diplomatic corps and immigration and border control agencies, also contributed. This acknowledgment was particularly significant in conveying how transnational terror drew upon all the available national resources, whether military or civilian, at the member states' disposal.

The tribunal thus firmly established that South America's criminal states had coordinated their repressive policies, and that "this alliance among the repressive forces, systematic and coordinated in its clandestine nature, was nothing less than a vast and transnational *asociación ilícita*."[84] The judges also noted that this transnational association coexisted concurrently with other national-level *asociaciones ilícitas,* set up locally inside each member country, and that they shared members and resources to perpetrate crimes.[85]

The Disappearance of Agustín Goiburú

The story of Agustín Goiburú, a Paraguayan doctor exiled in Argentina, offers an illustrative example of transnational operations. Goiburú, married and father of three children, was illegally detained on February 9, 1977, in the city of Paraná, northeast Argentina, after suffering decades of persecution from the Paraguayan dictatorship. As a young doctor, he had worked in the Rigoberto Caballero police hospital in Asunción. In 1958 he had been one of the founders of the MOPOCO, a political group opposing the Stroessner dictatorship. At the time, he also denounced the torture and inhuman treatment that regime opponents suffered. Eventually he was forced to resign from the hospital for refusing to sign false death certificates, which covered up the real circumstances of political prisoners dying during torture. The dictatorship ceaselessly harassed the doctor, and he finally sought refuge in the Uruguayan Embassy. In 1959 he settled in Posadas, a frontier city in Misiones province, Argentina.

From Argentina the doctor continued denouncing Stroessner's atrocities.

In the Paraná River Agustín saw firsthand the floating bodies of brutally tortured young men, dumped from Paraguayan Army planes.[86] Meanwhile, the dictatorship devised plans to detain Goiburú. In November 1969 the Stroessner regime's claws reached him for the first time: the Paraguayan Navy seized the doctor while he was fishing in the Paraná River, in Argentine territorial waters, with his son Rolando and two friends. Goiburú was immediately flown to Asunción, where his wife located him three months later.[87] Owing to international pressure, he was eventually moved to a police station from which, along with a group of fellow prisoners, he successfully escaped in December 1970 after digging an underground tunnel. Receiving asylum at the Chilean Embassy, Goiburú was later reunited with his family in Argentina.

This escape caused further embarrassment to Stroessner, and Goiburú became the dictatorship's number one enemy.[88] In 1974 his persecution worsened after he was accused of being the mastermind behind a foiled assassination attempt against the dictator. In December 1974 two armed men entered the family house; Goiburú's oldest son Rogelio, his brother, and some neighbors managed to capture one of them, Paraguayan policeman Bernardo Cocco, who later confessed that the head of the Paraguayan police had hired him to kill Goiburú. The doctor was no longer safe in Posadas and began recording in a diary all the cars and individuals following him.[89] In February 1975 the family moved to Paraná, 780 kilometers away from Asunción, but distance was no obstacle to the Stroessner regime. In 1975 another kidnapping failed at the last moment. A report that year by the Paraguayan Armed Forces corroborated the regime's fixation: it labeled Goiburú as "elusive and dangerous" and recommended that, should he be located and detained, "personnel working specifically on that case could travel [to Argentina]."[90]

After the Argentine coup of 1976, Goiburú's situation became even more precarious. Argentine and Paraguayan officers, as well as diplomatic officials, continually surveilled the doctor and his family. Indeed, Paraguayan consul Francisco Ortiz Tellez closely monitored the Paraguayan community of exiled opponents in northern Argentina, regularly reporting on their gatherings and whereabouts.[91]

By early 1977 yet another detention plan, code-named Safari,[92] was crafted, with every detail painstakingly arranged, since the security forces knew that Goiburú adopted safety measures and possessed weapons both at home and at his clinic.[93] The plot was that a group of four men, with two cars and appropriate weapons, would abduct the doctor on his way home from the clinic. The

day before, Goiburú was summoned to the local police station and kept waiting at length, before being told it had been a mistake.[94] While there he noticed
several people passing by and staring at him.[95]

The next day the abduction unfolded exactly as intended. Around midday,
on February 9, 1977, a green Ford Falcon crashed against Goiburú's parked
car. When the doctor exited to assess the damage, he was immediately grabbed
and forced into the car, which took off toward an unknown destination.[96] His
family immediately began a desperate search and eventually established that
he had been handed over to Paraguayan authorities shortly after his kidnapping. Various speculations concerning his fate circulated at the time.[97] A former political prisoner, Domingo Rolón, saw Dr. Goiburú inside Asunción's
Police Investigations Department in March 1977. The doctor asked him who
he was and later introduced himself, saying that he had been transferred from
Argentina.[98] An Argentine colonel also confirmed the doctor's clandestine rendition to Asunción. Despite the family's efforts, Goiburú was never released,
and his body was not found.

During the Condor trial, the Argentine judges considered Goiburú's detention and his ensuing repatriation to Paraguay to have taken place under Condor's framework. Undoubtedly, Paraguayan authorities had been interested in
ascertaining the doctor's whereabouts and in detaining him for several years
before his actual disappearance. Furthermore, the tribunal was fully convinced
that the Argentine and Paraguayan dictatorships had repeatedly exchanged
information about the victim.[99]

Goiburú's case plainly demonstrates the workings of transnational repression over the years, given that the doctor was recurrently targeted in 1969,
1974, and 1975 before his disappearance in 1977. His case also depicts the full
scope of regional collaboration that other exiles similarly faced: abandoning
one's country because of repeated political persecution, continued oppression
in the country of exile, and the victim's final silencing thanks to well-oiled
mechanisms of coordinated repression.

National and Regional Impact

By 2016, few doubted Condor's existence. Numerous journalists and academics had examined the terror network since the early 1990s, while survivors
had continually denounced its activities since the 1970s. The TOF1 verdict
provided the final missing piece in the long journey that justice seekers had

embarked upon decades earlier: a court of law formally acknowledged Condor's modus operandi and its legacy of atrocities throughout South America.

The Condor trial's proceeding was exceptional in five respects, owing to the transnational nature of the crimes probed. First, the tribunal collected and systematized possibly the largest corpus of evidence ever assembled concerning South America's extraterritorial atrocities. In a truly enormous and unparalleled undertaking, the judges collated in one place academic investigations, thousands of archival records, and hundreds of survivor and expert testimonies. According to Judge Adrián Grünberg, "We blended academic and journalistic research with archival records and, of course, witness statements: documents and books would have been incomplete without flesh-and-blood testimonies. This was the novelty of this trial."[100]

Carolina Varsky, a longtime human rights lawyer, formerly of CELS, observed that the extensive and rich documentary evidence had "allowed [the tribunal] to reveal what Condor had been, establish a juridical truth about it, and disclose the criminal arrangement amongst the dictatorships to eliminate common enemies."[101] Human rights trials usually draw exclusively upon the testimonies of survivors and victims' relatives.[102] But in this instance, thousands of archival records were scrutinized to better understand the complex system of transnational repression. As Judge Grünberg asserted, "in order to deliver a judgment on Condor, the tribunal symbolically and practically crossed borders too, assembling all the relevant evidence required."[103] Both the prosecutors and the magistrates methodically integrated the information that the archival records contained into their legal analyses. This unequaled archival evidence supplemented witness declarations in revealing the crimes perpetrated and uncovering the defendants' responsibility.[104]

Second, the tribunal did not merely accumulate evidence. Rather it assessed this evidentiary corpus according to strict legal criteria to confirm Condor's existence and its categorization as a transnational *asociación ilícita*, which had committed extraterritorial human rights violations in a systematic and coordinated fashion.[105] The tribunal proved beyond doubt the veracity of the *asociación ilícita*, since it had access to Condor's founding document—a very rare circumstance for this kind of case—which contained the signature of each country's representative on the November 28, 1975, agreement.[106] The court's recognition of a transnational criminal conspiracy represented "a remarkable juridical advancement."[107]

Some prior court cases relating to past atrocities had used the category of *asociación ilícita* to scrutinize the wrongdoings at the national level in Argentina and Chile. In 2004 Argentina's Supreme Court had established that Enrique Arancibia Clavel had been a member of the Chilean DINA, which had constituted an *asociación ilícita* dedicated to pursuing Pinochet's opponents beyond Chile's borders.[108] Several lower courts had also condemned defendants for participating in *asociaciones ilícitas* tasked with implementing political repression during the Argentine dictatorship.[109] Nevertheless, the 2016 verdict was the first in which a court probed an *asociación ilícita* at the international level, which had allowed the Condor states to jointly conduct repressive policies throughout the region.[110] This recognition was particularly remarkable if one recalls that this charge had been included in the original *querella* in 1999, a time when jurisprudence on these matters was still in its infancy.[111] The *asociación ilícita* accusation enabled the magistrates to release an extraordinary verdict on the very nature of Condor. Prosecutor Ouviña reflected that the tribunal "did not purely examine human rights violations committed against representative victims in a specific context, but also dissected and adjudicated *that very context*, deliberating [whether] it equaled an *asociación ilícita* and establishing the criminal responsibility of particular individuals within it."[112] Operation Condor had allowed South American dictatorships to exponentially amplify the strength, power, and effectiveness of their policies of political repression.

Third, the trial focused on the entire transnational network and its operations in six South American states. Earlier prosecutions generally focused on the atrocities that took place in a particular clandestine center, such as the Orletti prosecutions in Argentina, or specific episodes or subsets of victims in Chile. By focusing on the *asociación ilícita* itself, the tribunal portrayed the full lengths to which South America's criminal states went to hunt down opponents. By choosing illustrative cases involving different nationalities, political affiliations, and various crime locations, the judges examined Condor's entire modus operandi and better comprehended its geographical scope and brutality. By intentionally examining numerous transnational crimes, the court effectively put Operation Condor itself on trial.[113] The judges also carefully distinguished individual cases that clearly fell under Condor from those that formed part of local repression. Grünberg observed how, to qualify as a Condor case, evidence was required to prove information exchange among countries, joint operations, or clandestine renditions.[114]

Fourth, Cordero's extradition was a milestone, since he was the first foreign defendant to be sent to Argentina to face trial for human rights crimes. Previous extraditions always entailed Argentine citizens being repatriated—for instance, from Mexico and Spain—to stand trial in their native country.[115] Cordero's extradition also had a significant impact in Brazil. In authorizing the extradition in 2009, the Brazilian Federal Supreme Court accepted that disappearances amounted to kidnappings, and thus statutory limitations could not apply to these permanent crimes. This was a noteworthy achievement, since Brazil still remains the only Condor country where an amnesty law (sanctioned in 1979) has repeatedly hampered accountability efforts, and no final criminal verdict for dictatorship era atrocities has ever been achieved.[116]

Lastly, the prosecution further illustrated that domestic courts can effectively assess the extraterritorial conduct of states, and that state agents can be found criminally responsible for cross-border crimes. By entwining jurisdictional grounds based on territoriality and passive personality (i.e., victims' nationality, which envisages that states can initiate prosecutions, in limited cases, for offenses committed abroad against their citizens), the Argentine magistrates addressed transnational crimes for the first time and found state agents responsible for extraterritorial atrocities. The trial's cases encompassed offenses perpetrated against both foreign citizens in Argentina (territoriality) and Argentine victims in other Condor countries (passive personality). This novel double framing enabled the court to probe human rights violations in two complementary ways. First, when looking into atrocities against exiles in Argentina, the magistrates considered the role of Argentine agents operating in tandem with foreign counterparts, who intentionally traveled to Argentina from adjacent countries to seize refugees of interest to the dictatorial regimes. Second, when examining crimes perpetrated abroad against Argentines, the court evaluated the collaboration of Argentine security agents with local counterparts who apprehended Argentine citizens in exile in several South American countries. Overall, the judges exposed the whole machinery of transnational terror by combining the complementary lenses of territorial and passive personality jurisdictions. This probing of states' extraterritorial behavior was particularly groundbreaking in human rights and represented a noteworthy step forward when pitted against prior justice efforts, which had mainly considered a state's conduct inside territorial borders.

As expected, the verdict resonated widely across the region, where Argentina undoubtedly has stood out for its progress in accountability. Uruguayan lawyer Pablo Chargoñia affirmed that "Argentina is a sort of lighthouse," leading the way in accountability standards.[117] The day of the verdict, the courtroom on Comodoro Py Avenue in Buenos Aires was overflowing with people who had traveled from Uruguay, Paraguay, and Chile. The sentence was tremendously significant for these survivors and relatives, given that justice still remains hard to attain in their countries.

In 2016 human rights lawyers hoped that the Argentine verdict could further accountability attempts elsewhere, spurring neighboring countries to probe the responsibility of their own officials in Condor.[118] Lawyer Marcos Kotlick envisioned that owing to Uruguay's proximity to Argentina and the close relations between the two, a contagion effect and international pressure, similar to what Argentina had experienced when European trials shamed local judges into action, might encourage the Uruguayan judiciary to follow suit.[119]

The sentence undeniably set an important precedent and provided a formidable potential tool for regional activists and lawyers to pressure their local governments and judiciaries to begin similar prosecutions. Unfortunately, six years later, a renewal of accountability endeavors has not materialized. No significant developments have unfolded in Brazil or Paraguay, nor are they likely to, now that right-wing governments, closely connected to and nostalgic of the former dictatorships, govern both countries. In Uruguay only timid steps have been taken. The Argentine sentence was crucially relevant there, since half of the trial's victims were Uruguayan, as was the only foreign defendant. Uruguayan activists and lawyers have continually urged the judiciary and the government to promote accountability. However, a lack of political will and the still-powerful veto players—mostly the Supreme Court of Justice and the military—continue to contribute to maintaining a high rate of impunity: Uruguayan judges had delivered sentences in just sixteen cases as of November 2021.[120] There seems little hope for change, since a new center-right government coalition will govern until 2025, and it has shown little interest, if not outright opposition, to accountability.

Final Reflections

The Argentine Condor trial represented a pioneering moment in South America's search for truth and justice for the horrors of the recent past. According to lawyer Martín Rico, the verdict could potentially become a leading precedent in international jurisprudence, given its groundbreaking focus on a transnational network by criminal states.[121] Former Uruguayan judge Mariana Mota believes that the proceedings transcended the legal sphere, contributing to the construction of knowledge and collective memory about South America's transnational state terror. The verdict could help challenge justificatory narratives focusing on "internal or dirty wars" against subversion and demonstrate instead the existence of coordinated policies and a common doctrine shared by criminal states to violently repress political opposition.[122]

Survivors and victims' relatives welcomed the verdict and expressed satisfaction with the work of the tribunal and the public prosecution. Providing testimony during the trial was a cathartic experience for many non-Argentine relatives who had struggled to achieve justice in Chile, Paraguay, and Uruguay. Jorge Tamayo, whose brother Manuel disappeared in Argentina in 1976, asserted how "justice in Chile had been deaf, blind, and silent, while Argentina had instead opened a window of hope for the families."[123] Flor Hernández Zazpe, whose brother Juan was abducted with Manuel, particularly valued the opportunity to testify on the witness stand and contribute to revealing the juridical truth about what happened, observing that "for the first time in forty years, we know the names and surnames of those who were responsible for Juan's death."[124]

Likewise, Chilean Laura Elgueta Díaz, a Condor survivor herself and sister of Luis, who disappeared in Buenos Aires in 1976, noted that "this [the trial] was the first time we felt some justice: giving testimony in the courtroom, telling our truth, was a restorative experience for us." The trial helped to prove that in her brother's case there were no alternative interpretations: "it was a planned kidnapping, torture, and murder. They killed him and, year after year, they kill us a little too."[125] Paraguayan Federico Tatter, whose mother Idalina had been one of the women filing the original case and whose father had disappeared in Argentina, expressed mixed feelings. On one hand, the sentence culminated the persistent justice struggles of his family and more than satisfied the original objective of demonstrating Condor's existence, opening up additional avenues of investigation as a result. On the other, he reflected that after a forty-year delay it was difficult to speak of justice, but he hoped the verdict at least would inspire activists to continue demanding change in the future.[126]

Flor Hernández Zazpe highlighted a tension at the heart of criminal prosecutions: while the case contributed to fully revealing the secret deeds of the transnational terror, it could not repair what cannot be undone: "Knowing the truth allowed us to see how Juan had traveled [to Argentina] in search of protection and ended up being persecuted and disappeared. Our hearts are overwhelmed thinking about the pain Juan and his comrades must have lived through in a situation they had never imagined. . . . There is no justice for such great, permanent, and infinite sadness and heartbreak."[127]

This landmark trial would likely not have existed without the unrelenting prior struggles of justice seekers. In particular, impunity challengers critically filed the original lawsuit in 1999 and then sustained various proceedings over time through their twists and turns. Undoubtedly, the "legal creativity"[128] of lawyer Alberto Pedroncini played a fundamental role. Pedroncini was one of Argentina's historic human rights lawyers and a member of the APDH, as well as the driving force behind the two pioneering lawsuits of *plan sistemático* and Operation Condor, which had challenged impunity head-on in the 1990s. Decades earlier, at the height of the Videla dictatorship in the late 1970s, Pedroncini and other distinguished attorneys, including Emilio Mignone and Raúl Alfonsín, had already achieved unprecedented resolutions from the Supreme Court after they presented a habeas corpus writ regarding over four hundred desaparecidos. In a December 1978 verdict, the high court was forced to admit the existence of a denial of justice when courts could not investigate habeas corpus petitions because of the lack of information from the authorities; it further called on the executive branch to undertake all the necessary measures so that the requests concerning the whereabouts of victims of disappearances could be adequately addressed.[129] In May 1979 Pedroncini had taken part in an international colloquium in Paris, where he outlined one of the earliest proposals for the drafting of international treaties on enforced disappearances, which was at the time still a vaguely defined and poorly understood crime.[130] He had further participated in the Trial of the Juntas in 1985.[131]

The cases Pedroncini selected for the original Condor querella were emblematic of repression on a continental scale. For instance, the identification and location of Paula Logares in Buenos Aires by the Abuelas in the early 1980s undeniably demonstrated that the toddler and her parents had been illegitimately returned to Argentina after their kidnapping in Uruguay in 1978; her biological identity was confirmed in 1984 through pioneering DNA studies, used for the first time.[132] The Condor querella also initially included the case of Simón Riquelo (see chapter 7), which was representative of the many Uruguayan children who disappeared in Argentina.

Other impunity challengers sustained the trial at different junctures. Federico Tatter, who had been a member of the Paraguayan Truth and Justice Commission, helped the tribunal acquire crucial evidence from the Archives of Terror to be added to the proceedings. In September 2014, when Tatter gave testimony about his father's disappearance, he also handed over a copy of the "Rollo 143," which included 1,150 particularly relevant documents on Condor victims and perpetrators; the tribunal had failed to obtain these materials until then, despite several official requests transmitted to Paraguayan authorities.[133]

The trial also benefited from numerous strategic facilitators, including both the public and private prosecutors, as well as the judges, who went many extra miles working on this case. Survivor Elgueta Díaz considered the tribunal's work to be flawless, pointing to the professionalism, respect, and humanity with which they approached each victim's case. She especially noted "the seriousness of the work of the public prosecutors and their tireless search for evidence that allowed us to get closer to the truth" and convincingly prove regional collaboration in prisoners' detentions and renditions.[134] The work of Melisa Slatman, a historian who collaborated with the prosecutors in processing and understanding the unprecedented archival evidence, was particularly decisive. She was a crucial enabler who ploughed through thousands of archival documents "with the required historical outlook, bearing in mind the history of neighboring countries and their respective archives."[135] This interdisciplinary approach and the sustained presence of a historian benefited not just the public prosecution but the entire proceedings, as otherwise lawyers would have struggled to tackle and interpret the records on their own.

Carlos Osorio, director of the NSA's Southern Cone Documentation Project, was another strategic facilitator. He testified before the judges in March 2015 for over eleven hours, split over two hearings, during which he meticulously dissected over a hundred documents of the nine hundred he had officially deposited with the tribunal, containing much critical evidence. Further, the public prosecutors were continually in contact with the NSA; in their final pleas in the trial, they cited NSA-provided documents nearly 150 times.[136] Other strategic facilitators included investigative judge Rodolfo Canicoba Corral and prosecutor Miguel Ángel Osorio, who, despite the difficult political environment of the early 2000s, never shelved the investigation. Instead they employed the strategic litigation elements Pedroncini had provided in the original querella to keep the investigation open and compile the required evidence for future use.

Long-standing efforts by survivors, victims' relatives, human rights activists, lawyers, journalists, and historians from all corners of South America were vindicated by these historic verdicts. The 2016 sentences clearly affirmed that the region's criminal states had established in the mid-1970s a transnational network which committed unparalleled human rights violations against their citizens beyond state borders, and sowed unbounded terror in South America and beyond.

In May 2018 the Fourth Chamber of the Federal Court of Criminal Cassation, presided over by Judge Mariano Hernán Borinsky, rejected the appeals and unconstitutionality challenges filed by defense lawyers, thus ratifying the first-instance verdicts. As of mid-2021, the sentences dictated against eight of the condemned had become final; however, appeals filed by another five were still pending before the Supreme Court, and a resolution was expected by late 2021.

10 • Justice across the Atlantic

The Condor Trial in Italy

Per trovare la giustizia, bisogna esserle fedeli: essa,
come tutte le divinitá, si manifesta soltanto a chi ci crede.[1]
—*Piero Calamandrei*

July 8, 2019, was a typical stifling hot summer day in Rome. That afternoon at 5 p.m., the First Assize Appeals Court was scheduled to deliver its verdict in the Condor trial after over one year of appeal proceedings.[2] I reached the courtroom early at about 4 p.m. It was still empty. Outside, some fellow trial monitors, including journalists Janaina Cesar and Nadia Angelucci and historian and movie director Emanuela Tomassetti, were gathering, along with several lawyers and victims' relatives. The air was filled with a sense of anticipation that, after many years, justice might finally be within reach.

The courtroom was standing-room-only by the time the president of the court, Judge Agatella Giuffrida, began reading the tribunal's resolution.[3] The appeals judges upheld the life sentences previously dictated at first instance in 2017, and significantly overturned eighteen of the nineteen prior acquittals. Overall, twenty-four Uruguayan, Chilean, Bolivian, and Peruvian civilian and military officials were condemned to life imprisonment for the murders of thirty-eight Italian and Uruguayan victims committed between 1973 and 1980. Among those sentenced were former Bolivian interior minister Luis Arce Gómez, Peruvian ex-president Francisco Morales Bermúdez, and former Uruguayan foreign minister Juan Carlos Blanco. Twenty years to the day since proceedings had begun, neither victims' relatives nor their lawyers (fig. 6) could hide their joy and satisfaction at having successfully reversed the earlier acquittals and achieved such resounding condemnatory verdicts.

Figure 6. Lawyers and activists celebrate the appeals verdict in the Italian Condor trial on July 8, 2019, in Rome, Italy. From left to right: Nila Heredia, Mario Angelelli, Arturo Salerni, Jorge Ithurburu, and Andrea Speranzoni.

But why were the courts in Rome investigating atrocities committed in the 1970s over ten thousand kilometers away from Italy in the first place? This prosecution stemmed from the relentless and inspiring efforts by numerous relatives of Condor's victims, who had for decades strived to achieve justice and eventually crossed the Atlantic Ocean in order to do so. This trial in Italy exemplifies a second type of strategic litigation discussed in this book, namely foreign trials: prosecutions regarding human rights violations that were perpetrated in another country. The possibility of litigating cases in foreign courts, particularly in Europe, was especially advantageous for victims' relatives, owing to the prevailing impunity in South America. This chapter recounts the history of the Italian Condor prosecution by retracing its origins in the mid-1990s and its subsequent evolution, as well as its central features, including victims, defendants, charges, and the appeals phase. It especially highlights the network of justice seekers who worked tirelessly over the years in both South America and Italy to achieve this unprecedented result.

The Cradle of Impunity

As with the Argentine trial, the Italian Condor proceedings arose from the scenario of tight impunity in the Southern Cone and especially from the fact that the Ley de Caducidad had forestalled all judicial investigations of past atrocities in Uruguay since 1986. It was indeed in Montevideo that the idea to file a complaint before the Italian courts first emerged. This had been attempted in 1981, when victims' relatives and exiles living in Italy had requested justice from local courts for all the desaparecidos who were Italian nationals, but with no success.[4] In the late 1990s, however, the possibility of resorting to the Italian tribunals resurfaced with greater strength, as former Uruguayan public prosecutor Mirtha Guianze recalled: "There were seemingly insurmountable obstacles standing in the way of justice in Uruguay: first, the Ley de Caducidad and, second, the attitude of the Executive, which systematically shelved all investigation requests. Further, the Supreme Court of Justice had deemed that law to be constitutional and lower courts consequently closed down all proceedings. This context offered no hope for change. It was then that a group of mothers and relatives decided to look abroad for the justice that was being denied to them at home."[5]

According to former Representative Felipe Michelini, a son of slain Senator Zelmar Michelini, a group of Argentine survivors linked to the CELS had traveled to Montevideo in the mid-1990s in an effort to present a joint complaint in Italy.[6] The subsequent London arrest of General Pinochet reenergized activists to employ European tribunals, thereby reactivating their demands for truth and justice in South America and beyond.[7] Raúl Olivera, a Uruguayan activist of the PIT-CNT's Human Rights Secretariat, noted that "it was unsurprising that we ventured down the path of international justice, especially at the historical moment when Spanish Judge Garzón had given a qualitative leap forward using international law."[8]

The first concrete step occurred in March 1999, when Felipe Michelini convened a meeting of victims' relatives, lawyers, and activists on the premises of the SERPAJ NGO in Montevideo.[9] Numerous emblematic figures participated, including Aurora Meloni, María Bellizzi, Luz Ibarburu, Marta Casal, Filomena Narducci, Javier Miranda, Raúl Olivera, and Guillermo Paysee.[10] Cristina Mihura, a Uruguayan exile living in Italy since the 1970s, also joined these efforts, as she frequently collaborated with Luz Ibarburu and María Esther Gatti in presenting criminal cases in Argentina, given that their loved ones had disappeared in Argentina just a few days apart.[11]

This network of impunity challengers had two main objectives. First, they aimed to mount foreign trials to help document the atrocities perpetrated by South America's dictatorships that were not being investigated locally.[12] Second, relatives hoped that criminal responsibility for the murders or disappearances of their loves ones would finally be established, given the lack of effective inquiries in either Argentina or Uruguay.[13] The total impunity in Uruguay had pushed these justice seekers toward finding alternative avenues on the other side of the Atlantic.[14]

The Italian Path against Impunity[15]

Prior legal experience in Italy probing the atrocities suffered by Italian citizens during the Argentine dictatorship favored the filing of the 1999 Operation Condor case and its subsequent evolution.[16] Since 1982, through various ups and downs, the Italian judiciary had strived to peruse the crimes of the Argentine dictatorship. In 1988, after Argentina had relapsed into impunity, Italian prosecutors reopened the proceedings that had lain dormant for the previous five years.[17] Italian justice seekers faced an uphill struggle in gathering evidence to push these investigations forward, including a complicated trip to Argentina undertaken in February 1994 by lawyers Marcello Gentili and Giancarlo Maniga, human rights activist Jorge Ithurburu, judge Antonio Cappiello, and public prosecutor (pubblico ministero; hereafter, PM) Antonio Marini. Despite a lack of cooperation and even outright obstruction by Argentine courts, numerous testimonies were eventually collated in Buenos Aires and other provinces.

In April 1998 the appointment of PM Francesco Caporale gave fresh impetus to the investigations. On October 21, 1999, the first trial against seven Argentine military officers, including former General Carlos Suárez Mason—the head of the First Army Corps—began in Rome on seven counts of murders of Italian citizens (committed between 1976 and 1978) and the kidnapping of a baby born during his mother's illegal detention.[18] In December 2000 Rome's Second Assize Court condemned two defendants to life imprisonment in absentia, and the remaining five to twenty-four-year terms—sentences confirmed by the Court of Appeals and the Court of Cassation in 2003 and 2004, respectively. On June 8, 2006, a second trial probed the assassinations of three Italian citizens at the ESMA between 1976 and 1977, crimes that involved five emblematic navy officials including Jorge Acosta and Alfredo Astiz. On March 14, 2007, Rome's Second Assize Court sentenced the defendants to life imprisonment in absentia,[19] and the Court of Appeals and Court of Cassation ratified these verdicts in 2008 and 2009, respectively.

These two lawsuits formed a critical backdrop against which the Condor proceedings should be read. Lawyer Maniga, who participated in all these actions, commented that "in the wake of the Argentine investigations, it was easier to convince the PM to continue with these inquiries, expanding beyond Argentina—our focus until then—in order to also examine similar events in other South American countries, especially those linked to Operation Condor."[20] Similarly, Ithurburu recalled how, when the start date for the first trial had finally been set in April 1999, it spurred the "rather emboldened" activists and lawyers to file two additional lawsuits, namely Condor and ESMA.[21] The group of impunity challengers also included Argentine lawyer Carlos Slepoy in Madrid, Gregorio Dionis of the international human rights NGO network Equipo Nizkor, and other allies in France and South America.[22]

A notable point relates to the legal instrument that allowed these trials to unfold: article 8 of the Italian Criminal Code, which stipulates that "the citizen or the foreigner, who commits political crimes on a foreign territory . . . will be punished according to Italian law, upon request of the Minister of Justice. . . . For the purpose of criminal law, a political crime is a crime that offends a political interest of the State, namely a political right of the citizen."[23] According to PM Caporale, article 8 "embodies an absolutely revolutionary principle" that provides an important exception to the general norm of the "territoriality of criminal law," permitting courts to initiate criminal proceedings against defendants physically located outside of Italy.[24] Ironically, article 8 had been added to the Italian Criminal Code in 1930 under the reforms of Alfredo Rocco, the minister of justice during Mussolini's fascist regime. Maniga observed that until the 1990s, this norm had rarely been used "because of its association with fascist legislation," but in practice it turned into an extremely beneficial tool that offered a legal basis for action in these cases.[25]

A Long Investigation

Over the first six months of 1999, a transnational network of impunity challengers in Italy, Uruguay, and Argentina drafted the Condor complaint. This initial group comprised, in Italy, relatives and activists Meloni, Mihura, and Ithurburu, together with lawyer Maniga; meanwhile, another group of relatives of victims and activists led efforts in Argentina and Uruguay.

On June 9, 1999, Maniga filed the criminal case in Rome, accompanied by

Meloni, Mihura, and another five women who traveled from South America: Argentine Claudia Allegrini and Uruguayans Marta Casal, Luz Ibarburu, and María Bellizzi, who was accompanied by her daughter Silvia.[26] The women accused former Chilean dictator Augusto Pinochet of the murders of their loved ones:[27] five Italo-Uruguayan victims (Daniel Banfi, Gerardo Gatti, Bernando Arnone, Juan Pablo Recagno, and Andrés Bellizzi), who had disappeared or been slain between 1974 and 1977 in Argentina,[28] and one Italo-Argentine (Lorenzo Viñas) who had disappeared in Brazil in 1980. All these crimes were explicitly framed as part of Operation Condor.[29]

Since the allegation unequivocally named Pinochet, Rome's chief prosecutor assigned the case to PM Giancarlo Capaldo, who was already conducting an investigation on the general.[30] On October 29, 1998, after his arrest in London, two Italian left-wing Green Party senators, Stefano Boco and Giovanni Lubrano, had initiated a criminal case in Rome regarding the disappearances and murders in Chile between 1973 and 1976 of three Italian citizens.[31] Consequently, Capaldo led both investigations.

After the filing of the complaint, the second crucial step was obtaining the authorization to proceed against Pinochet from the left-wing government Minister of Justice Oliviero Diliberto (1998–2000), who granted it a month later on July 8, 1999. Afterward the investigation grew exponentially: other relatives, human rights NGOs, and Italian diplomatic missions began transmitting information regarding twenty-five additional politically motivated murders of Italian citizens perpetrated in the 1970s in South America.[32] Subsequently, Minister of Justice Piero Fassino (2000–2001) approved in February and March 2001 the start of proceedings against another seventy-nine South American officials.[33]

Between 1999 and 2006 Capaldo conducted extensive pretrial inquiries to assemble the necessary evidence, and received numerous statements by victims' relatives and experts in South America. He traveled extensively to gather information and to collaborate with judges scrutinizing the same crimes, particularly French judge Roger Leloir and Spanish judge Baltasar Garzón, as well as relevant authorities in the US, Canada, the Netherlands, Belgium, Sweden, and Uruguay. The prosecutor's strategy focused on the "moment of the kidnapping, to demonstrate that the victim had been detained against his/her will" and, consequently, to link "the individual detention to a broader pattern of repressive operations against the members of a specific political group targeted at the time."[34] The PM reconstructed the political, intelligence, and military hierarchies in several South American countries to fully comprehend the terror structures in place and identify the individuals responsible within the chain of command.[35]

Capaldo concluded his preliminary investigations in the Chilean lawsuit on July 19, 2005, narrowing the case down to four murders of Italo-Chilean victims. The Condor pretrial proceedings were finalized a year later, on June 26, 2006, focusing on twenty-one murders. On July 6 he merged the two case files and, four days later, requested the detention of 146 South American civilian and military officials (sixty-one Argentines, thirty-three Uruguayans, twenty-three Chileans, eleven Brazilians, seven Bolivians, seven Paraguayans, and four Peruvians) on charges of massacre, kidnapping and murder against twenty-five victims.[36] Eventually, in December 2007, Judge Luisanna Figliolia endorsed the PM's request regarding 140 accused, given that six had passed away.[37]

At the time, only former Uruguayan Navy Captain Jorge Troccoli was immediately arrested in the Italian city of Salerno, where he then lived.[38] He was one of the thirty-three Uruguayan defendants who faced accusations of kidnapping and murdering six Italo-Uruguayan exiles.[39] In parallel, Uruguay had filed an extradition request for him, since earlier in 2007 Troccoli had absconded to Italy—the land of his great-grandfather—to flee a criminal investigation in Uruguay.[40] An international arrest warrant was issued in December 2007.

In April 2008, however, the Italian courts released Troccoli because there was insufficient proof to retain him in pretrial detention.[41] Separately, Uruguay had also failed to submit extradition papers by the required deadline in March. In October 2008, despite Uruguay's repeated appeals, Italian Minister of Justice Angelino Alfano definitively denied the extradition request, on the grounds that Troccoli was an Italian national who resided in Italy. The 1881 extradition treaty between Italy and Uruguay (applicable at the time) provided that should either country reject an extradition request, the denying state had to begin criminal proceedings regarding the alleged crimes.[42] In February 2009 Minister Alfano thus authorized the start of proceedings against Troccoli regarding the murder of twenty Uruguayan victims; investigations occurred in parallel to the main Condor case and required the PM to engage in additional evidence-gathering efforts.[43]

Pretrial investigations continued for over ten years. On January 31, 2013, PM Capaldo finally concluded his inquests and asked for trial proceedings to start for thirty-five Bolivian, Chilean, Peruvian, and Uruguayan defendants accused of the murder of twenty-three Italian citizens.[44] By then Argentina had resumed its own prosecutions for past atrocities, and accordingly all the Argentine defendants were removed from the Italian proceedings.[45] In addition, many of the original defendants had passed away during the lengthy pretrial phase, and only thirty-five remained. In July 2014 Capaldo completed the Troccoli investigation and took it to trial too.[46]

Several factors contributed to generating such prolonged delays. Lawyer Maniga explained that the complex nature of the cases resulted in a much longer and more difficult inquiry than initially foreseen.[47] Other difficulties also intervened, such as the identification of potential witnesses and the locations of numerous defendants scattered across South America. Lawyer Arturo Salerni noted that "the Italian judiciary has a well-known reputation for being slow,"[48] and pointed to additional time-consuming factors, including the fact that the crimes under scrutiny had been perpetrated four decades earlier and thousands of kilometers away from Italy. Salerni also observed that the PM had some discretion in the timing of the trial; he speculated that Capaldo might have required additional time to finalize such a complex investigation and prepare for the trial as best as possible.

First Instance

On October 11, 2013, preliminary trial hearings finally started in Rome before Judge Alessandro Arturi. That day the judge accepted the constitution of the *parte civile* (civil party; plural: parti civili) plaintiffs,[49] which included the Presidency of the Italian Council of Ministers and the Oriental Republic of Uruguay. Uruguay's participation as a parte civile was especially remarkable, since it was the only South American country to be actively involved in the proceedings in that capacity. At the time, lawyer Fabio Maria Galiani observed that this decision underscored the country's commitment to support the victims and attempt to redress human rights violations.[50]

The preliminary hearings lasted for almost a year, during which time the tribunal evaluated several issues, including the presentation of further parti civili requests, the translation of charges into Spanish to notify the defendants, the rectification of some indictment details, statements by the victims' lawyers and defense attorneys, and the presentation of supplementary documentation by both prosecution and defense. Postponements in this phase were mainly attributable to the slowness of international judicial and diplomatic channels and the processing of international rogatory letters: indeed, all the defendants in South America had to be formally notified of the relevant charges made against them and then respond. Eventually, in October 2014, Judge Arturi ordered the start of the proceedings against the thirty-three remaining defendants.[51]

On February 12, 2015, the trial's oral phase began before Rome's Third Assize Court, presided over by Judge Evelina Canale, Assistant Judge Paolo Colella, and six lay judges.[52] For the prosecution, PM Tiziana Cugini assisted PM Capaldo, who was by then close to retiring. That day the court merged the separate lawsuits comprising Troccoli and other Uruguayan defendants into the main investigation, which became known as *Procedimento penale 2/15 R.G.—Contro Arce Gómez, Luis ed altri 32* (Criminal proceeding 2/15 against Arce Gómez, Luis and 32 others). The thirty-three Chilean, Bolivian, Peruvian, and Uruguayan defendants were accused of forty-three murders perpetrated against Italian and Uruguayan nationals in Chile, Argentina, Bolivia, Brazil, and Paraguay.

The original complaint had expanded significantly over the years, and the trial proceedings now comprised three sets of cases. The oldest dossier, initiated in October 1998, related to the murders between 1973 and 1976 of Italo-Chileans Juan Montiglio, Omar Venturelli, Jaime Donato, and Juan Maino, which were charged to eleven defendants including some of the masterminds of political repression in Chile, such as General Sergio Arellano Stark and DINA's head, Manuel Contreras. The second segment, originally filed in June 1999, covered the murders of six Italo-Argentines and thirteen Italo-Uruguayans. The Italo-Argentines were Luis Stamponi and his mother, Mafalda Corinaldesi, who disappeared in 1976 in Bolivia and in Argentina, respectively; Alejandro Logoluso and his girlfriend, Marta Landi, abducted in Paraguay in 1977; and Horacio Campiglia and Lorenzo Viñas, kidnapped in Brazil in 1980. These crimes were attributed to eight Chilean, Bolivian, Peruvian, and Uruguayan officials. The Italo-Uruguayan cases had unfolded in Argentina and encompassed, in 1974, Daniel Banfi; in 1976, Gerardo Gatti, María Emilia Islas, Bernardo Arnone, and Juan Pablo Recagno; in 1977, Andrés Bellizzi, Ileana García, Edmundo Dossetti, Julio D'Elía, Yolanda Casco, Raúl Borelli, and Raúl Gámbaro; and in 1978, Héctor Giordano. These murders were charged against fifteen Chilean and Uruguayan officials, encompassing high-ranking civilian and military figures such as Uruguay's foreign minister Juan Carlos Blanco and navy intelligence officer Juan Carlos Larcebeau. The third file related to the murder of twenty Uruguayans—Alberto Corchs, Elena Lerena, Alfredo Bosco, Guillermo Sobrino, Gustavo Goycochea, Noemí Basualdo, María Castro, José Martínez, Aída Sanz, Elsa Fernández, Atalivas Castillo, Miguel Río Casas, Eduardo Gallo, Gustavo Arce, Juvelino Carneiro, Carolina Barrientos (Argentine-Uruguayan), Carlos Cabezudo, María Artigas, Alfredo Moyano (Argentine-

Uruguayan), and Célica Gómez—in Argentina between late 1977 and early 1978; these were added to the proceedings in 2009, and Troccoli was the sole defendant.

The trial's oral phase before Rome's Third Assize Court lasted sixty-one hearings during almost two years, because of the large number of victims and defendants under examination. Forty-seven hearings were devoted to the examination of oral witnesses who had been requested by the public prosecution, the parti civili, and the defense. Between April 2015 and October 2016, the court heard the testimonies of 135 people, including some of the women who had initially presented the complaint in 1999. Survivors of political repression in Argentina, Chile, and Uruguay, such as Nicasio Romero, Ángel Gallero, Silvia Tolchinsky, and Cristina Fynn, delivered poignant, powerful testimonies to the court. The magistrates also listened to the particularly moving stories of stolen children who had been illegally adopted by families loyal to the dictatorships in Argentina and Uruguay, including those of Carlos D'Elía and María Victoria Moyano. Victims' relatives, including Uruguayans Zelmar Michelini, Chilean Alejandro Montiglio, and Argentine María Campiglia, narrated to the tribunal the events surrounding the disappearances and murders of their loved ones, as well as their subsequent searches for justice.

The judges relied on the expertise of South American public prosecutors who had conducted criminal investigations into Operation Condor, such as Argentine Pablo Ouviña and Uruguayan Mirtha Guianze. Several document analysts, including Italian Giulia Barrera and Chilean Carlos Osorio, and historians such as Italian Gennaro Carotenuto and Uruguayan Oscar Destouet, crucially helped the justices better comprehend the historical context in South America, the complex repressive dynamics inside each country, and Condor's modus operandi. A few former military officers, such as Uruguayan Rubí Veliz and Julio César Barboza, testified as well, as did human rights activists from Uruguay and Brazil.

The second phase of the proceedings began on October 13, 2016, when PMs Capaldo and Cugini presented their final statements to the court. They requested life imprisonment sentences for twenty-six Bolivian, Chilean, Peruvian, and Uruguayan defendants, and acquittals for the six Chilean and Uruguayan accused who had passed away, as well as for Uruguayan Ricardo Chávez, who had not committed the crimes he had been charged with. The prosecution's strategy revolved around two core and complementary elements: first, a careful reconstruction of each victim's circumstances and the identification of the individuals responsible; and second, the demonstration of Condor's existence. On the latter point, the prosecution especially noted how the fact that military agents of one state could operate on the territory of another could only be explained by the existence of specific agreements at the highest levels that sanctioned such arrangements.[53] Between late October and late December 2016, the parti civili lawyers presented their conclusions to the judges, followed by the defense attorneys.

Inside the Courtroom

The first-instance phase tackled several subjects of importance, and two are analyzed here. First, the judges categorically established that the persecution of political exiles in South America predated the 1975 official founding of Operation Condor. The murder of Daniel Banfi in Buenos Aires was especially important in revealing the close collaboration between the Argentine and Uruguayan police forces in September 1974 (see chapter 2). Banfi's wife persuasively asserted that "Uruguayan police commissioner Hugo Campos Hermida moved around Buenos Aires like he owned the place."[54] Further, the disappearance of Italo-Uruguayan Andrés Bellizzi in April 1977, also in Buenos Aires, helped corroborate this point. On September 25, 2015, Uruguayan investigative journalist Roger Rodríguez, who helped shed light on several cases of disappeared babies and other atrocities, testified as an expert witness and presented numerous documents to show that Condor-like practices were already occurring in 1974. He unequivocally affirmed that Andrés Bellizzi "had been sentenced to disappear on June 2, 1974."[55] Rodríguez explained to the judges how Operativo Gris had unfolded that day, describing how the PFA had detained and booked 100 Uruguayans and one Argentine in Buenos Aires (see chapter 2). He stressed to the tribunal that, out of the detainees on that day, eight people were later targeted again: one survived, five remained disappeared, including Andrés, and two were the brothers of Condor victims. The journalist noted that the list of prisoners in 1974 later turned into a "list of potential suspects for the future Operation Condor."[56]

Moments of tension characterized Rodríguez's testimony. The journalist had brought many documents from Uruguay to exhibit to the judges, but the court's president often interrupted him or asked him to summarize their contents instead. At one point, the journalist made a powerful plea, asserting that he had traveled over fifteen thousand kilometers to deliver records the court lacked. Rodríguez knew that the main defendant for Bellizzi's murder had passed away, and thus no criminal responsibility could be attributed in that case. However, the journalist was displeased with the way the tribunal was treating him, as well as María and Silvia Bellizzi on the previous day, by repeatedly telling them to condense a forty-year-long fight for justice down to ten minutes. For the Bellizzis in particular, the hearing had been the first opportunity they had ever had to appear before a court of law to speak about Andrés's disappearance. The journalist implored the judges: "We could not obtain justice for Andrés either in Argentina or Uruguay. . . . For these reasons, I insist, please let me hand in these documents, . . . not for the court to sentence or condemn anyone but so that, at least, we can gather in one place all the documents that prove Andrés Bellizzi was the victim of a crime against humanity."[57] Rodríguez's appeal powerfully exposed the expectations that victims and relatives have regarding judicial proceedings. For them, giving testimony in court constitutes a form of symbolic reparations for the crimes suffered and a crucial step in their enduring search for accountability. Conversely, tribunals have to comply with tight schedules and limit their analysis of cases to the defendants still included in the proceedings. These diverging priorities can at times clash in the courtroom. Eventually, however, the tribunal accepted Rodríguez's request and received all his documents.

A second subject extensively addressed by the tribunal was the persecution of Uruguayan exiles belonging to the GAU, MLN, and PCR in Argentina, at the hands of Argentine and Uruguayan officers between late 1977 and early 1978. These abductions had unfolded after the arrest in Uruguay of Montoneros leader Oscar De Gregorio and the ensuing capture of over fifty GAU activists in Montevideo (see chapter 5). Systematic operations had begun in Buenos Aires on December 21, when five GAU militants (Alfredo Bosco, Edmundo Dossetti and his wife Ileana García, and Alberto Corchs and his wife Elena Lerena), were first apprehended. A day later, Raúl Borelli, Julio D'Elía and his wife Yolanda Casco—also GAU activists—and Guillermo Sobrino of the Socialist Militant Groups (AMS) were kidnapped. On December 23 Argentine and Uruguayan officers seized another seven exiles: four GAU activists, namely Noemí Basualdo and her husband Gustavo Goycochea, and Antonia Castro and her husband José Martínez, and two Tupamaros, Atalivas Castillo and Aída Sanz; Aída's mother, Elsa Fernández, was visiting from Uruguay for the birth of her grandchild and was not politically active, but she was nonetheless taken. On Christmas Day 1977, Tupamaro militants Eduardo Castro and Miguel Río Casas were apprehended in a large-scale military operation. Two days later the final two GAU militants were abducted: Raúl Gámbaro and Gustavo Arce. On December 30 Asunción Artigas and Alfredo Moyano of the Tupamaros, and

Federico Cabezudo and Carolina Barrientos and her husband Juvelino Carneiro of the PCR were also captured. Célica Gómez, who was not a political militant but was linked to the PCR, was apprehended on January 3, 1978. The GAU, MLN, AMS, and PCR were at that time coalescing resistance efforts against the Uruguayan dictatorship as part of the UAL.

Vital survivor testimonies helped determine that these prisoners were illicitly held in three secret prisons, part of the so-called Circuito Camps in Buenos Aires province. Luis Taub, abducted in September 1977, testified that security officers initially confined the Uruguayans in the Tactical Operations Command (Comando de Operaciones Tácticas 1; COT1 Martínez), in the locality of Martínez, north of the capital. Taub was captive there on Christmas Day 1977 and spoke to Alfredo Bosco.[58] Uruguayan officers tortured and interrogated prisoners, assisted by their Argentine counterparts. Taub moreover recounted to the judges how on Christmas Eve, security officers had organized an *asado* (a typical South American barbeque), probably to celebrate the success of the operations against the Uruguayans.[59]

Rosa Barreix, a GAU militant concurrently imprisoned at the FUSNA in Montevideo, narrated that just before Christmas 1977, Jorge Troccoli had explicitly told her that some of her comrades had been captured (*han caído*) in Buenos Aires, mentioning Corchs, Lerena, Borelli, and D'Elía.[60] He also showed her a statement given by José Michelena, another militant arrested in June 1977. Three passenger lists that journalist Rodríguez brought to Rome clearly demonstrated that FUSNA officials Troccoli, Ricardo Dupont, and José Uriarte had flown from Montevideo to Buenos Aires on December 20, 1977—on the eve of the operations—and then returned on December 22.

At an undefined moment between January and February 1978, Uruguayan officers transferred some prisoners to Uruguay, crossing the River Plate at its narrowest point by boat in the Paraná River Delta. Adriana Chamorro, another Argentine survivor, explained to the Italian magistrates that she had shared her prison cell with Asunción (Mary) Artigas, who had recounted to her the transfer of the small group of Uruguayans from COT1 Martínez. Mary related that "they were ordered to prepare *milanesa* sandwiches [a South American meat-based sandwich], because the following day some prisoners would be sent to Uruguay."[61] According to Mary, five prisoners were transferred, including Gallo and D'Elía. Corroborating this assertion, former Uruguayan Navy Prefecture officer Rubí Veliz affirmed to the judges that during Carnival of 1978 he had indeed seen some navy officers disembark a few prisoners, including a crying woman and a wounded person, from a boat docked in a secluded coastal area between the cities of Nueva Palmira and Carmelo, just opposite Argentina.[62] Further, Uruguayan survivor Ángel Gallero confirmed the presence in Uruguay of some of these prisoners. During his incarceration at La Tablada in Montevideo in February 1978, Gallero recognized PCR leader Carlos Cabezudo, whom he personally knew from their shared militancy.[63] He also heard the names "Gallo" and "Célica" being mentioned repeatedly.

Between January and February 1978, the remaining detainees in Argentina were moved from COT1 Martínez to Pozo de Banfield. The latter secret center had been operating since October 1974 in Lomas de Zamora, in the building of the Buenos Aires Provincial Police Investigations Brigade for Crimes against Property and Personal Security. Banfield was labeled the "maternity ward," since many pregnant women gave birth there, including Aída Sanz's daughter Carmen, born on December 27, 1977, and Yolanda Casco's son Carlos on January 26, 1978. On August 25, 1978, Argentine witness Eduardo Corro and his wife Adriana accompanied Mary throughout her labor until the very last moment, when she was taken away to give birth to Maria Victoria.[64] Between late 1976 and 1978, Banfield functioned as "a deposit for prisoners coming from different clandestine prisons within Buenos Aires province, until a definitive decision on their destiny was taken."[65]

From there, Uruguayan detainees were frequently taken to be interrogated at another prison, Pozo de Quilmes, before being returned to Banfield. It operated between 1975 and 1979 on the premises of the Police Investigations Brigade in the city of Quilmes. Washington Rodríguez, a Uruguayan exile kidnapped in April 1978, talked with Aída Sanz during his imprisonment there and she told him that, if he was ever freed, he should seek asylum and inform the UNHCR about the group of twenty-two Uruguayans incarcerated in Quilmes.[66] Sanz also recounted to him how Uruguayan OCOA agents, commanded by a navy official, regularly tortured Uruguayan prisoners.[67] Teresa Serantes, another Uruguayan survivor, confirmed to the Italian magistrates the presence of numerous Uruguayan prisoners in Quilmes, including Jorge Martínez and Guillermo Sobrino, and that Uruguayan officers, including a woman nicknamed "Sergeant Peters," participated in all their interrogations.[68]

Six months after their abduction, on May 16, 1978, all the remaining Uruguayans in Banfield—except for Mary, who was six months pregnant, and Ileana García, who was suspected to be pregnant—were *trasladados* ("transferred," a jargon expression used by officers to mean extrajudicial executions).[69] Ileana and Mary were included in prisoner transfers in June and October 1978, respectively.[70] The final fate of these prisoners remains unknown: they could

have been sent to Uruguay, but given the long time elapsed since their detention, it is likely they were included instead in the death flights that routinely
occurred in Argentina.[71] The court ascertained that, on the date of the large
May transfer, the FUSNA head of intelligence Juan Carlos Larcebeau and his
commander Jorge Jaunsolo were in Buenos Aires.

The Verdicts

On January 17, 2017, Rome's Third Assize Court sentenced to life imprisonment eight high-ranking officials and acquitted nineteen defendants. It concluded that former Bolivian dictator Luis García Meza, his head of intelligence
Luis Arce Gómez, and former Peruvian dictator Francisco Morales Bermúdez,
his prime minister Pedro Richter Prada, and his head of military intelligence
Germán Ruiz Figueroa were guilty of the murders of Campiglia and Viñas in
1980.[72] Former Uruguayan foreign minister Blanco also received a life term
for the murders of Daniel Banfi in 1974 and of Gerardo Gatti, María Emilia
Islas, Bernando Arnone, Juan Pablo Recagno, Luis Stamponi, and Mafalda
Corinaldesi in 1976.[73] Likewise, Chilean colonel Hernán Ramírez and Tacna
Military Base commander Rafael Ahumada were condemned to the same sentence for the murders of Omar Venturelli and Juan Montiglio.[74] The court ruled
that Uruguayan Ricardo Chávez was not responsible for any charged crimes,
and it also acquitted twelve Uruguayans,[75] five Chileans,[76] and one Peruvian[77]
on murder charges, while sentences for kidnapping—for which the tribunal
found them guilty—could not be dictated because of statutory limitations.[78]
The deaths of six defendants meant that the judges could not ultimately deliver verdicts regarding four victims, Italo-Uruguayans Andrés Bellizzi and
Héctor Giordano and Italo-Argentines Alejandro Logoluso and Marta Landi,
whose murders had been charged to the deceased.[79]

The tribunal was the first in Europe to acknowledge the existence of Operation Condor in a criminal verdict and, in particular, to affirm how "complex
and illegal international repressive operations . . . could not have been carried
out without an agreement put in place at the highest political levels."[80] Condor
had in fact strengthened the existing collaborations among South American
intelligence services, which had previously unfolded on an ad hoc basis and
gradually became more systematic and efficient. It had further provided a
guarantee of impunity, since no security agent was ever investigated for the
atrocities committed at the time, neither in his own country nor where the
crimes had been perpetrated.

The justices clearly demarcated between South America's political and military leaders and the actual executioners of the crimes. The tribunal considered that the former bore "full moral and material responsibility for each murder," having planned and actively contributed to them.[81] For the latter, the investigations had identified the material authors of the kidnappings and imprisonment, but had failed to uncover those of the murders.[82] Accordingly, these middle-rank officers were judged to have contributed to some segments of the operations, "namely, the identification, kidnapping, illegal detention, interrogation, and torture of the prisoners, but not their deaths."[83] Therefore, while the magistrates were fully convinced of the role of the top military, intelligence, and civilian echelons in masterminding and allocating the necessary resources to eliminate political exiles, they could not determine which of the other defendants had provided the necessary and additional causal contributions to perpetrate the murders, the so-called *quid pluris* (additional element).[84]

This judgment generated mixed reactions. The tribunal had resoundingly condemned several South American dictators and government ministers for orchestrating transnational political repression.[85] Some victims' relatives, such as the Venturelli and Montiglio families, had finally achieved justice. Aurora Meloni, who had spent forty years seeking justice for her husband's murder, believed that the verdict was the finale of a lifetime dedicated to demanding accountability for her family. The nineteen acquittals, however, left a bittersweet taste: justice had somehow been incomplete.

Criticisms quickly poured in against the sentences, both in Italy and abroad. Paraguayan human rights activist Martín Almada publicly expressed his disappointment and contended that the acquittals were beyond comprehension. The Uruguayan government and victims' families also voiced their disenchantment and surprise; Nilo Patiño, spokesperson of the Uruguayan NGO Madres y Familiares, asserted that the acquittals had felt like a "bucket of cold water," since "they were expecting a different outcome."[86] Former prosecutor Guianze observed that, most likely, "the judges had incorrectly evaluated the available evidence and failed to understand the powers that security agents had over detainees' life and death within South America's clandestine repressive systems."[87] Many parti civili lawyers pointed to similar shortcomings. Andrea Speranzoni argued that the tribunal had overlooked several elements of the available archival documents, and he maintained that a closer reading of those records would have led to different conclusions on the middle ranks.[88] Another judicial actor observed that the court had neglected to properly interpret the evidence by only focusing on command roles.[89] Alessia Liistro, a parte civile lawyer, affirmed that Condor's very existence, understood as a shared plan to physically elimi-nate opponents, meant that all the defendants, despite implementing different criminal segments, nevertheless shared responsibility for the entire operation.[90]

Soon after, Rome's Public Prosecutor's Office appealed the judgments and requested that the Appeals Court reappraise the roles of the middle and lower ranks, especially emphasizing how those defendants had contributed to differ-ent portions of the criminal actions under scrutiny and therefore should be held accountable for the victims' assassinations.[91] The defense attorneys and parti civili lawyers filed their respective appeals.

On Appeal

Proceedings before Rome's First Assize Appeals Court began on April 12, 2018. One judge immediately declared a conflict of interest with one of the lawyers involved, and therefore a new composition of the tribunal had to be arranged. On June 21, 2018, the new court, presided over by Judge Agatella Giuffrida, Assistant Judge Caterina Brindisi, and six predominantly female lay judges, initiated the appeals phase. By this time there were twenty-five defen-dants remaining, since two had died in the preceding months. In 2018 the Uruguayan government replaced Galiani with Speranzoni as its lawyer, after some Uruguayan activists and relatives criticized Galiani's performance.

A central issue under discussion on appeal was the possibility of renewing investigations. According to the Italian Code of Criminal Procedure, the sur-facing of new evidence after a first-instance verdict is one of the grounds that permits the reopening of investigations. In October 2018 Speranzoni, who also represented several Chilean and Uruguayan families, presented such a request to the court in a written memo, in which he asked the judges to incorporate thirteen new archival records from Uruguay, the US, and Argentina that had become publicly available after the first-instance sentencing.[92] Speranzoni par-ticularly underscored the significance of the Uruguayan records, which con-tained information directly relevant to the murders under consideration and could potentially help overturn some of the acquittals.[93] Speranzoni's petition was widely supported by his colleagues.[94]

Conversely, defense attorneys attempted to convince the judges to deny this request, raising technical objections regarding compliance with appeal dead-lines and questioning the Italian nationality of the victims. Francesco Guzzo, Troccoli's defense lawyer, argued that the supposedly novel documents were not really so, since "they had always been in their 'natural home,' namely Uruguayan military archives."[95] Guzzo accused Uruguay of rendering these records available with a significant delay, stating that "they now expect us to believe that Uruguay did not previously have access to those archives."[96] In December 2018 the Appeals Court agreed to partially reopen investigations, allowing the incorporation of twelve new documents but denying additional witnesses.

Beginning on March 18, 2019, all trial parties presented their final statements. General prosecutor Francesco Mollace and PM Tiziana Cugini contended that "the first-instance tribunal had failed to deliver justice and that the appeals phase was an opportunity to remedy that error."[97] The prosecution requested that the magistrates overturn all the acquittals and sentence all twenty-five defendants to life terms. Luca Ventrella, the lawyer representing Italy, drew the judges' attention to the contradictions of the first-instance verdicts, which had only condemned Condor's leaders. He argued that the lower court judges had displayed a "surprising shyness" at the moment of delivering justice and labeled the acquittals "juridical aberrations."[98] In his opinion, the first-instance court had adopted a fragmentary approach when considering the relevant structures and responsibilities in the perpetration of the murders, producing verdicts "in which none was, in the end, responsible for aberrant crimes."[99]

Hearings continued throughout April, May, and June. On May 13, 2019, Speranzoni presented in detail the new records he had gathered in South America, especially from the Uruguayan Ministry of Foreign Affairs and FUSNA's Computadora archive. He emphasized that these additional documents complemented what had been found in Troccoli's military file—extensively scrutinized during the first-instance trial—and that this corpus of evidence clearly demonstrated both Troccoli's stationing in Argentina between late 1977 and 1979 and FUSNA's pivotal role in the repression unleashed against Uruguayans in Buenos Aires.[100]

Between June 21 and 28, 2019, the remaining parti civili lawyers and defense attorneys presented their pleas. Lawyer Mario Angelelli lamented "the passing of time, which had deprived the trial of many culprits," specifically mentioning the death of Condor's mastermind, Manuel Contreras. He further recalled the bravery of the victims' relatives, especially María Bellizzi, who had never faltered in the search for her son. Lawyer Alicia Mejía observed how "this extermination plan had targeted political and social leaders, but also rank-and-file militants: the dictatorships had in fact eliminated anyone who represented a threat to the status quo."[101] In her concluding plea, Mejía urged the judges "to read together all the various facts and proofs, to avoid committing the same mistake as the first-instance court, which had approached them in a disjointed and fragmented manner."[102]

Afterward, it was the turn of the defense. Lawyer Luca Milani, who was defending three Peruvians and two Uruguayans, questioned the work of the public prosecution's office and asserted that "the objective of a criminal trial was not to find the truth nor write history, but only to attribute criminal responsibilities."[103] Similarly, lawyer Marco Bastoni, defending three Chileans, claimed that "this had been a political trial and, consequently, elements outside criminal procedures, such as political ideologies, had influenced it."[104] Bastoni exhorted the magistrates to approach their decision with a "moral, almost surgical distance regarding the facts under scrutiny."[105] Lastly, Troccoli's lawyer, Francesco Guzzo, spoke for over an hour, describing the first-instance verdict as "fair, wise, and well-balanced in its evaluation of every element."[106] Guzzo then reproached the PM and the parti civili lawyers for placing his defendant permanently at the center of attention, "as if everything was dependent upon him . . . when, in fact, he was an obscure inferior officer." He tried to challenge the many clues that pointed to Troccoli's command role within FUSNA and reprimanded the prosecution for "generating the image of a monster, who had to be condemned at all costs." Guzzo attempted to depict a different image of Troccoli as "a simple and insignificant officer, who spent the majority of his time sitting at a desk, filling out bureaucratic paperwork, and who had a secondary role in fighting subversion,"[107] lacking all decision-making power. The court adjourned until July 8, 2019, to deliver its verdicts.

The Appeals Sentences

On July 8 the judges confirmed the first-instance life sentences handed down to the six remaining Uruguayan, Bolivian, Peruvian, and Chilean high-ranking officers and, further, reversed eighteen of the nineteen acquittals, thereby sentencing to life terms an additional twelve Uruguayan defendants,[108] five Chileans,[109] and one Peruvian.[110] Chávez's first-instance acquittal was also ratified.

The Appeals Court explained in painstaking detail the reasons for its dramatically different evaluation of the role of the middle ranks and stressed how the lower tribunal had failed to take into consideration a significant portion of the existing evidence that related to the defendants' military files, their duties at the time, and the repressive apparatuses in each Condor country.[111] Consequently, the first-instance analysis, which had separated Condor's masterminds from the middle ranks, had been incomplete, and its conclusions had not fully grasped the significance of the available evidence; its decisions had turned out "to be hasty and contradictory vis-à-vis the correct premises voiced."[112]

This legal reasoning, released on December 27, 2019, illustrates how the judges had carefully evaluated all the evidence collated both at first instance and on appeal. The magistrates particularly observed how Condor practices, such as close intelligence exchanges and joint abduction operations, had rendered political asylum completely ineffective, since the dictatorships could effectively control the movement of exiles and arrest targeted individuals outside their countries of origin.[113] Directly challenging the first-instance court's stance, the appeals judges stressed how middle-rank officers had implemented repressive policies "with expertise, determination, and produced a high number of victims."[114] These officers were far from being subordinate and unaware of what was happening: "to the contrary, although they operated further down the hierarchy from the military command and the heads of state, they were their closest collaborators," the magistrates stated.[115] They had played significant roles within intelligence and coordination structures, "endowed with decision-making autonomy regarding the organization of operations, means, personnel and economic resources."[116] The judges notably commented:

> After all, it is reasonable to believe that the creators of Operation Condor, having set out its objectives, would rely for their accomplishment on individuals of recognized trust, who shared their intentions and who could translate into action what they had theorized and, since repressive activities had been planned on a large scale, its implementation necessarily required autonomy in the choice of the timing [of operations], places of action and victims to target (always belonging to opposition groups under watch), ample powers, spirit of initiative and abilities to face any contingencies in order to ensure the overall success of the operation that was based on, essentially, surprising the victim and the speed of detention.[117]

The tribunal concluded that the murders had to be framed under the legal category of "participation by several individuals in a crime" (*concorso di persone nel reato continuato*).[118] This was because the defendants, encompassing both Condor's architects and the material authors who had executed the indispensable tasks of gathering intelligence, conducting arrests, and illegally imprisoning the victims, had all contributed to the realization of the final goal, namely the victims' murder.

Lawyers and activists enthusiastically welcomed the verdict and praised the magistrates' work. Activist Ithurburu observed that the "conscious participation of the defendants in the plan that clearly envisioned the elimination of political opponents" had been evidently recognized.[119] Lawyer Giancarlo Maniga pointed out that the judges had accepted that all the defendants had been accomplices to the murders, whatever the exact role they had fulfilled within the coordinated set of actions leading to the assassinations. Regardless of their intermediary ranks, these officers had consciously and voluntarily undertaken the duties and tasks assigned to them, thereby providing functional contributions to each criminal act.[120]

Lawyer Speranzoni particularly praised the tribunal for thoroughly dissecting the wide-ranging documentation, which included hundreds of witness statements, archival records, and verdicts by Uruguayan criminal courts. Ventrella, who had previously questioned the first-instance court and its lack of "juridical courage," affirmed that the higher judges had listened to the parti civili pleas regarding the middle-rank officers' roles and their autonomous decision-making power.[121] Lawyer Arturo Salerni pointed to the historical relevance of the trial, which brought back to life the countless untold stories of desaparecidos, explicitly referring to the courage of Juan Montiglio, who had remained at Salvador Allende's side in La Moneda Palace until the last minute and whose story—without this trial—would have "remained hidden in the darkness of torture chambers and constituted deaths without culprits."[122]

Final Reflections

Coming exactly twenty years after the first authorization had been granted to open investigations against Pinochet, the appeals verdicts constituted a landmark achievement. The Italian Condor trial was significant in four respects. First, it represented the apex of a lifetime of struggle by justice seekers scattered across Italy and South America. Alejandro Montiglio, Juan's son, reflected how the prosecution had "brought to an end an emotional page of his family history."[123] Zelmar Michelini, son of the homonymous Uruguayan senator, noted the significant reparative aspects of trials and pondered the importance of providing his testimony before the Italian magistrates, especially because of Rome's fundamental prominence in his father's life: "My father's speech [at the 1974 Russell Tribunal in Rome] was of great international relevance and allowed the world to learn for the first time in detail what [crimes] the Uruguayan dictatorship had been perpetrating."[124]

Second, the conviction of the middle-rank officers demonstrated their crucial role as necessary cogs in the implementation of repression, both inside each South American country and through the repressive coordination. The verdicts dictated against Uruguayan defendants Troccoli and Pedro Mato Narbondo meant that they finally were facing justice after having both fled Uruguay to avoid prosecution for human rights violations years earlier. To avoid a second potential escape, the Appeals Court instituted a travel ban and confiscated Troccoli's passport in July 2019.[125] Mato Narbondo (also a Brazilian national) lives in Santana do Livramento; he is unlikely to serve his sentence in Italy since Brazil never permits the extradition of its citizens.

Third, the Italian prosecution stands out when compared to other foreign trials previously conducted, which were restricted to probing only cases of European nationals. Italy's refusal to extradite Troccoli to Uruguay and the ensuing duty for Italy to prosecute the defendant for the additional twenty murders of Uruguayan-only nationals widened the court's original jurisdiction beyond the original Italian victims. This was an exceptional occurrence, since the Italian courts thus investigated the murders of the citizens of a second state (Uruguay), which were committed in the territory of a third (Argentina).

Lastly, the verdict also sent a stark warning to today's abusers of human rights. Despite delays and obstacles, none is beyond the reach of justice, and there will be tribunals willing to embark on investigations, no matter how much time has elapsed.

The transnational network of justice seekers, which encompassed impunity challengers on both sides of the Atlantic and sustained these proceedings for two decades, from the filing of the original complaint in 1999 until the appeals verdict in 2019, was especially remarkable. Victims' relatives played a fundamental role in two respects. First, the Argentine and Uruguayan women who personally filed their lawsuit provided the initial cases to begin proceedings, and they subsequently identified other potential victims whose cases could also be added.[126] Second, they helped the prosecution and lawyers compile and process the required evidence so that proceedings could move forward. Aurora Meloni, Cristina Mihura, and Filomena Narducci were closely involved for geographical reasons, since they lived in Italy or regularly traveled there.[127] Mihura in particular worked hand in hand with PM Capaldo over several years and was part of a group of around twenty volunteers from twelve countries who aided the preliminary inquiry, particularly by translating numerous documents from Spanish and English into Italian and compiling relatives' statements when the PM traveled to Argentina and Uruguay.[128] Mihura also actively worked to keep the investigation alive in the late 2000s, when it seemed to have come to a standstill. Her lawyer, Paolo Sodani, regularly put pressure on the prosecutor's office to advance to the trial phase,[129] while Mihura herself repeatedly and publicly deplored the slowness of the investigations before the Italian government, including Parliament.

Another impunity challenger was Ithurburu, who helped coordinate efforts behind all the trials that unfolded in Italy: he gathered economic resources to cover legal costs, assigned lawyers to follow victims' cases, located potential witnesses, and traveled to collect evidence and testimonies.[130] He also ensured that young Italian lawyers would be involved in the trial, giving them an opportunity to litigate before the prestigious assize courts, and that female lawyers would act as parte civile lawyers for female victims.[131]

Numerous human rights lawyers, particularly Maniga, Salerni, Speranzoni, and Angelelli, pushed for the proceedings to move forward at different crucial junctures, and some worked pro bono for years. Speranzoni in particular undertook a special effort to overturn the first-instance acquittals when, in August and September 2018, he traveled with his colleague Mejía to Uruguay and Argentina to conduct additional investigations and unearth potential new evidence for the appeals phase. The selection of new documents from the recently declassified Computadora archives that Speranzoni filed before the Appeals Court was undoubtedly instrumental in overturning the acquittals. Impunity challengers also included committed individuals and institutions located in Uruguay, especially Raúl Olivera, Felipe Michelini, the PIT-CNT's Human Rights Secretariat, and SERPAJ, among many others.[132]

Their efforts were buttressed by a wide network of other institutional actors that functioned as strategic facilitators and comprised, among others, the three biggest Italian trade unions, the regions of Emilia Romagna and Calabria, the Waldensian Church, and Rome's municipal government, which supported the proceedings and covered some legal costs. The Italian state also participated as a parte civile and contributed to 20 percent of the expenses associated with bringing some key witnesses to Rome.[133] The Basso Foundation collaborated and provided facilities to hold meetings and press conferences throughout the trial.

Giancarlo Capaldo, a prestigious PM in Rome's public prosecution office with a long-standing history of investigating some of the darkest pages of recent Italian history, including Mafia-related cases and the mysterious 1983 kidnapping of fifteen-year-old Emanuela Orlandi in the Vatican City, played a fundamental role. Given that he had not been involved in probing crimes against humanity before, Capaldo closely collaborated with historians and archivists in working on this case, "since normal technical instruments were insufficient in these circumstances."[134] As in the Argentine trial, archivists and document analysts, especially Giulia Barrera and Carlos Osorio of the NSA, strategically contributed to and facilitated the work of the tribunal, helping the Italian judges understand the complex machinery of South America's transnational terror through appropriate archival records. The collaboration with the NSA dated back to the early days of the investigation, when in 2001 PM Capaldo and Mihura traveled to Washington to unearth relevant documentary evidence.[135]

Uruguay contributed by hiring two lawyers over a long period of time, sending relevant archival documentation, helping with translations, and covering travel expenses for some witnesses. While the Uruguayan government clearly supported the successful completion of Italian proceedings, this proactive attitude stood in marked contrast to its approach to justice within its own borders, which has been defined by a high rate of impunity for dictatorship-era crimes.

Unquestionably, this transnational network of justice seekers was the driving motor behind the Italian Condor trial and ensured its ultimate success in delivering justice for the victims and families who had awaited this moment for over forty years. On July 9, 2021, the Court of Cassation (Italy's highest court) ratified the life sentences of eleven Uruguayan and three Chilean officials; consequently, Troccoli (the only convict who lives in Italy) was arrested the following day and taken to Salerno's prison. Meanwhile, the final appeals hearing regarding the last two Peruvian defendants was scheduled for January 2022. In August 2021 Italy's minister of justice, Marta Cartabia, signed the provisional arrest and extradition requests regarding another three Chilean military officers whose sentences had become final in February 2020.

Conclusion

Forty-five years since their parents' disappearance in Argentina in 1976, justice finally seems to be within reach for Anatole and Victoria Julién. In November 2020 Buenos Aires's TOF1—the same tribunal that handed down verdicts in the Condor and Orletti prosecutions—sentenced to life imprisonment four civilian intelligence officers in the so-called *Orletti V* trial, for their responsibility in the homicides, torture, and abductions perpetrated against eleven victims. For the first time, an Argentine criminal court also probed and convicted the defendants for crimes that Anatole and Victoria suffered, including their abduction, detention, and concealment.[1]

Besides the proceedings in Argentine courts, in May 2019 the Inter-American Commission released its decision regarding the family's case and found that Argentina had violated several of the rights of Mario Julién, Victoria Grisonas, and their children, including the right to life and to judicial protection, as expressed in the American Convention on Human Rights, the Inter-American Convention on Forced Disappearance of Persons, and the Inter-American Convention to Prevent and Punish Torture.[2] The commission recommended that Argentina, among other things, should investigate these violations and provide reparations for material and moral damages suffered. After determining that Argentina had not sufficiently complied with these recommendations, in December 2019 the commission referred the proceedings to the Inter-American Court. In December 2021, the Court condemned Argentina for Mario and Victoria's disappearance, and for breaching Anatole and Victoria's rights to justice and truth.

Anatole and Victoria's enduring quest for accountability epitomizes a broader set of justice-seeking efforts that have occurred throughout South America, some of which have been documented in this book. Hundreds of other victims, however, are still waiting for justice to be delivered and for the atrocities of transnational terror to be fully revealed.

This conclusion reviews the main findings of the book and identifies lessons learned from the justice process for South American transnational crimes that could be relevant to justice-seeking efforts for contemporary manifestations of cross-border violations, so that other victims can be supported in their demands for accountability.

Transnational Repression in South America

Since the 1992 discovery of the Archives of Terror in Paraguay, scholars and investigative journalists have considered Operation Condor to be the principal embodiment of South America's transnational terror. In this book, I have suggested that Condor can be better understood when placed within a broader historical continuum, one that accounts for the phenomenon of extraterritorial repression before and after the mid-1970s. I have proposed the concept of "transnational repression" to denote lasting and diverse, yet interconnected, processes of coordination in place between 1969 and 1981 among South America's security forces, which facilitated the cross-border targeting of political opponents. By focusing on transnational repression and enlarging the time frame, one can appreciate that Condor was the product of a wider set of historical and political dynamics that transcended the period of 1975 to 1978 normally associated with it.

The database I have compiled revealed that Condor-like practices were taking place as early as 1969, and these progressively became more sophisticated and widespread. Condor undeniably represented the most institutionalized, sophisticated, and lethal period of transnational terror, which unfolded between March 1976 and December 1978. However, the repressive coordination on the continent had four additional phases beyond Condor itself. The five-phase model discussed in chapter 1 allowed us to unravel the complex dynamics and the set of actors that operated in each moment, the processes leading up to Condor's official establishment, and its subsequent downfall, as well as the evolving nature of the multifaceted terror collaboration over the decade.

The first part of the book illuminated how the shifting and gradually deepening nature of transnational terror reflected the objectives of the South American criminal states and their desire to confront the perceived "subversive" threat represented by opponents in exile. From the late 1960s onward, these regimes developed ever more elaborate methods of cooperation that effectively

silenced many opposing voices. This strategy initially relied on traditional practices of collusion, comprising information exchange and the monitoring of
suspected individuals, which had existed among South America's police forces
since the early twentieth century. The persecution of Brazilian refugees Wilson Barbosa and Jefferson Cardim illustrated how, in the late 1960s and early
1970s, Uruguayan, Argentine, and Brazilian agents were already closely sur-
veilling individuals of interest abroad. Subsequently such agents coordinated
operations to arrest and interrogate targets under torture before secretly returning them to their countries of origin, where they disappeared or were
imprisoned. Pinochet's coup in Chile in September 1973, which followed the
military takeover in Uruguay three months earlier, marked an unprecedented
turning point in the escalation of transnational repression.

As outlined in chapter 2, in February 1974 the gathering of the heads of the
region's police forces established a new system that facilitated the harassment
of thousands of refugees in Argentina and marked the start of transnational
repression's second stage. Bilateral operations were the functional heart of
this new arrangement, which innovatively contemplated, among other things,
a secret communications channel and the permanent stationing of foreign
officers in Buenos Aires, including the infamous Uruguayan police commissioner Hugo Campos Hermida. As Argentina spiraled further into political violence, victims of cross-border operations substantially increased. Between late
1974 and early 1975, transnational repression evolved yet again, and a complex
web of actors undertook both bilateral and multilateral repressive actions.
Concurrently, military agents began to take center stage, in collaboration with
the police forces that were by that point under military operational control. The
Fuentes Alarcón–Santucho episode described in chapter 3 is representative of
the third phase.

By late 1975 conditions were ripe for the formal creation of the most ambitious and institutionalized phase of transnational repression yet to be seen in
the region. Argentina, Bolivia, Chile, Paraguay, and Uruguay formally endorsed
Manuel Contreras's master plan for the Condor System at its founding meeting in November 1975. This novel and ambitious scheme of transnational
intelligence exchange and operations became fully functioning just months
later. By the time of the military takeover in Argentina in March 1976, the
country quickly turned into a hunting ground, where previously protected
political refugees found themselves cornered, given that all neighboring countries were now living under restrictive military rule. Brazil joined Condor in
mid-1976.

Chapter 4 described the core features of the Condor System—transnational repression's fourth phase—which relied on two main institutional pillars: the secret communications system, Condortel, and its operational arm, Condoreje. The Teseo unit, mainly composed of agents from Argentina, Chile, and Uruguay, was established to hunt down opponents beyond the continent and particularly in France. By late 1978 Condor began to unravel. The success of brutal policies of political repression, which drastically reduced the strength of both domestic and exiled opposition, combined with the return of traditional territorial animosities between core member countries, exemplified by the Beagle Channel dispute between Argentina and Chile, spelled the end of transnational repression's deadliest phase. After 1979, as chapter 5 explained, the fifth phase of collaboration returned to its original ad hoc and bilateral format, and mainly targeted Montoneros militants returning to Argentina.

This five-phase interpretation better discerns the shifting dynamics in terms of key actors and the gradually strengthening nature of the repressive coordination. The analysis of the database aided in the drawing of three conclusions: First, although victims came from all South American countries, Uruguayans constituted the largest group by nationality, amounting to 48 percent of the total. Indeed, from the early 1970s thousands of Uruguayans had been escaping political persecution and settling in nearby Chile and Argentina. Ironically, repression in Uruguay was initially less lethal than it was later in Chile and Argentina, where activists had fewer chances to flee due to the ruthless policies of persecution aiming to immediately silence all opposition. In the mid-1970s, however, hundreds of Uruguayans remained politically active from exile. In the eyes of the dictatorship in Montevideo, they embodied a direct threat: this is what turned them into prime targets of transnational repression operations.

Second, Argentina was the key theater of transnational terror operations, given that this is where 69 percent of the victims were targeted (fig. 7). Starting in the 1960s, Argentina had provided a safe refuge for exiles from Paraguay and Brazil, the countries in which the earliest military takeovers had taken place. In late 1973, thousands of Uruguayans and Chileans who were escaping repression in the aftermath of their respective coups also found relative safety in Argentina. After 1976, however, Argentina turned from a sanctuary into a deadly trap from which there was no escape.

Third, although transnational repression pursued members of both peaceful and armed organizations, the largest group of victims were activists belonging to political parties (40 percent of the total), followed by militants of guerrilla

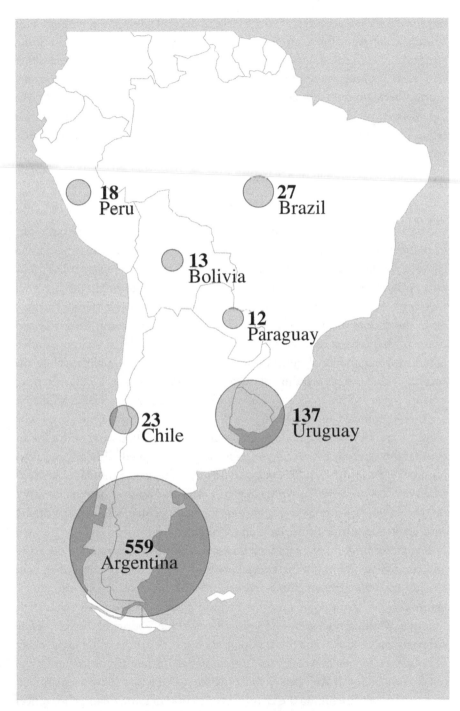

Figure 7. Map of transnational terror victims by country in South America, 1969–81.

organizations (36 percent), of which only 14 percent were JCR members. This finding challenges the arguments in numerous declassified US and South American government documents that attempted to justify the onset of South America's repressive coordination in the early 1970s as a response to coop-eration between guerrilla groups on the continent, particularly the JCR. The database shows that, in practice, regional terror targeted any voices dissenting from South America's regimes, whether they belonged to traditional political parties or to armed organizations.

Justice for Transnational Crimes

The story of transnational terror in South America ultimately became one of justice seeking. A network of survivors, victims' relatives, lawyers, human rights activists, and journalists joined forces with various judges, prosecutors, and political and religious leaders, working tirelessly to untangle the inner workings of the repressive coordination and ensure that the perpetrators would sit in the dock to answer for the atrocities that had been committed. The sec-ond part of the book retraced the domestic and international attempts under-taken by a transnational network of justice seekers to gradually disclose the secrets behind the perpetration of extraterritorial atrocities by South America's criminal states. The analytical framework anchored in the notion of justice seekers—proposed in chapter 6—drew attention to those individuals who played a crucial role in denouncing human rights violations and strove for ac-countability, thereby embarking on especially complicated, difficult, and risky long-term commitments. In the same way that the transnational terror abol-ished borders to commit unspeakable crimes in the name of national security, justice seekers have transcended borders to obtain justice, achieving landmark verdicts in Argentina, Chile, Italy, and Uruguay.

The remaining chapters applied this framework to illustrate the proactive and courageous efforts by justice seekers over time. Chapter 7 described how, already in 1976—transnational repression's deadliest year—the courageous testimonies of Uruguayan survivors including Senator Wilson Ferreira, trade unionist Washington Pérez, and journalist Enrique Rodríguez Larreta before Amnesty International and the US Congress began to call attention to the plight of political refugees in Argentina. Subsequently, the democratic openings and transitions in South America enabled justice seekers to achieve some impor-tant milestones, including the criminal conviction of a Brazilian police officer in 1981 for his role in the abduction of a Uruguayan family, and the recognition in 1984 by Argentina's truth commission that a repressive coordination had existed among South America's regimes.

Chapter 8 then turned to outlining justice seekers' uphill struggle to investigate transnational crimes through criminal prosecutions in Chile and Uruguay, starting in the late 1990s. There a network of impunity challengers—including victims and their lawyers—and strategic facilitators—judges and prosecutors—achieved exceptional steps forward. Investigations in the Chilean Condor case demonstrated for the first time that the DINA's participation in the terror network could have not gone ahead without General Pinochet's knowledge and approval. This evidence permitted Judge Juan Guzmán Tapia to successfully indict the former dictator for a second time in 2004, after a previous failed attempt in 2001. In Uruguay, proceedings probing the disappearance of twenty-eight Uruguayan exiles in Buenos Aires resulted in 2009 in the first conviction to be handed down in the country regarding dictatorship-era atrocities against eight retired police and military officers.

These litigation efforts frequently relied on the strategic argument by victims and their lawyers that disappearances constituted a permanent crime that would continue to be committed until the fate of the victim(s) had been completely established. This stance, which was eventually endorsed by courts in Argentina, Chile, and Uruguay, allowed the circumvention of amnesty laws that had been preventing the elucidation of past atrocities throughout the Southern Cone until that point. In an ironic twist of fate, as journalist Giles Tremlett noted, the very crime of disappearance, which security forces had devised as a tool to ensure their impunity, was exactly what enabled criminal courts to open up investigations, given that such offenses could not be subject to statutes of limitations or amnesties.[3] Starting in 1998, then, a combination of both domestic and international factors, including a renewal of efforts by South American justice seekers, the powerful reverberations from Pinochet's arrest in London, and the creation of the International Criminal Court (ICC), reactivated global accountability struggles.

Two major justice-seeking endeavors in Argentina and Italy regarding the crimes of Operation Condor were also discussed. Chapter 9 focused on the Argentine Condor trial, which was emblematic of efforts to obtain justice in domestic courts by identifying a set of crimes and employing legal arguments to overcome judicial obstacles in order to successfully start investigations. Indeed, this case was one of just two criminal proceedings that Argentine criminal tribunals could investigate in the early 2000s. Lawyers Alberto Pedroncini and David Baigún deliberately deployed the permanent crime thesis, the *aso-*

ciación ilícita charge, and the inclusion of foreign defendants to ensure that their case could not be easily shelved. Eventually, several years later, the 2016 first-instance verdict produced fifteen criminal convictions for crimes against 173 victims, which were confirmed on appeal in 2018. This verdict constitutes the first judicial recognition that Condor amounted to a transnational criminal enterprise, through which South America's criminal states had perpetrated human rights violations beyond borders.

Finally, the discussion of the Italian Condor trial in chapter 10 elucidated how a transnational network of impunity challengers tactically used the domestic courts of other countries—Italy, in this case—to obtain the justice being denied to them in South America. A group of Uruguayan, Italian, and Argentine justice seekers strategically presented in 1999 a complaint before Rome's Public Prosecutor Office regarding the murder of Italian citizens perpetrated under Operation Condor. In 2017 Rome's Third Assize Court was the first European tribunal to officially acknowledge the existence of Condor and its lethal consequences. In 2019 the Assize Appeals Court condemned twenty-four Uruguayan, Chilean, Peruvian, and Bolivian defendants to life terms for the murders of thirty-eight Italian and Uruguayan citizens. In July 2021 seventeen verdicts became final: the Court of Cassation upheld fourteen of them, while another three Chilean officers did not appeal. Two appeals pending before the Court of Cassation were scheduled for review in January 2022.

Since the first criminal prosecution, which occurred in Washington, DC, in 1978 for the assassination of Chilean politician Orlando Letelier and his colleague Ronni Moffitt, 107 South American civilian and military officers, including former dictators, heads of state, and government ministers, have been convicted for transnational human rights violations committed against 262 victims. These Condor trials encompass, so far, a total of forty-five criminal proceedings at various stages of the judicial process. One is currently at the trial phase, four were shelved after the accused's deaths, and eleven are under preliminary investigations. Sentences have been dictated in twenty-nine proceedings (see table 1), conducted in Argentina (twelve trials), Chile (six trials), Uruguay (five trials), Italy (two trials), and one each in Brazil, France, Paraguay, and the US.[4]

As of November 2021, one criminal trial is taking place in Montevideo's criminal court of the 26th Circuit, investigating the role of Uruguayan officers José Ricardo Arab and Jorge Silveira in the 1976 abduction in Argentina of siblings Anatole and Victoria. An offshoot of the original Italian Condor prosecution, the so-called Condor Brazil trial, unfolding before Rome's First Assize

Table 1. Criminal Proceedings with At Least a First-Instance Verdict

Country	Case Name	Charge(s)	Victim(s)	Convicted	Status
USA (1976)	Letelier and Moffitt	Murder	2	4	First Instance (1978; 1987; 1990; 1991)
Argentina (1978)	Arancibia Clavel	Murder; Joint criminal enterprise	2	1	Supreme Court (2004)
Brazil (1979)	Kidnapping of the Uruguayans	Abuse of authority	4	1	Appeals Court (1981)
Italy (1983)	Leighton	Attempted murder	2	2	Appeals Court (1995)
Uruguay (1985)	Michelini and others	Murder	4	2	First Instance (2011)
Uruguay (1990)	Elena Quinteros	Murder	1	1	Supreme Court (2012)
Chile (1978/1990)	Orlando Letelier	Murder	2	2	Supreme Court (1995)
Argentina (1996)	Systematic Plan of Baby Kidnapping	Identity theft; Forgery; Appropriation of minors	34	9	Appeals Court (2014)
Chile (1998)	Carlos Prats	Murder; Joint criminal enterprise	2	7	Supreme Court (2010)
Chile (1998)	Uruguayans in Tejas Verdes	Kidnapping	2	14	Supreme Court (2015)

(continued)

Table 1. *continued*

Country	Case Name	Charge(s)	Victim(s)	Convicted	Status
Chile (1998)	Uruguayans	Kidnapping	3	6	Supreme Court (2015)
France (1998)	Disappearance of French-Chileans	Disappearance; Torture	4	14	First Instance (2010)
Italy (1999)	Luis Arce Gómez and 32 others	Political crimes abroad; Murder	43	17	Supreme Court (2021)
Chile (1999)	Operation Condor	Kidnapping; Murder	12	20	First Instance (2018)
Argentina (1999)	Plan Condor	Kidnapping; Joint criminal enterprise	106	14	Appeals Court (2018)
Chile (2001)	Coyhaique	Kidnapping	3	4	Supreme Court (2014)
Uruguay (2002)	María Claudia García Gelman	Murder	1	5	Supreme Court (2020)
Uruguay (2006)	Soba and others	Murder	28	8	Supreme Court (2011)
Argentina (2006)	Contraofensiva I	Kidnapping	6	8	Supreme Court (2013)

Country (year)	Case	Charges			Court (year)
Argentina (2007)	Contraofensiva II	Kidnapping	6	4	Appeals Court (2012)
Uruguay (2007)	Unifying Action Groups (GAU)	Murder	37	2	Appeals Court (2010)
Argentina (2011)	Automotores Orletti III and IV	Murder; Kidnapping; Torture	9	3	Appeals Court (2019)
Argentina (2012)	Contraofensiva III	Kidnapping	6	3	First Instance (2012)
Argentina (2014)	Contraofensiva Montonera	Murder; Kidnapping; Torture	94	6	First Instance (2021)
Argentina (no exact date)	Laura Elgueta Díaz and Sonia Díaz	Kidnapping	2	1	First Instance (2004)
Paraguay (no exact date)	Agustín Goiburú	Kidnapping	1	1	First Instance (2007)
Argentina (no exact date)	Automotores Orletti I	Murder; Kidnapping; Torture	65	4	Appeals Court (2013)
Argentina (no exact date)	Automotores Orletti II	Kidnapping; Torture	67	1	Appeals Court (2018)
Argentina (no exact date)	Automotores Orletti V	Murder; Kidnapping; Torture; Hiding of minors	11	4	Appeals Court (2021)

Table 2. Criminal Proceedings at the Pretrial Stage

Country	Case Name	Crime(s) Alleged	Victim(s)
Uruguay (1984)	Orletti ("*primer vuelo*")	Torture; Disappearance; Kidnapping	25
Uruguay (1984)	Universindo Rodríguez and Lilián Celiberti	Torture; Kidnapping	4
Chile (1999)	Operation Condor BIS	Kidnapping; Murder	11
Uruguay (2006)	"Fusilados de Soca"	Murder; Kidnapping; Appropriation of minors; Identity theft	5
Uruguay (2011)	Antonio Viana	Torture	1
Argentina (2012)	Plan Condor IV	Kidnapping	348
Uruguay (2012)	Montoneros	Appropriation of minors; Torture; Kidnapping; Enforced disappearance; Kidnapping; Joint criminal enterprise; Appropriation of minors	26
Peru (2015)	Condor	Kidnapping	13
Uruguay (2016)	Héctor Giordano	Enforced disappearance	1
Uruguay (2017)	Nueva Palmira	Torture; Disappearance; Kidnapping	2
Italy (2019)	Filipazzi, Potenza, and Quinteros	Murder	3

Court, was shelved in October 2021 after the death of the only remaining defendant in the case, Brazilian military intelligence chief Átila Rohrsetzer. Finally, eleven case files (see table 2) were still in the phase of preliminary investigations: seven in Uruguay, and one each in Argentina, Chile, Italy, and Peru.

Some of these cases are slowly moving toward the trial stage. In May 2018 the Uruguayan specialized prosecutor for crimes against humanity, Ricardo

Perciballe, asked Montevideo's criminal judge of the 23rd Circuit to indict four military officers for the illegal deprivation of liberty of Lilián Celiberti and Universindo Rodríguez.[5] As chapter 7 noted, this was the first criminal complaint ever filed in Uruguay for human rights violations—in February 1984, when the dictatorship was still in power. A judicial resolution remains pending. Meanwhile, victims and relatives continue to file new allegations.

Lessons Learned

Transnational crimes are neither unique to South America nor distant historical events. On June 4, 2020, a group of unidentified armed men abducted thirty-seven-year-old Wanchalearm Satsaksit—a prominent Thai prodemocracy activist who lived in exile in Cambodia—in front of his Phnom Penh flat.[6] A year later, he was still missing. Since the 2014 military coup in Thailand, many political exiles have taken refuge in nearby Laos, Vietnam, and Cambodia, and Thai authorities have intensively pursued these antimonarchy activists and repeatedly demanded their return from neighboring countries.[7] Thailand, Laos, Vietnam, and Cambodia have engaged in practices that closely resemble those of Condor, including the harassment, surveillance, arbitrary arrest, and forcible repatriation of exiled dissidents, including UNHCR refugees. At least nine Thai activists have been forcibly disappeared in neighboring countries; in 2019 the mutilated bodies of two of them, with hands cuffed and ankles tied, were found floating in the Mekong River on the Thai–Laos border. This modus operandi closely resembles that of South America's repressive coordination, and the accompanying impunity is strikingly similar too; Southeast Asian authorities never properly investigated any of these cases, feigning ignorance and lack of involvement.

Geographies of terror and impunity still torment our world today, and transnational atrocities by both state and nonstate actors are taking place well beyond Southeast Asia, including in Latin America, Europe, Africa, and the Middle East. What lessons can be learned from the Condor trials and potentially applied to the quest for justice for contemporary cross-border atrocities?

Four key insights can be cited. First, these unprecedented prosecutions would not have occurred without the persistent and unrelenting determination of justice seekers. Throughout South America and beyond, these activists have shouldered the burden of speaking out against atrocities while they were taking place and have also methodically assembled the evidence required to enable criminal proceedings to get under way. As chapters 7 to 10 recounted, the creative minds of progressive legal professionals—such as Argentine Alberto Pedroncini, Uruguayan Pablo Chargoñia, and Chilean Eduardo Contreras—identified innovative ways to overcome impunity and seemingly unbreakable amnesty laws, eventually compelling the judiciary to finally investigate past atrocities. These actors bolstered the permanent struggles of survivors and victims' relatives—including Uruguayan Aurora Meloni, Paraguayan Idalina Radice, and Chilean Flor Hernández Zazpe—who sought to expose the horrors endured and achieve justice for their loved ones. Strategic facilitators including Italian Giancarlo Capaldo, Chilean Juan Guzmán Tapia, Argentine Daniel Rafecas, and Uruguayan Mirtha Guianze buttressed these pioneering endeavors by impunity challengers and helped legal cases move forward and reach the courtroom. This transnational network of actors was especially important in probing the crimes of the repressive coordination, since although abundant evidence existed, it was generally scattered throughout the continent and needed to be effectively compiled and transmitted from one country to another to be successfully used in criminal courts.

Second, the Condor trials have proven that domestic courts can effectively scrutinize cross-border atrocities. These prosecutions, carried out by ordinary magistrates, corroborated that neither ad hoc nor international courts are required to probe complex crimes, as often advocated in the past—unless some exceptional circumstances materialize. This is also in line with the ICC's complementarity principle, whereby it steps in only when national jurisdictions are unable or unwilling to investigate and prosecute serious crimes. The tribunals in Argentina, Chile, Uruguay, and Italy creatively blended different jurisdictional grounds—territoriality or nationality—to better capture and adequately investigate the geographies of transnational crimes. There is no specific prescription that can be recommended; rather, varying combinations should be designed in reflecting the circumstances and nature of any given situation. Further, universal jurisdiction provides an additional potential tool for justice seekers. Since the late 2010s, investigations based on this principle have resurfaced and particularly focused on the atrocities committed by the government of Syrian President Bashar al-Assad. In February 2021 a criminal court in Koblenz, Germany, convicted a former agent of the Syrian intelligence services to four and a half years for abetting the torture of civilians; this constituted the world's first verdict regarding crimes during the Syrian civil war.[8] Similar investigations of serious crimes through universal jurisdiction are occurring in the domestic courts of another dozen countries.

Third, international judicial cooperation in gathering and sharing the necessary evidence, both testimonial and documentary, so that it can be incorporated in different criminal prosecutions is a crucial prerequisite for the successful conclusion of such proceedings. A wealth of evidentiary sources was marshaled to ground the verdicts in the Condor trials. Nevertheless, existing channels— regarding both the transmission of evidence and extradition requests—often proved extremely slow and generated significant unacceptable delays, which totaled months or even years, and greatly slowed down the resolution of the proceedings. The availability of modern technology, particularly regarding the digitization of documents and the possibility of immediate communication through videoconferencing, should be further promoted to avoid such unjustified delays. A smooth and fluid exchange of information and evidence should be facilitated in order to speed up investigations regarding cross-border crimes, which are likely to increase in a globalized and interconnected world.

Fourth, the creation of multidisciplinary teams within relevant institutional structures, such as the judiciary or public prosecutor's offices, is fundamental to the effective completion of such complex criminal investigations. These should include historians and document analysts to carefully examine archival evidence; psychologists and social workers to support witnesses and victims through the different stages of the judicial process; forensic anthropologists and doctors to assist with locating, searching for, and identifying victims of enforced disappearance; and translators to help with processing documentation in various languages.

There is no blueprint or model that can be automatically applied to contemporary extraterritorial human rights violations. The conviction of over a hundred former state officials in the Condor trials shows that justice is possible even in such intricate circumstances. Scholars and policymakers working on contemporary transnational crimes can draw hope, inspiration, and insights from the stories of resilience and hope narrated in these pages, as they seek to help today's victims in their justice-seeking endeavors.

Although this book has unraveled some of the untold secrets of Condor and South America's transnational repression, much more remains to be uncovered, especially the fate of hundreds of its remaining victims. New declassification rounds of government documents, increasing access to state archives in the Americas, and continued criminal investigations are essential steps in recovering these still missing pieces of the puzzle. Only then will justice have been fully served.

NOTES

Introduction

1. "Valparaiso, of earthquakes and staircases, / where each step is a house on tenterhooks. / Valparaiso, of sailors and markets, /and shores of icy clear waters, / had sheltered Anatole and Eva Lucía / when in December 1976 / they appeared in O'Higgins Square, / adrift and holding hands." This poem forms part of the poetry book *Viento del exilio* of 1981. The reprint of this stanza of Benedetti's poem has been authorized by the Mario Benedetti Foundation. This and all subsequent translations from Spanish are the author's own.

2. Unless otherwise specified, this section draws on the author's interview with Anatole Larrabeiti Yáñez, Operation Condor survivor, Santiago, Chile, September 12, 2013.

3. SDHPR, Personal File of Julién Grisonas, Victoria Eva, p. 9, available at www .gub.uy/secretaria-derechos-humanos-pasado-reciente/sites/secretaria-derechos -humanos-pasado-reciente/files/documentos/publicaciones/JULI%C3%89N%20 GRISONAS%2C%20Victoria%20Eva%20Ficha%20accesible_0.pdf (accessed August 22, 2020).

4. Inter-America Commission on Human Rights, *Report No. 56/19, Case 13.392, Julien-Grisonas Family,* OEA/Ser.L/V/II.172, Doc. 65, May 4, 2019, paragraph 59.

5. Buenos Aires Federal Criminal Court No. 1, Trial Proceedings No. 2.261, "Ferrer, José Néstor; Nerone, Rolando Oscar, and Gutiérrez, Oscar Roberto, illegal deprivation of liberty, aggravated by violence or threats and homicide aggravated by treachery," and No. 2.390, "Enciso, César Alejandro, illegal deprivation of liberty, aggravated by violence or threats," November 3, 2017, 851.

6. Ibid., 987–88.

7. Ibid., 1008–9.

8. Ibid., 878.

9. Ibid., 988.

10. Ibid., 863.

11. *A todos ellos: Informe de Madres y Familiares de Uruguayos Detenidos Desaparecidos* (Montevideo: Caligraficos, 2004).

12. Inter-America Commission, *Report 56/19*, paragraph 63.

13. UYFRM, Documentation submitted to the Tribunal in Rome (hereafter Rome Tribunal Documentation), Box 6, Envelope 9/7, Victims' Declarations (Part III), "Testimony of Julio César Barboza," n.d.

14. Documentary, "Los Huérfanos del Cóndor," by Emilio Pacull (2003), minutes 23:00 onward, available at www.youtube.com/watch?v=v9SL6sVYmaA (accessed August 22, 2020).

15. Inter-America Commission, *Report 56/19*, paragraph 65.

16. Buenos Aires Federal Criminal Court No. 6, Trial Proceeding No. 1.531, "Franco, Rubén and others, abduction of minor children," September 17, 2012, 928.

17. SDHPR, File of Victoria Julién.

18. Phone interview with Belela Herrera, August 20, 2020.

19. UYFRM, Historical and Diplomatic Archive, 2. Diplomatic Missions and Embassies, 2.1, Embassy of the Republic in Argentina, Consulate General Reports, Box 1-Conf, Folder E, Report 2/977/863 to General Consul Alfredo Manini Terra, July 22, 1977. [Hereafter, UYFRM references contain a first code that always relates to the box; if there is a second, this refers to the folder consulted, unless otherwise noted. "Box" and "Folder" are not repeated each time.]

20. SDHPR, File of Victoria Julién.

21. Phone interview with Herrera.

22. UYFRM, 2.1, Subversion, Information about Individuals, 3-Conf, H3-2, "Debate sobre la identidad de dos niños aparecidos en Chile," *La Nación*, August 4, 1979.

23. UYFRM, 2.4, Embassy of the Republic in Chile, Reports Issued, 7, Envelope 8, Report A-547/79, "Appearance of Uruguayan children in Valparaíso," to Minister of Foreign Relations Adolfo Folle Martínez, August 2, 1979.

24. Ibid., Report A-580/79, "Uruguayan children," to Minister of Foreign Relations Adolfo Folle Martínez, August 10, 1979.

25. Phone interview with Herrera.

26. NSA, Clamor, Press bulletin, July 31, 1979.

27. Luciana Bertoia, "Cuatro condenados a prisión perpetua en un caso emblemático del Plan Cóndor," *Página12*, November 28, 2020.

28. Amy Ross and Chandra Lekha Sriram, "Closing Impunity Gaps: Regional Transitional Justice Processes?," *Transitional Justice Review* 1, no. 1 (2013): 3–30.

29. Pierre Hazan, "'Beyond Borders: The New Architecture of Transitional Justice?," *International Journal of Transitional Justice* 11, no. 1 (2017): 1.

30. Neil J. Kritz, *Transitional Justice: How Emerging Democracies Reckon with Former Regimes* (Washington, DC: United States Institute of Peace Press, 1995).

31. Ezequiel González Ocantos, *Shifting Legal Visions: Judicial Change and Human Rights Trials in Latin America* (New York: Cambridge University Press, 2016).

32. Priscilla Hayner, *Unspeakable Truths: Transitional Justice and the Challenge of Truth Commissions,* 2nd ed. (New York: Routledge, 2011); Eugenia Allier-Montaño and Emilio Crenzel, eds., *The Struggle for Memory in Latin America: Recent History and Political Violence* (New York: Palgrave Macmillan, 2015).

33. Geoff Dancy et al., "Behind Bars and Bargains: New Findings on Transitional Justice in Emerging Democracies," *International Studies Quarterly* 63, no. 1 (2019): 99–110.

34. Monika Heupel, "How Do States Perceive Extraterritorial Human Rights Obligations? Insights from the Universal Periodic Review," *Human Rights Quarterly* 40, no. 3 (2018): 521–46; Mark Gibney and Sigrun Skogly, eds., *Universal Human Rights and Extraterritorial Obligations* (Philadelphia: University of Pennsylvania Press, 2010).

35. Donatella Della Porta and Sidney G. Tarrow, *Transnational Protest and Global Activism* (Lanham, MD: Rowman & Littlefield, 2005); Sidney G. Tarrow, *The New Transnational Activism* (New York: Cambridge University Press, 2005).

36. Richard Goldstone and Adam M. Smith, *International Judicial Institutions: The Architecture of International Justice at Home and Abroad* (London: Routledge, 2008), 295–310.

37. Margaret E. Keck and Kathryn Sikkink, *Activists beyond Borders: Advocacy Networks in International Politics* (Ithaca, NY: Cornell University Press, 1998).

38. Ellen Lutz and Kathryn Sikkink, "The Justice Cascade: The Evolution and Impact of Foreign Human Rights Trials in Latin America," *Chicago Journal of International Law* 2, no. 1 (2001): 1–33; Ellen Lutz and Caitlin Reiger, *Prosecuting Heads of State* (Cambridge: Cambridge University Press, 2009).

39. Universal jurisdiction contemplates that a national court may prosecute individuals for serious crimes against international law—crimes against humanity, war crimes, genocide, and torture—based on the principle that they harm the international community, which individual states may act to protect. Generally, this principle is invoked when other, traditional bases of criminal jurisdiction are not available.

40. Terry Lynn Karl and Philippe C. Schmitter, "Modes of Transition and Types of Democracy in Latin America, Southern and Eastern Europe," *International Social Science Journal* 128 (1991): 269–84; Francesca Lessa et al., "Overcoming Impunity: Pathways to Accountability in Latin America," *International Journal of Transitional Justice* 8, no. 1 (2014): 75–98.

41. Verónica Michel, *Prosecutorial Accountability and Victims' Rights in Latin America* (New York: Cambridge University Press, 2018); Leigh A. Payne, Gabriel Pereira, and

Laura Bernal-Bermudez, *Transitional Justice and Corporate Accountability from Below: Deploying Archimedes' Lever* (New York: Cambridge University Press, 2020).

42. Jo-Marie Burt, "Guilty as Charged: The Trial of Former Peruvian President Alberto Fujimori for Grave Violations of Human Rights," *International Journal of Transitional Justice* 3, no. 3 (2009): 384–405; Richard A. Wilson, *Writing History in International Criminal Trials* (New York: Cambridge University Press, 2011), 214–32; Susana Kaiser, "Argentina's Trials: New Ways of Writing Memory," *Latin American Perspectives* 42, no. 3 (2015): 193–206.

43. Fernando Butazzoni, *Las cenizas del Cóndor* (Montevideo: Planeta, 2014).

44. Caterina Preda, "The Transnational Artistic Memorialisation of Operation Condor: Documenting a 'Distribution of the Possible,'" *Journal of Latin American Cultural Studies* 29, no. 2 (2020): 251–69.

45. Giles Tremlett, "Operation Condor: The Cold War Conspiracy That Terrorised South America," *Guardian*, September 3, 2020.

46. See, among others, John Dinges, *The Condor Years: How Pinochet and His Allies Brought Terrorism to Three Continents* (New York: New Press, 2004); J. Patrice McSherry, *Predatory States: Operation Condor and Covert War in Latin America* (Lanham, MD: Rowman & Littlefield, 2005).

47. See, among others, Samuel Blixen, *El vientre del Cóndor: Del Archivo del Terror al caso Berríos* (Montevideo: Ediciones de Brecha, 1994); Nilson Mariano, *Operación Cóndor: Terrorismo de estado en el Cono Sur* (Buenos Aires: Lohlé Lumen, 1998); Francisco Martorell, *Operación Cóndor: El vuelo de la muerte* (Santiago: LOM Ediciones, 1999); Stella Calloni, *Los años del lobo: Operación Cóndor,* 2nd ed. (Buenos Aires: Ediciones Continente, 1999).

48. MMDH, ed., *Operación Cóndor: Historias personales, memorias compartidas* (Santiago: Museo de la Memoria y de los Derechos Humanos, 2015); Fernando López, *The Feathers of Condor: Transnational State Terrorism, Exiles and Civilian Anticommunism in South America* (Newcastle upon Tyne: Cambridge Scholars Publishing, 2016).

49. George E. Marcus, "Ethnography in/of the World System: The Emergence of Multi-Sited Ethnography," *Annual Review of Anthropology* 24 (1995): 95–117.

50. Archival documents are cited in the notes, and each archive is identified through a unique abbreviation. Please refer to the abbreviations list in the front matter for details.

Chapter 1. Five Phases of Transnational Repression

1. I thank Analia Banfi for sharing this expression with me.

2. Unless otherwise referenced, this section is based on communications with Wilson Barbosa, February 28, 2019, and March 26, 2020.

3. Silvia Whitaker, "A repressão além-fronteiras—A participação do Itamaraty," Brazilian Truth Commission (hereafter CNV), July 2013 to July 2014, 5, http://cnv

.memoriasreveladas.gov.br/images/documentos/Capitulo6/Nota%2018%2019%20 20%2021%2039%2041%2042%2093%20-%2000092_003073_2014_85%20Relatorio %20de%20Pesquisa.pdf (accessed March 27, 2020).

4. The DOPS, created in 1924, was Brazil's oldest political police force, tasked with preventing and combating political and social crimes that could jeopardize state security. São Paulo's DOPS (DOPS/SP), the country's most active branch, specialized in using informants. Its officers stood out for their extensive experience in interrogation and torture. See CNV, "Órgãos e procedimentos da repressão política," in *Relatório da Comissão Nacional da Verdade* (Brasilia: Comissão Nacional da Verdade, 2014), 161.

5. Whitaker, "A repressão além fronteiras," 5.

6. Ibid., 6, 7.

7. Cláudio Antônio Weyne Gutiérrez, "O fim das fronteiras policiais entre Brasil e Uruguai," in *Conexão repressiva e Operação Condor*, ed. Enrique Serra Padrós et al., vol. 3, *A ditadura de Segurança Nacional no Rio Grande do Sul (1964–1985): História e memória* (Porto Alegre: Corag, 2010), 125–40.

8. Established in 1957, CENIMAR was Brazil's oldest military intelligence organ and became involved in political repression in 1971. CENIMAR centralized information production within the navy, and its agents infiltrated opposition groups and ran torture centers. See CNV, "Órgãos e procedimentos da repressão política," 159.

9. See Federal Decree 68.050, January 13, 1971, available at www.jusbrasil.com .br/diarios/2887933/pg-1-secao-1-diario-oficial-da-uniao-dou-de-13–01–1971 (accessed March 27, 2020).

10. Alfonso Correa, "Uruguay–Brasil: El fin de las fronteras policiales," *Marcha* (Montevideo), November 28 1969. The author thanks Maria Cláudia Moraes Leite for sending this article on July 4, 2019.

11. Interview with Sara Méndez, survivor of Operation Condor, Montevideo, October 8, 2013.

12. David Pion-Berlin, "The National Security Doctrine, Military Threat Perception, and the 'Dirty War' in Argentina," *Comparative Political Studies* 21, no. 3 (1988): 385.

13. National Security Council Report 68, "United States Objectives and Programs for National Security," April 14, 1950, History and Public Policy Program Digital Archive, US National Archives, available at http://digitalarchive.wilsoncenter.org/document /116191 (accessed March 27, 2020).

14. DOS, "ARA Monthly Report (July)—The 'Third World War' and South America," August 3, 1976.

15. López, *Feathers of Condor.*

16. Pion-Berlin, "National Security Doctrine."

17. López, *Feathers of Condor.*

18. NACLA, "Uruguay Police Agent Exposes U.S. Advisors," *NACLA's Latin America and Empire Report* 6, no. 6 (1972): 20–25.

19. Clara Aldrighi, *La intervención de Estados Unidos en Uruguay (1965–1973): El caso Mitrione* (Montevideo: Trilce, 2007).

20. Khatchik DerGhougassian and Leiza Brumat, "The Argentine Military and the Antisubversivo Genocide: The School of Americas' Contribution to the French Counterinsurgency Model," *Genocide Studies International* 12, no. 1 (2018): 48–71.

21. Daniel H. Mazzei, "La misión militar francesa en la escuela superior de Guerra y los orígenes de la Guerra Sucia, 1957–1962," *Revista de Ciencias Sociales* 13 (2013): 105–37.

22. Marie-Monique Robin, *Escuadrones de la Muerte: La Escuela Francesa* (Buenos Aires: Editorial Sudamericana, 2004).

23. Mazzei, "La misión," 117.

24. Diego Galeano, "Traveling Criminals and Transnational Police Cooperation in South America, 1890–1920," in *Voices of Crime: Constructing and Contesting Social Control in Modern Latin America*, ed. Luz E. Huertas, Bonnie A. Lucero, and Gregory J. Swedberg (Tucson: University of Arizona Press, 2016), 17–50.

25. Gabriel Périès, "De la lucha contra la delincuencia interior a la coalición de los Estados contra la subversión internacional: La normativa de la tecnología de identificación dactiloscópica," *Derecho Penal y Criminología* III, no. 8 (2013): 37–47.

26. Ibid., 38.

27. Galeano, "Traveling Criminals," 35.

28. Proceedings of the October 1905 police conference, 175 and subsequent pp., http://bdh-rd.bne.es/viewer.vm?id=0000072559&page=1 (accessed August 24, 2020).

29. Galeano, "Traveling Criminals," 38.

30. Articles 8 and 9 of the agreement and proceedings of the conference of February 20–29, 1920, 13–15, http://bdh-rd.bne.es/viewer.vm?id=0000072559&page=1 (accessed August 24, 2020).

31. Enrique Serra Padrós, "Rio Grande do (Cone) Sul: La conexión represiva de Seguridad Nacional (1960–1985)," *Revista de Sociedad, Cultura y Política en América Latina* 1, no. 1 (2012): 67–85.

32. Ananda Simões Fernandes, "A perseguição além da fronteira: Os órgãos de repressão e espionagem da ditadura brasileira para o controle dos exilados brasileiros no Uruguai," *Estudios Historicos* 1 (2009): 1–10.

33. José Baumgartner, Jorge Durán Mattos, and Mario Mazzeo, *Desaparecidos: Informe especial* (Montevideo: Centro de Estudios de América Latina, 1986).

34. Tanya Harmer, "Brazil's Cold War in the Southern Cone, 1970–1975," *Cold War History* 12, no. 4 (2012): 659–81.

35. Simões Fernandes, "A perseguição."

36. Express cable 2066/394 from the Italian Embassy in Montevideo to the Ministry of Foreign Affairs, "Brazilian Politics," June 11, 1964. Document sent by Janaina Cesar on March 22, 2019.

37. Pio Penna Filho, "O Itamaraty nos anos de chumbo: O Centro de Informações do Exterior (CIEX) e a repressão no Cone Sul (1966–1979)," *Revista Brasileira de Política Internacional* 52, no. 2 (2009): 43–62.

38. Enrique Serra Padrós, "Conexão repressiva internacional: O Rio Grande do Sul e o Brasil na rota do Condor," in *Conexão Repressiva e Operação Condor*, ed. Enrique Serra Padrós et al., vol. 3, *A ditadura de Segurança Nacional no Rio Grande do Sul (1964–1985): História e memória* (Porto Alegre: Corag, 2010), 125–40.

39. Ananda Simões Fernandes, "A conexão repressiva entre a ditadura brasileira e o Uruguai (1964–1973): A atuação do Departamento de Ordem Política e Social do Rio Grande do Sul," *Revista de Sociedad, Cultura y Política en América Latina* 1, no. 1 (2012): 87–102.

40. Simões Fernandes, "A perseguição."

41. CNV, "Órgãos e procedimentos da repressão política."

42. Caroline Silveira Bauer, "O controle sobre argentinos no Brasil e brasileños na Argentina: Vigilância e repressão extraterritoriais," *Revista de Sociedad, Cultura y Política en América Latina* 1, no. 1 (2012): 103–17.

43. Serra Padrós, "Rio Grande do (Cone) Sul."

44. MJDH, "CIEX Secret Cable 102, João Calixto-Leonel Brizola, Activities," February 16, 1972.

45. Enrique Serra Padrós and Fábio Azambuja Marçal, "O Rio Grande do Sul no cenário da coordenação repressiva de segurança nacional," in *Conexão Repressiva e Operação Condor*, ed. Enrique Serra Padrós et al., vol. 3, *A ditadura de Segurança Nacional no Rio Grande do Sul (1964–1985): História e memória* (Porto Alegre: Corag, 2010), 35–48.

46. Simões Fernandes, "A conexão."

47. Glenda Mezarobba, "Between Reparations, Half Truths and Impunity: The Difficult Break with the Legacy of the Dictatorship in Brazil," *Sur—International Journal on Human Rights* 7, no. 13 (2010): 7–26.

48. Gissele Cassol, "Uruguai 'verde-amarelo': Brasileiros presos em terra estrangeira," *Estudios Historicos* 1, no. 1 (2009): 1–13. Speculations surround Goulart's death and whether he was poisoned as part of Condor operations; in December 2014 an autopsy on the exhumed body of the former president did not find traces of any toxic medication or poison.

49. Serra Padrós, "Conexão repressiva internacional."

50. Simões Fernandes, "A conexão repressiva."

51. Aldo Marchesi, *Latin America's Radical Left: Rebellion and Cold War in the Global 1960s* (Cambridge: Cambridge University Press, 2018), 101.

52. The origins of the ELN were in 1966, when Ernesto "Che" Guevara chose Bolivia as the country from where to unleash his planned South American revolution. Che's guerrilla movement was also known as Ñancahuazú. The ELN attempted to set up a second *foco* in Bolivia in 1969 and later turned to urban guerrilla warfare in 1971.

See Richard Gott, "La experiencia guerrillera en Bolivia," *Estudios Internacionales* 2, no. 1 (1968): 85–114; Régis Debray, *Che's Guerrilla War* (Harmondsworth: Penguin, 1975).

53. Clara Aldrighi and Guillermo Waksman, "Chile, la gran ilusión," in *El Uruguay del exilio: Gente, circunstancias, escenarios,* ed. Silvia Dutrénit Bielous (Montevideo: Trilce, 2006), 33–97.

54. Aldo Marchesi, "Geografías de la protesta armada: Nueva izquierda y latino-americanismo en el cono sur. El ejemplo de la Junta de Coordinación Revolucionaria," *Sociohistórica* 25 (2009): 41–72.

55. Aldrighi and Waksman, "Chile," 44.

56. The origins of the Tupamaros National Liberation Movement (MLN-T) date back to the early 1960s, when radical left-wing activists, led by law student Raúl Sendic, created the Coordinador to undertake armed struggle to improve the conditions of sugarcane workers (*los cañeros*) in the northern Artigas province. Formally established in 1966, its founders were disillusioned members of the Socialist Party. They believed that an independent country could only be achieved through socialism and that armed struggle was an essential revolutionary tactic, since ruling elites would not willingly relinquish power. See Clara Aldrighi, *La izquierda armada: Ideología, ética e identidad en el MLN-Tupamaros* (Montevideo: Trilce, 2001); Alfonso Lessa, *La revolución imposible: Los Tupamaros y el fracaso de la vía armada en el Uruguay del siglo XX* (Montevideo: Editorial Fin de Siglo, 2002); Leonardo Haberkorn, *Historias tupamaras: Nuevos testimonios sobre los mitos del MLN* (Montevideo: Editorial Fin de Siglo, 2008).

57. Jimena Alonso, "Uruguayos en Chile: De la solidaridad al exilio (1970–1973)," IX Jornadas de Sociología de la UNLP, La Plata, Argentina, December 5–7, 2016.

58. Clara Aldrighi and Guillermo Waksman, *Tupamaros exiliados en el Chile de Allende: 1970–1973* (Montevideo: Mastergraf, 2015).

59. The MIR was created in 1965 and brought together several left-wing currents, including Marxists and anarchists. Despite differences, the MIR defined itself as a Marxist-Leninist avant-garde movement and believed that only a government of workers and *campesinos* (rural workers) could overthrow capitalism and construct socialism. Miguel Enríquez was elected its secretary general in 1967 and a new central committee, with a large base of students from Concepción University, was assembled. See Andrés Pascal Allende, *El MIR chileno: Una experiencia revolucionaria: A los 36 años del surgimiento del MIR* (Buenos Aires: Cucaña, 2003); Inés Nercesian, "Cambio social, modernización y surgimiento de la lucha armada en Brasil, Chile y Uruguay (1950–1970)," *PolHis* 5, no. 10 (2012): 211–25; Marian E. Schlotterbeck, *Beyond the Vanguard: Everyday Revolutionaries in Allende's Chile* (Oakland: University of California Press, 2018).

60. Guillermo O'Donnell, *Bureaucratic Authoritarianism: Argentina, 1966–1973, in Comparative Perspective* (Berkeley: University of California Press, 1988).

61. Express cable 2183 from the Italian Embassy in Rio de Janeiro to the Ministry

of Foreign Affairs, "Press Conference by Magalhães Pinto," August 24, 1967. Document sent by Janaina Cesar on March 29, 2019.

62. ADT, Note 85 from the Secretary General of the Ministry of Interior to Antonio Campos Alum, Director of the National Office of Technical Matters, R00186F1446, June 17, 1969, MJDH Archive.

63. UYFRM, 2.1, Subversive Activities, 4, A12-13, Letter from the Embassy in Buenos Aires to the Minister of Foreign Affairs, April 15, 1970.

64. Interview with Jair Krischke, president of the Justice and Human Rights Movement NGO, Porto Alegre, Brazil, November 22, 2017.

65. Roger Rodriguez, "El Cóndor ya aleteaba en 1970," Caras y Caretas, February 3, 2012.

66. See CNV, "Conexões internacionais: A aliança repressiva no Cone Sul e a Operação Condor," in Relatório da Comissão Nacional da Verdade (Brasilia: Comissão Nacional da Verdade, 2014), 219–73.

67. Avegno was a CIEX agent known as "Altair," one of Brazil's most important infiltrated agents, who participated in meetings of the Association of Brazilian Exiles in Uruguay in 1968 and several operations including Cardim's abduction and Pires Cerveira's disappearance. See CNV, "Conexões internacionais," 230.

68. MJDH, "Report 388/ADIBAIRES—2.2.2.1—Imprisonment of Jefferson Cardim and his son," December 19, 1970, paragraph 1.

69. CNV, "Conexões internacionais."

70. MJDH, Jefferson Lopetegui de Alencar Osorio—Depoimento 160113, Serviço Público Federal, Brasilia, March 2013, 11.

71. The site of the Coordinación Federal has been emblematic of political repression in Argentina since the days of General Juan Perón. Starting in 1974, and most forcefully after the 1976 coup, it turned into one of the most active clandestine detention centers. In 1971 the name of Coordinación Federal was officially changed to Superintendencia de Seguridad Federal. Carlos Rodríguez, "La historia de Coordinación Federal," Página12, March 16, 2008.

72. MJDH, Report 388/ADIBAIRES, paragraph 2.

73. Ibid., paragraph 3.

74. Ibid., paragraph 6.

75. Ibid., paragraph 4.

76. MJDH, Depoimento 160113, p .12.

77. CNV, "Conexões internacionais."

78. MJDH, "Report 388/ADIBAIRES," paragraph 5.

79. Secret-Urgent Telegram 38 to the Brazilian Embassy in Buenos Aires, dated January 18, 1971, cited in Whitaker, "A repressão além-fronteiras."

80. Secret-Very Urgent Telegram 72 from the Brazilian Embassy in Buenos Aires, dated January 18, 1971, cited in Whitaker, "A repressão além-fronteiras," 3.

81. MJDH, "CIEX Secret Report 429, Chile, Activities of Brazilian exiles and refugees, Edmur Camargo Document," October 21, 1971, paragraph 1(a).

82. MJDH, "Secret Report 213(240571) of the Air Force Attaché in Montevideo, Imprisonment of Edmur Camargo in Argentina," June 23, 1971.

83. CNV, "Conexões internacionais."

84. MJDH, "CIEX Secret Report 104, Activities of Cuban G-2 in Chile, Sonia Lafoz, Edmur's case," February 16, 1972; and "CIEX Secret Report 090, Chile, Situation of Buenos Aires' Air Force Attaché, Case Edmur Pericles Camargo," February 16, 1972.

85. CNV, "Conexões internacionais."

86. MJDH, "CIEX Secret Report 429," paragraph 1(e).

87. UYFRM, 2.1, Subversive Action, 2-Conf, H12-4, Telex C563/10 of December 13, 1971, and C570/18 of December 16, 1971, to Minister of Foreign Affairs.

88. Ibid., Letter 1571 from the Embassy to the Foreign Ministry, June 4, 1971, and Letter 1589, June 7, 1971.

89. UYFRM, 2.1, Subversive Activities, 1A, A6-1, clipping of *La Nación* newspaper article, June 14, 1972.

90. UYFRM, 2.1, Subversive Action, 3-Conf, H12-4, Letter 3189 from the Ambassador in Buenos Aires to the Foreign Minister, "Tupamaros in Argentina," December 1, 1972.

91. Ibid., Letter 1310 from the Ambassador in Buenos Aires to the Foreign Minister, "Connections between the Tupamaros and Argentine terrorists," June 14, 1972.

92. The PRT-ERP emerged in 1965 when Mario Roberto Santucho's Popular Indo-American Revolutionary Front and Nahuel Moreno's Workers' Word united. In 1968 Moreno's group established PRT-La Verdad (The Truth), while militants associated with Santucho called themselves PRT-El Combatiente (The Fighter), reflecting their decision to embrace armed struggle. In 1970 the PRT established its armed wing, the ERP, becoming the PRT-ERP. See Pablo A. Pozzi, *Por las sendas argentinas: El PRT-ERP, la guerrilla marxista* (Buenos Aires: Eudeba, 2001); Vera Carnovale, *Los combatientes: Historia del PRT-ERP* (Buenos Aires: Siglo XXI, 2011).

93. UYFRM, 2.4, Confidential Notes 1970–1973, 77, 9, Note 74/72, "Designation of a Military Attaché before the Government of Chile," January 26, 1972.

94. ADT, "Bilateral Intelligence Agreement between the Paraguayan Armed Forces and Argentine Army," R00186F1573–1580, September 12, 1972.

95. Marchesi, "Geografías," 43.

96. "Message to the Tricontinental," available at https://www.marxists.org/archive/guevara/1967/04/16.htm (accessed August 24, 2020).

97. López, *Feathers of Condor.*

98. Marchesi, "Geografías," 47.

99. Melisa Slatman, "Para un balance necesario: La relación entre la emergencia de la Junta de Coordinación Revolucionaria y el Operativo Cóndor. Cono Sur, 1974–1978,"

Testimonios: Revista de la Asociación de Historia Oral de la República Argentina 2, no. 1 (2010): 1–24.

100. The name recalled the September 1915 meeting in Zimmerwald, Switzerland, where leading socialists from ten countries, including Vladimir Lenin and Leon Trotsky, had participated opposing the First World War.

101. JCR document published in *Che Guevara,* No. 2, February 1975, CEIU Archive, David Cámpora Collection, available in Alvaro Rico, ed., *Investigación histórica sobre detenidos desaparecidos,* vol. 1 (Montevideo: IMPO, 2007), 263–64.

102. SID, Third Department, Memorandum I-08/1975, "Revolutionary Coordinating Junta," August 1, 1975, 2. Document sent by Samuel Blixen on June 15, 2020.

103. Marco A. Sandoval, "La Junta de Coordinación Revolucionaria (JCR): El internacionalismo proletario del Cono Sur, 1972–1977" (master's thesis, Centro de Investigación y Docencia Económicas, Mexico, 2016).

104. Slatman, "Balance necesario."

105. SID, Memorandum I-08/1975, 3.

106. Marco A. Sandoval, "Un fruto del exilio: La Escuela Internacional de Cuadros de la JCR (Junta de Coordinación Revolucionaria)," III Jornadas de Trabajo sobre Exilios Políticos del Cono Sur en el siglo XX, Santiago, November 9–11, 2016.

107. SID, Memorandum I-08/1975, 5; Marchesi, "Geografías."

108. Dinges, *Condor Years,* 56.

109. Ibid., 86.

110. Sandoval, "La Junta."

111. SID, Memorandum I-08/1975, 4.

112. Sandoval, "La Junta"; Aerogram 97, sent by the Chilean Embassy in Buenos Aires to the Ministry of Foreign Affairs' Department South America—Argentina, April 5, 1974. Document sent by John Dinges on July 2, 2019. According to a report redacted by Uruguayan Major Manuel Cordero, however, there were two meetings in Mendoza in early 1974. The first unfolded in January and involved the MIR, PRT-ERP, MLN, and ELN leadership, who agreed to create a general command composed of the top leaders from each group. The second occurred in February and counted on the participation of other revolutionary groups from Brazil, Argentina, Cuba, and France. See Confidential Report 8-2-44, Third Army Corps, Army General Staff, n.d., 48, available at https://www.gub.uy/secretaria-derechos-humanos-pasado-reciente/sites/secretaria-derechos-humanos-pasado-reciente/files/documentos/publicaciones/MLN-T%20unificado%20Cronolog%C3%ADa%20documental.pdf (accessed March 14, 2021).

113. SID, Memorandum I-08/1975, 7.

114. "Primer Comunicado de la Junta de Coordinación Revolucionaria," *Che Guevara* magazine, November 1, 1974, www.latinamericanstudies.org/terrorism/JCR-comunicado-1974.htm (accessed April 3, 2019).

115. Dinges, *Condor Years.*

116. See the five lawsuits relating to the Caravan's crimes at https://expedientes delarepresion.cl/base-de-datos/?_sf_s=caravana%20muerte (accessed April 25, 2020).

117. Pascale Bonnefoy, *Terrorismo de Estadio: Prisioneros de guerra en un campo de deportes,* 2nd ed. (Santiago: Editorial Latinoamericana, 2016).

118. Aldrighi and Waksman, *Tupamaros exiliados.*

119. *La Tercera* newspaper, September 16, 1973, available in Bonnefoy, *Terrorismo de Estadio,* 168.

120. "Vinculaciones extremistas con Bolivia y el Uruguay," *El Mercurio,* October 5, 1973.

121. Created in 1965, the SID centralized information and intelligence production within the armed forces and advised the Ministry of Defense. The SID conducted counterintelligence military tasks, communicated with foreign intelligence organs, and coordinated with the police regarding "terrorist activities." Its Third Department (plans, operations, and liaison) carried out operations in Argentina between 1976 and 1977. See Nilo Patiño, Luciano Costabel, and Samuel Blixen, *Una máquina (casi) perfecta: El SID como usina de inteligencia y soporte de la represión durante la dictadura militar,* Proyecto de extensión sobre archivos militares FIC—UDELAR (Montevideo: Universidad de la República, 2018), and the 2015 Final Statement of the Public Prosecution in the Operation Condor Trial (hereafter OCT Public Prosecution's Final Statement), 398–404. Document sent by Cristina Mihura on December 16, 2017.

122. SID, Memorandum I-12/973, "Analysis of current possibilities of action of the MLN (Tupamaros)," April 26, 1973.

123. Press Office of the Joint Forces, "Special Communique 947," September 24, 1973. Document sent by Felipe Michelini on October 11, 2019.

124. SID, Memorandum 291, "Elements linked to the MLN (Tupamaros) alleged to be in Chile," Department I, September 14, 1973. Document sent by Felipe Michelini on October 9, 2019. The DNII, established in 1967, was a police intelligence organ reporting to the police headquarters and tasked with preventing and repressing actions that could subvert or destroy state institutions. Since 1971 the police and the DNII had been militarized and subject to the military penal code and discipline. The DNII had a lead role in repressing the Tupamaros and direct responsibility over foreigners in Uruguay. See the OCT Public Prosecution's Final Statement, 407–9.

125. CNV, "Conexões internacionais."

126. DOD, Intelligence Information Report, "Close liaison with Chilean Army to investigate Uruguayans in Chile," September 24, 1973.

127. MAC, Memorandum 12-A, December 16, 1974.

128. Patrick Keatley, "Brazilian Rebels 'Tortured after Being Abducted,'" *Guardian,* February 19 1974.

129. List by Colonel Manuel Contreras, cited in Bonnefoy, *Terrorismo de Estadio,* 164n1.

130. See the declarations of Sergio Manuel Fernández Carranza in Chilean Lawsuit 179-2011, "Murder of José Wannio Mattos Santos," July 4, 2012, 196–99, and of Raúl Aníbal Jofré González in 3120-2009, "Kidnapping and other crimes against Luis Alberto Corvalán Castillo," May 11, 2015, 306–12 (both documents sent by Pascale Bonnefoy on March 2, 2019). See also Investigations Police of Chile, Police Report 669 to San Miguel's Appeals Court in Lawsuit 02-2005-VE, "Jorge Ruz Zúñiga y Juan Ampuero Gómez," June 17, 2009, 2928 (document sent by Cristian Cruz on March 8, 2019).

131. Fernández's declaration, Chilean Lawsuit 179-2011, 198.

132. CNV, "Public Hearing of the Permanent Sub-commission of Memory, Truth, and Justice on the participation of the Brazilian Political Police during the coup in Chile," April 14, 2014, http://cnv.memoriasreveladas.gov.br/images/documentos/Capitulo6/Nota %20789%20-%20Nota0%20Taquigraficas.pdf (accessed April 8, 2020).

133. Testimony of Osni Geraldo Gomes to the Brazilian CNV, November 7, 2013, line 660, http://cnv.memoriasreveladas.gov.br/images/documentos/Capitulo6/6-79 -00092.002434_2013–95-Osni%20Geraldo%20Gomes.pdf (accessed April 8, 2020).

134. Ibid., line 710. See also CNV, "Public Hearing," 4, 7, 14.

135. Bonnefoy, *Terrorismo de Estadio.*

136. Silvia Whitaker, "A atuação do Ministério das Relações Exteriores com relação aos cidadãos brasileiros que se encontravam no Chile por ocasião do Golpe de Estado de 11 de setembro de 1973," CNV, September 2014, 9, http://cnv.memoriasreveladas.gov .br/images/documentos/Capitulo6/Nota%2058%2059%2060%2061%2063%2064 %2065%2066%2067%2068%2069%2070%2071%2072%2073%2074%2085%20 86%2087%2091%2095%20-%2000092_003072_2014_31%20Relatorio%20de%20 Pesquisa.pdf (accessed April 8, 2020).

137. *Chile: An Amnesty International Report,* AMR 22/001/1974 (London: Amnesty International Publications, 1974), 25.

138. DOS, Santiago 5356, October 31, 1973, paragraph 1.

139. Bonnefoy, *Terrorismo de Estadio;* email communications with Heber Corbo, March 15 and 22, 2019.

140. Testimony of Carlos Capelán sent to Clara Aldrighi on March 2, 2019, upon the author's request.

141. Aldrighi and Waksman, *Tupamaros exiliados.*

142. CNV, *Relatório da Comissão Nacional da Verdade,* vol. 3, *Mortos e desaparecidos políticos* (Brasilia: Comissão Nacional da Verdade, 2014), 1452–67.

143. Keatley, "Brazilian Rebels."

144. CNV, "Conexões internacionais."

145. UYFRM, 2.1, Sent Telegrams, 1-Conf, A, Telex C465/5 to Foreign Minister Blanco, June 28, 1973.

146. Ibid., Received Telegrams, 1-Conf, B, Telex C233/18G.

147. Ibid., Citizens: Aldunate, Michelini, Ruiz, Erro, 1-Conf, H7–1, Telex 438/3, Au-

gust 14, 1973; Letter 2105 to the Minister of Foreign Affairs, August 21; and Telex 596/21, October 24; Received Telegrams, 1-Conf, B, Telex C222/21G, September 5, 1973; Individual Procedures, 1-Conf, H7, Confidential Letter 1494 from Consulate to the Ambassador, October 29, 1973; and Sent Telegrams, 1-Conf, A, Telex C299/24 to Foreign Minister Blanco, August 30, 1973.

148. Chilean Ministry of Foreign Relations, International Relations Directorate, Confidential Circular 37, December 11, 1973. Subsequent guidelines from Confidential Circular 5 of December 18 identified four areas missions should report on: press articles from antijunta discrediting campaigns; the creation of solidarity and support committees; activities of Marxist Chileans abroad; and any other relevant information on overseas anti-Chile activities. Documents sent by John Dinges on July 2, 2019.

149. CNV, "Public Hearing," 3.

150. MJDH, Letter 004579 from the head of the Foreigners' Specialized Branch of São Paulo Police to the general director of São Paulo Police, May 21, 1973, and accompanying receipt from Iguazú Police Precinct, May 17, 1973.

151. Interview with Jair Krischke.

152. M. Jandyra Cavalcanti Cunha and Jair Krischke, "Operação Condor: O Voo sem Fim da Impunidade no Cone Sul," *Revista FSA* 9, no. 7 (2020): 135–64.

153. José Mitchell, "Brasil antecipou Operação Condor," *Jornal do Brasil,* May 9, 2000.

Chapter 2. Police Coordination in the Southern Cone

1. Interview with Antonio Viana Acosta, former Tupamaros militant, Uruguay, August 4, 2014.

2. DOS, "A Report on the Situation of Refugees in Argentina," Amnesty International, NS 193/76, September 6, 1976.

3. CODEPU, Embassy of Chile in Buenos Aires, Strictly Confidential Circular No. 1 to the Chilean Consul in Buenos Aires, January 15, 1974. Document sent by John Dinges on July 2, 2019.

4. Ibid., Aerogram No. 22 to the Directorate of International Relations, South American Department—Argentina, January 29, 1974.

5. Founded by General Juan Perón in 1946 as a civilian intelligence agency, the SIDE was tasked in 1973 with producing intelligence and conducting information activities regarding national security. In late 1975 it began playing an important role in political repression and also closely collaborated with foreign agents based in Argentina. In 1976 its name was changed to the State Intelligence Secretariat but retained SIDE as its acronym. See the verdict in Buenos Aires Federal Criminal Court No. 1, Trial Proceeding 1.627, "Guillamondegui, Nestor Horacio and others, aggravated illegal deprivation of liberty, torments, and murder," hereafter Orletti I, May 31, 2011, 884–94, www.cij.gov.ar/nota-6923-Lesa-humanidad—difundieron-fallo-que-conden-a-cuatro-acusados-por-delitos-en-Automotores-Orletti.html (accessed April 29, 2020).

6. CODEPU, Aerogram No. 46, February 19, 1974. Document sent by John Dinges on July 2, 2019.

7. UYFRM, 2.4, Received Telegrams, 17, 14, Cable A 187P, November 6, 1973.

8. UYFRM, Administrative Archive, Embassy of the Republic in Chile, Doc. No. 24, Nomina 1974, Box 6, January 22, 1974.

9. Aldrighi and Waksman, *Tupamaros exiliados*.

10. Aldo Marchesi, "'La partida decisiva de la revolución en América Latina': Militantes bolivianos, chilenos y uruguayos en la Argentina peronista, Buenos Aires, 1973–1976," *PolHis* 5, no. 10 (2009): 227.

11. Cristina Porta and Diego Sempol, "En Argentina: Alguna escenas posibles," in *El Uruguay del exilio: Gente, circunstancias, escenarios*, ed. Silvia Dutrénit Bielous (Montevideo: Trilce, 2006), 98.

12. Jimena Alonso and Magdalena Figueredo, "¿Exilio o reorganización? Un análisis de la experiencia del Movimiento de Liberación Nacional: Tupamaros en Argentina," I Jornadas de Trabajo sobre Exilios Políticos del Cono Sur en el siglo XX, La Plata, Argentina, September 26–28, 2012.

13. Porta and Sempol, "En Argentina."

14. Alonso and Figueredo, "Exilio."

15. Marchesi, "La partida decisiva."

16. Martín Sivak, *El asesinato de Juan José Torres: Banzer y el Mercosur de la muerte* (Buenos Aires: Ediciones del Pensamiento Nacional, 1997).

17. Dinges, *Condor Years*.

18. Interview with Carlos Osorio, Director of the National Security Archive's Southern Cone Documentation Project, Washington DC, April 16, 2018.

19. Roger Rodríguez, "1974: La conexión con la Triple A de Gordon y la Federal argentina," *La República*, September 8, 2008.

20. Interview with Francisco Martorell, Operation Condor expert, Santiago, November 28, 2016.

21. Kate Zoglin, "Paraguay's Archive of Terror: International Cooperation and Operation Condor," *University of Miami Inter-American Law Review* 32, no. 1 (2001): 57–82.

22. Unless otherwise referenced, this section draws upon the author's 2014 interview with Antonio Viana Acosta and the articles by Roger Rodríguez, "El vía crucis del Negro Viana Acosta," *La República*, September 14, 2008, and Irina Hauser, "Me torturaron en Coordinación Federal durante 15 días sin descanso," *Página12*, August 12, 2007.

23. Ignacio González Jansen, *La Triple A* (Buenos Aires: Editorial Contrapunto, 1986).

24. UYFRM, 2.1, Subversive Activities, 3, A12-13, Cable A-113, February 23, 1974.

25. McSherry, in *Predatory States*, claimed that this summit was called the "First Police Seminar on the Anti-subversive Struggle in the Southern Cone" (Primer Seminario de Policía sobre la Lucha Antisubversiva en el Cono Sur), 78.

26. DOS, "Memorandum of conversation, meeting with Comisario Margaride, Chief of Argentine Federal Police," March 4, 1975. Document sent by John Dinges on December 3, 2019.

27. Letter from Ernesto Baeza Michaelsen to the Minister of Interior, February 25, 1974. Brad Eidahl found this document in Chile's National Archive of Administration. Document sent by John Dinges on April 13, 2018.

28. "Historia de la Triple A: Aniquilar a los asilados," *El Auténtico*, December 10, 1975, 4. Document sent by Roger Rodríguez on October 5, 2015.

29. Edwin Harrington and Mónica González, *Bomba en una calle de Palermo* (Santiago: Editorial Emisión, 1987).

30. "Historia de la Triple A," 4.

31. Ibid.

32. Ibid.

33. A US State Department document that Martin Anderson discovered proves that Perón had authorized the Argentine PFA and intelligence agencies to cooperate with Chilean intelligence to seize left-wing activists in exile in Argentina; similar arrangements also existed with Bolivian, Uruguayan, and Brazilian security services. These arrangements used Argentina as a base for counterinsurgency operations and the clandestine transfer of detainees. DOS, "Summary of Argentine Law and Practice on Terrorism," March 1976. Document sent by John Dinges on March 22, 2020.

34. DOS, Santiago 2716, May 17, 1974, paragraph 4.

35. CIA, "Counterterrorism in the Southern Cone," May 9, 1977; CIA, "Classified reading material re 'CONDOR' for Ambassador Landau and Mr. Propper," August 22, 1978.

36. CIA, "Latin American Trends, Staff Notes," section on "Counterterrorism in South America," June 23, 1976, 4. Document sent by John Dinges on October 20, 2020. Also see CIA, "S. America: Anti-Refugee Action," *National Intelligence Daily*, June 23, 1976.

37. Interview with Viana Acosta.

38. The OCOA was the Uruguayan dictatorship's principal operative instrument of repression. Inspired by the French experience in Indochina and Algeria, the Army General Command created it in September 1971, tasking it with coordinating and centralizing the antisubversive struggle. It especially persecuted the Tupamaros and ran three secret prisons: 300 Carlos within the Thirteenth Infantry Battalion, La Tablada Military Base, and the Castillo de Carrasco. See the OCT Public Prosecution's Final Statement, 404–7, and Samuel Blixen and Nilo Patiño, *Un modelo de guerra sucia: El rol operativo del OCOA en la represión,* Proyecto de extensión sobre archivos militares FIC—UDELAR (Montevideo: Universidad de la República, 2018).

39. UYFRM, 2.1, Negotiations Regarding Specific Individuals, 1—Confidential, H7, Letter to the Minister of Foreign Affairs H7/1974 (637), May 3, 1974.

40. DOS, "Report on the Situation of Refugees in Argentina."

41. CODEPU, Ministry of Foreign Relations of Chile, Directorate of International Relations, South American Department, strictly confidential, No. 00813/27, "On the activities of Chilean exiles in Argentina," April 1, 1974. Document sent by John Dinges on July 2, 2019.

42. "Habeas corpus para varios extranjeros," *La Nación*, May 8, 1974. Document sent by Argentina's National Library on September 16, 2019. On the Bolivian exiles, see Hugo Rodas Morales, *Marcelo Quiroga Santa Cruz: El socialismo vivido (1969–1977)*, vol. 2 (La Paz: Plural, 2008), 644–49.

43. UYFRM, 2.1, Telegrams Sent, 9, Cable A-236, April 26, 1974.

44. ARFRM, National Directorate of Immigration, Letter to the Ministry of Foreign Affairs 1129/74 DDR, Collection 1971–1975 ACNUR, September 23, 1974; UYFRM, 2.1, Citizens' Interests, 10a, F3, Cable A-258, May 9, 1974.

45. ARFRM, "Aga Khan declarations on refugees: Regarding four Uruguayan citizens expelled from our country," Collection 1971–1975 ACNUR, May 13, 1974; UYFRM, 2.1, Telegrams Sent, 9, Cable A-264, May 14, 1974.

46. Written testimony by Leandro Despouy presented to Case File No. 1075/2006, "Almirón, Rodolfo Eduardo and others, illicit association." Document sent by Aurora Meloni on June 2, 2014.

47. URFRM, 2.1, Citizens' Interests, 10a, F3, Letter to the Ambassador in Argentina A-442/974, August 13, 1974.

48. Ibid., Letter to the Ambassador in Argentina A-618/974, October 17, 1974.

49. NSA, Senate Subcommittee on International Operations, "Activities of certain foreign intelligence agencies in the United States," top secret, January 18, 1979, 9.

50. Charles Gillespie, *Negotiating Democracy: Politicians and Generals in Uruguay* (Cambridge: Cambridge University Press, 1991).

51. URFRM, 2.1, Sent Telegrams, 8, Telex A542 of October 4 and Telex A578 of October 18, 1973.

52. Ibid. Negotiations Regarding Specific Individuals, 1—Confidential, H7, Letter to the Minister of Foreign Affairs H7/974 (843), May 30, 1974.

53. The PCR was founded in 1972, and its ideology was Marxist-Leninist-Maoist. It was especially involved in the fight against the dictatorship in Uruguay. Numerous members were arrested and murdered.

54. URFRM, Letter to the Minister of Foreign Affairs (843).

55. Part 2, from minute 11:10 onward of the audio recordings of Zelmar Michelini's speech in 1974 are available at https://fzelmarmichelini.org/web/index.php/tribunal -russell (accessed March 26, 2019).

56. URFRM, 2.1, Negotiations Regarding Specific Individuals, 1—Confidential, H7, Cable C316/24, June 3, 1974.

57. Ibid., Negotiations and Denunciations, 1—Confidential, H7-1, Letter to the Con-

sular Section H7–1/1974 (919), June 21, 1974; Letter C/974/548 to the Immigrations Office of June 24, 1974; and Letter H7–1/1974 (938) to the Ministry of Foreign Affairs, June 25, 1974.

58. Press conference, Operation Condor Verdict, Basso Foundation, Rome, July 9, 2019, www.radioradicale.it/scheda/578904/operazione-condor-la-sentenza-del-procedi mento-di-appello (accessed July 18, 2019). Michelini's speech starts at 1:05:30.

59. Testimony of Zelmar Michelini, son of Zelmar Michelini, before Rome's Third Assize Court, Trial Proceedings R. G. 2/15, Hearing of June 5, 2015, 10. All R. G. 2/15 hearings transcriptions are available at www.24marzo.it/index.php?module=pagemaster &PAGE_user_op=view_page&PAGE_id=553&MMN_position=87:87 (accessed January 21, 2020).

60. Ibid., 14.

61. Ibid., 13.

62. OCT Public Prosecution's Final Statement, 110.

63. Álvaro Rico, ed., *Investigación histórica sobre dictadura y terrorismo de Estado en el Uruguay (1973–1985)*, vol. 2 (Montevideo: Universidad de la República, 2008), 33.

64. Testimony of Roger Rodríguez before Rome's Third Assize Court, Trial Proceedings R. G. 2/15, Hearing of September 25, 2015, 27.

65. Interview with Nicasio Washington Romero Ubal, survivor of transnational repression, Milan, Italy, June 4, 2018.

66. DNII, Department No. 4, "Memorandum—Monthly Report on Terrorist Activities," June 6, 1974. This list was received by the Uruguayan SID on June 8, 1974.

67. Testimony of Claudia Bellingeri of the DIPPBA Archive, Operation Condor Trial in Buenos Aires, hearing of April 4, 2015, author's notes.

68. DOD, Intelligence Information Report, "Official Decree on the Creation of the National Intelligence Directorate (DINA)," July 2, 1974.

69. OCT Public Prosecution's Final Statement, 99–100, 918.

70. Ibid., 919.

71. The Exterior Department was created in late 1973 and operated within DINA's headquarters at 11 Belgrado Street in Santiago. See the report by Chile's Investigations Police on the DINA Exterior requested by Judge Juan Guzmán in Chilean Lawsuit 2182-98, "Operation Condor," September 1, 2003, vol. 10, 2223–24.

72. Dinges, *Condor Years*.

73. CIA, report no. redacted, August 20, 1974.

74. Alejandro Carrió, *Los crímenes del Cóndor: El caso Prats y la trama de conspiraciones entre los servicios de inteligencia del Cono Sur* (Buenos Aires: Sudamericana, 2005).

75. CIA, report no. redacted, Chile Declassification Project Tranche I (1973–1978), November 27, 1973.

76. Stella Calloni, *Operación Cóndor: Pacto criminal* (La Habana: Fondo Cultural del ALBA, 2006).

77. CODEPU, Ministry of Foreign Relations of Chile, Cable 655 from Embassy of Chile in Buenos Aires, n.d., September 1974. Document sent by John Dinges on July 2, 2019.

78. Interview with John Dinges, Washington DC, April 11, 2018.

79. Richard Gott, "Allende Army Chief Killed in Argentina," *Guardian*, October 1 1974.

80. CIA, report no. redacted, Chile Declassification Project Tranche I (1973–1978), October 25, 1974, paragraph 2.

81. Testimony of Zelmar Michelini, 22.

82. Guillermo Jabif appeared as no. 956 in a list of wanted individuals circulated in October 1974 by UYFRM. 2.3, Embassy of the Republic in Brazil, Confidential Correspondence, 9, 5, Letter 104/74-1446 to the General Consul of Porto Alegre, December 23, 1974.

83. Unless otherwise specified, this section draws upon the author's interview with Aurora Meloni, Banfi's wife, Milan, Italy, May 5, 2014.

84. Testimony of Aurora Meloni before Rome's Third Assize Court, Trial Proceedings R. G. 2/15, Hearing of June 4, 2015, 30.

85. Interview with Nicasio Romero.

86. Testimony of Nicasio Romero before Rome's Third Assize Court, Trial Proceedings R. G. 2/15, Hearing of June 4, 2015, 70.

87. Quoted in Carlos Romero, "El inicio de la represión coordinada del Cóndor," *Tiempo Argentino*, September 9, 2012. Libertad was located in Montevideo's outskirts.

88. "Uruguayos: Hay 6 desaparecidos," *La Razón*, September 20, 1974. Document sent by Aurora Meloni on March 30, 2019.

89. URFRM, 2.1, Negotiations Regarding Specific Individuals, 1—Confidential, H7, Cable C316/8P and Cable A596, October 9, 1974.

90. Testimony of Aurora Meloni, 49.

91. Interview with Nicasio Romero.

92. Testimony of Oscar Bonilla before Rome's Third Assize Court, Trial Proceedings R. G. 2/15, Hearing of June 4, 2015, 89.

93. "Eran Tupamaros los muertos en San Antonio de Areco," *Clarín*, November 1, 1974. Document sent by Aurora Meloni on March 30, 2019.

94. Testimony of Zelmar Michelini, 17.

95. DOS, Montevideo 3707, December 20, 1974.

96. Sergio Israel, *El enigma Trabal: La conexión francesa* (Montevideo: Editorial Fin de Siglo, 2011).

97. Roger Rodríguez, "El sobreviviente de los fusilados de Soca rompe un silencio de 30 años," *La República*, November 7, 2005.

98. Unless otherwise specified, this section draws on the author's interview with Julio Abreu, survivor of transnational repression, Montevideo, March 26, 2014.

99. Alberto Silva, *Julio Abreu: Sobreviviente del vuelo cero* (Montevideo: Editorial Primero de Mayo, 2013), 79.

100. Lawsuit 173-318/2006, "García Floreal; Estefanell Maria Graciela; Brum Corbo Héctor Daniel; Corbo María de los Ángeles, su muerte," was filed in 2006. For more details, see the webpage of the Observatorio Luz Ibarburu, www.observatorioluzibarburu.org/causas/86 (accessed May 7, 2020).

101. Israel, *El enigma Trabal*, 177.

102. Patiño, Costabel, and Blixen, *Una máquina*.

103. SDHPR, personal file of María Rosa Aguirre, www.gub.uy/secretaria-derechos-humanos-pasado-reciente/sites/secretaria-derechos-humanos-pasado-reciente/files/documentos/publicaciones/AGUIRRE%2C%20Maria%20Rosa%20Ficha%20accesible.pdf (accessed April 2, 2019).

104. Personal file of Guillermo Roberto Beausire Alonso, available from the database of the Chilean Museum of Memory and Human Rights, https://interactivos.museodelamemoria.cl/victimas/?p=2994 (accessed April 2, 2019).

105. ARFRM. "Machine-gun attack against refugee center in Santa Fe. Threats to Mr Marmet, of Caritas," Collection 1971–1975 ACNUR, December 6, 1974.

106. Ibid., "Arrest of two Chilean refugees. Valenzuela Soto, Quinteros Celis, who were put on a plane bound for Santiago," Collection 1971–1975 ACNUR, December 13, 1974.

107. Ibid., "Kidnapping of refugee Natalio Dergan, house raid by an armed group. Note from the Ministry to the Ministry of Interior, Institutional Matters Section," Collection 1971–1975 ACNUR, December 4, 1974.

108. SDHPR, personal file of Natalio Dergan, www.gub.uy/secretaria-derechos-humanos-pasado-reciente/sites/secretaria-derechos-humanos-pasado-reciente/files/documentos/publicaciones/DERGAN%2C%20Natalio%20Ficha%202018%20accesible.pdf (accessed April 2, 2019).

109. SID, Department III—Plans—Operations—Liaison, Memorandum I-32/74, September 24, 1974. Document sent by Samuel Blixen on March 27, 2019.

110. Ibid., Memorandum I-33/974, October 9, 1974. Document sent by Samuel Blixen on April 2, 2019.

111. Montevideo Police, DNII, Department IV, "Information on Uruguayan Citizens who died in the Republic of Argentina," November 1, 1974. Document sent by Samuel Blixen on March 27, 2019.

112. Melisa Slatman, "Un espía chileno en Buenos Aires: Los documentos de Arancibia Clavel y la multiplicidad de niveles de la participación argentina en las redes de coordinación represiva," in *Cone Sul em tempos de ditadura: Reflexões e debates sobre a história recente,* ed. Enrique Serra Padrós (Porto Alegre: Evangraf, UFRGS, 2013), 197.

113. Dinges, *The Condor Years,* 79.

114. Interview with Carlos Osorio.

Chapter 3. Dynamics of Hybrid Cooperation

1. Gabriel Salazar, *Villa Grimaldi (Cuartel Terranova): Historia, testimonio, reflexión* (Santiago, Chile: LOM Ediciones, 2013).

2. There is no exact figure for the total number of prisoners. The number cited was calculated by Pedro Matta, a survivor and expert on the site. Email by Pedro Matta to John Dinges dated October 8, 2019, and shared with this author by Dinges.

3. Pascale Bonnefoy, "Los tres de Arica," *The Clinic,* September 11, 2013.

4. OCT Public Prosecution's Final Statement, 928–32.

5. VDS, folder on Jorge Fuentes Alarcón, sworn statements, Renán Gregorio Castillo Urtubia, DJUR 05-10-90, September 14, 1990.

6. Ibid., Patricio Bustos Streeter, DJUR 09-01-91, January 8, 1991.

7. Ibid., Gladys Angelica Ledezma Maturana, DJUR 01-10-78, October 28, 1976; Selva Ivonne Hidalgo Fuentes, DJUR 21-07-90, July 24, 1990.

8. Ibid., Sergio Carlos Requeña Rueda, DJUR 23-11-78, November 30, 1978.

9. Buenos Aires Federal Criminal Court No. 1, Trial Proceedings 1.504, "Videla, Jorge Rafael and others, illegal deprivation of personal liberty"; 1.951, "Lobaiza, Humberto José Román and others, illegal deprivation of liberty"; 2.504, "Falcón, Néstor Horacio and others, illicit association and illegal deprivation of liberty"; and 1.976, "Furci, Miguel Angel, illegal deprivation of liberty and torments," all August 9, 2016, hereafter OCT 2016 Verdict, 1218.

10. Marchesi, *Latin America's Radical Left,* 150.

11. Testimony of Carlos Osorio of the NSA (hereafter Osorio's 2015 testimony), Operation Condor Trial in Buenos Aires, hearings of March 6 and 7, 2015, author's notes.

12. ADT, "Information obtained on the MIR and Chilean Resistance in Argentina," November 3, 1974, R00080F0735 to R00080F0742.

13. SID, Department III—Plans—Operations—Liaison, Memorandum I-32/74, "Activities undertaken in the Republic by the MLN (Tupamaros)," September 24, 1974.

14. ADT, "Seventh bilateral intelligence conference between Paraguay and Argentina," n.d., R00143F0706 to R00143F0739. References in the document (such as p. 9 on the "Situation in Latin American countries until July 1975") permit one to date this document to the second half of 1975.

15. SID, Third Department, Memorandum I-08/1975, "Revolutionary Coordinating Junta," August 1, 1975.

16. Samuel Blixen, "La justificación de la estructura represiva," *Brecha,* June 23 2006.

17. This information analyzed in the SID memorandum reproduced information originally confiscated from Amilcar Santucho, which had most likely been circulated across the region. See CIA, Intelligence Information Cable 603116, June 20, 1975.

18. DOS, confidential memorandum, "Ninety-first meeting of the Working Group/

Cabinet Committee to Combat Terrorism, Wednesday, September 3, 1975, 2:30 pm, Department of State, Room 7516," September 5, 1975.

19. ADT, Intelligence Directorate of the Paraguayan Armed Forces' Chiefs of Staff, report no. 64, "Combined Subversive Action," October 20, 1975, R00I430221 to R00I43F0224.

20. DOS, Buenos Aires 5479, August 14, 1975.

21. ARFRM, "Raid by Police Station 50 on February 18 in the Shelter, Fray Cayetano 649. UNHCR requests the intervention of the Ministry of Interior," Collection 1971–1975 ACNUR—Refugees and Stateless, February 24, 1975; and "Memorandum no. 548 on the Meeting with UNHCR regarding the Raid at Fray Cayetano Shelter," Collection 1971–1975 ACNUR, February 20, 1975.

22. Ibid., Letter from the UNHCR Latin America's Regional Representative to Argentine Foreign Minister, Alberto J. Vignes, Collection 1971–1975 ACNUR, November 19, 1974.

23. Ibid., "Declaration regarding the operation in the UNHCR refuge: Arrest of Héctor Acuña Fernández, Amando Vara Vera (Chileans) and Luis Miguel Abella, Francisco Varela Borga (Uruguayans)," Collection 1971–1975 ACNUR, February 19, 1975.

24. When a victim was not found at home, the security forces waited inside until the person sought appeared and was immediately trapped.

25. DOS, Buenos Aires 5331, August 7, 1975.

26. Ibid., State 171175, July 21, 1975.

27. MAC, Memorandum 69-I, October 31, 1975.

28. Horacio Verbitsky, "La investigación inconclusa de Rodolfo J. Walsh López Rega, la CIA y la Triple A," *El Periodista*, March 21–27, 1986.

29. In his 1977 open letter to the Argentine military junta, Walsh publicly revealed some of his findings regarding the murders of refugees in Argentina and the role of Commissioners Gattei and Gettor.

30. Vania Markarian, *Left in Transformation: Uruguayan Exiles and the Latin American Human Rights Network, 1967–1984* (New York: Routledge, 2005).

31. URFRM, 2.1, Subversive Activities, 2-Confidential, 12-4, Letter to the Minister of Foreign Affairs H12-4/1975 (460), "Transfer of Erro to Villa Devoto," April 3, 1975.

32. See Decree S 614/1975 of March 7, 1975, Secret and Reserved Decrees, Arrests, available at http://servicios.infoleg.gob.ar/infolegInternet/verNorma.do?id=215447 (accessed September 9, 2019).

33. URFRM, 2.1, "Transfer of Erro to Villa Devoto."

34. Ibid., and also Cable C108/3P, April 4, 1975.

35. Ibid., Letter to the Minister of Foreign Affairs H12-4/1975 (493), "Alleged trip by Michelini," April 7, 1975.

36. Ibid., Letter to the Uruguayan Ambassador Adolfo Folle Martínez from the Ar-

gentine Foreign Minister Adolfo Maria Savino, April 23, 1975; Cable C288/19 to the Minister of Foreign Affairs, April 25, 1975.

37. UYFRM, 2.6, Embassy of the Republic in the USA, 18, Packet 1, Coded Cables from URUWASHI C240/12, November 12, 1975; C265 and C266, December 12, 1975.

38. Ibid., Coded Messages from the Ministry, Cable C307/24A, November 24, 1975.

39. SDHPR, "Operativos represivos—Movimiento de Liberación Nacional-Tupamaros (MLN-T)," available at www.gub.uy/secretaria-derechos-humanos-pasado-reciente /sites/secretaria-derechos-humanos-pasado-reciente/files/documentos/publicaciones /Operativo%20MLN.pdf, 41 (accessed September 9, 2019).

40. Marchesi, *Latin America's Radical Left*.

41. SID, Memorandum I-09/975, "Report on operations against the National Liberation Movement (Tupamaros) conducted by Argentine security forces in the months of March and April this year," n.d. Document sent by the Photographic Archive and Documentation Center of *Brecha* magazine (Uruguay) on October 16, 2018.

42. The Tupamaros never fully recovered from the internal crisis suffered in late 1972. The meeting of the MLN's central committee on October 8, 1974, was another turning point that exposed profound differences within its members and resulted in its disintegration, with two factions emerging in the aftermath. The *peludos*, supporters of continuing armed struggle in Uruguay, were endorsed by the PRT-ERP and assumed the party's leadership. Conversely, *los burgueses* opposed armed struggle and eventually distanced themselves from the group, privileging the development of the resistance to the Uruguayan dictatorship by strengthening the alliances with Uruguayan exiles in Buenos Aires. See Marchesi, "Geografías," and Aldrighi and Waksman, *Tupamaros exiliados*.

43. See also DOD, Intelligence Information Report, "MLN—Tupamaro Reorganization," January 9, 1975.

44. DOS, Argentina Declassification Project, "Brief description of the torture inflicted upon Andres Cultelli in Argentina," CU 154D, n.d.

45. SDIIPR, personal file of Alfredo Moyano Santander, available at www.gub.uy /secretaria-derechos-humanos-pasado-reciente/sites/secretaria-derechos-humanos -pasado-reciente/files/documentos/publicaciones/MOYANO%20SANTANDER%2C %20Alfredo%20Ficha%20accesible.pdf (accessed September 9, 2019).

46. UYFRM, Rome Tribunal Documentation, National Army, personal military file of Infantry Officer Don José Nino Gavazzo Pereira (hereafter Gavazzo's military file), 009299.

47. Ivonne Trías, *Hugo Cores: Pasión y rebeldía en la izquierda uruguaya* (Montevideo: Trilce, 2008).

48. CIA, Intelligence Information Cable 992369, July 28, 1976; and CIA Intelligence Information Cable 122075, December 7, 1976.

49. Dinges, *Condor Years*, 86.

50. Ibid.

51. ADT, "Police Record 2626, Amilcar Latino Santucho Juarez," May 16, 1975, R0016F1117 to R0016F1118.

52. Ibid., tourist card of Ariel Nodarse (Jorge Fuentes), entry point Itá Enramada, May 16, 1975, R0080F00779.

53. Ibid., typed notes on the monitoring of Jorge Fuentes, n.d., R0080F0776.

54. OCT Public Prosecution's Final Statement, 118.

55. ADT, Capital Police, Investigations Department, "Preliminary Statement—Ariel Nodarse Ledesma," May 19, 1975, R0208F1123 to R0208F1125.

56. DOS, Office of the Legal Attaché, Letter from Robert W. Scherrer to General Ernesto Baeza Michaelsen, director general of the Chilean Investigations Police, June 6, 1975.

57. Dinges, *Condor Years,* 90.

58. FBI, Communications from the Buenos Aires Legal Attaché to the Director, No. 097–06, June 6, 1975.

59. CIA, Cable 603116.

60. ADT, Questionnaire for Nene (Jorge Fuentes), 38 questions, n.d., R0080F0730 to R0080F0733.

61. Ibid., Interrogation of Jorge Fuentes, n.d., R0080F0710 to R0080F0713; ibid., Handwritten Questionnaire for Alicia (Amilcar Santucho), 10 questions, n.d., R0080-F0746 to R0080F0747; ibid., "Questionnaire for Nene," n.d., R00046F1537.

62. Ibid., Interrogation of Nene, n.d., R0080F0755 to R0080F0766.

63. Ibid., Interrogation of Jorge Fuentes, n.d., R0080F0798 to R0080F0807.

64. Ibid., Questionnaire for Montenegro (Amilcar Santucho), n.d., R00080F0895 to R00080F0899.

65. Ibid., Preliminary Statement—Jorge Isaac Fuentes Alarcón, July 14, 1975, R00028F1021 to R00028F1022.

66. Ibid., Questionnaire for Montenegro and Interrogation of Alicia, n.d., R0225-F1449 to R0225F1450.

67. Ibid., Questionnaire for Alicia, n.d., R0080F0719 to R0080F0720.

68. Riveiro was one of the most emblematic figures in the Argentine repressive apparatus; beyond operating in Buenos Aires and Mendoza, he was in charge of the Argentine military mission in Central America in the 1980s, especially in Honduras.

69. Battalion 601, established in 1968 during a restructuring of the intelligence apparatus, was entrusted in late 1975 with centralizing all intelligence information received from the military zones, areas, and subareas into which Argentina had been divided. Its Reunion Center, composed also of intelligence agents from the three military branches, the penitentiary police, the SSF, and SIDE, among others, compiled all the information. Battalion 601 had eight working groups (*grupos de tarea,* GT) and re-

ported directly to the ruling military junta. See DOS, "Organizational Chart of '601,'" February 7, 1980, 0000AE97; Anibal García Fernández, "El Batallón 601 de inteligencia del Ejército Argentino y su participación en la represión en América Latina (1976–1983)," Colloquium on the Armed Forces and Social Control, National School of Anthropology and History (ENAH), Mexico City, August 22–24, 2016; Melisa Slatman, "Actividades extraterritoriales represivas de la Armada Argentina durante la última dictadura civil-militar de Seguridad Nacional (1976–1983)," Anos 90 19, no. 35 (2012): 237–60; InfoJus, El Batallón de Inteligencia 601 (Buenos Aires: Ministerio de Justicia y Derechos Humanos de la Nación, 2015).

70. ADT, Handwritten List of 15 Questions for Nene, n.d., R00021F1755 to R00021F1756.

71. Ibid., Questionnaire for Nene, n.d., R0080F0721 to R0080F0722; ibid., Answers to 20 Questions by Jorge Fuentes, n.d., R00102F1746 to R00102F1747.

72. Ibid., Questionnaire for Alicia, 50 questions, n.d., R0080F0752 to R0080F0754.

73. VDS, REL 135-79, "Exito de la Solidaridad Internacional," Denuncia, November 1979.

74. ADT, Investigations Department, Political and Related Directorate, Technical Section, Police File 2628, May 16, 1975, R00016F1121 to R00016F1122.

75. ADT, Letter from Manuel Contreras to Pastor Coronel, September 25, 1975, R022F0152.

76. ADT, Interrogation of Jorge Fuentes, n.d., R0080F0799.

77. John Dinges and Saul Landau, Assassination on Embassy Row (London: Writers and Readers, 1981), 155–57.

78. Ibid., 156.

79. McSherry, Predatory States.

80. OCT Public Prosecution's Final Statement, 169–72.

81. Declaration of Carlos Hernan Labarca Sanhueza in Chilean Lawsuit 2182-98, "Operation Condor," vol. 10, August 28, 2003, 2285–2287.

82. OCT Public Prosecution's Final Statement, 170.

83. MAC, Memoradum 58-G, August 27, 1975.

84. This section is based on this author's communications with Edén Echenique, February 11 and 14, and September 17, 2019.

85. UYFRM, Gavazzo's personal military file, 009298.

86. ADT, Investigations Department, Capital Police. "List of political opponents based in border cities to our country," February 15, 1974, R209F1332.

87. Dinges, Condor Years.

88. Vito Ruggiero, "Il Neofascismo Italiano in America Latina: Network anticomunisti transnazionali nel Cono Sur (1977–1982)" (PhD Thesis, Roma Tre, 2019).

89. Dinges, Condor Years.

90. Ruggiero, "Il Neofascismo italiano."

91. Dinges and Landau, *Assassination on Embassy Row.*

92. Dinges, *Condor Years.*

93. Police Declaration by Mario Ernesto Jahn Barrera, Chilean Lawsuit 2182-98, "Operation Condor," vol. 10, August 26, 2003, 2277–78.

94. Dinges, *Condor Years*, 107.

95. ADT, Invitation from General Manuel Contreras to General Francisco Brítez, October 1975, R00143F0011.

96. Ibid., report no. 696 by the police headquarters, November 6, 1975, R00143-F0023.

97. Cavalcanti Cunha and Krischke, "Operação Condor," 135–64.

98. MAC, Memorandum 66-I, October 10, 1975.

99. Ibid., Memorandum 69-I, October 31, 1975.

100. Interview with AR001-2018, member of the Taub family, Buenos Aires, July 13, 2018.

101. MMDH, Operación Cóndor.

102. MAC, Memoranda 72-J and 73-J, November 17, 1975.

103. Ibid., Memorandum 74-J, November 21, 1975.

104. Official Decree S3511/1975 acknowledging the arrest of Rubio Farias and Espinosa Machiavello on November 22, 1975, available at https://www.argentina.gob.ar /normativa/nacional/decreto-3511-1975-215464; Official Decree S3604/1975 regarding Bustos Ramírez on November 26, 1975, available at https://www.argentina.gob.ar/nor mativa/nacional/decreto-3604-1975-215590 (both accessed August 26, 2021).

105. Official Decree S787/1976 ordering the expulsion of Palma Herrera on June 10, 1976, available at https://www.argentina.gob.ar/normativa/nacional/decreto-787-1976 -210715; Official Decree S2059/1976 for the expulsion of Letelier Sotomayor on September 15, 1976, available at https://www.argentina.gob.ar/normativa/nacional/decreto -2059-1976-210911 (both accessed August 26, 2021).

106. Declaration of Gertrudis Elizabeth Rubio Farias to the Santiago Court of Appeals in Chilean Lawsuit 2182-98, "Operation Condor," vol. 27, August 16, 2006, 8714–16.

107. Patricia Collyer Canales, "Catalina Palma y la Operación Cóndor: 'Los Agentes Argentinos que llegaron a detenernos, dijeron que le estaban haciendo un "favorcito" a Pinochet,'" *Página19*, October 19, 2018.

108. Declaration of Sergio Muñoz Martínez to the Santiago Court of Appeals, August 24, 2006, 8729–8730.

109. Vicky Baker, "Exposing History's Faultlines," *Index on Censorship* 45, no. 1 (2016): 68–71.

110. Declaration of Rosa Adriana Catalina Palma Herrera to the Santiago Court of Appeals, July 11, 2006, 8560–62.

111. Declarations of Sergio Enrique Letelier Sotomayor, August 24, 2006, 8731–33;

Gabriel Alfonso Salinas Alvarez, August 25, 2006, 8742–45; Juan José Bustos Ramírez, vol. 28, January 15, 2007, 8951–52.

112. Declarations of Roberto Guillermo Pizarro Hofer, vol. 27, August 25, 2006, 8739–41; Guillermina Alicia Gariazzo Gavilán, August 25, 2006, 8736–38; Juan Bustos.

113. ADT, Program of the First Working Meeting on National Intelligence, October 29, 1975, R00143F0012 to R00143F0022.

114. ADT, Invitation to the First Working Meeting on National Intelligence, October 29, 1975, R00143F0014.

115. Ibid., R00143F0015.

116. Ibid., R00143F0017.

117. Ibid., R00143F0018.

118. The document with "Minutes of the Conclusions of the First InterAmerican Meeting on National Intelligence" is reproduced in Peter Kornbluh, *The Pinochet File: A Declassified Dossier on Atrocity and Accountability*, updated ed. (New York: New Press, 2013), 365–68.

119. In December 1975, but effective February 1976, General Otto Paladino was designated as SIDE's new head, and the entire body—which at the time of signing the Condor agreement was still in the hands of the navy—was then placed under the functional control of the army. I thank Melisa Slatman for clarifying this point.

120. Interview with Luiz Cláudio Cunha, investigative journalist, Brasilia, November 10, 2017.

121. Luiz Cláudio Cunha, "As garras do Brasil na Operação Condor," *Sul21*, July 9, 2012.

122. ADT, High Command of the Paraguayan Armed Forces, report no. 64, "Combined Subversive Action," October 20, 1975, R00143F0221–24.

123. Through decrees 2770, 2771, and 2772 of October 6, 1975, the Argentine police was also placed under the operational control of the army. This arrangement implied that while the police retained their autonomy, they had to be available to operate with the army when required. I thank Melisa Slatman for clarifying this point.

124. They were Argentina, Bolivia, Brazil, Colombia, Chile, Ecuador, El Salvador, the US, Honduras, Nicaragua, Panama, Paraguay, Peru, Uruguay, and Venezuela. A preparatory gathering preceded the conference on August 26, 1975, also held in Uruguay and presided over by General Luis Queirolo, the army chief of staff, with the participation of delegates from Argentina, Bolivia, Brazil, Colombia, Chile, Ecuador, the US, Honduras, Nicaragua, Panama, Paraguay, Peru, and Venezuela.

125. UYFRM, 2.4., 33, 6, Conference of American Armies, press releases of October 20, 21, and 24, 1975.

126. Ibid.

127. Kornbluh, *Pinochet File*, 367–68.

128. Ibid.

Chapter 4. The Condor System

1. Leonardo Haberkorn, "Punta Rieles: La cárcel de emprendedores que parece un pueblo en miniatura," *La Nación*, June 12, 2019.

2. Rico, *Investigación histórica sobre dictadura*, 302.

3. Unless otherwise referenced, this section is based on the author's 2013 interview with Sara Méndez.

4. CELS, Testimony of Sara Méndez at the Argentine Military Commanders' Trial on June 14, 1985, "The Newspaper of the Trial (*El diario del juicio*)," Year 1, no. 9, July 23, 1985, 202.

5. CIA, Intelligence Information Cable 136305, January 10, 1977, paragraph 1.C.

6. José Mitchell, "Coronel confirma ação conjunta," *Jornal do Brasil*, May 8, 2000, 7.

7. See the letter by the director of the Chilean CNI (General Odlier Mena) to the Chilean Minister of Foreign Affairs, dated March 2, 1979 (n. 205193), to notify the designation of two military officers to the functions of administrative advisor and secretary of the Chilean Embassy in Brasilia. General Mena affirmed that this replacement would be reported to the Brazilian SNI, in accordance with the provisions of Plan Condor. Document sent by John Dinges on July 2, 2019.

8. UYFRM, 2.1, Confidential Notes Received and Sent, 1-Conf, C, Note H3-3/1976 (1538), sent to the Argentine Ministry of Foreign Affairs. Three cell-like rooms were also found in the Embassy's first underground floor, but these allegations were never investigated.

9. SID's Request for Personal Particulars no. 03/76 sent to the National Director of the Technical Police on January 22, 1976. The police responded the same day, providing information that included last known address and photos. The SID and police regularly exchanged information on many Uruguayans subsequently targeted in Buenos Aires, including Cecilia Trías and Raúl Altuna (report no. 299/76) and Hugo Méndez and Raúl Borrelli (report no. 38/76). Documents sent by Melisa Slatman on March 24, 2020.

10. Sandoval, "La Junta."

11. Gladys Meilinger de Sannemann, *Paraguay en el Operativo Cóndor: Represión e intercambio clandestino de prisioneros políticos en el Cono Sur* (Asunción: RP Ediciones, 1989).

12. Francisco Peregil, "Gladys Meilinger, víctima y verdugo del horror en Paraguay," *El País*, February 1, 2014.

13. Interview with CL001-2017, former militant and friend of Luis Muñoz, Santiago, May 9, 2017.

14. Interview with Flor Hernández Zazpe, sister of Juan Hernández Zazpe, Santiago, November 23, 2016.

15. OCT Public Prosecution's Final Statement, 378–82.

16. Memo 019 from Luis Gutierrez to L. F. Alemparte, Santiago, December 23, 1975, in OCT Public Prosecution's Final Statement, 175.

17. MAC, Response to Memo 019 of 23/12/1975, Buenos Aires, January 8, 1976.

18. NSA, Monthly Special Intelligence Report 4/76, Task Force 1, strictly secret and confidential, Detection of the Meeting of the PRT-ERP "Central Committee," dated by analyst Carlos Osorio as April 1, 1976.

19. OCT 2016 Verdict, 1882.

20. OCT Public Prosecution's Final Statement, 931. Miguel Ángel Athanasiú Jara's and Frida Laschan Mellado's son, Pablo, was illegally appropriated and recovered his identity in 2013.

21. DOS, Santiago 4325, May 7, 1976.

22. PFA, Report SSF DAE "S" 5543, September 15, 1976, 3, hereafter Obregón's report, www.mpf.gob.ar/plan-condor/files/2019/04/36.pdf (accessed May 20, 2020).

23. According to Juan Raúl Ferreira, Michelini had labeled the situation in Argentina as *una trampa mortal* (death trap) the night of the kidnapping. See *D. F.*, documentary by Mateo Gutiérrez and Taxi Films (2008), minute 1:01:06.

24. UYFRM, 2.1, Uruguay's Internal Politics, 2-Confidential, H12, Confidential Note to the Consular Section in Buenos Aires, H12/1975 (1827), November 25, 1975.

25. CELS, Testimony of Matilde Esther Rodríguez Piñeyrua de Gutiérrez to Federal Judge Juan Edgardo Fegoli, Buenos Aires, April 16, 1984.

26. Testimonies of Matilde Rodríguez and Juan Pablo Gutiérrez in *D. F.*, minutes 1:02:52 and 1:04:06, respectively.

27. Matilde Rodríguez's 1984 testimony.

28. Juan Pablo Gutiérrez, in *D. F.*, minute 1:03:44.

29. Ibid.

30. Montevideo's Criminal Court of the Eleventh Circuit, Sentence No. 68 in Lawsuit 100-10592/1985, June 30, 2011, 9, https://www.observatorioluzibarburu.org/media/uploads/7.%20%20Sent_68_condena_Bordaberry_Blanco_30-6-2011%20Penal%2011.pdf (accessed July 30, 2020).

31. CELS, "Denuncia hechos: Promueve la reapertura del proceso," by lawyers Augusto Conte, Emilio Mignone, Luis Zamora, and Marcelo Parrilli, January 18, 1983.

32. Ibid.

33. CELS, Testimony of Zelmar Michelini to Federal Judge Juan Fegoli, Buenos Aires, May 10, 1984.

34. Ibid.

35. CELS, Federal Criminal and Correctional Court No.1 of the Federal Capital, "19147 Gutiérrez Ruiz, Héctor; Michelini, Zelmar R; Barredo de Schroeder, Rosario del Carmen; Whitelaw, William s/homicidio," Judge Juan Edgardo Fegoli, 1976.

36. Ibid.

37. 1984 testimonies of Matilde Rodríguez and Zelmar Michelini.

38. SERPAJ, *Uruguay Nunca Más: Human Rights Violations, 1972–1985* (Philadelphia: Temple University Press, 1992), 335.

39. Testimony of Matilde Rodríguez in *D. F.*, minute 1:13:14.

40. DOS, Letter from Wilson Ferreira Aldunate to General Don Jorge Rafael Videla, president of the Republic of Argentina, Buenos Aires, May 24, 1976, NSA Argentina Declassification Project document 0000A05D.

41. Testimony of Julio Traibel, in *D. F.*, minute 1:14:30.

42. Letter from Wilson Ferreira to General Videla, 5.

43. CELS, "19147 Gutiérrez Ruiz, Héctor et al., s/homicidio."

44. Testimony of Cecilia Michelini in *D. F.*, minute 1:31:12.

45. UYFRM, 2.6, international press articles on amnesty, 21, 5; Flavio Tavares, "Bárbaras torturas sufrieron los cuatro asesinados en B. Aires," *Excelsior*, May 24, 1976.

46. DOS, Usun 2156, May 18, 1976, paragraph 3.

47. DOS, Buenos Aires 3343, May 20, 1976, paragraph 6.

48. DOS, Buenos Aires 3465, May 25, 1976, paragraph 1.

49. DOS, State 131390, May 27, 1976, paragraph 2.

50. CELS, Testimony of Juan Raúl Ferreira to Federal Judge Juan Fegoli, Buenos Aires, May 9, 1984.

51. DOS, Buenos Aires 3465.

52. Claudio Trobo, *Asesinato de estado: Quién mató a Michelini y Gutiérrez Ruiz?* (Buenos Aires: Ediciones Colihue, 2005).

53. Walter de León Orpi, "Juan María Bordaberry: El dictador latinoamericano condenado por delitos de lesa humanidad," in *Luchas contra la impunidad: Uruguay 1985–2011*, ed. Gabriela Fried-Amilivia and Francesca Lessa (Montevideo: Trilce, 2011), 175–88.

54. CELS, Testimony of Margarita Michelini to Federal Judge Juan Fegoli, Buenos Aires, April 25, 1984.

55. Testimony of Gabriela Schroeder in *D. F.*, minute 1:36:15.

56. Testimony of Juan Ignacio Azarola Saint before the 1985 Uruguayan Parliamentary Investigative Commission on the Situation of Disappeared Persons and Its Causes (hereafter Uruguayan Commission on the Disappeared) in *A todos ellos*, 418–20.

57. 1984 testimony of Margarita Michelini; testimony of Enrique Rodríguez Larreta (son) in *D. F.*, minute 1:44:51.

58. Interview with Ricardo Poggio, Research and Conservation Division of the National Memory Archive, Human Rights and Cultural Pluralism Secretariat, Ministry of Justice, Buenos Aires, June 22, 2018.

59. CELS, "Comienza un nuevo juicio por Automotores Orletti," September 30, 2016, available at www.cels.org.ar/web/2016/09/comienza-un-nuevo-juicio-por-automotores-orletti/ (accessed November 13, 2019).

60. Task force agents referred to secret prisons by calling them *cuevas* (caves), from which people never emerged. Interview with Ricardo Poggio.

61. Buenos Aires Federal Criminal Court No. 1, Orletti I, 905.

62. OCT Public Prosecution's Final Statement, 381.

63. Ibid., 903.

64. Ibid., 911.

65. CELS, "Admitió Gordon que actuó en un centro clandestino," *Clarín*, April 1, 1986.

66. DOS, Buenos Aires 3465.

67. UYFRM, 2.1, Information about Individuals, 3-Confidential, H3-2, packet II, Confidential Report from Ambassador Gustavo Magariños to Foreign Minister Blanco, H3-2/1976 (957), May 28, 1976.

68. Sivak, *El asesinato de Juan José Torres*.

69. UYFRM, 2.6, New York General Consulate/Confidential, 3, 8; Stan Lehman, "Argentine Cops Find Body of Ex-President," *San Juan Star*, June 4, 1976.

70. DOS, Buenos Aires 3664, June 3, 1976, paragraph 5.

71. Ibid.

72. Gerardo Irusta, *Espionaje y servicios secretos en Bolivia: 1930–1980* (La Paz: self-pub., 1995).

73. DOS, Buenos Aires 3664, paragraph 4.

74. UYFRM, 2.1, Information about Individuals, 3-Confidential, H3-2, packet II, Confidential Cable Received by the Embassy in Buenos Aires C194/24Z, June 2, 1976.

75. Ibid.

76. Osorio's 2015 testimony.

77. DOS, State 137156, June 4, 1976.

78. DOS, Briefing Memorandum 7611578, To the Secretary from INR Harold H. Saunders, "Murders in Argentina—No Intergovernmental Conspiracy," June 4, 1976.

79. DOS, Santiago 5434, June 7, 1976.

80. DOS, Buenos Aires 3741, June 7, 1976.

81. Ibid., paragraph 4.

82. Ibid.

83. DOS, Montevideo 2046, June 7, 1976, paragraph A.

84. Osorio's 2015 testimony.

85. DOS, State 209192, August 23, 1976, paragraphs 1, 3.A, 3.B, and 3.C.

86. Dinges, *Condor Years*.

87. DOS, San Jose 4526, September 20, 1976.

88. Dinges and Landau, *Assassination on Embassy Row*.

89. UYFRM, 2.6, international press articles on amnesty, 21, 5; "25 Political Refugees Abducted in Argentina," *San Juan Star*, June 12, 1976.

90. "Theft in Argentina of List of Refugees Stirs Slaying Fears," *New York Times*, June 11, 1976.

91. Unless otherwise referenced, this section is based on the author's interview with

Brenda Falero, survivor of Operation Condor, Montevideo, October 2, 2013, and the OCT 2016 Verdict, 3205–14.

92. Ibid., 3208.

93. Letter from Robert J. Muller, regional representative for Latin America, to Foreign Relations Minister César Augusto Guzzetti, ARG/089/76, June 11, 1976. Document sent by UNHCR Records and Archives Office on February 22, 2019.

94. UYFRM, "25 Political Refugees Abducted in Argentina."

95. Interview with Brenda Falero.

96. Interview with Ricardo Poggio.

97. Ibid.

98. DOS, Buenos Aires 3960, June 15, 1976.

99. DOS, "Memorandum of conversation," Santiago de Chile, June 6, 1976. During his 2015 testimony in the Operation Condor Trial in Buenos Aires, NSA analyst Osorio affirmed that the correct meeting date was June 10.

100. DOS, Buenos Aires 3918, June 13, 1976, paragraph 3.

101. DOS, Buenos Aires 3960, paragraph 7; CIA, Latin American Trends, Staff Notes, secret, "Counterterrorism in South America," June 23, 1976.

102. UYFRM, 2.1, Information about Individuals, 3-Confidential, H3-2, packet II, Confidential Cable Sent C336/2, July 7, 1976.

103. Ibid., Confidential Cable Received C218/14Z, June 16, 1976.

104. Ivonne Trías and Universindo Rodríguez, *Gerardo Gatti: Revolucionario* (Montevideo: Trilce, 2012).

105. The FUSNA was the navy's operational and elite unit, modeled after the French army paratroopers, and was dedicated to political repression. It was officially created in 1972 and initially focused on the repression of the Tupamaros. See OCT Public Prosecution's Final Statement, 409–10, and "Por primera vez, el Fusna por dentro," *La República,* January 31, 2006.

106. This secret clandestine center, also known as *infierno grande* (big hell), operated inside storehouse no. 4 of the army's Materials and Armaments' Service. See https://sitiosdememoria.uy/smlg-uymo-07 (accessed May 20, 2020).

107. UYFRM, Rome Tribunal Documentation, 5, 7, Victims' Declarations, Testimony of Ricardo Gil Iribarne before Criminal Judge of the 19th Circuit in Montevideo (hereafter 19th Criminal Judge), August 20, 2006.

108. Ibid.

109. SDHPR, Special Information Report 8/976, Junta of the Commanders in Chief, SID, June 25, 1976, cited on p. 19 of "PVP—Operativos represivos," available at www.gub.uy/secretaria-derechos-humanos-pasado-reciente/comunicacion/publicaciones/operativos-represivos (accessed December 3, 2019).

110. Orletti I, 315.

111. UYFRM, Victims' Declarations, Testimony of Washington Pérez before the Uruguayan Commission on the Disappeared, July 8, 1985.

112. OCT Public Prosecution's Final Statement, 427.

113. Amnesty International, "Uruguay: Testimony on kidnapping in Argentina, torture, and illegal transfer to Uruguay: Nelson Eduardo Dean Bermudez," AI Index, AMR 52/18/79, February 27, 1979. Document sent by Maria José Parada on February 2, 2015.

114. UYFRM, Rome Tribunal Documentation, Victims' Declarations, Testimony of Sergio López Burgos before 19th Criminal Judge, August 9, 2006, 585; interview with Gastón Zina, survivor of Operation Condor, Montevideo, Uruguay, August 8, 2014; testimonies of Ariel Soto and Alicia Cadenas in Orletti I, and email exchange with Raúl Altuna, June 9, 2020.

115. Orletti I, Testimony of Laura Anzalone, 651, and of Enrique Rodríguez, 324.

116. Interview with Melisa Slatman, University of Buenos Aires and Public Prosecutor's Office, Buenos Aires, September 16, 2013.

117. Interview with Ricardo Poggio.

118. Eduardo Dean's 1979 testimony, 3.

119. Testimony of Alicia Cadenas in Alvesta, Sweden, April 22, 1979. Document sent by Alicia Cadenas on March 28, 2014.

120. Orletti I, Testimony of José Felix Díaz, 655.

121. Interview with Gastón Zina.

122. Orletti I, Testimony of Pilar Nores, 511.

123. Alicia Cadenas testimony, 429; Eduardo Dean's 1979 testimony.

124. Orletti I, Enrique Rodríguez testimony, 327; Ana Salvo testimony, 443.

125. Orletti I, Testimony of Ana Ines Quadros, 377.

126. Interview with Elba Rama, survivor of Operation Condor, Montevideo, March 21, 2014.

127. Eduardo Dean's 1979 testimony, 4; Orletti I, Testimonies of Pilar Nores, 511; Sergio López Burgos, 404; and Enrique Rodríguez, 316.

128. Montevideo's Criminal Court of the 19th Circuit, Sentence No. 36 in Lawsuit 98-247/2006, March 26, 2009, 22, www.observatorioluzibarburu.org/media/uploads/98_247_2006.pdf (accessed August 27, 2020).

129. Orletti I, Testimony of Ana Salvo, 437.

130. Interview with Sara Méndez.

131. Orletti I, Testimonies of López Burgos, 405–6; Pilar Nores, 516; Roger Rodríguez, 567; and Ricardo Gil Iribarne, 484; OCT Public Prosecution's Final Statement, 435.

132. La Cason secret prison in Punta Gorda was called *infierno chico* to distinguish it from *infierno grande,* or 300 Carlos.

133. Interview with Sara Méndez.

134. Alicia Cadenas's 1979 testimony.

135. UYFRM, 2.1, Information about Individuals, 3-Confidential, H3-2, packet I, Cable C364/11, July 16, 1976.

136. Ibid., Cable C367/24, July 19, 1976.

137. Email exchange with UY001-2019, former PVP activist, December 3, 2019.

138. DOS, Buenos Aires 4740, July 20, 1976, paragraph 2.

139. DOS, Buenos Aires 5637, August 27, 1976.

140. CIA, Intelligence Information Cable, 990638, July 26, 1976, paragraph 1.

141. Ibid., paragraph 2.

142. SIDE No. 3258, Intelligence Brief 05/76, May 24, 1976, strictly secret and confidential, available at www.mpf.gob.ar/plan-condor/files/2018/12/Biedma-3.pdf (accessed May 30, 2020).

143. OCT Public Prosecution's Final Statement, 1000.

144. Orletti I, Testimony of María de la Luz Lagarrigue Castillo, 225.

145. ADT, Interrogation of Jorge Fuentes, n.d., R00080F0712.

146. Dinges, *Condor Years*.

147. Orletti I, Testimony of José Luis Bertazzo, 193.

148. Interview with José Luis Bertazzo, survivor of Orletti, Buenos Aires, July 21, 2014. *Señor*, rather than *caballero*, is normally used in Argentina.

149. José Luis Méndez Méndez, *La Operación Cóndor contra Cuba* (Buenos Aires: Instituto Espacio para la Memoria, 2011).

150. OCT Public Prosecution's Final Statement, 1008; and interview with José Luis Bertazzo.

151. CIA, "Background on the August 1976 disappearance of two Cuban Embassy security men," July 27, 1985, paragraph 5. Also see FBI, Memorandum for Ambassador John Sears from Legal Attaché Robert Scherrer, secret/eyes only, October 19, 1976.

152. In 2012 and 2013 the Argentine Forensic Anthropology Team discovered and identified their bodies.

153. CIA, SNLA 76-050, "Staff notes. Argentina-Cuba: Castro support for local subversion?" September 22, 1976; CIA, Intelligence Information Cable 020110, August 25, 1976.

154. NSA, Interagency Intelligence Memorandum, "Cuban support for nationalist movements and revolutionary groups," July 1977.

155. OCT Public Prosecution's Final Statement, 1007.

156. Ibid., 996–97.

157. Obregón's report, 5–7. The inspector refers to the PVP by calling it OPR-33. Many US declassified government documents also call the PVP OPR-33, an organization which had predated it.

158. Orletti I, Testimony of José Felix Díaz, 659; UYFRM, Rome Tribunal Documentation, 6, 8/4, Declarations to the 19th Criminal Judge by José Gavazzo, October 25, 2007, 3073, and by Jorge Silveira, August 14, 2006, 670.

159. OCT Public Prosecution's Final Statement, 437.

160. After the first wave of detentions in June–July 1976, Mechoso and Adalberto Soba had taken over from Gatti and Duarte as PVP leaders.

161. José Gavazzo's 2007 testimony, 3069–76.

162. Besides conducting operations in Buenos Aires, the SID also illegally detained and tortured almost fifty PVP activists in Montevideo between May and December 1976. Information provided by Raúl Olivera on February 6, 2020.

163. Gil Iribarne's 2006 testimony, 623.

164. OCT Public Prosecution's Final Statement, 435.

165. Orletti I, testimony of Pilar Nores, 691.

166. Ibid., testimony of Beatriz Castellonese, 530–33. Mechoso's remains were identified in 2012, hidden in a drum recovered from San Fernando, the same modus operandi as in the Cubans' assassination.

167. Sentence No. 36 in Lawsuit 98-247/2006, 17.

168. OCT Public Prosecution's Final Statement, 438.

169. Orletti I, Testimony of Maria Elena Laguna, 461.

170. OCT Public Prosecution's Final Statement, 669.

171. Ibid., 682.

172. François Graña, *Los padres de Mariana: María Emilia Islas y Jorge Zaffaroni: La pasión militante* (Montevideo: Trilce, 2011).

173. UYFRM, Rome Tribunal Documentation, Victims' Declarations, Testimony of Maria Elena Laguna, November 13, 2000, 063033–34.

174. Ibid., Testimony of Beatriz Barboza, December 9, 1999.

175. Interview with UY001-2014, former PVP activist, Montevideo, November 24, 2014.

176. Orletti I, Testimony of Beatriz Barboza, 473; interview with UY002-2014, former PVP activist, Montevideo, December 11, 2014.

177. UYFRM, Rome Tribunal Documentation, Victims' Declarations, Testimony of Alvaro Nores Montedonico, Toronto, September 20, 1984, 1600.

178. Ibid., Testimony of Ricardo Gil Iribarne to the 1985 Uruguayan Commission on the Disappeared.

179. Interview with José Luis Bertazzo.

180. Roger Rodríguez, "El destino del 'segundo vuelo' sigue enterrado en impunidad," *La República*, October 5, 2009.

181. Marcelo's body also appeared in the San Fernando drums, and was identified in 1989.

182. SDHPR, personal file of María Macarena Gelman García, available at www.gub .uy/secretaria-derechos-humanos-pasado-reciente/sites/secretaria-derechos-humanos -pasado-reciente/files/documentos/publicaciones/GELMAN%20GARC%C3%8DA %2C%20Mar%C3%ADa%20Macarena%20Ficha%20accesible.pdf (accessed November 29, 2019).

183. Orletti I, testimonies of Monica Soliño, 347; Elba Rama, 399; Ariel Soto, 421; Gastón Zina, 457; and Laura Anzalone, 653.

184. UYFRM, Rome Tribunal Documentation, 6, 9/7, Testimony of Julio César Barboza to the 1985 Uruguayan Commission on the Disappeared, n.d.

185. Roger Rodríguez, "La República descubrió la infame 'Base Valparaíso,' donde mataron a María Claudia, la nuera de Gelman," *La República,* May 29, 2005.

186. UYFRM, Rome Tribunal Documentation, Folder 8/4, Testimony of Gilberto Vazquez before 19th Criminal Judge, August 22, 2006, 1775.

187. Roger Rodríguez, "El nido escondido del Cóndor," *La República,* October 12, 2009.

188. Email exchange with Raúl Altuna, June 5, 2020.

189. Enrique Rodríguez Larreta, *El informe Orletti: Conexión internacional* (Montevideo: Pressur, 2013), 26.

190. URFRM, 2.1, Subversive Activities, 2, A6-1, Press Office of the Joint Forces, Special Communique 21, October 28, 1976; Joint Forces Communiques, 1, A1-2-1, Press Office of the Joint Forces, Special Communique 22, October 29, 1976.

191. They were Sergio López Burgos, Sara Méndez, Asilú Maceiro, Elba Rama, Ana Inés Quadros, Gastón Zina, Cecilia Gayoso, Mónica Soliño, Ariel Soto, Ana Salvo, Alicia Cadenas, Edelweiss Zahn, Victor Lubian, and Marta Petrides.

192. DOS, Montevideo 4161, November 1, 1976.

193. Ibid., Buenos Aires 7203, November 2, 1976.

194. Interviews conducted in Montevideo in 2014 with PVP militants: Elba Rama on March 21, Ariel Soto on March 27, and Edelweiss Zahn on April 1.

195. Dinges, *Condor Years.*

196. DOD, Intelligence Information Report no. 6804033476, "Special Operations Forces," October 1, 1976, paragraph "COMMENT."

197. In 1971 Banzer's dictatorship entrusted the fight against subversion to the police; the intelligence and repressive apparatuses were restructured, creating the DOP and the DOS (Department of Social Order). The DOP operated throughout Bolivia and centralized various repressive operations, from information gathering, surveillance, and infiltration operations to abductions and interrogations in clandestine prisons. OCT Public Prosecution's Final Statement, 1196.

198. Ibid., 1205.

199. The SIE reported to Army Intelligence and primarily dealt on Condor matters with the Ministry of the Interior. OCT Public Prosecution's Final Statement, 1194, and Irusta, *Espionaje y servicios secretos en Bolivia.*

200. Irusta, *Espionaje y servicios secretos en Bolivia,* 344.

201. SIE's radiogram 136/76 to the Ministry of the Interior and the DOP confirmed the expulsion at 10:15 a.m. CELS, press release, "Serious international denunciation filed," February 26, 1985.

202. Interview with José Luis Bertazzo.

203. OCT Public Prosecution's Final Statement, 801. Only Lila's body, which had been buried in a mass grave in Avellaneda's municipal cemetery, was identified in 2014.

204. Testimony by Cristoph Georg Paul Willeke Floel in Chilean Lawsuit 2182-98, "Operation Condor," vol. 40, July 10, 2012, 13158–65.

205. US Government Memorandum, June 7, 1976, to David E. Simcox (counselor for political affairs in Brasilia at the time) from Program Studies Section, re state telegram 137156. Document sent by André Saboia Martins on November 14, 2017.

206. UYFRM, Rome Tribunal Documentation, José Gavazzo's military file, 009311.

207. SID, Department III, Plans—Operations—Liaison, August 16, 1976. Document sent by Giulia Barrera, December 15, 2017.

208. José Gavazzo's military file, 009320.

209. CIA, Intelligence Information Cable 017078, December 28, 1977.

210. CIA, Intelligence Information Cable 935174, June 25, 1976, paragraph 2.

211. Ibid., paragraph 4. Since that paragraph has been heavily redacted, the information on the three Condor countries operating in Paris is derived from another CIA document, Weekly Summary, No. 1396, July 2, 1976, 7.

212. CIA, Intelligence Information Cable 978420, July 21, 1976.

213. Ibid., 992369, July 28, 1976.

214. McSherry, *Predatory States*.

215. "Conclusions of the First InterAmerican Meeting," in Kornbluh, *Pinochet File*, 365–68.

216. CIA, Intelligence Information Cable 169805, February 1, 1977.

217. Defense Intelligence Agency (hereafter DIA), Intelligence Appraisal, "Latin America: Counterterrorism and trends in terrorism (U)," DIAIAPPR 189-78, August 11, 1978.

218. Ibid., 3.

219. Cable of the Uruguayan Ministry of Defense "Parte Nro. J-02677/1385," April 9, 1976, confidential, very urgent. Document sent by Jorge Ithurburu on December 17, 2017.

220. ADT, Ministry of the Interior, Telex number [cannot be read clearly but likely 02550/269], April 21, 1976, R00132F2129; also see Armed Forces Central Command, General Staff, Search Order 23/76, July 6, 1976, R021F1522.

221. Interview with Roger Rodríguez, journalist, Montevideo, October 4, 2013. Scholars and journalists, including Dinges, McSherry, and Stella Calloni, erroneously believed in the early 2000s that Condor 1 was Chile.

222. DIA, Intelligence Appraisal, "Counterterrorism."

223. DOS, Asuncion 4451, October 13, 1978. Ambassador White connected this encrypted system to Operation Condor and "advised the Carter administration to recon-

sider whether this linkage was in the U.S. interest." J. Patrice McSherry, "Tracking the Origins of a State Terror Network: Operation Condor," *Latin American Perspectives* 29, no. 1 (2002): 52.

224. CIA, 992369, paragraph 2.

225. Dinges bases this conclusion on two sources: the testimony of Chile's representative Cristoph Willeke Floel, and the 1990s interviews by journalist Jorge Boimvaser with SIDE officer Colonel Rubén Visuara. See John Dinges, *Los años del Cóndor: Operaciones internacionales de asesinato en el Cono Sur* (Santiago: Debate, 2021), 354.

226. Ibid.

227. DOD, "Special Operations Forces" report.

228. Willeke Floel's 2012 testimony, 13159–60.

229. Ibid., 13160–61.

230. FBI, Cable from Buenos Aires to FBI director, September 28, 1976, also known as "Chilbom," 2.

231. Willeke Floel's 2012 testimony, 13163.

232. DOS, "ARA Monthly Report (July): The 'Third World War' and South America," August 3, 1976; CIA, Intelligence Information Cable 999039; and Marcelo Godoy, "General admite que Brasil fez parte da Operação Condor," *O Estado de São Paulo*, December 30, 2007.

233. According to Greek mythology, Teseo (Theseus) was the son of Aegeus, the king of Athens, and a great hero. Teseo killed several evildoers, most famously, the Cretan Minotaur, enclosed in the legendary labyrinth of Knossos.

234. CIA, Intelligence Information Cable 187182, February 16, 1977, and CIA, Intelligence Information Cable 413973, October 7, 1977.

235. FBI, "Chilbom" cable, 2.

236. CIA, Intelligence Information Cable 999039, August 5, 1976.

237. CIA, Intelligence Information Cable 413973, paragraph 2.

238. CIA, Intelligence Information Cable 187182.

239. CIA, Intelligence Information Cable 986766, July 23, 1976.

240. CIA, "Latin American Trends," August 11, 1976.

241. CIA, Intelligence Information Cable 413973, paragraph 4.

242. CIA, 992369. Also see CIA, "Counterterrorism in the Southern Cone," Secret, May 9, 1977. Dinges specifically mentions Edy Kaufman as a potential target of Teseo in *Los años del Cóndor*, 403, 614.

243. CIA, Intelligence Information Cable 413973; Dinges, *Condor Years*.

244. CIA, Intelligence Information Cable 187182.

245. CIA, Intelligence Information Cable 999039.

246. CIA, Intelligence Information Report, "Text of the agreement by Condor Countries regulating their subversive targets" (hereafter Teseo Agreement), August 16, 1977.

247. Ibid., paragraph VI.1–2.

248. FBI, "Chilbom" cable, 2–3.

249. CIA, Teseo Agreement.

250. DOD, "Special Operations Forces" report; CIA, Intelligence Information Cable 122075.

251. CIA, Intelligence Information Cable 999039; Intelligence Information Cable 048376, September 23, 1976; Intelligence Information Cable 105881, November 22, 1976.

252. Kornbluh, *Pinochet File.*

253. For a discussion of the contacts between the CIA and French intelligence, see Dinges, *Los años del Cóndor,* chaps. 13 and 14.

254. DOS, Montevideo 4755, December 10, 1976.

255. CIA, Intelligence Information Cable 122075; and DOS, State 065403, March 25, 1977.

Chapter 5. Condor's Demise

1. Unless otherwise referenced, this section is based on the author's interview with Laura Elgueta Díaz, survivor of Operation Condor, Santiago, November 26, 2016, and her testimony in the Operation Condor Trial in Buenos Aires, hearing of March 25, 2014, author's notes.

2. OCT 2016 Verdict, 1999.

3. Ibid.

4. VDS, written testimony of Sonia Magdalena Díaz Ureta de Elgueta, Ruth Elena Díaz Vargas de Elgueta, and Laura Ruth Elgueta Díaz, before notary Luis De Angoitia y Gaxiola, Mexico City, DJUR-10-02-79, February 13, 1979, 4.

5. ARFRM, General Director for Information, International Organizations Department, "Intrusion complaint in the office on Venezuela Street," 80AH/0146, Refugees and Stateless People, March 18, 1977.

6. DOS, Buenos Aires 3096, April 27, 1977.

7. DOS, Memorandum of Conversation, UNHCR Headquarters, Buenos Aires, March 31, 1977.

8. Sandoval, "La Junta."

9. CIA, International Issues Review, "Terrorist links in Latin America: Post-mortem on the JCR," June 29, 1979, 35, 39.

10. DIA, Intelligence Appraisal, "Latin America: Counterterrorism and Trends in Terrorism (U)," DIAIAPPR 189–78, August 11, 1978, 6.

11. Delegations comprised, among others, Ciro García, SIDE director of communication and army captain (ret.); Jorge Cayo, chief of communications intelligence (Argentina); Victor Barrenechea, chief of delegation and chief of Operation Condor psychology (Bolivia); Lt. Colonel Enrique Cowell, from DINA's Department of Psychological Operations (Chile); Commander Ruben Sosa, chief of foreign intelligence and psychology

representative (Paraguay); and Captain Horacio Sasson, of the SID (Uruguay). CIA, Intelligence Information Cable 145221, January 7, 1977.

12. CIA, Intelligence Information Cable 249827, April 18, 1977.

13. CIA, Intelligence Information Cable 249827; for instance, two Chilean-produced movies were to be shown on television in Argentina and Uruguay. CIA. Intelligence Information Cable 170209, February 2, 1977.

14. DOS, INR analysis, "Human rights in Latin America," n.d., 13.

15. CIA, Intelligence Information Cable 249827.

16. DOS, "Memorandum for the record—ARA/INR/CIA weekly meeting," June 27, 1977.

17. CIA, Intelligence Information Cable 170209.

18. CIA, Intelligence Information Cable 158629, January 25, 1977.

19. CIA, Intelligence Information Cable 158629.

20. DOS, State 292202, December 1, and Montevideo 4652, December 2, 1976.

21. DOS, Montevideo 4755, December 10, 1976.

22. CIA, Intelligence Information Cable 158629.

23. The DINA had enjoyed significant autonomy and had responded directly to Pinochet; conversely, the CNI operated under the jurisdiction of the Ministry of Defense. Pablo Policzer, *Los modelos del horror: Represión e información en Chile bajo la Dictadura Militar* (Santiago: LOM Ediciones, 2017).

24. CIA, Intelligence Information Cable 136305, January 10, 1977, paragraph 1.A.

25. Ibid.

26. DOS, State 065403, March 25, 1977.

27. Ibid.; CIA, Intelligence Information Cable 247101, April 12, 1977, paragraph 1.A.

28. CIA, "Counterterrorism in the Southern Cone," May 9, 1977.

29. According to CIA Intelligence Information Cable 986766 of July 23, 1976, paragraph 1, a senior Bolivian official had commented that the Condor program was developing "an effective organization" and would be able to operate against the forces and leaders of the JCR.

30. DOS, State 065403, paragraph 4.

31. ADT, Capital Police, Investigations Department, "Memorandum from the Head of Investigations to His Excellency the President of the Republic," March 29, 1977, R00008F1742–45.

32. OCT Public Prosecution's Final Statement, 768.

33. ADT, Capital Police, Investigations Department, "Gustavo Edison Inzaurralde Melgar," n.d., R00008F1371–73.

34. See ADT, Capital Police, Investigations Department, Directorate of Foreigners' Registration, Police Record 3.850 of Dora Marta Landi Gil, R00017F1317–18, and Police Record 3.851 of Alejandro Jose Logoluso, R00017F1320–22, March 29, 1977.

35. OCT Public Prosecution's Final Statement, 764; ADT, Capital Police, Investiga-

tions Department, Directorate of Foreigners' Registration, Police Record 3.845 of José Nell, R00017F1308–11, March 29, 1977. On April 6, 1977, a joint Argentine–Chilean task force broke into Nell's house in Flores's neighborhood, where Chilean refugee Jorge Sagaute Herrera was living. Sagaute was murdered, and his family recovered his remains in 2019. "El equipo Argentino de antropología forense identificó los restos de un desaparecido chileno," *Pagina12*, December 23, 2019.

36. ADT, Argentine Intelligence Report, secret, "Summary of intelligence activities April 5–6, 1977," n.d., R00143FR0932–35; Uruguayan National Army, II Department (Information), "F A II.-R,O,E.-O.P.R.-33," n.d., R008FF1755–60; and "List of O.P.R. (33) wanted," n.d., R0008F1755–60.

37. ADT, Capital Police, Investigations Department, Report to Pastor M. Coronel, April 9, 1977, R00172F0570.

38. DOS, Buenos02002, March 15, 1977, paragraph 2.

39. Interview with Federico Tatter, Paraguayan exile and relative of Condor victim, Asunción, September 6, 2016.

40. OCT Public Prosecution's Final Statement, 1087.

41. DOS, Memorandum of Conversation at the UNHCR headquarters in Buenos Aires, March 31, 1977.

42. ADT, Capital Police, Investigations Department, Report on the Declarations by Sotero Franco Benegas, transmitted from Encarnación, February 2, 1977, R208F25947. In 2009 Vera Baéz's remains were found buried on police grounds and positively identified in 2016. He became the fourth desaparecido to be recovered in Paraguay. "El cuarto desaparecido con nombre," *ABC*, October 20, 2016.

43. ADT, Capital Police, Investigations Department, n.d., R00011F0540.

44. OCT Public Prosecution's Final Statement, 771; interview with Lidia Cabrera, survivor of Operation Condor, September 18, 2016.

45. Interview with Lidia Cabrera.

46. Ibid.

47. OCT Public Prosecution's Final Statement, 777.

48. ADT, Capital Police, Investigations Department, Report to Pastor M. Coronel, May 16, 1977, R00172F0398.

49. Interview with Lidia Cabrera; DOS, Memorandum of Conversation at the US Embassy in Asunción, "Released political prisoner interview," July 21, 1978.

50. OCT 2016 Verdict, 2347.

51. Alejandra Dandan, "Los crímenes del Circuito Camps," *Página12*, September 12 2011.

52. SDHPR, personal file of Raúl Tejera, available at https://www.gub.uy/secretaria -derechos-humanos-pasado-reciente/comunicacion/publicaciones/ficha-perteneciente -tejera-llovet-raul-nestor (accessed August 26, 2020).

53. Ibid.

54. AI, *Testimony on Secret Detention Camps in Argentina,* AMR 13/79/79 (London: Amnesty International Publications, 1980).

55. Ibid.

56. "History of El Olimpo," available at https://www.exccdolimpo.org.ar/historia (accessed August 26, 2021).

57. "Los crímenes del centro Protobanco." *Página12,* December 29, 2011.

58. OCT Public Prosecution's Final Statement, 1047–52.

59. Interview with CL001-2016, close relative of Alexei Jaccard, Santiago, November 18, 2016.

60. Interview with CL002-2017, close relative of Ricardo Ramírez, Santiago, May 16, 2017.

61. OCT Public Prosecution's Final Statement, 1048.

62. Ibid.

63. VDS, Vicaría file on Jaccard Siegler, Alexei Vladimir, REL 542–77, n.d.

64. OCT 2016 Verdict, 2106.

65. VDS, report on the case of Alexei Jaccard, including background, representations made, and evaluation, REL 371–78, June 1978.

66. OCT Public Prosecution's Final Statement, 1052.

67. Interview with CL002-2017.

68. OCT Public Prosecution's Final Statement, 1051.

69. Ibid.

70. VDS, Letters from Juan Salinas of the Chilean Investigations Police to Santiago's Appeals Court, RA 06-06-77, June 29 and July 1, 1977, 13–15.

71. MAC, Memo from Buenos Aires–Luis Felipe to Santiago–Cristian, *informes varios,* July 17, 1977.

72. Juan Pablo Figueroa, "Operación Cóndor: Hallan restos en Chile de tres detenidos desaparecidos secuestrados en Argentina," *Centro de Investigación Periodística (CIPER),* June 16, 2015.

73. Ibid.

74. Interview with CL001-2016.

75. VDS, "El trágico final del ex marido de Paulina Veloso," *La Nación,* RELP 01-207, October 14, 2007.

76. DOS, Brasilia 5662, July 8, 1977.

77. DOS, Rio de Janeiro 4065, August 25, 1977.

78. MJDH, Army Ministry, Army I, Confidential Search Request 771/76-11, October 5, 1976.

79. MJDH, State Department for Political and Social Order, São Paulo, "Monitoring and Security Together with the Argentine Consulate in São Paulo," April 20, 1977.

80. DOS, Brasilia 5566, July 6, 1977.

81. Ibid.

82. MJDH, State Department for Political and Social Order, São Paulo, "Of. N. 733/77," from Delegate Sergio Fleury to the Argentine consul in São Paulo, June 24, 1977.

83. DOS, Brasilia 5994, July 20, 1977.

84. DOS, State 163308, July 13, 1977.

85. DOS, Rio de Janeiro 4146, August 30, 1977.

86. CIA, Memorandum, "Transmittal of intelligence items," September 10, 1977.

87. CIA, Memorandum, "Transmittal of intelligence items," December 2, 1977.

88. CIA, "Weekly situation report on international terrorism—Ecuador joins Condor," March 1, 1978.

89. Ibid.

90. CIA, report number blacked out, February 14, 1978.

91. CIA, Intelligence Information Cable 413973, October 7, 1977.

92. Ibid.

93. CIA, Intelligence Information Cable 0170784A, December 28, 1977.

94. DIA, Intelligence Appraisal, "Latin America: Counterterrorism and trends in terrorism (U)," DIAIAPPR 189 78, August 11, 1978.

95. CIA, Intelligence Information Cable 0170784A.

96. Rico, *Investigación histórica sobre detenidos desaparecidos.*

97. Slatman, "Actividades extraterritoriales."

98. The Navy Prefecture both in Argentina and Uruguay is a branch of the security forces tasked with protecting the country's rivers and maritime territory.

99. UYFRM, Rome Tribunal Documentation, 3, Envelope 4/3, Report by the General Command of the Navy to the President on Uruguayan Citizens Disappeared in Argentina, September 26, 2005, 8–9.

100. Interview with Roger Rodríguez; DOS, Montevideo 5244, January 23, 1978, and UYFRM, Rome Tribunal Documentation, 1, Envelope 2/2, Technical Historian Report on Troccoli's Military File, "Secretos de la dictadura II," *Posdata,* April 26, 1996.

101. UYFRM, Rome Tribunal Documentation 1, Envelope 1/4, Navy Witnesses, Testimony of Juan Heber Fernandez Maggio before the 19th Criminal Judge, September 20, 2007, 063716.

102. UYFRM, Rome Tribunal Documentation, 3, Envelope 4/3, Report by the Uruguayan Navy to the Presidency Office, September 26, 2005, 15–16.

103. Witness statements by María Paula, María Elvira, María Virginia Herrero, and Rosario Evangelina Quiroga, in Lawsuit 2-15129/2012, May 7, 2012, available at www.observatorioluzibarburu.org/media/uploads/20151292012_-_Testimonios.pdf (accessed December 16, 2019).

104. UYFRM, 2005 Uruguayan Navy report, 10.

105. Lawsuit 2-15129/2012, "Ley 18.026 Delitos de genocidio, lesa humanidad, crímenes de guerra y otros," filed on April 30, 2012, available at www.observatorioluzi

barburu.org/media/uploads/20151292012_-_Denuncia_penal.pdf (accessed December 16, 2019).

106. Testimony of Rosario Quiroga in *Sonata en Si menor*, documentary by Patricio Escobar (2014), minute 8:44, available at www.youtube.com/watch?time_continue=3 &v=iyUft9Vv9pQ&feature=emb_logo (accessed December 16, 2019).

107. UYFRM, Rome Tribunal Documentation, 3, Envelope 4/3, FUSNA Record of De Gregorio Marconi, Oscar Ruben, copy of a letter by Aida Marconi De Gregorio to the Uruguayan President, Junta of the Military Commanders, and Minister of the Interior, November 21, 1977, SID—III Dept.—P.O.E., 061080.

108. Quiroga's testimony, *Sonata en Si menor*, minutes 17–21.

109. "Recuerdos de la ESMA," July 7, 2014, available at www.lavaca.org/notas/recuer dos-de-la-esma/ (accessed December 16, 2019).

110. UYFRM, Rome Tribunal Documentation, 1, Envelope 1/4, Navy Witnesses, Testimony of Jorge Saravia Briano before the 19th Criminal Judge, October 1, 2007, 063756. Also see Box 1, Envelope 2, Navy, personal military file of Navy Lieutenant Jorge Néstor Troccoli Fernandez, 063826.

111. Testimony of Martín Gras before the 19th Criminal Judge, September 28, 2007, available from Rome's First Assize Appeals Court, 2.

112. UYFRM, 2005 Uruguayan Navy report, 11.

113. "Recuerdos de la ESMA"; Martín Gras's testimony, 4.

114. Ibid., 5.

115. "Recuerdos de la ESMA."

116. Witness statement by Jaime Feliciano Dri in Lawsuit 2-15129/2012, May 28, 2012, available at www.observatorioluzibarburu.org/media/uploads/20151292012_-_ Testimonio_Jaime_Feliciano_DRI.pdf (accessed December 16, 2019).

117. Quiroga's testimony in Rico, *Investigación histórica sobre dictadura*, 523.

118. Testimony of Jaime Dri, *Sonata en Si menor*, minute 19.

119. Lawsuit 2-15129/2012.

120. Testimony of Miguel Ángel Estrella, *Sonata en Si menor*, minute 41:30.

121. Lawsuit 2-15129/2012.

122. Witness statements by Quiroga and her daughters in Lawsuit 2-15129/2012.

123. Ibid.

124. Dri's witness statement in Lawsuit 2-15129/2012.

125. UYFRM, 2.1 Subversion, 2-Confidential, H311, Circular 57AD transmitting Joint Forces Communiques 1.378, December 23, and Circular 60AD transmitting Joint Forces Communiques 1.3789, December 26, 1977; Laws, Decrees, Resolutions, and Circulars, 1, A1-2-1, Circular 1/78 transmitting Joint Forces Communiques 1.380 on January 1, 1978.

126. Slatman, "Actividades extraterritoriales"; Alejandrina Barry's testimony, *Sonata en Si menor*, minute 55:35; Lawsuit 2-15129/2012.

127. DOS, Montevideo 5244.

128. DOS, Montevideo 0022, January 4, 1978, paragraph 1D.

129. Testimony of Giulia Barrera, archival expert, before Rome's Third Assize Court, Trial Proceedings R. G. 2/15, Hearing of February 26, 2016, 29.

130. Final statement by lawyer Andrea Speranzoni before Rome's First Assize Appeals Court, Procedimento penale 40/17 R. G. contro "Arce Gómez Luis ed altri 26," hearing of May 13, 2019, author's notes.

131. UYFRM, personal military file of Navy Lieutenant Troccoli, 063867–063868.

132. OCT Public Prosecution's Final Statement, 902–3.

133. CNV, "Conexões internacionais."

134. Ibid.

135. Rio's Cardenal Eugênio Sales warned Florinda Castro by letter about the presence of Argentine police officers in Rio, February 19, 1979, available at www.mpf.gob.ar/plan-condor/files/2018/12/Habegger-8-2.pdf (accessed December 17, 2019); also see DOS, State 132608, May 24, 1979.

136. "Relatório da Operação Gringo/CACO no. 11/79," compiled by the Brazilian CIE, December 31, 1979, available at http://cnv.memoriasreveladas.gov.br/images/documentos/Capitulo6/Nota%20128%20-%2000092_003255_2014_56.pdf (accessed May 31, 2020), 160.

137. Ibid., 1778.

138. OCT Public Prosecution's Final Statement, 1240.

139. Interview with Andrés Habegger, Norberto Habegger's son, Buenos Aires, July 9, 2018.

140. Chico Otavio and Raphael Kapa, "Salen a la luz en Brasil nuevas evidencias sobre el Plan Cóndor," La Nación, November 26, 2014.

141. OCT 2016 Verdict, 1778.

142. CIA, Intelligence Information Cable 2158813, April 12, 1979.

143. OCT Public Prosecution's Final Statement, 1243.

144. Interview with Andrés Habegger.

145. AI, Testimony on Secret Detention Camps.

146. "Relatório da Operação Gringo."

147. CNV, "Conexões internacionais."

148. Testimony of Nadine Monteiro Borges, Operation Condor Trial in Buenos Aires, hearing of March 17, 2015, author's notes. In November 1978 prisoners in "El Olimpo" secret torture center saw photo albums linked to the pursuit of Argentines in Brazil; one contained the names of 100 UNHCR Argentine refugees and their photos. AI, Testimony on Secret Detention Camps.

149. Nadine Borges's deposition.

150. Ibid.

151. Luiz Cláudio Cunha, Operación Cóndor: El secuestro de los uruguayos (Montevideo, Uruguay: Servicio Paz y Justicia, 2017).

152. Interview with Jair Krischke.

153. Omar Ferri, *Seqüestro no Cone Sul: O caso Lilian e Universindo* (Porto Alegre: Mercado Aberto Editora, 1981).

154. MJDH, Testimony of Hugo Walter García Rivas to the International Secretariat of Jurists for Amnesty in Uruguay (hereafter SIJAU testimony), São Paulo, May 19, 1980.

155. MJDH, Testimony of Hugo Walter García Rivas to MJDH, Porto Alegre, May 3, 1980.

156. Cunha, *Operación Cóndor.*

157. SIJAU testimony, 5.

158. Hugo García's MJDH testimony, 3.

159. MJDH, Lawsuit filed before Montevideo's Criminal Judge of the Sixth Circuit, February 23, 1984, paragraph 2.

160. Ibid.

161. SIJAU testimony, 6.

162. MJDH, 1984 Lawsuit.

163. Cunha, *Operación Cóndor,* 77.

164. UYFRM, 2.3, Confidential Notes Sent, 16, 3, "Seqüestrador revela que Uruguai buscou ação conjunta com o DOPS," *Jornal do Brasil,* June 14, 1980.

165. Interview with Luiz Claudio Cunha, journalist, Brasilia, November 13, 2017.

166. MJDH, "Desaparecimento misterioso de uruguaios no Sul," *Jornal de Brasília,* November 22, 1978.

167. UYFRM, 2.3, Confidential Notes Sent, 14, 3, Letter from Porto Alegre Consul Daniel Frias to Ambassador General (ret.) Eduardo Zubía 1050/978, November 24, 1978, accompanied by letter from Omar Ferri and *Zero Hora* and *Folha da Tarde* newspaper clippings.

168. Interview with Omar Ferri, lawyer, Porto Alegre, November 19, 2017.

169. MJDH, "Sequestrado implica Dops gaúcho," *Folha de São Paulo,* November 30, 1978.

170. DOS, Montevideo 4179, December 4, 1978, paragraph 2.

171. UYFRM, 2.3, Confidential Notes Sent, 13, 5, Letter from Porto Alegre Consul Hamlet Goncalvez to Ambassador General (ret.) Eduardo Zubía 74/979-caas, January 30, 1979.

172. UYFRM, 2.1, Laws, Decrees, Resolutions and Circulars, Box 1, Folder A1-2-1, Joint Forces Communiques 1400 and 1401, November 25 and December 12, 1978.

173. SIJAU testimony, 9.

174. DOS, Asuncion 4451, October 13, 1978.

175. DOS, Asuncion 4237, October 2, 1978.

176. CIA, Current Intelligence Weekly Summary, November 17, 1978, 5.

177. CIA, Intelligence Information Cable 1646108, December 15, 1978, paragraph 3.

178. DOS, Buenos Aires 9248, November 22, 1978; Buenos Aires 9630, December 7, 1978; and CIA, Memorandum of Conversation between Carlos Fernandez of *Convicción* and APAO John Corr, December 5, 1978.

179. DOS, Briefing Memorandum, "Your luncheon with DOD representatives," May 22, 1980, 3.

180. DOD, Intelligence Information Report, "Political conversations with Argentine leaders," January 23, 1979, transmitting Buenos Aires Embassy memo, DOS, "Memorandum of conversation—politics, The Beagle and human rights," January 9, 1979.

181. DOS, "Memorandum of conversation—politics, The Beagle and human rights," 1–2.

182. Hernán Confino, "Tensiones de un retorno: La Contraofensiva Estratégica Montonera de 1979 y 1980 en Argentina," *Izquierdas* 28 (2016): 274–91.

183. Juan Manuel Mannarino, "Roberto Perdía habló en el juicio Contraofensiva Montonera: 'Nuestro plan era atacar al grupo económico de Martínez de Hoz,'" *Infobae*, April 16, 2019.

184. Interview with Nilson Mariano, Operation Condor expert, Porto Alegre, November 21, 2017.

185. DOD, "International terrorism: A compendium, Volume III—Latin America," DJS-2630-9A-80, March 30, 1980.

186. ADT, Armed Forces High Command, report no. 009/79, April 16, 1979, R00019F1014.

187. ADT, Armed Forces High Command, "Entry of Argentine terrorists to Argentina via Paraguay," July 10, 1980, R00143F0880.

188. MJDH, "Morte na barca," *Veja*, August 13, 1980.

189. Interview with Edgardo Binstock, a *contraofensiva* militant and relative of Condor victim, Buenos Aires, July 11, 2018.

190. DOS, Memorandum from RSO/James J. Blystone, "Conversation with Argentine Intelligence Source," April 7, 1980.

191. DOS, Buenos Aires 2953, April 9, 1980.

192. Unless otherwise referenced, this section is based on the interview with AR001-2018, former *contraofensiva* militant, Buenos Aires, July 10, 2018.

193. CELS, Comisión Argentina de Derechos Humanos, "Secuestran y torturan en Perú a exiliados argentinos," June 25, 1980.

194. DOS, Memorandum from RSO/James J. Blystone, "Meeting with Argentine Intelligence Service," June 19, 1980; Memorandum from Townsend Friedman, "The case of the missing Montoneros," August 19, 1980.

195. DOS, Lima 5570, June 20; Lima 5964, July 3, 1980; and CIA, Weekly Situation Report on International Terrorism, "Strange deaths of Montonero terrorists," August 20, 1980.

196. DOS, Lima 6226, July 11, 1980, paragraph 2.

197. Ibid.

198. CELS, Comisión Argentina de Derechos Humanos, Urgent Action, "Argentine state terror without borders," August 1, 1980; DOS, Madrid 11686, August 7, 1980.

199. CELS, "Los hijos de Noemí Gianotti creen que su madre fue trasladada de Perú a Argentina," *El País*, August 27, 1980.

200. Interview with Nilson Mariano.

201. MJDH, List of passengers of Expreso Gral. Urquiza S.R.L., from Buenos Aires to São Paulo, 12:30 pm; interviews with Jair Krischke and Nilson Mariano.

202. Nilson Cezar Mariano, "Montoneros no Brasil: Terrorismo de Estado no seqüestro-desaparecimento de seis guerrilheiros argentinos" (master's thesis, Pontifical Catholic University of Rio Grande do Sul, 2006).

203. Interview with Edgardo Binstock.

204. Mariano, "Montoneros no Brasil."

205. Letters from Silvia Tolchinsky to Claudia Allegrini (Viñas's wife) dated October 10, 1994, and January 1995. Documents sent by Nilson Mariano on November 22, 2017.

206. Marcelo Godoy, "General admite que Brasil fez parte da Operação Condor," *O Estado de São Paulo*, December 30, 2007.

207. Testimony of John Dinges, Operation Condor Trial in Buenos Aires, hearing of March 27, 2015, author's notes; ADT, Report from Pastor Coronel to Don Francisco Brítez, April 13, 1981, R00081F0689.

208. Interview with Carlos Osorio.

209. Interview with Melisa Slatman.

Chapter 6. Justice Seekers

1. Samuel P. Huntington, *The Third Wave: Democratization in the Late Twentieth Century* (Norman: University of Oklahoma Press, 1991).

2. The Inter-American Commission is a principal and autonomous organ of the Organization of American States, which promotes and protects human rights in the Americas. The commission, created in 1959, is composed of seven independent members serving in a personal capacity. See Par Engstrom, ed., *The Inter-American Human Rights System: Impact beyond Compliance* (Cham, Switzerland: Palgrave Macmillan, 2019).

3. Dustin N. Sharp, "Emancipating Transitional Justice from the Bonds of the Paradigmatic Transition," *International Journal of Transitional Justice* 9, no. 1 (2015): 159.

4. Colleen Murphy, *The Conceptual Foundations of Transitional Justice* (Cambridge: Cambridge University Press, 2017).

5. Ruti Teitel, *Globalizing Transitional Justice* (Oxford: Oxford University Press, 2014).

6. Geraldo L. Munck and Carol Skalnik Leff, "Modes of Transition and Democratization: South America and Eastern Europe in Comparative Perspective," *Comparative Politics* 29, no. 3 (1997): 343–62.

7. Scott Mainwaring, "Transitions to Democracy and Democratic Consolidation: Theoretical and Comparative Issues," in *Issues in Democratic Consolidation: New South American Democracies in Comparative Perspective,* ed. Scott Mainwaring, Guillermo O'Donnell, and J. Samuel Valenzuela (Notre Dame, IN: University of Notre Dame Press, 1992), 294–341.

8. Elin Skaar, "Truth Commissions, Trials—or Nothing? Policy Options in Democratic Transitions," *Third World Quarterly* 20, no. 6 (1999): 1109–28.

9. Cath Collins, *Post-transitional Justice: Human Rights Trials in Chile and El Salvador* (University Park: Pennsylvania State University Press, 2010).

10. David Pion-Berlin, "To Prosecute or to Pardon? Human Rights Decisions in the Latin American Southern Cone," *Human Rights Quarterly* 16, no. 1 (1994): 105–30.

11. Terence Roehrig, "Executive Leadership and the Continuing Quest for Justice in Argentina," *Human Rights Quarterly* 31, no. 3 (2009): 721–47.

12. David Backer, "Civil Society and Transitional Justice: Possibilities, Patterns and Prospects," *Journal of Human Rights* 2, no. 3 (2003): 297–313.

13. Mara Loveman, "High-Risk Collective Action: Defending Human Rights in Chile, Uruguay, and Argentina," *American Journal of Sociology* 104, no. 2 (1998): 477–525.

14. Elin Skaar, "Puede la independencia judicial explicar la justicia postransicional?," *America Latina Hoy* 61 (2012): 15–49.

15. Lisa Hilbink, *Judges beyond Politics in Democracy and Dictatorship Lessons from Chile* (Cambridge: Cambridge University Press, 2007).

16. González Ocantos, *Shifting Legal Visions.*

17. Naomi Roht-Arriaza, "The Role of International Actors in National Accountability Processes," in *The Politics of Memory: Transitional Justice in Democratizing Societies,* ed. Alexandra Barahona de Brito, Carmen González-Enríquez, and Paloma Aguilar (Oxford: Oxford University Press, 2001), 40–64.

18. Keck and Sikkink, *Activists beyond Borders.*

19. Thomas Risse, Steve C. Ropp, and Kathryn Sikkink, eds., *The Power of Human Rights: International Norms and Domestic Change* (Cambridge: Cambridge University Press, 1999).

20. Kathryn Sikkink, "The Transnational Dimension of the Judicialization of Politics in Latin America," in *The Judicialization of Politics in Latin America,* ed. Rachel Sieder, Line Schjolden, and Alan Angell (New York: Palgrave MacMillan, 2005).

21. Kathryn Sikkink, *The Justice Cascade: How Human Rights Prosecutions Are Changing World Politics* (New York; London: W. W. Norton, 2011).

22. Collins, *Post-transitional Justice,* 3.

23. Jo-Marie Burt, Gabriela Fried-Amilivia, and Francesca Lessa, "Civil Society and the Resurgent Struggle against Impunity in Uruguay (1986–2012)," *International Journal of Transitional Justice* 7, no. 2 (2013): 306–27.

24. Elin Skaar and Eric Wiebelhaus-Brahm, "The Drivers of Transitional Justice:

An Analytical Framework for Assessing the Role of Actors," *Nordic Journal of Human Rights* 31, no. 2 (2013): 127–48.

25. Leigh A. Payne, Francesca Lessa, and Gabriel Pereira, "Overcoming Barriers to Justice in the Age of Human Rights Accountability," *Human Rights Quarterly* 37, no. 3 (2015): 728–54.

26. Francesca Lessa, *Memory and Transitional Justice in Argentina and Uruguay: Against Impunity* (New York: Palgrave Macmillan, 2013), 228.

27. Pamela E. Oliver and Gerald Marwell, "Mobilizing Technologies for Collective Action," in *Frontiers in Social Movement Theory*, ed. Aldon D. Morris and Carol McClurg Mueller (New Haven, CT: Yale University Press, 1992), 252.

28. Howard S. Becker, *Outsiders: Studies in the Sociology of Deviance* (New York: Free Press, 1963).

29. Elizabeth Jelin, *State Repression and the Labors of Memory* (Minneapolis: University of Minnesota Press, 2003), 33.

30. Martha Finnemore and Kathryn Sikkink, "International Norm Dynamics and Political Change," *International Organization* 52, no. 4 (1998): 896.

31. Ibid., 897.

32. Keck and Sikkink, *Activists beyond Borders*.

33. R. Charli Carpenter, "Setting the Advocacy Agenda: Theorizing Issue Emergence and Nonemergence in Transnational Advocacy Networks," *International Studies Quarterly* 51, no. 1 (2007): 104.

34. Ezequiel González Ocantos, "Communicative Entrepreneurs: The Case of the Inter-American Court of Human Rights' Dialogue with National Judges," *International Studies Quarterly* 62, no. 4 (2018): 737–50.

35. Michael Mintrom, *Policy Entrepreneurs and Dynamic Change* (Cambridge: Cambridge University Press, 2019), 1–2.

36. Lorena Balardini, "State Actions after State Crimes: The Monitoring Role of the Public Prosecutors in the Transitional Justice Process in Argentina," XXXVII International Congress of the Latin American Studies Association, Boston, May 24–27, 2019.

37. I would like to thank Risa Kitagawa, Jo-Marie Burt, Stephen Meili, and Leigh Payne for raising these points.

38. Carlos S. Nino, *Radical Evil on Trial* (New Haven, CT: Yale University Press, 1996).

39. Raúl Alfonsín, "Confronting the Past: 'Never Again' in Argentina," *Journal of Democracy* 4, no. 1 (1993): 16.

40. The Full Stop Law established a sixty-day deadline for summoning alleged human rights violators, otherwise all criminal investigations would be closed down. The Due Obedience Law instituted the legality of following orders and thereby prevented the prosecution of all subordinate officers except for rape, theft, appropriation of property, and child stealing.

41. De León Orpi, "Juan María Bordaberry."

42. Interview with Mariana Mota, criminal judge, Montevideo, April 4, 2014.

43. Francesca Lessa and Pierre-Louis Le Goff, "Uruguay's Culture of Impunity Continues to Rear Its Head," *Al Jazeera*, February 22, 2013.

44. Elin Skaar, *Judicial Independence and Human Rights in Latin America: Violations, Politics, and Prosecution* (New York: Palgrave MacMillan, 2011).

45. See Report 21/00, Case 12.059, Carmen Aguiar de Lapacó, February 29, 2000, available at www.cidh.org/annualrep/99eng/Friendly/Argentina12.059.htm (accessed May 4, 2019).

46. Ibid., paragraph 17.

47. Helen Duffy, *Strategic Human Rights Litigation: Understanding and Maximising Impact* (Oxford: Hart, 2018).

48. Naomi Roht-Arriaza, "After Amnesties Are Gone: Latin American National Courts and the New Contours of the Fight against Impunity," *Human Rights Quarterly* 37, no. 2 (2015): 341–82.

49. Cath Collins and Boris Hau, "Chile: Incremental Truth, Late Justice," in *Transitional Justice in Latin America: The Uneven Road from Impunity towards Accountability*, ed. Elin Skaar, Jemima García-Godos, and Cath Collins (New York: Routledge, 2016), 135.

50. Ibid.

51. Information kindly provided by Boris Hau, Diego Portales University's Transitional Justice Observatory, August 3, 2021.

52. Kathryn Sikkink and Carrie Booth Walling, "The Impact of Human Rights Trials in Latin America," *Journal of Peace Research* 44, no. 4 (2007): 430.

53. Jeffrey Davis, *Seeking Human Rights Justice in Latin America: Truth, Extra-territorial Courts, and the Process of Justice* (New York: Cambridge University Press, 2014).

54. Lawrence Weschler, *A Miracle, A Universe: Settling Accounts with Torturers* (Chicago: University of Chicago Press, 1998).

55. "Brazilian human rights evidence preserved in the Nunca Mais project," Center for Research Libraries, June 2011, available at www.crl.edu/impact/brazilian-human -rights-evidence-preserved-nunca-mais-project (accessed June 8, 2020).

56. Louis Bickford, "Unofficial Truth Projects," *Human Rights Quarterly* 29, no. 4 (2007): 994–1035.

57. Weschler, *A Miracle*, 10.

58. Francesca Lessa, "Barriers to Justice: The Ley de Caducidad and Impunity in Uruguay," in *Amnesty in the Age of Human Rights Accountability: Comparative and International Perspectives*, ed. Francesca Lessa and Leigh A. Payne (Cambridge: Cambridge University Press, 2012), 123–51.

59. Burt, Fried-Amilivia, and Lessa, "Civil Society."

60. The Inter-American Court, created as an autonomous legal institution by the 1969 American Convention on Human Rights, interprets and applies the American

Convention. I/A Court H.R., Case of Gelman v. Uruguay, Merits and Reparations, Judgment of February 24, 2011, Series C, No. 221.

61. Burt, Fried-Amilivia, and Lessa, "Civil Society."

62. Glenda Mezarobba, "Brazil: The Tortuous Path to Truth and Justice," in Skaar, García-Godos, and Collins, *Transitional Justice,* 103–25.

63. I/A Court H.R., Case of Gomes Lund et al. v. Brazil, Preliminary Objections, Merits, Reparations, and Costs, Judgment of November 24, 2010, Series C, No. 219.

64. Paulo Abrão and Marcelo D. Torelly, "Resistance to Change: Brazil's Persistent Amnesty and Its Alternatives for Truth and Justice," in Lessa and Payne, *Amnesty in the Age of Human Rights Accountability,* 152–81.

Chapter 7. Condor Unveiled

1. See 1978 Annual Report of the Inter-American Commission (OEA/Ser.L/V/II.47, Doc. 13, rev. 1), June 29, 1979.

2. Lilian Celiberti de Casariego v. Uruguay, Communication No. 56/1979, CCPR/C/13/D/56/1979, July 29, 1981. Italian lawyer Francesco Cavallaro submitted the petition in July 1979.

3. Email exchange with Professor Christian Tomuschat, member of the committee (1977–86), May 10, 2020.

4. Celiberti v. Uruguay, paragraph 10.2.

5. The victim's wife filed the case in June 1979, Delia Saldias de Lopez v. Uruguay, Communication No. 52/1979, CCPR/C/13/D/52/1979, July 29, 1981.

6. Marko Milanovic, *Extraterritorial Application of Human Rights Treaties: Law, Principles, and Policy* (Oxford: Oxford University Press, 2011).

7. Nehal Bhuta, "The Frontiers of Extraterritoriality—Human Rights as Global Law," in *The Frontiers of Human Rights: Extraterritoriality and Its Challenges,* ed. Nehal Bhuta (Oxford: Oxford University Press, 2016), 1–19.

8. Richard Gott, "Shots and Plots," *Guardian,* June 4 1976.

9. DOS, Washington Office on Latin America, Legislative Update, May–June 1976, Argentina Declassification Project document 00009F97.

10. Ibid., 3.

11. *Human Rights in Argentina: Hearings before the Subcommittee on International Organisations of the Committee on International Relations,* House of Representatives, 94th Congress, Second Session, September 28 and 29, 1976 (Washington, DC: US Government Printing Office, 1977).

12. UYFRM, Documentation sent to Rome, 5, Envelope 7, "Victims' declarations," transcription of the testimony by Washington Pérez in Alvesta, Sweden, recorded on September 1 and transcribed in London on September 3 and 4, 1976.

13. Ibid., 2.

14. Ibid., 6.

15. Ibid., 8.

16. Testimony of Jorge Washington Pérez Carrozo, son of Washington Pérez, Operation Condor Trial in Buenos Aires, hearing of September 27, 2013, author's notes.

17. UYFRM, Rome Tribunal Documentation, Victims' Declarations, Testimony of Washington Pérez, July 8, 1985, 18–19.

18. David Watts, "Argentine Population Terrorized, Amnesty Says," *Times* (London), March 24 1977.

19. Testimony of Enrique Rodríguez Larreta Piera, London, March 18, 1977, paragraph 7, in Rodríguez Larreta, *El informe Orletti.*

20. Ibid., paragraphs 11, 12, 18, and 19.

21. Ibid., 33.

22. Ibid., 35–38.

23. Ibid., 57–60.

24. Ibid., 62.

25. Ibid., 20.

26. Ibid., 21–23.

27. Declarations were reproduced in the *Monthly Bulletin of the International Press Report* 26, no. 8 (September 1977), "The Larreta file," 11, 15; and as Enrique Rodríguez Larreta, "Kidnapped in Buenos Aires," *Index on Censorship,* 6, no. 4 (July 1, 1977), 22–29.

28. Resolution No. 20/78, Case 2155, Argentina, November 18, 1978, available at www.cidh.org/annualrep/79.80eng/Argentina2155.htm (accessed May 12, 2020).

29. Rodríguez Larreta, *El informe Orletti.*

30. "Aseguran que en México operan bandas para secuestrar a los asilados políticos de 6 países," *El Día,* April 24, 1977, in Rodríguez Larreta, *El informe Orletti,* 127.

31. "The Uruguayan military dictatorship continues its repression of human rights but no longer with the support of the United States," *Congressional Record–House,* May 11, 1977, H4326, in Rodríguez Larreta, *El informe Orletti,* 129.

32. Inter-American Commission on Human Rights, "Report on the Situation of Human Rights in Argentina," OEA/Ser.L/V/II.49, Doc. 19, corr. 1, April 11, 1980, available at www.cidh.org/countryrep/Argentina80eng/chap.3b.htm (accessed May 14, 2020).

33. Amnesty International, "Uruguay: Testimony on kidnapping in Argentina, torture, and illegal transfer to Uruguay," February 27, 1979. Interview with Eduardo Dean Bermúdez, Operation Condor survivor, Montevideo, November 24, 2014.

34. Testimony of Alicia Cadenas, April 22, 1979. Document sent by Alicia Cadenas on March 28, 2014.

35. "Amnesty International says testimony of former military officer confirms practice of torture in Uruguay," news release issued by the Amnesty International Swiss Section, AMR 52/18/79, February 27, 1979.

36. UYFRM, Documentation sent to Rome, 6, Envelope 9/8, "Declarations of Julio Cesar Cooper," January 11, 1979, 4.

37. Interview with Jair Krischke.

38. MJDH, Testimony of Hugo Walter García Rivas, Porto Alegre, May 3, 1980.

39. SIJAU testimony.

40. "Case 4529: Kidnapping in Brazil of four persons later taken to Montevideo," Annual Report of the Inter-American Commission on Human Rights 1978, OEA/Ser.L/V/II.47, Doc. 13 rev. 1, June 29, 1979, available at http://cidh.org/annualrep/78eng/section.4c.htm (accessed May 12, 2020).

41. Interview with Omar Ferri.

42. Dinges, *Condor Years*.

43. CELS, "Chile: An Innocuous Murder," *Latin American Political Report* 13, no. 5 (February 2, 1979): 36.

44. Jack Anderson, "'Condor': South American Assassins," *Washington Post*, August 2, 1979. Anderson wrote other articles on the deteriorating human rights situation in South America, including one in which he criticized US financial support and backing of several military takeovers, and the training of thousands of Latin American officers at the School of the Americas. See Anderson, "The Rise of Latin Dictators," *Washington Post*, October 10, 1976.

45. FBI, "[Condor: Chilbom]," secret, September 28, 1976, available at https://assets.documentcloud.org/documents/5817666/National-Security-Archive-Doc-05-FBI-cable.pdf (accessed May 10, 2020). The report was declassified fully unredacted only in 2019.

46. DOS, State 201355, August 4, 1979.

47. Ibid., paragraph 3.

48. See Miguel Angel Estrella v. Uruguay, Communication No. 74/1980, CCPR/C/18/D/74/1980, March 29, 1983; Maria del Carmen Almeida de Quinteros v. Uruguay, Communication No. 107/1981, CCPR/C/19/D/107/1981, July 21, 1983; and Antonio Viana Acosta v. Uruguay, Communication No. 110/1981, CCPR/C/21/D/110/1981, March 29, 1984.

49. Scott Mainwaring, "The Transition to Democracy in Brazil," *Journal of Interamerican Studies and World Affairs* 28, no. 1 (1986): 149–79.

50. Mezarobba, "Brazil."

51. Interview with Jair Krischke.

52. Ferri, *Seqüestro no Cone Sul;* MJDH, "O que faziam no Brasil os uruguaios seqüestrados," *Jornal da Tarde*, May 30, 1979.

53. Ferri, *Seqüestro no Cone Sul*.

54. Interview with Omar Ferri.

55. Interview with Jair Krischke.

56. Cunha, *Operación Cóndor*.

57. Interview with Jair Krischke.

58. MJDH, Lawsuit filed before Montevideo's Criminal Judge of the Sixth Circuit, February 23, 1984, paragraph 18.

59. Ferri, *Seqüestro no Cone Sul.*

60. MJDH, "Para que esto no vuelva a suceder," *Jaque,* March 2, 1984.

61. Interview with Omar Ferri.

62. Cunha, *Operación Cóndor.*

63. Interview with Jair Krischke.

64. Interview with Federico Tatter.

65. Pamela Lowden, *Moral Opposition to Authoritarian Rule in Chile, 1973–90* (London: Palgrave Macmillan, 1996).

66. Patricio Orellana and Elizabeth Q. Hutchinson, *El movimiento de derechos humanos en Chile, 1973–1990* (Santiago: Centro de Estudios Políticos Latinoamericanos Simón Bolívar, 1991).

67. Oriana Bernasconi, Elizabeth Lira, and Marcela Ruiz, "Political Technologies of Memory: Uses and Appropriations of Artefacts that Register and Denounce State Violence," *International Journal of Transitional Justice* 13, no. 1 (2019): 11.

68. Interview with Flor Hernández Zazpe.

69. The habeas corpus filed by Jaime Nuguer regarding the disappearance of Inés Ollero was the first to be addressed by the Supreme Court in April 1978. See Jaime Nuguer, *Un hábeas corpus en dictadura: Las acciones judiciales por Inés Ollero que culminaron con el encarcelamiento del jefe de la ESMA* (Buenos Aires: Lenguaje claro Editora, 2013).

70. Alison Brysk, *The Politics of Human Rights in Argentina: Protest, Change, and Democratization* (Stanford, CA: Stanford University Press, 1994).

71. CELS, "Report on the human rights situation in Argentina, October 1979–October 1980," 12.

72. CELS, "Uruguay–Argentina: Coordinación represiva," Colección Memoria y Juicio, August 1983.

73. CELS, "Revelan las conexiones entre los aparatos represivos del Cono Sur," *La Voz,* September 1, 1983.

74. Markarian, *Left in Transformation.*

75. Marisa Ruiz, *La piedra en el zapato: Amnistía y la dictadura uruguaya* (Montevideo: Universidad de la República, 2006).

76. UYFRM, 2.6, international press articles on amnesty, 21, 5, "Michelini y Gutierrez Ruiz asesinados," Comité de Defensa de los Prisioneros Políticos en Uruguay, Year 1, No. 1, June 1976.

77. Communication with Mariana Errandonea, relative of an Operation Condor victim, May 12, 2020.

78. Ibid.

79. Gabriel Bucheli et al., *Vivos los llevaron . . . Historia de la lucha de Madres y Familiares de Uruguayos Detenidos Desaparecidos (1976–2005)* (Montevideo: Trilce, 2005).

80. Ibid., 29; Trías and Rodríguez, *Gerardo Gatti.*

81. "Our history," Mothers and Relatives of Uruguayan Disappeared Detainees, available at https://desaparecidos.org.uy/nuestra-historia/ (accessed May 16, 2020).

82. Interview with Federico Tatter.

83. Ibid.

84. Ibid.

85. Interview with Lidia Cabrera.

86. Case 2291, Argentina—Esteban Cabrera, Eduardo Sotero Franco Venegas, and Lidia Esther Cabrera de Franco, March 5, 1979, available at www.cidh.org/annualrep /78sp/Argentina2291.htm (accessed May 17, 2020).

87. Interview with Lidia Cabrera.

88. Interview with Federico Tatter.

89. Personal archive of Idalina Tatter, Folder 2, Subfolder Commission of Relatives of Paraguayans Disappeared in Argentina, images 31 and 32, n.d., estimated between 1981 and 1983.

90. Interview with Federico Tatter.

91. Nino, *Radical Evil on Trial.*

92. CONADEP, *Informe de la Comisión Nacional sobre la Desaparición de Personas—Nunca Más,* anniversary ed. (1984; repr., Buenos Aires: Editorial Universitaria de Buenos Aires, 2006).

93. Ibid., 269.

94. In February 1985 CELS lawyer Baños filed another lawsuit to denounce the 1976 kidnapping, torture, and clandestine rendition from Bolivia to Argentina of three Argentine citizens. The suit accused Bolivian former dictator Hugo Banzer, his Ministry of Interior, and the head of DOP as well as Argentine Minister of Interior Albano Harguindeguy. See CELS, "Serious international denunciation filed," February 26, 1985.

95. CELS, "Press release and criminal lawsuit," February 22, 1984.

96. Ibid., 3–5.

97. Ibid., 4.

98. Ibid., 13.

99. Ibid., 14.

100. This section on the trip to Buenos Aires and the Orletti inspection is based on the author's interviews with Sara Méndez, Gastón Zina, and Ana Inés Quadros.

101. CELS, press release, "Submission by the Uruguayan Consulate in the 'Rodriguez Larreta' proceedings," November 30, 1985.

102. Ibid., press releases, "Immediate arrest of Raul Guglielminetti sought," January 9, 1986; "Aníbal Gordon identified," March 24, 1986; "Gordon confesó haber trabajado durante 16 años en la SIDE," *La Razón,* May 12, 1986.

103. Ibid., "General Otto Paladino, Raul Guglielminetti, Anibal Gordon, Eduardo Alfredo Ruffo, and high-ranking Uruguayan officials accused," March 26, 1986.

104. Ibid., "Former Uruguayan military officer denounced repressive coordination and individuals responsible in Argentina and Uruguay," April 1, 1986.

105. Ibid., "Indictment and capture ordered for four Uruguayan military and security officers," August 5, 1986.

106. Sentence 13/84 of December 1985 is available at www.derechos.org/nizkor/arg /causa13/index.html (accessed February 15, 2021).

107. CELS, "The Newspaper of the Trial (*El diario del juicio*)," Year 1, no. 9, July 23, 1985, and no. 10, July 30, 1985.

108. Interview with Elba Rama.

109. Interview with UY001-2017, Uruguayan survivor of Condor, Buenos Aires, September 12, 2017.

110. CELS, Rodolfo Zibell, "Una cedula falsa para salvar la vida de su hijo," in "The Newspaper of the Trial, (*El diario del juicio*)," Year 1, no. 5, June 25, 1985.

111. Interview with Sara Méndez.

112. Lawsuit No. 88-36/1984, Rodríguez Díaz Universindo y Celiberti Lilián, su denuncia, available at https://observatorioluzibarburu.org/causas/100 (accessed May 23, 2020); MJDH, *Jaque*, March 2, 1984.

113. MJDH, "Presentan denuncia penal en Montevideo de secuestro en Brasil y traslado a Uruguay," *Busqueda*, February 29, 1984.

114. Email exchange with Lilian Celiberti, May 15, 2020.

115. Mauro César Silveira, "Acabou o pesadelo de Lilian e Universindo," *Zero Hora*, December 30, 1983. Document sent by Lilian Celiberti on May 15, 2020.

116. Email exchange with Celiberti.

117. MJDH, Lawsuit filed before Montevideo's Criminal Judge of the Sixth Circuit, February 23, 1984, paragraph 20.

118. Email exchange with Celiberti.

119. "90-190/1984, Rodríguez Larreta Enrique, su denuncia," available at https:// observatorioluzibarburu.org/causas/24 (accessed May 23, 2020); CELS, "Informe sobre el viaje al Uruguay realizado el día 17 de abril en representación del CELS," n.d., but most likely April 1985 or soon thereafter.

120. "94-10384/1984, Alba Rosa Blanco de Badano, su denuncia," available at https:// observatorioluzibarburu.org/causas/108 (accessed May 23, 2020).

121. Francesca Lessa, "No hay que tener los ojos en la nuca: The Memory of Violence in Uruguay, 1973–2010," in *The Memory of State Terrorism in the Southern Cone: Argentina, Chile, and Uruguay,* ed. Francesca Lessa and Vincent Druliolle (New York: Palgrave Macmillan, 2011), 179–208.

122. The number of lawsuits was calculated (based on information on dictatorship-era criminal cases) by the Uruguayan Observatorio Luz Ibarburu, available at www .observatorioluzibarburu.org/causas/ (accessed February 15, 2021).

123. Lawsuit No. 100/1985, Gerardo Gatti y otros, su desaparición, available at https://observatorioluzibarburu.org/causas/278 (accessed May 23, 2020).

124. Lawsuit No. 519/1985, Malugani Violeta; Gonzalez de Prieto Milka; Gatti de Islas Ester; Hernandez Irma; Ibarburu Luz María; Recagno Ademar; Gonzalez Souza Asunción, su denuncia, available at https://observatorioluzibarburu.org/causas/220 (accessed May 23, 2020).

125. CELS, "Informe sobre el viaje al Uruguay."

126. On the commissions, see Francesca Lessa, "Investigative Commission on the Kidnapping and Assassination of Former National Representatives Zelmar Michelini and Héctor Gutiérrez-Ruiz," in *Encyclopedia of Transitional Justice,* ed. Lavinia Stan and Nadya Nedelsky (New York: Cambridge University Press, 2013), vol. 3, 255–60.

127. Francesca Lessa, "Parliamentary Investigative Commission on the Situation of Disappeared Persons and Its Causes," in Stan and Nedelsky, *Encyclopedia of Transitional Justice,* 353–57.

128. Lessa, "Investigative Commission."

129. Alexandra Barahona de Brito, *Human Rights and Democratization in Latin America: Uruguay and Chile* (Oxford: Oxford University Press, 1997).

130. SERPAJ, *Uruguay Nunca Más.*

131. Ibid., 343.

132. Ibid., 329.

133. Communication with Francisco Bustamante, SERPAJ, July 21, 2020.

134. Lessa, "Barriers."

135. Interview with Laura Elgueta Díaz.

136. See Dinges's numerous articles in the *Washington Post,* including "Figure Sought in Letelier Case Called U.S. Citizen," March 6, 1978; "Dossier Said to Report Chile Hired Cuban Hit Men," October 24, 1978; and "The Unresolved Questions in the Letelier Case," June 29, 1980.

137. Interview with Federico Tatter.

Chapter 8. Eluding Amnesty

1. "Not a leaf moves in this country if I'm not moving it." Pinochet's famous statement was given to journalists in October 1981. Patrick Guillaudat and Pierre Mouterde, *Los movimientos sociales en Chile, 1973–1993* (Santiago: LOM Ediciones, 1998), 99.

2. Juan Guzmán Tapia, *En el borde del mundo: Memorias del juez que procesó a Pinochet* (Barcelona: Editorial Anagrama, 2006).

3. Interview with CL003-2016, criminal judge, Santiago, November 24, 2016, and Cath Collins et al., "Jurisprudential Milestones in Human Rights Cases: Chile 1990–2020," *Transitional Justice Observatory,* Diego Portales University, June 9, 2020, 3, available at https://derechoshumanos.udp.cl/cms/wp-content/uploads/2020/12/CHILEjurisprudentialmilestones90-20ENG9jun2020-1.pdf (accessed July 5, 2020).

4. Larry Rohter, "Judge Declares Pinochet Fit to Face Human Rights Charges," *New York Times*, December 14 2004.

5. Interview with Eduardo Contreras, lawyer, Santiago, November 25, 2016.

6. Interview with Sandro Gaete, Human Rights Brigade of Chile's Investigations Police, Santiago, May 18, 2017.

7. Barahona de Brito, *Human Rights and Democratization*, 176.

8. These include, among others, Collins, *Post-transitional Justice*, and Luis Roniger and Marjo Sznajder, *The Legacy of Human Rights Violations in the Southern Cone: Argentina, Chile, and Uruguay* (Oxford: Oxford University Press, 1999).

9. Alexandra Barahona de Brito, "Truth, Justice, Memory, and Democratization in the Southern Cone," in Barahona de Brito, González-Enríquez, and Aguilar, *Politics of Memory*, 133.

10. Brian Loveman and Elizabeth Lira, *Poder judicial y conflictos políticos (Chile: 1973–1990)*, vol. 3 (Santiago: LOM Ediciones, 2020).

11. Elizabeth Lira, "Chile: Dilemmas of Memory," in Lessa and Druliolle, *Memory of State Terrorism*, 109.

12. Cath Collins, "Human Rights Trials in Chile during and after the 'Pinochet Years,'" *International Journal of Transitional Justice* 4, no. 1 (2010): 67–86.

13. Ibid., 74.

14. Collins, "Jurisprudential Milestones," 3.

15. Steve J. Stern, *Reckoning with Pinochet: The Memory Question in Democratic Chile, 1989–2006* (Durham, NC: Duke University Press, 2010).

16. Collins "Jurisprudential Milestones," 5.

17. Loveman and Lira, *Poder judicial*.

18. Stern, *Reckoning with Pinochet*, 139.

19. Ibid.

20. "Historic Verdicts: The Murder of Orlando Letelier," YouTube channel of the Chilean Judiciary, May 4, 2017, available at www.youtube.com/watch?v=GZs93xAe9Vk (accessed July 4, 2020).

21. William R. Long, "Letelier Murder Case Sentences Upheld in Chile," *Los Angeles Times*, May 31, 1995. The mitigating circumstance (*atenuante*) of half statute of limitations (*prescripción gradual*) (article 103 of the Criminal Code) was applied at sentencing and reduced the prison-term length; see Collins, "Jurisprudential Milestones," 5.

22. "Historic Verdicts," interview with Nelson Caucoto, minute 03:30 onward.

23. Ibid.

24. Ibid., interview with Cristian Cruz, minute 03:48 onward. DINA agents Townley and Fernández Larios, who materially participated in the assassination, entered a US witness protection program in exchange for their collaboration and so avoided extradition to Chile.

25. Alexander Wilde, "Irruptions of Memory: Expressive Politics in Chile's Transition to Democracy," *Journal of Latin American Studies* 31, no. 2 (1999): 473–500.

26. Roniger and Sznajder, *Legacy of Human Rights Violations.*

27. Lessa, *Memory and Transitional Justice.*

28. Data from the Observatorio Luz Ibarburu, available at www.observatorioluzi barburu.org/causas/ (accessed July 5, 2020).

29. Rafael Michelini, "La Operación Zanahoria," *La Republica*, September 16, 2019.

30. Felipe Michelini, "El largo camino de la verdad," *Revista IIDH* 24, julio-diciembre de 1996 (1997): 157–72.

31. "Tres expedientes en trámite que apuntan hacia el Ejecutivo," *La Republica*, April 11, 2000, www.lr21.com.uy/politica/7974-tres-expedientes-en-tramite-que-apuntan -hacia-el-ejecutivo (accessed July 6, 2020).

32. Felipe Michelini, "El largo camino."

33. Skaar, *Judicial Independence.*

34. Collins, "Human Rights Trials."

35. Karinna Fernández Neira, "Breve análisis de la jurisprudencia chilena, en relación a las graves violaciones a los derechos humanos cometidos durante la dictadura militar," *Estudios Constitucionales* 8, no. 1 (2010): 467–88.

36. Collins, "Human Rights Trials."

37. Skype interview with Karinna Fernández Neira, human rights lawyer, July 14, 2017.

38. Interview with Eduardo Contreras.

39. Interview with CL003-2016.

40. Ibid.

41. Ibid.

42. Collins "Jurisprudential Milestones," 6–7.

43. See the Extension and Foundation for an Order of Unconditional Provisional Imprisonment of Augusto Pinochet and His Arrest, Fifth Central Magistrate's Court, *Audiencia Nacional*, Madrid, October 18, 1998, available at http://www.derechos.org /nizkor/chile/juicio/funda.html (accessed March 3, 2021). On July 1, 1996, the Association of Progressive Prosecutors of Spain filed, in a private capacity, criminal charges against Pinochet and other leaders of the Chilean military junta, thereby originating the Spanish case. See Richard J. Wilson, "Prosecuting Pinochet: International Crimes in Spanish Domestic Law," *Human Rights Quarterly* 21, no. 4 (1999): 927–79; Reed Brody and Michael Ratner, eds., *The Pinochet Papers: The Case of Augusto Pinochet Ugarte in Spain and Britain* (Boston: Kluwer Law International, 2000); Madeleine Davis, ed., *The Pinochet Case: Origins, Progress and Implications* (London: Institute of Latin American Studies, 2003).

44. El juez más famoso de Chile," *BBC Mundo*, May 5, 2005, available at http://

news.bbc.co.uk/hi/spanish/latin_america/newsid_4113000/4113275.stm (accessed July 8, 2020).

45. Collins and Hau, "Chile."

46. Interview with CL003-2016.

47. Email exchange with Francisco Bustos, human rights lawyer, July 21, 2020.

48. Interview with Sandro Gaete. The *amparo* is a typically Mexican procedure, also found in other Latin American countries; it may be invoked by any person who believes that any of his or her rights protected by the Constitution or any applicable international treaties are being violated.

49. *Amparo* writ filed by Elba Rosa Alarcón Muñoz, October 6, 1975, consulted in May 2017 at the archive of the Foundation for Social Assistance of the Christian Churches (Fundacion de Ayuda Social de las Iglesias Cristianas), Santiago.

50. Indictment Charge in Lawsuit 2182-98, "Operation Condor," February 16, 2016, available at www.pjud.cl/documents/396533/0/Acusacion+Condor.pdf/89c5c894 -2ec8-4841-8cd6-6e6bef1aaf98 (accessed July 7, 2020).

51. Interview with Karinna Fernández Neira.

52. Email exchange with Francisco Bustos.

53. Interview with Paulina Zamorano Valenzuela, human rights lawyer, Santiago, November 28, 2016; 2016 Indictment Charge.

54. Interview with Paulina Zamorano.

55. Interview with CL002-2016, judicial clerk, Santiago, November 28, 2016.

56. "Abren un juicio de desafuero a Pinochet por la 'Operación Cóndor,'" *ABC Internacional,* December 12, 2003, available at www.abc.es/internacional/abci-abren-juicio -desafuero-pinochet-operacion-condor-200312230300-228366_noticia.html?ref= https:%2F%2Fwww.google.com%2F (accessed July 7, 2020).

57. "Chile: Pinochet Escapes Justice," Human Rights Watch, July 1, 2002, available at www.hrw.org/news/2002/07/01/chile-pinochet-escapes-justice (accessed August 21, 2020).

58. "Fallo completo de la Corte de Apelaciones sobre el desafuero Augusto Pinochet," *Radio Cooperativa,* July 7, 2004, available at www.cooperativa.cl/noticias/pais /augusto-pinochet/fallo-completo-de-la-corte-de-apelaciones-sobre-el-desafuero-de -augusto/2004-07-07/104424.html and "Operación Cóndor: Suprema desaforó a general (R) Pinochet," *El Mostrador,* August 26, 2004, available at www.elmostrador.cl /noticias/pais/2004/08/26/operacion-condor-suprema-desaforo-a-general-r-pinochet/ (both accessed July 7, 2020).

59. Collins, *Post-transitional Justice,* 92.

60. Indictment in the Operation Condor episode, December 13, 2004. Document sent by Boris Hau on November 26, 2016.

61. "Corte confirma proceso a Pinochet," *BBC Mundo,* January 4, 2005, available

at http://news.bbc.co.uk/hi/spanish/latin_america/newsid_4146000/4146315.stm (accessed July 8, 2020).

62. "La Justicia de Chile anula el procesamiento contra Augusto Pinochet por la 'Operación Cóndor,'" *El Mundo,* June 7, 2005, available at www.elmundo.es/elmundo /2005/06/07/internacional/1118168421.html (accessed July 8, 2020).

63. "La Corte Suprema ratifica el sobreseimiento definitivo de la causa contra Pinochet por la Operación Cóndor," *La Vanguardia,* September 15, 2005, available at www .lavanguardia.com/internacional/20050915/51262814172/la-corte-suprema-ratifica-el -sobreseimiento-definitivo-de-la-causa-contra-pinochet-por-la-operacion.html (accessed July 8, 2020).

64. At least eighteen Chilean judges had endeavored to probe human rights violations, and many were also removed from their posts. "Los jueces que sacaron la cara por la justicia durante el régimen militar," *El Mostrador,* March 20, 2005, available at https://www.elmostrador.cl/noticias/pais/2005/03/20/los-jueces-que-sacaron-la-cara -por-la-justicia-durante-el-regimen-militar/ (accessed March 2, 2021).

65. Zoom interview with Magdalena Garcés, human rights lawyer, September 15, 2020.

66. Interviews with CL002-2016 and Eduardo Contreras.

67. John Dinges's interview in *El Juez y el General,* documentary by Patricio Lanfranco and Elizabeth Farnsworth (2008), minute 57:20.

68. Indictment in the Operation Condor episode, 22.

69. Interview with CL003-2016.

70. Ibid.

71. Pablo Chargoñia, "Avances, retrocesos y desafíos en la lucha judicial contra la impunidad," in Fried-Amilivia and Lessa, *Luchas contra la impunidad,* 165.

72. "Tres expedientes en trámite."

73. "Desparecidos y ETA, centro de la visita de Aznar," *Inter Press Service,* March 19, 1998, available at www.ipsnoticias.net/1998/03/uruguay-desparecidos-y-eta-centro-de -la-visita-de-aznar/ (accessed July 18, 2020).

74. Raúl Ronzoni, "Abogada francesa pide captura de ex dictador Alvarez," *Inter Press Service,* November 27, 1998.

75. Skaar, *Judicial Independence.*

76. Ibid.

77. Interview with Pablo Chargoñia, human rights lawyer, Montevideo, April 8, 2014.

78. "Secuestro y desaparición de María Claudia García de Gelman," Institución Nacional de Derechos Humanos y Defensoría del Pueblo, April 29, 2019, available at www.gub.uy/institucion-nacional-derechos-humanos-uruguay/node/196 (accessed July 17, 2020).

79. Lessa, *Memory and Transitional Justice.*

80. "Sanguinetti: 'En Uruguay no desapareció ningún niño,'" *La República,* January 29, 2000, available at www.lr21.com.uy/politica/1627-sanguinetti-en-uruguay-no-desaparecio-ningun-nino (accessed July 17, 2020).

81. Interview with Juan Errandonea, lawyer, Montevideo, March 23, 2012.

82. Interview with Raúl Olivera, human rights activist, Montevideo, October 3, 2013.

83. Mirtha Guianze, "La Ley de Caducidad, las luchas por la Justicia y por la jurisdicción universal de los derechos humanos en Uruguay," in Fried-Amilivia and Lessa, *Luchas contra la impunidad,* 189–202.

84. Sentence No. 991 in Lawsuit 17-414/2003, October 18, 2002, available at https://observatorioluzibarburu.org/media/uploads/14142003.pdf (accessed July 17, 2020).

85. Guianze, "La Ley."

86. Chargoñia, "Avances," 166.

87. Petitioner's original complaint, July 19, 2002, available at https://observatorioluzibarburu.org/media/uploads/1001985.pdf (accessed July 17, 2020).

88. "Apareció Simón en Argentina," *La República,* March 12, 2002, available at www.lr21.com.uy/politica/73355-aparecio-simon-en-argentina (accessed July 18, 2020).

89. Roger Rodríguez, "El tercer secreto . . . ," *La República,* March 21, 2010.

90. Interview with Mirtha Guianze, former criminal prosecutor and director of Uruguay's National Institute of Human Rights, Montevideo, April 4, 2014.

91. "Discurso del Presidente de la República, Tabaré Vázquez, en el acto realizado en el Palacio Legislativo," March 1, 2005, available at http://archivo.presidencia.gub.uy/_web/noticias/2005/03/2005030111.htm (accessed July 18, 2020).

92. Chargoñia, "Avances."

93. Interview with Federico Álvarez, former criminal judge, Montevideo, March 12, 2012.

94. Interview with Pablo Chargoñia.

95. Petitioner's original complaint, September 19, 2005. Document sent by Silvia Ocaña, Observatorio Luz Ibarburu, July 20, 2020.

96. Ibid., 9.

97. I/A Court H.R., Case of Barrios Altos v. Peru, Merits, Judgment March 14, 2001, Series C, No. 75.

98. Petitioner's original complaint, 12–13.

99. Interview with Pablo Chargoñia.

100. Indictment Resolution, September 11, 2006, 1–2. Document sent by Silvia Ocaña, Observatorio Luz Ibarburu, July 20, 2020.

101. Data elaborated from the Observatorio Luz Ibarburu's online database, available at www.observatorioluzibarburu.org/causas/ (accessed July 20, 2020).

102. Interview with Federico Álvarez.

103. Interview with Pablo Chargoñia.

104. Speech delivered by Gonzalo Fernández during a seminar on "Memory, Truth,

and Justice," November 17, 2005, available at http://archivo.presidencia.gub.uy/_web/noticias/2005/11/2005111712.htm (accessed July 28, 2020).

105. Interview with Pablo Chargoñia.

106. "La 'orden explícita y directa' de Vázquez era 'no tocar' la ley de Caducidad," *Sudestada,* April 11, 2019, available at www.sudestada.com.uy/articleId__77b9e835-a129-4bef-926d-ae24b129e71f/10893/Detalle-de-Noticia (accessed July 28, 2020).

107. Interview with Mariana Mota.

108. Interview with Pablo Chargoñia.

109. 2006 Indictment Resolution, 14.

110. Ibid., 3, 12–13.

111. As Mirtha Guianze explained during our interview, ultimately Barrios's disappearance was excluded from the investigations, since no evidence could be found of Uruguayan agents' participation.

112. Sentence No. 36 in Lawsuit 98-247/2006, March 26, 2009, 13, 24, available at www.observatorioluzibarburu.org/media/uploads/98_247_2006.pdf (accessed July 29, 2020). The remaining six defendants in the same case were included in a separate but basically identical verdict dictated on the same day: Sentence No. 37 in Lawsuit 2-43332/2005, available at www.observatorioluzibarburu.org/media/uploads/2.%20Silveira%20Ramas%20Medina%20Vazquez%20Maurente%20Sande%2026.03.2009.pdf (accessed July 29, 2020).

113. Sentence No. 36 in Lawsuit 98-247/2006, 24–25.

114. Ibid., 69.

115. Ibid., 80.

116. Indictment in Lawsuit 2-20415/2007, December 17, 2007, available at www.observatorioluzibarburu.org/media/uploads/2204152007_-_Decreto_01142.pdf (accessed July 29, 2020).

117. Petitioner's original complaint, May 28, 2007, available at www.observatorioluzibarburu.org/media/uploads/2211522007_-_Denuncia.pdf (accessed July 29, 2020).

118. Ibid., 19.

119. Prosecutor's plea in Lawsuit 2-21152/2007, n.d., 8–22, available at www.observatorioluzibarburu.org/media/uploads/2211522007_-_Dictamen_Fiscal.pdf (accessed July 30, 2020).

120. Interview with Mariana Mota.

121. Indictment Charge in Lawsuit 2-21152/2007, September 17, 2010, 21, available at www.observatorioluzibarburu.org/media/uploads/2211522007b_1.pdf (accessed July 30, 2020).

122. Resolution of the Appeals Tribunal in Lawsuit 2-21152/2007, July 28, 2011, 35, available at www.observatorioluzibarburu.org/media/uploads/2211522007_-_Sentencia_Tribunal_Apelaciones.pdf (accessed July 30, 2020).

123. Ibid., 44.

124. Interview with Mariana Mota.

125. Francesca Lessa and Jo-Marie Burt, "New Ruling by Uruguay's Supreme Court of Justice Once Again Jeopardizes the Search for Truth and Justice for Dictatorship-Era Crimes," *WOLA Commentary,* November 7, 2017, available at www.wola.org/analysis/new-ruling-uruguays-supreme-court-justice-jeopardizes-search-truth-justice-dictatorship-era-crimes/ (accessed July 30, 2020).

126. Supreme Court's Verdict No. 1501 in Lawsuit 98-247/2006, May 6, 2011, available at www.observatorioluzibarburu.org/media/uploads/982472006a.pdf and Verdict in Lawsuit 2-43332/2005, July 20, 2011, available at www.observatorioluzibarburu.org/media/uploads/24333220005a.pdf (both accessed July 30, 2020).

127. Ariela Peralta, "El caso Gelman y los desafíos a la Ley de Caducidad," in Fried-Amilivia and Lessa, *Luchas contra la impunidad,* 203–15.

128. Interview with UY001-2012, human rights lawyer, Montevideo, March 13, 2012.

129. See Barrios Altos v. Peru; and I/A Court H.R., Case of Almonacid Arellano et al. v. Chile, Preliminary Objections, Merits, Reparations and Costs, Judgment of September 26, 2006, Series C, No. 154.

130. Gelman v. Uruguay, paragraph 232.

131. Burt, Fried-Amilivia, and Lessa, "Civil Society."

132. Interview with Magdalena Garcés.

133. Ibid.

134. "Ministro Mario Carroza dicta acusación por secuestros y homicidios calificados en 'Operación Cóndor,'" February 23, 2016, available at https://www.araucaniacuenta.cl/ministro-mario-carroza-dicta-acusacion-por-secuestros-y-homicidios-calificados-en-operacion-condor/ (accessed August 27, 2021).

135. Patricio Antonio Biedma, José Campos Cifuentes, Cristina Carreño Araya, Jean Ives Claudet Fernández, Humberto Cordano López, José De La Maza Asquet, Luis Elgueta Díaz, Edgardo Enríquez Espinoza, Cecilia Magnet Ferrero, Víctor Oliva Troncoso, and Luis Quinchavil Suarez.

136. Interview with Paulina Zamorano.

137. Interview with CL002-2016.

138. Interview with CL003-2017, lawyer, Santiago, May 19, 2017.

139. "Ministro Carroza condena a 20 exagentes de la DINA por Operación Cóndor," *La Tercera,* September 21, 2018, available at https://www.latercera.com/nacional/noticia/ministro-carroza-condena-20-exagentes-la-dina-operacion-condor/326486/ (accessed August 27, 2021). In April 2019 Demóstenes Eugenio Cárdenas Saavedra was absolved in the case.

140. "Operación Cóndor: Condenan a 20 ex DINA, entre ellos Gladys Calderón, alias 'El ángel del cianuro,'" *El Mostrador,* September 21, 2018, available at www.elmostrador.cl/noticias/pais/2018/09/21/operacion-condor-condenan-a-20-ex-dina-entre-ellos-gladys-calderon-alias-el-angel-del-cianuro/ (accessed July 9, 2020).

141. Sentence in Lawsuit 2182-98, "Operation Condor," September 21, 2018, 898–900. Document sent by lawyer Francisco Bustos on June 26, 2020.

142. Ibid., 379–427.

143. Ibid.; testimony of former DINA agent Samuel Fuenzalida Devia, 341–42.

144. Sentence in Lawsuit 2182-98, 392.

145. Interview with Sandro Gaete.

146. Sentence in Lawsuit 2182-98, 307–8.

147. Ibid.; testimony of Guillermo Ferrán Martínez, 242–44.

148. Sentence in Lawsuit 2182-98; testimony of Eduardo Oyarce Riquelme, 514–15.

149. Email exchange with Boris Hau, researcher, Transitional Justice Observatory, Diego Portales University, July 18, 2020.

150. Interviews with CL003-2017 and Paulina Zamorano.

151. Interview with Paulina Zamorano.

152. Interview with CL001-2016, member of Alexei Jaccard's family, Santiago, November 18, 2016.

153. Interview with Karinna Fernández Neira.

154. Interview with CL001-2016.

155. Ibid.

156. Interviews with CL003-2016 and Magdalena Garcés.

157. Interview with Magdalena Garcés.

158. Interview with Flor Hernández Zazpe.

159. Email exchange with Boris Hau.

160. Francisco Bustos, "La circunstancia agravante del artículo 12 No 8 del Código Penal y su (in)aplicación en causas sobre crímenes contra el Derecho internacional: Un análisis de la jurisprudencia chilena (1993–2018)" (master's thesis, Universidad de Chile, 2019).

161. Email exchange with Boris Hau.

162. Interview with Magdalena Garcés.

163. Email exchange with Francisco Bustos, March 4, 2021.

164. Interview with Karinna Fernández Neira.

165. Interview with Nelson Caucoto, lawyer, Santiago, May 10, 2017.

166. The archives of the Vicaria were extensively used in human rights trials in Chile. See Boris Hau, Francesca Lessa, and Hugo Rojas, "Registration and Documentation of State Violence as Judicial Evidence in Human Rights Trials," in Resistance to Political Violence in Latin America: Documenting Atrocity, ed. Oriana Bernasconi (New York: Palgrave MacMillan, 2019), 197–227.

167. Interview with Mariana Mota.

168. Interview with Mirtha Guianze.

169. Interview with CL002-2016.

170. Email exchange with Francisco Bustos, July 13, 2020; "Tribunal Constitucional

rechaza requerimiento de acusado en Operación Cóndor," *La Tercera,* July 19, 2018, available at www.latercera.com/nacional/noticia/tribunal-constitucional-rechaza-requeri miento-acusado-operacion-condor/249789/ (accessed July 13, 2020).

171. Interviews with CL002-2016 and with Pablo Chargoñia.

172. Interview with Alejandro Solís, judge, Santiago, November 23, 2016.

173. Interview with Pablo Chargoñia.

174. Ibid.

175. Data on prosecutions in Chile and Uruguay are from calculations based on the information compiled in the author's project database.

176. Interview with Alejandro Solís.

177. Mónica González, "Fallo del caso Prats: Una travesía de 36 años que estalla en el corazón del Ejército," *Centro de Investigación Periodística, (CIPER),* July 8, 2010.

178. See verdicts in Rol 16.996-AyB, Caso Coyhaique; Rol 2182-98, Episodio "Uruguayos: Ariel Arcos y otros," and Rol 2182-98, Episodio "Julio Cesar Fernández y otros," all available at https://expedientesdelarepresion.cl/ (accessed July 12, 2020).

179. Sentence No. 157 in Lawsuit 2-20415/2007, October 21, 2009, available at www .observatorioluzibarburu.org/media/uploads/3.%20Alvarez_y_Larcebeau%20sent %20157%20%2021.10.2009.pdf (accessed August 1, 2020).

180. Sentence No. 68 in Lawsuit 100-10592/1985, June 30, 2011, available at www .observatorioluzibarburu.org/media/uploads/7.%20%20Sent_68_condena_Borda berry_Blanco_30-6-2011%20Penal%20II.pdf (accessed July 30, 2020).

181. Ibid., 27–28.

182. "Suprema Corte ratificó la condena a Gavazzo, Silveira, Arab, Medina y Vázquez por el homicidio de María Claudia García de Gelman," *La Diaria,* September 5, 2020 (accessed September 9, 2020).

183. Interview with CL002-2016.

184. Interview with Mirtha Guianze.

185. Ibid.

186. Interview with Pablo Chargoñia.

187. Ibid.

Chapter 9. Against Impunity

1. OCT 2016 Verdict, 15–26 and 58–86.

2. Argentina Public Prosecutor's Office, "A diez años del fallo 'Simón': Un balance sobre el estado actual del proceso de justicia por crímenes de lesa humanidad," Buenos Aires, 2015, 2, available at www.fiscales.gob.ar/lesa-humanidad/wp-content /uploads/sites/4/2015/06/20150612-Informe-Procuradur%C3%ADa-de-Cr%C3% ADmenes-contra-la-Humanidad.pdf (accessed February 21, 2020).

3. Interview with AR001-2013, federal investigative prosecutor, Buenos Aires, September 26, 2013.

4. Interview with Pablo Ouviña and Mercedes Moguilansky, Operation Condor prosecutors, Buenos Aires, September 26, 2013.

5. Interview with Pablo Llonto, human rights lawyer, Buenos Aires, September 26, 2013.

6. Dora Sala, "'Si commuoveva se raccontavo il mio rapimento,'" *Il Manifesto*, February 11, 2020.

7. "El militar argentino Alfredo Astiz, condenado en rebeldía por un tribunal francés," *El País*, March 17, 1990, available at https://elpais.com/diario/1990/03/17/internacional/637628424_850215.html (accessed February 22, 2020).

8. Interview with Marcos Kotlik, former CELS lawyer, Buenos Aires, September 19, 2013.

9. CELS, *Derechos humanos en Argentina: Informe anual 2000* (Buenos Aires: CELS–EUDEBA, 2000).

10. "Querella por el robo de bebes," *La Nación*, March 2, 1999, available at www.lanacion.com.ar/politica/querella-por-el-robo-de-bebes-nid129728 (accessed February 22, 2020).

11. *Argentina—Country Summary, 2002* (New York: Human Rights Watch, 2002).

12. Alejandra Dandan, "Una práctica sistemática y generalizada," *Página12,* July 6, 2012.

13. Interview with Carolina Varsky, director of the Program on Memory and Fight against Impunity between 1998 and 2013, and subsequently of litigation of the CELS, Buenos Aires, September 16, 2013.

14. Interview with Daniel Rafecas, Judge at the Third Federal Court for Criminal Correctional Matters of the Federal Capital, Buenos Aires, October 30, 2013.

15. Other crimes included criminal actions against the constitutional order, sovereignty, and territorial integrity of each Condor country; criminal action to ensure impunity for the crimes; and conspiracy against the right of people's self-determination. Copy of the querella on file with the author, 2–3. Document sent by lawyer Jaime Nuguer on November 21, 2013.

16. Interview with Jaime Nuguer, lawyer of the original lawsuit, Buenos Aires, July 17, 2018.

17. Interview with AR001-2013.

18. Argentine Criminal Code, Second Book, VIII, "Crimes against Public Order," available at http://servicios.infoleg.gob.ar/infolegInternet/anexos/15000-19999/16546/texact.htm#22 (accessed August 20, 2018).

19. Interview with Jaime Nuguer.

20. Copy of the querella on file with the author.

21. Interview with Daniel Rafecas.

22. Interview with Pablo Ouviña and Mercedes Moguilansky.

23. Interview with Pablo Llonto.

24. Interview with Federico Tatter.

25. Ibid.

26. Interview with Marcos Kotlik.

27. Interview with Daniel Rafecas.

28. CELS, *Derechos humanos en Argentina: Informe anual 2002* (Buenos Aires: Siglo Ventiuno, 2002).

29. Lessa, *Memory and Transitional Justice*.

30. Interview with Luz Palmás Zaldua, CELS lawyer in the Condor case (2014–18), Buenos Aires, June 12, 2018.

31. Victoria Ginzberg, "El Cóndor sería la próxima causa en librarse de leyes de impunidad," *Página12*, June 16, 2002.

32. Naomi Roht-Arriaza, *The Pinochet Effect: Transnational Justice in the Age of Human Rights* (Philadelphia: University of Pennsylvania Press, 2006).

33. "Piden extradición de Pinochet," *BBC Mundo*, July 20, 2001.

34. Lourdes Heredia, "Operación Cóndor: Videla procesado," *BBC Mundo*, September 27, 2001.

35. Roht-Arriaza, *Pinochet Effect*, 152.

36. Irinia Hauser, "Crímenes que no borra el paso del tiempo," *Página12*, August 25, 2004.

37. María José Guembe, "Reopening of Trials for Crimes Committed by the Argentine Military Dictatorship," *Sur—International Journal on Human Rights* 2, no. 3 (2005): 114–31.

38. Prosecutor Osorio, cited in Alejandra Dandan, "El plan de la represión sin fronteras," *Página12*, March 4, 2013.

39. Interviews with Marcos Kotlik and Luz Palmás Zaldua.

40. Interview with Luz Palmás Zaldua.

41. I thank Lorena Balardini for clarifying this point. Also see CELS, *Derechos humanos en Argentina: Informe 2010* (Buenos Aires: Siglo Veintiuno–CELS, 2010).

42. Interview with Pablo Ouviña and Mercedes Moguilansky.

43. Interviews with Marcos Kotlik and Luz Palmás Zaldua.

44. Interview with Daniel Rafecas.

45. Interview with Jair Krischke.

46. Roger Rodríguez, "Cordero fue extraditado a Argentina," *La República*, January 24, 2010.

47. Argentina Public Prosecutor's Office, Coordinating and Monitoring Unit for Human Rights Trials, December 2012, 5–6, available at www.mpf.gov.ar/docs/Links/DDHH/causas_elevadas_diciembre_2012.pdf (accessed July 15, 2020).

48. Ibid. Condor II encompassed three defendants, including Uruguayan Cordero, and the cases of eleven victims, while Condor III encompassed eleven defendants, including former dictator Bignone, and sixteen victims.

49. Interview with Pablo Ouviña and Mercedes Moguilansky.

50. Interview with Luz Palmás Zaldua.

51. Interview with Carolina Varsky.

52. Alejandra Dandan, "Una condena que atraviesa fronteras," *Página12*, April 1, 2011.

53. Argentina Public Prosecutor's Office, Informe de la Procuraduría de Crímenes contra la Humanidad, *La judicialización de la Operación Cóndor*, November 2015, available at www.fiscales.gob.ar/wp-content/uploads/2015/11/Informe-ProcuLesa-Op-C%C3 %B3ndor-Final.pdf (accessed February 27, 2020).

54. Interview with Luz Palmás Zaldua.

55. Miguel Ángel Furci and his wife were sentenced in 1994 to five and three years, respectively, for hiding and detaining Mariana Zaffaroni, the daughter of Uruguayan exiles disappeared in Buenos Aires in 1976 (see chapter 4).

56. For details about each accused and the charges, see the Argentina Public Prosecutor's Office webpage at www.mpf.gob.ar/plan-condor/imputados-y-areas-de-actuacion/ (accessed February 27, 2020).

57. Argentina Public Prosecutor's Office, *La judicialización*, 6.

58. "Operación Cóndor: Con el veredicto previsto para el viernes próximo, llegará el final de un juicio histórico," May 20, 2016, available at www.fiscales.gob.ar/lesa -humanidad/operacion-condor-con-el-veredicto-previsto-para-el-viernes-proximo-llegara -el-final-de-un-juicio-historico/ (accessed February 27, 2020).

59. Ibid.

60. Interview with Pablo Ouviña and Mercedes Moguilansky.

61. Interview with Marcos Kotlik.

62. Interview with Adrián Grünberg, judge in TOF1, Buenos Aires, October 26, 2016.

63. Ibid.

64. Author's notes, trial hearing, June 5, 2016.

65. Private prosecution refers to the right that "allows victims and their lawyers, including domestic human rights organizations, to open a criminal investigation and actively participate throughout every stage of the criminal proceedings." Veronica Michel and Kathryn Sikkink, "Human Rights Prosecutions and the Participation Rights of Victims in Latin America," *Law and Society Review* 47, no. 4 (2013): 874.

66. Author's notes, trial hearing, June 16, 2015.

67. Ibid., July 3, 2015.

68. "Se desdibujaron las fronteras para propiciar un plan criminal," *InfoJus*, August 18, 2015, available at www.infojusnoticias.gov.ar/nacionales/se-desdibujaron-las -fronteras-para-propiciar-un-plan-criminal-9468.html (accessed February 27, 2020).

69. Author's notes, trial hearing, October 16, 2015.

70. Interview with Pablo Ouviña and Mercedes Moguilansky.

71. Author's notes, trial hearing, December 1, 2015.

72. Defendants: Cordero, Olea, Tragant, Minicucci, De Lio, and Falcón.

73. Defendants: Furci, Lobaiza, Sadi Pepa, Vañek, Feroglio, Menéndez, Guañabens, Caggiano, Riveros, Alespeiti, and Bignone.

74. Author's notes, trial hearing, February 23, 2016.

75. For details on each defendant, see Francesca Lessa, "Operation Condor on Trial: Justice for Transnational Human Rights Crimes in South America," *Journal of Latin American Studies* 51, no. 2 (2019): 438.

76. "Operation Condor: Former Argentine Junta Leader Jailed," *BBC News*, May 28, 2016, available at www.bbc.co.uk/news/world-latin-america-36403909; "Argentine Court Confirms a Deadly Legacy of Dictatorships," *New York Times*, May 28, 2016, available at www.nytimes.com/2016/05/29/world/americas/argentine-court-confirms-a-deadly-legacy-of-dictatorships.html (both accessed February 28, 2020).

77. Carlos Cué, "Argentina, primer país que condena a los jerarcas del Plan Cóndor," *El País*, May 28, 2016.

78. Interview with Pablo Ouviña, June 9, 2016.

79. "Operación Cóndor: Se probó la asociación ilícita y se impusieron penas de 8 a 25 años de prisión," May 27, 2016, available at www.fiscales.gob.ar/lesa-humanidad/operacion-condor-se-probo-la-asociacion-ilicita-y-se-impusieron-penas-de-8-a-25-anos-de-prision/ (accessed February 27, 2020).

80. Full text of the verdict, "Lesa humanidad: Difundieron los fundamentos de la sentencia por el 'Plan Cóndor,'" August 9, 2016, is available at www.cij.gob.ar/nota-22663-Lesa-humanidad-difundieron-los-fundamentos-de-la-sentencia-por-el-Plan-C-ndor.html (accessed February 27, 2020).

81. Ibid., 1.222.

82. Ibid., 1.221.

83. Ibid., 1.225–1.226.

84. Ibid., 5.097.

85. Ibid., 5.098.

86. Alfredo Boccia Paz, *Goiburú: La odisea del insumiso* (Asunción: Servilibro, 2014).

87. Alfredo Boccia Paz et al., *En los sotanos de los Generales: Los documentos ocultos del Operativo Condor* (Asunción: Servilibro, 2002).

88. OCT 2016 Verdict, 2.309.

89. Interview with Rogelio Goiburú, victim's son, Asunción, September 9, 2016.

90. OCT 2016 Verdict, 2.324.

91. Ibid., 2.323.

92. Ibid., 2.299.

93. Ibid., 2.312.

94. Ibid., 2.300.

95. Interview with Rogelio Goiburú.

96. OCT 2016 Verdict, 2.301.

97. Interview with Rogelio Goiburú

98. Interview with Domingo Rolón, Operation Condor survivor, Asunción, September 8, 2016.

99. OCT 2016 Verdict, 2.325.

100. Interview with Adrián Grünberg.

101. Interview with Carolina Varsky.

102. "Operation Condor: Landmark Human Rights Trial Reaches Finale," *BBC News*, May 27, 2016, available at www.bbc.co.uk/news/world-latin-america-36394820 (accessed March 10, 2020).

103. Interview with Adrián Grünberg.

104. Francesca Lessa, "Remnants of Truth: The Role of Archives in Human Rights Trials for Operation Condor," *Latin American Research Review* 56, no. 1 (2021): 183–99.

105. 2016 interview with Pablo Ouviña.

106. Interview with Adrián Grünberg.

107. Interview with Jaime Nuguer.

108. Hauser, "Crímenes."

109. See MPF, "Dossier de sentencias pronunciadas en juicios de lesa humanidad en Argentina," March 2016, available at www.fiscales.gob.ar/wp-content/uploads/2016/03/LH_Dossier_23-3.pdf (accessed February 27, 2020).

110. Interviews with Pablo Llonto, and Pablo Ouviña and Mercedes Moguilansky.

111. Interview with Jaime Nuguer.

112. 2016 interview with Pablo Ouviña.

113. Ibid.

114. Interview with Adrián Grünberg.

115. "El Gobierno autoriza la extradición a Argentina del represor Ricardo Miguel Cavallo," *El Mundo*, March 1, 2008, available at www.elmundo.es/elmundo/2008/02/29/espana/1204288296.html (accessed August 29, 2020).

116. Mezarobba, "Brazil."

117. Interview with Pablo Chargoñia.

118. Interview with Martín Rico, lawyer for the Human Rights and Cultural Pluralism Secretariat, Buenos Aires, October 1, 2013.

119. Interview with Marcos Kotlik.

120. Data provided by the Observatorio Luz Ibarburu via email, December 18, 2020.

121. Interview with Martín Rico.

122. Interview with Mariana Mota.

123. Interview with Jorge Tamayo, brother of a Condor victim, Santiago, May 17, 2017.

124. Interview with Flor Hernández Zazpe.

125. Interview with Laura Elgueta Díaz.

126. Interview with Federico Tatter.

127. Interview with Flor Hernández Zazpe.

128. Interview with Jaime Nuguer.

129. See "Pérez de Smith, Ana María y otros," Argentina Supreme Court of Justice, 96–106, available at https://sj.csjn.gov.ar/sj/suplementos.do?method=ver&data=habeas corpus (accessed July 16, 2020).

130. Interview with Jaime Nuguer.

131. "Murió Alberto Pedroncini," *Página12*, August 6, 2017, available at www.pagina 12.com.ar/54892-murio-alberto-pedroncini (accessed February 22, 2020).

132. Abuelas, Casos Resueltos, "Paula Eva Logares," available at www.abuelas.org.ar /caso/logares-paula-eva-243 (accessed March 11, 2020).

133. Alejandra Dandan, "Pruebas de una represión sin límites," *Página12*, September 7, 2014.

134. Interview with Laura Elgueta Díaz.

135. Interview with Luz Palmás Zaldua.

136. "Operation Condor Verdict: GUILTY!: National Security Archive Provided Declassified Evidence; Hails Historic Ruling," National Security Archive, May 27, 2016, available at https://nsarchive.gwu.edu/briefing-book/southern-cone/2016-05-27/operation -condor-verdict-guilty (accessed February 11, 2021).

Chapter 10. Justice across the Atlantic

1. "In order to find justice, one must be faithful to it: like all deities, it manifests itself only to those who believe in it." Phrase by Italian jurist Piero Calamandrei, cited by lawyer Luca Ventrella during the seminar "Analysis of the Condor Appeals Verdict" at Università degli Studi Roma Tre Law School, on February 6, 2020, author's notes.

2. The courts of assize (*corte d'assise*) are special sections of the Italian judicial system that deal with the most serious crimes, such as murder and terrorism. They are composed of two professional judges and six lay judges, whose members are chosen to serve for short periods and represent various sectors of society.

3. The text of the resolution in Italian and Spanish is available at www.24marzo.it /index.php?module=pagemaster&PAGE_user_op=view_page&PAGE_id=578&MMN _position=200:200 (accessed January 14, 2020).

4. Interview with Silvia and María Bellizzi, relatives of Condor victim, Montevideo, February 13, 2018.

5. Interview with Mirtha Guianze.

6. Email exchange with Felipe Michelini, January 16, 2020.

7. Interview with Arturo Salerni, human rights lawyer, Rome, December 15, 2017.

8. Interview with Raúl Olivera.

9. Analia Banfi Vique, "Felipe Michelini y su legado en pos de la justicia internacional," *La Diaria*, April 20, 2020.

10. Nadia Angelucci, "Juicio por Plan Cóndor: 40 años y 11.000 kilómetros en busca de justicia," *La Diaria*, July 6, 2019.

11. Interview with IT004-2017, relative of Uruguayan victim, Rome, December 15, 2017.

12. Interview with Raúl Olivera.

13. Interview with Mirtha Guianze. Analia Banfi kindly informed me that in December 2016 an investigative judge in Buenos Aires shelved the investigation into Daniel Banfi's murder, because its authors could not be determined.

14. Interview with Silvia and María Bellizzi.

15. Interview with Jorge Ithurburu, president of the human rights NGO 24marzo Onlus, December 17, 2017.

16. Ibid.

17. Ibid.

18. Francesco Caporale, *Desaparecidos: Note a margine di tre processi*, 2nd ed. (Bologna: qudulibri, 2015).

19. Anna Maria De Luca, "Roma, 5 ergastoli agli ufficiali argentini che torturarono e uccisero durante il regime," *La Repubblica*, March 14, 2007.

20. Interview with Giancarlo Maniga, lawyer, Milan, June 4, 2018.

21. Interview with Jorge Ithurburu.

22. Ibid.

23. The full text of article 8 is available at www.brocardi.it/codice-penale/libro -primo/titolo-i/art8.html (accessed January 14, 2020).

24. Caporale, *Desaparecidos*, 22

25. Interview with Giancarlo Maniga.

26. Interview with Aurora Meloni.

27. Text of the 1999 lawsuit, 21–39. Document sent by Jorge Ithurburu on January 15, 2020.

28. Interview with Aurora Meloni.

29. 1999 lawsuit, 9–13.

30. Interview with Jorge Ithurburu.

31. Text of the 2006 arrests requests by PM Capaldo in case 31079/2005, "Pinochet Ugarte, Augusto José Ramón + 145," (hereafter 2006 arrests request) July 10, 2006, 85–90, available at www.24marzo.it/index.php?module=pagemaster&PAGE_user_op =view_page&PAGE_id=482&MMN_position=185:185 (accessed January 15, 2020).

32. Ibid., 90.

33. Ibid., 91.

34. Interview with IT001-2017, former public prosecutor, Rome, December 13, 2017.

35. Ibid.

36. 2006 arrests request, 1003–12.

37. "Plan Cóndor: Italia ordena arrestos," *BBC Mundo*, December 25, 2007.

38. Interview with IT002-2017, lawyer, Rome, December 18, 2017.

39. Namely, Ileana García, Edmundo Dossetti, Julio D'Elía, Yolanda Casco, Raúl Borelli, and Raúl Gámbaro.

40. Lawsuit 2-20415/2007, available at www.observatorioluzibarburu.org/causas /138 (accessed January 21, 2020).

41. Lourdes Rodríguez, "Piano se va lontano," *La Diaria,* October 24, 2013.

42. The treaty reflected the international law principle *aut dedere aut judicare* (obligation to extradite or prosecute). Interview with Andrea Speranzoni, lawyer, Milan, June 4, 2018.

43. Rodríguez, "Piano."

44. See Capaldo's request dated January 31, 2013, available at www.24marzo.it /index.php?module=pagemaster&PAGE_user_op=view_page&PAGE_id=182&MMN _position=185:185 (accessed January 17, 2020).

45. Interview with Mario Antonio Angelelli, lawyer, Rome, December 18, 2017.

46. "Avviso della conclusione delle indagini preliminary," July 23, 2014, copy sent by Arturo Salerni on January 18, 2020.

47. Interview with Giancarlo Maniga.

48. Interview with Arturo Salerni.

49. Italian law allows victims to submit requests for moral and material damages as part of criminal trials, without filing a separate civil case. This permits victims to anticipate civil compensation requests, without waiting for the completion of criminal proceedings.

50. Rodríguez, "Piano."

51. Paolo Brogi, "Desaparecidos, il giudice rinvia a giudizio venti militari," *Corriere della Sera,* October 13, 2014.

52. In Italy ordinary citizens between the ages of thirty and sixty-five and of good moral conduct can be called to participate as lay judges in deciding cases together with professional judges in mixed decision-making bodies. When hearing particularly serious cases of crimes against the state or where the defendants risk prison terms of at least twenty-four years, six lay judges sit alongside two professional judges. Toby S. Goldbach and Valerie P. Hans, "Juries, Lay Judges, and Trials," *Cornell Law Faculty Working Papers,* paper 122, 2014.

53. Interview with IT003-2017, public prosecutor, Rome, December 19, 2017.

54. *La memoria del Cóndor,* documentary by Emanuela Tomassetti and produced by Land Comunicazioni, 2018, minute 0:39:42.

55. Rome's Third Assize Court, Trial Proceedings R. G. 2/15 (hereafter R. G. 2/15), hearing of September 25, 2015, 24. All hearings transcriptions are available at www .24marzo.it/index.php?module=pagemaster&PAGE_user_op=view_page&PAGE_id =553&MMN_position=87:87 (accessed January 21, 2020).

56. Ibid., 27.

57. Ibid., 41

58. R. G. 2/15, hearing of November 20, 2015, 24.

59. Ibid., 26.

60. R. G. 2/15, hearing of October 20, 2015, 86–87.

61. R. G. 2/15, hearing of March 17, 2016, 65.

62. R. G. 2/15, hearing of June 9, 2016, 50–51.

63. R. G. 2/15, hearing of October 21, 2015, 57–60.

64. R. G. 2/15, hearing of March 17, 2016, 46.

65. *Trabajo de recopilación de datos: Pozo de Banfield,* Asociación de Ex Detenidos Desaparecidos, Argentina, July 2004, 10. Document sent by Ana Maria Parnas on February 14, 2019.

66. R. G. 2/15, hearing of October 21, 2015, 71.

67. Ibid., 72.

68. R. G. 2/15, hearing of November 20, 2015, 90.

69. R. G. 2/15, hearing of March 17, 2016, 44.

70. Ibid., 45.

71. The death flights (*vuelos de la muerte*) were an extermination method whereby detainees were told they were being transferred to other prisons in the south of Argentina. Instead they were sedated, stripped naked, and loaded onto planes from which they were then thrown to their deaths in the Atlantic Ocean.

72. Verdict by Rome's Third Assize Court (hereafter First-instance verdict), January 17, 2017, 146–47, available at www.24marzo.it/index.php?module=pagemaster&PAGE _user_op=view_page&PAGE_id=573&MMN_position=196:196 (accessed January 22, 2020).

73. Ibid., 147.

74. Ibid., 148.

75. José Arab, José Gavazzo, Juan Carlos Larcebeau, Pedro Mato, Luis Maurente, Ricardo Medina, Ernesto Ramas, José Sande, Jorge Silveira, Ernesto Soca, Jorge Troccoli, and Gilberto Vázquez.

76. Pedro Espinoza, Daniel Aguirre, Carlos Luco, Orlando Moreno, and Manuel Vázquez.

77. Martín Martínez.

78. First-instance verdict, 149.

79. The defendants were Sergio Arellano Stark, Manuel Contreras, Luis Ramírez, and Marcelo Moren (Chile), and Iván Paulós and Gregorio Álvarez (Uruguay). First-instance verdict, 50, 92, 100.

80. Ibid., 3.

81. Ibid., 11.

82. Ibid., 12.

83. Ibid., 45.

84. Ibid., 12.

85. Interview with Arturo Salerni.

86. "Fallo fue 'balde de agua fría' para Familiares de Desaparecidos," *Ecos,* January 17, 2017.

87. Interview with Mirtha Guianze.

88. Interview with Andrea Speranzoni.

89. Interview with IT003-2017.

90. Interview with Alessia Liistro, lawyer, Rome, December 14, 2017.

91. Interview with Giancarlo Maniga.

92. Memo by Andrea Speranzoni to the Court of Appeals, October 8, 2018. Document sent by Arturo Salerni on November 9, 2018.

93. Rome's First Assize Appeals Court, Procedimento penale 40/17 R. G. contro "Arce Gómez Luis ed altri 26" (hereafter R. G. 40/17), hearing of November 8, 2018, author's notes.

94. Ibid.

95. Ibid.

96. Ibid.

97. R. G. 40/17, hearing of March 18, 2019, author's notes.

98. Ibid.

99. Ibid.

100. R. G. 40/17, hearing of May 13, 2019, author's notes.

101. Angelelli's and Mejía's pleas on June 21, 2019, available at www.radioradicale .it/scheda/577330/processo-dappello-contro-i-responsabili-delloperazione-condor (accessed February 11, 2020).

102. Ibid.

103. R. G. 40/17, hearing of June 28, 2019, author's notes.

104. Ibid.

105. Ibid.

106. Ibid.

107. Ibid.

108. Pedro Mato, José Gavazzo, José Arab, Ricardo Medina, Luis Maurente, José Sande, Ernesto Soca, Ernesto Ramas, Jorge Silveira, Gilberto Vázquez, Jorge Troccoli, and Juan Carlos Larcebeau.

109. Pedro Espinoza, Daniel Aguirre, Carlos Luco, Orlando Moreno, and Manuel Vásquez.

110. Martín Martínez.

111. Appeals verdict of Rome's First Assize Appeals Court, December 27, 2019, 26, available at www.24marzo.it/index.php?module=pagemaster&PAGE_user_op=view _page&PAGE_id=578&MMN_position=200:200 (accessed February 11, 2020).

112. Ibid.

113. Ibid., 97–98.

114. Ibid., 99.

115. Ibid., 100.

116. Ibid.

117. Ibid., 99.

118. Ibid., 104–5.

119. Luca Veloz, "Corte de Roma confirma condena a Troccoli y Gavazzo," *La Radio Cooperativa,* January 7, 2020.

120. Email exchange with Giancarlo Maniga, January 12, 2020.

121. "Analysis of the Condor Appeals Verdict," author's notes.

122. Ibid.

123. *La memoria del Cóndor,* minute 0:19:50.

124. Ibid., minutes 32:00–33:45.

125. "Ordenan cierre de fronteras para el represor Troccoli en Italia tras condena por Plan Cóndor," *El Observador,* July 30, 2019.

126. Interview with Mario Angelelli.

127. Interview with Silvia and María Bellizzi.

128. Interview with IT004-2017.

129. Ibid.

130. Interview with Jorge Ithurburu.

131. Ibid.

132. Interview with Raúl Olivera.

133. Interview with Jorge Ithurburu.

134. Interview with IT001-2017.

135. "Operation Condor: Condemned to Life!," National Security Archive, January 17, 2017, available at https://nsarchive.gwu.edu/briefing-book/southern-cone/2017-01-17/operation-condor-condemned-life (accessed February 11, 2021).

Conclusion

1. Buenos Aires Federal Criminal Court No. 1, Trial Proceedings No. 3.002, "Martínez Ruíz, Honorio Carlos; Cabanillas, Eduardo Rodolfo; Ruffo, Eduardo Alfredo; and Furci, Miguel Ángel, illegal deprivation of liberty, aggravated by violence or threats; torture; concealment and retention of minors under the age of 10; and homicide aggravated by treachery and the crimes of conspiracy by one or more people," November 27, 2020.

2. Inter-America Commission on Human Rights, *Report No. 56/19, Case 13.392, Admissibility and Merits, Julien-Grisonas Family,* Argentina, OEA/Ser.L/V/II.172, Doc. 65, May 4, 2019, paragraph 204.

3. "Operación Condor: A 45 años de su fundación," roundtable presentation by

Giles Tremlett, December 1, 2020, minute 1:19:47, available at https://www.youtube
.com/watch?v=MuXqwOxlGCY (accessed August 26, 2021).

4. In table 1 I listed in the "Victim(s)" column the number of victims at the start
of each criminal trial, and in the "Convicted" column the number of defendants found
guilty, based on the highest available verdict. Many victims and perpetrators appear in
more than one criminal proceeding; for example, the victims in Orletti I (65) and II
(67) are essentially the same, with just two new victims added in the second Orletti trial.

5. "Fiscal pide procesamiento con prisión de cuatro militares retirados," *La Diaria,* June 1, 2018, available at https://ladiaria.com.uy/politica/articulo/2018/6/fiscal
-pide-procesamiento-con-prision-de-cuatro-militares-retirados/ (accessed September
7, 2020).

6. George Wright and Issariya Praithongyaem, "Wanchalearm Satsaksit: The Thai
Satirist Abducted in Broad Daylight," *BBC News,* July 2, 2020, www.bbc.com/news
/world-asia-53212932 (accessed September 10, 2020).

7. "Cambodia: Investigate Thai Activist's 'Disappearance,'" Human Rights Watch,
July 3, 2020, www.hrw.org/news/2020/07/03/cambodia-investigate-thai-activists-dis
appearance (accessed September 10, 2020).

8. Stephanie Nebehay, "U.N. Says Has Helped 12 Jurisdictions Prepare Syrian War
Crimes Cases," *Reuters,* March 15, 2021.

INDEX

Page numbers followed by f or t denote figures or tables.